The Palgrave Handbook of Urban Development Planning in Africa

Meleckidzedeck Khayesi · Francis Nyongesa Wegulo
Editors

The Palgrave Handbook of Urban Development Planning in Africa

Editors
Meleckidzedeck Khayesi
Geneva, Switzerland

Francis Nyongesa Wegulo
Department of Geography
Egerton University
Egerton, Kenya

ISBN 978-3-031-06088-5   ISBN 978-3-031-06089-2 (eBook)
https://doi.org/10.1007/978-3-031-06089-2

© The Editor(s) (if applicable) and The Author(s), under exclusive license to Springer Nature Switzerland AG 2022

This work is subject to copyright. All rights are solely and exclusively licensed by the Publisher, whether the whole or part of the material is concerned, specifically the rights of translation, reprinting, reuse of illustrations, recitation, broadcasting, reproduction on microfilms or in any other physical way, and transmission or information storage and retrieval, electronic adaptation, computer software, or by similar or dissimilar methodology now known or hereafter developed.
The use of general descriptive names, registered names, trademarks, service marks, etc. in this publication does not imply, even in the absence of a specific statement, that such names are exempt from the relevant protective laws and regulations and therefore free for general use.
The publisher, the authors, and the editors are safe to assume that the advice and information in this book are believed to be true and accurate at the date of publication. Neither the publisher nor the authors or the editors give a warranty, expressed or implied, with respect to the material contained herein or for any errors or omissions that may have been made. The publisher remains neutral with regard to jurisdictional claims in published maps and institutional affiliations.

Cover illustration: © AfriPics.com/Alamy Stock Photo

This Palgrave Macmillan imprint is published by the registered company Springer Nature Switzerland AG
The registered company address is: Gewerbestrasse 11, 6330 Cham, Switzerland

This book is dedicated to the memory of Mary Khanyanji Khayesi and Joan Fairhurst, two contributors who passed on while the book was under preparation.

Foreword

I launched the preparation of this book at Egerton University in Kenya on 30 July, 2018. At that time, I was the Deputy Vice-Chancellor for Academic Affairs at Egerton University in Kenya. Since then, Egerton University has facilitated the preparation of the book through the Department of Geography.

The key contribution of this book is not in publishing new research on urban development planning in Africa but in distilling and making available in a synthesized form the findings of existing research to provide an information resource for use by policymakers, practitioners, decision-makers and researchers. While there is a need for new research, it is important to consolidate existing research in an easy form that can be utilized by several people.

The details covered in the chapters reveal the rich knowledge resource available for overall urban development planning in Africa or for specific issues such as population, poverty, energy, transport, water and recreation. The authors have synthesized several studies to provide key insights on methods, theories, core findings and case studies that should inform current urban development planning in African countries.

I congratulate the editors and authors for bringing this book to a good conclusion and challenge them to update it from time to time. I look at this edition as the first step in a process that should see the editors and authors of this book and/or other researchers updating the chapters and even adding new themes in the coming years.

Alexander Kahi
Egerton University
Njoro, Kenya

Acknowledgements We are grateful to the authors, Egerton University, Felicia Yieke, staff of Palgrave MacMillan and our families for their contributions and support that made it possible for this handbook to come to fruition.

Contents

1	**Navigating the Urban Development Planning Landscape in Africa** Meleckidzedeck Khayesi and Francis Nyongesa Wegulo	1
2	**Planning Cultures** Andrea Garfinkel-Castro, Winnie V. Mitullah, and Michael A. Larice	17
3	**Political Management and Governance** Felix Kiruthu	49
4	**Agriculture** Reniko Gondo and Joseph E. Mbaiwa	75
5	**Financial Resources** Raphael Ngolo and Rodney Asilla	105
6	**Population Planning and Management** Reniko Gondo	141
7	**Managing Poverty** Humphreys W. Obulinji	165
8	**Public Transport Services** Meleckidzedeck Khayesi	197
9	**Water Management** Gladys Moraa Marie Nyachieo and Martin M. Magu	225
10	**Rural–Urban Linkages** Francis Nyongesa Wegulo	247
11	**Recreation Planning and Management** Wycliffe W. Simiyu Njororai	291

12 Air Quality 327
William S. W. Busolo and Victor Isanda Njabira

Index 373

Notes on Contributors

Asilla Rodney is a trained teacher and social science researcher by profession. He holds a Master of Research and Public Policy degree from Egerton University, Nakuru, Kenya; and a Bachelor of Education degree from Kenyatta University, Nairobi, Kenya. He teaches the French Language and Literature in English, as well as Research Methods at Egerton University, Kenya.

Busolo William S. W. holds a M.Sc. degree in Architecture from the University of London, United Kingdom and a Bachelor of Architecture, University of Nairobi, Kenya. He is currently the Principal Architect and Director at Intershelter Sullivan Architects. He is also a lecturer at Jomo Kenyatta University of Agriculture and Technology in the school of Architecture and Building Sciences, Department of Landscape Architecture, where his interests are in urban design, regional planning and housing.

Garfinkel-Castro Andrea is a doctoral candidate at the University of Utah. Her research focuses on planning culture—the ideas and beliefs planners draw on as they carry out the work of planning. Her dissertation focuses on understanding how planning in the United States differs at the national and local levels and how these cultures respond to changing socio-spatial contexts. The Black Lives Matter movement provides a temporal context to change by examining ways planners are addressing planning's aspirations-outcomes equity gap, an unreconciled discrepancy between stated intentions to plan equitably and outcomes that fall short of these aspirations and community needs. She is also launching a non-profit organization to carry out a pedestrian safety research and education project that seeks to implement and test low-cost pedestrian safety measures.

Gondo Reniko holds a Ph.D. degree from the University of Botswana. He obtained his M.Sc. and B.Sc. Degrees at Bindura University of Science Education and Zimbabwe Open University (Zimbabwe), respectively. He is a Senior Research Fellow at the Okavango Research Institute (ORI), University of

Botswana (UB) in southern Africa. He worked as a Primary school teacher for six years and as a secondary school teacher of Geography up to Advanced level for ten years in Zimbabwe. He also worked as a part-time lecturer for 10 years (Zimbabwe Open University) and for 3 years at Bindura University of Science Education. He joined Okavango Research Institute, University of Botswana in February 2016. He has 20 publications addressing the interface between Indigenous and Western knowledge in the governance of natural resources. He serves as a reviewer for the Journal of Sustainable Development, Scientific African and Sustainable Water Resources Management.

Khayesi Meleckidzedeck is a teacher by profession. He holds a Ph.D. degree in Transport Geography. His research focus is on road safety, walking, cycling, public transport and transport policy change. He loves transformative pedagogy and local level-led development change. He greatly supports individuals to nurture their talents to become the best they can be.

Kiruthu Felix holds a Ph.D. degree in History. He teaches in the Department of Public Policy and Administration at Kenyatta University in Nairobi, Kenya. He has keen scholarly interest in the history of political economy of Africa and in particular, the informal sector. He has published several research articles and book chapters especially on conflict, history and decentralized governance.

Larice Michael A. holds a Ph.D. degree in City Planning from the University of California at Berkeley. He is a Lecturer in the Department of City and Regional Planning at the University of California, Berkeley, where he teaches planning, urban theory, urban design and pedagogy for built environment educators. He has taught at the Universities of British Columbia, Pennsylvania, and Utah where he directed their urban design programmes. He has worked as an architect, planner and urban designer, including work for Eswatini's Ministry of Housing and Urban Development in slum upgrading. His research interests focus on liveability and quality of life in dense urban settlements. He is the co-editor of two editions of *The Urban Design Reader* (Routledge 2006 and 2012) with Professor Elizabeth Macdonald. He is currently in production on *The Routledge Handbook of Urban Design Practice* (forthcoming 2023).

Magu Martin M. holds a Ph.D. degree in Computational Chemistry from University of Johannesburg, South Africa. He is a chemistry lecturer who works with Multimedia University of Kenya to train, mentor, do research and disseminate research findings to students and the community surrounding the university. He has attracted research funds from different funding organization locally, nationally, regionally and internationally. Furthermore, he has worked with Water Research Commission of the Republic of South Africa in finding solutions to Volatile Organic Compounds in various water systems in South Africa and was able to develop a mobile 'app' for use in geochemical modelling of these pollutants and monitoring their fate and transport within the environment. He has undertaken numerous projects in Environmental Impact

Assessment & Environmental Audit (EIA/EA) within the country on waste management and water quality.

Mbaiwa Joseph E. is the Director of the Okavango Research Institute (ORI), University of Botswana and Professor of Tourism Studies. He graduated with a Ph.D. degree in Recreation, Park & Tourism Sciences at Texas A&M University (USA) in 2008. Prof Mbaiwa has over two decades of research and consultancy experience in tourism and natural resource management research and consultancy in Botswana. He has over 150 publications addressing tourism development, rural livelihoods and biodiversity conservation issues with focus on the Okavango Delta in Botswana. He serves in editorial boards of journals such as Journal of Sustainable Tourism, Journal of Ecotourism and South African Geographical Journal.

Mitullah Winnie V. holds a Ph.D. degree in Political Science. She is a Research Professor at the Institute for Development Studies, University of Nairobi with a background in political science and public administration. She is specialized in the areas of policy, institutions and governance, with research focusing on provision and management of urban services, including decentralization, housing, informality, social protection, transport and identity. Mitullah has researched, taught, consulted and collaborated with several academic colleagues across regions, countries, and globally. Her 2020 publications include two book chapters: 'Africa and the Global Economy', and 'African Cities and Competitiveness', in Kresl, P. K. (Ed.) Urban Competitiveness in Developing Economies, Routledge; and 'Gender Mainstreaming and Campaign for Gender Equality', in Nic Cheeseman, Karuti Kanyinga and Gabrielle Lynch (Eds.), Oxford Handbook of Kenya Politic.

Ngolo Raphael is an aspiring academic and freelance research analyst. He got his Bachelor of Commerce (Finance) degree from the Jomo Kenyatta University of Agriculture and Technology (JKUAT), Juja, Kenya, and an M.Sc. Degree in Banking and Finance from the Università Cattolica del Sacro Cuore of Milan, Italy. His research interests are in public finance.

Njabira Victor Isanda holds a Bachelor's degree in Landscape Architecture from Jomo Kenyatta University of Agriculture and Technology, Kenya. He is an associate at Intershelter Sullivan Architects. His research and practice interests are in urban and regional planning.

Njororai Wycliffe W. Simiyu has a Ph.D. degree in Physical Education and Sports from Kenyatta University in Kenya and has a research focus on race and sport, international soccer, track and field, sport labour migration, physical activity and health, performance sport, sociology of sport, pedagogy and leadership in Kinesiology. He is a professor of Kinesiology at The University of Texas at Tyler, Texas, U.S.A. He has taught at universities in Kenya (Egerton and Kenyatta University), Uganda (Kyambogo) and USA (Wiley and UTTYLER). He has previously served as president of the US-based Kenya

Scholars and Studies Association (KESSA) and as President of faculty Senate at The University of Texas at Tyler, Texas, USA. He has published over 120 peer-reviewed articles, book chapters and proceedings. He has presented papers at many US and international conferences. He frequently delivers keynote speeches at both local and international conferences on various themes pertaining to Physical Activity/Education and Sport. He also frequently writes opinion pieces for 'The Conversation' on various aspects of sports in Africa. On the leisure front, he loves running, reading and watching sports.

Nyachieo Gladys Moraa Marie holds a Doctorate degree in Sociology from Kenyatta University (with a specialization in transport) and a Masters in sociology from University of Nairobi and Bachelors (sociology) from Egerton University. She is a senior lecturer of sociology at Multimedia University of Kenya. She has published a book titled *Road safety in Kenya: Knowledge, Attitudes, Practices of Drivers of Passenger Service Vehicles* (MA Thesis), and journal papers among them, *Creating Employment through Transport* and a book chapter on Rural Development Planning in Africa published by Palgrave Macmillan. She has presented a number of papers in both national and international conferences. Dr. Nyachieo is a member of the Kenya Transport and Research Network (KTRN). Her interests are in social, economic, political and cultural factors that influence road safety, mobility and travel behaviour in public transport.

Obulinji Humphreys W. holds a Ph.D. degree in Geography. He is currently the Chairperson of Geography Department and lecturer of economic geography at Egerton University, Kenya. His research interests are mainly in urban informal sector activities, microfinance and livelihoods.

Wegulo Francis Nyongesa is a retired professor of Geography at Egerton University, Kenya. He has a Ph.D. degree in Economic Geography from Clark University, United States of America. His research focus is on regional development, rural to urban linkages, small towns and market centres and their role in local level development, informal sector and livelihoods and urban development. He has a long history of teaching and mentoring students at universities in Kenya. He has been an external examiner in many universities in Kenya and neighbouring countries. He has made substantial contribution to knowledge harvesting and publication with over 35 peer-reviewed articles, book chapters and proceedings. He has served as a visiting professor at Western University in London, Canada (2015), and Nanjing Agricultural University, China (2019).

LIST OF FIGURES

Fig. 7.1	Livelihoods framework (*Source* DFID, 2000)	168
Plate 1.1	A determined author, leaving no stone unturned	9
Plate 1.2	Felicia Yieke doing thorough editing of the handbook text	10

List of Tables

Table 3.1	Summary of findings	51
Table 4.1	Summary of research on urban agriculture in African cities	78
Table 5.1	Summary of the research on financing urban development programmes in Africa	107
Table 5.2	Examples of non-tax own-source revenues	113
Table 5.3	The comparative fiscal role of local governments	127
Table 5.4	Some of Africa's sovereign wealth funds	133
Table 6.1	Summary of research designs on urban population and planning in African cities	145
Table 6.2	Summary of research on population and planning in African cities	147
Table 7.1	Criteria for inclusion and exclusion of studies	167
Table 7.2	Summary of review of empirical research studies on urban poverty in Africa	170
Table 8.1	Results of anchoring studies on public transport services	199
Table 8.2	A summary of some key bus rapid transit projects in African cities	219
Table 9.1	Summary of findings of studies reviewed	227
Table 10.1	Results of reviewed studies	250
Table 10.2	Geographical focus of reviewed studies	277
Table 10.3	Designs used for collection of data/information in the sample studies	278
Table 10.4	Concepts and theories used in the reviewed studies	279
Table 11.1	Summary of results on recreation in African cities	294
Table 12.1	Summary of review of empirical research studies on urban air quality	330

CHAPTER 1

Navigating the Urban Development Planning Landscape in Africa

Meleckidzedeck Khayesi and Francis Nyongesa Wegulo

Why This Handbook?

Knowledge, wisdom and insight are needed in planning different aspects of development and environmental protection in Africa, both in rural and urban areas. The two of us are among the experts and practitioners who for long have underscored the importance of raw material-based development for Africa. Even though this emphasis is necessary, we have since learnt that we were missing out on the opportunity to call for the exploitation of existing knowledge as a vital development resource. Moreover, both of us were convinced that genuine research is that which was focused and driven by primary investigation; and in our research undertakings, we were guided by this philosophy. To this extent, we engaged in knowledge synthesis mainly to define research problems, design methods and discuss results. Along the way, we came to the realization that we could make significant contributions to research and policy through harvesting both codified and tacit knowledge. Serrat (2017) identifies several benefits associated with knowledge harvesting as follows:

M. Khayesi (✉)
Geneva, Switzerland
e-mail: mkhayesi@yahoo.com

F. N. Wegulo
Department of Geography, Egerton University, Egerton, Kenya

© The Author(s), under exclusive license to Springer Nature
Switzerland AG 2022
M. Khayesi and F. N. Wegulo (eds.), *The Palgrave Handbook of Urban Development Planning in Africa*, https://doi.org/10.1007/978-3-031-06089-2_1

1. the knowledge of individuals (but also groups) is made available to those who might need it independently of human memory;
2. a wide range of solutions to organizational issues is produced;
3. the ability to manage change is increased;
4. the likelihood of repeated mistakes is reduced;
5. the learning curve of new personnel is shortened;
6. precious knowledge is not lost when personnel leave; and
7. the tangible knowledge assets of the organization can be increased to create organizational value.

Following on to the argument made by Serrat (2017), we recognize that a dedicated effort at harvesting and investing existing knowledge is inadequately organized in the African urban development planning community. In most cases, researchers stop at publishing findings with the assumption that users will find the time and interest in searching journal articles and other documents for answers and solutions to problems and challenges that bedevil society.

Our premise is that besides publishing their findings from primary research, scholars need to engage in harvesting and investing the knowledge so gained in relevant and appropriate forms to support efforts towards sustainable urban development policy in Africa. This form of knowledge production should by all means transcend conventional literature review commonly found in most research reports. The focus should be on harvesting both tacit and codified knowledge for current and further use.

Thousands of journal articles and books are published each year worldwide. These publications constitute an important resource that researchers and practitioners need to mine and must do so while also ensuring that it is made readily available for use in sustainable urban development initiatives in Africa. While preparing this chapter, we conducted a basic search on Google for documents on urban development planning in Africa. To our surprise, the search yielded 116 million sources consisting of documents with varying scientific quality. This finding suggests that there is a large amount of information that needs to be sieved and used for both research and policy guidance on urban development planning in Africa. We also conducted a quick search in the Web of Science that yielded about 82,200 documents on urban development planning in Africa for the period 1945–2021. This finding is an additional indicator of how much information exists on this subject.

African citizens and leaders optimistically get excited whenever a new mineral is discovered in any of the countries on the continent. And this excitement is for good reasons given the potential of minerals to bring about positive economic development. It is for this and other reasons that every effort must be made to conserve and utilize Africa's diverse natural resources. This notwithstanding, it is important to recognize that knowledge is perhaps the most important economic resource. Powell and Snellman (2004) and

Aberkane (2015) have outlined why it is worth exploiting the knowledge economy, pointing out that knowledge is:

a. infinite-remaining inexhaustible compared with raw materials that are finite;
b. collegial-requiring collective effort in its production; and
c. prolific-generating positive returns when exchanged.

There are several insightful publications on urban development in Africa and African development in general by scholars such as Akin Mabogunje, Robert Obudho, William Banyikwa, Peter Ngau, Simeon Ominde, Diana Lee-Smith, Kwesi Darkoh, Poul Ove Pedersen, Dorothy McCormick, Garth Myers, Meshack Khosa, Elliot Sclar, Jennifer Robinson, Yinka Adebayo, Roger Behrens, Winnie Mitullah, Edgar Pieterse, Ben Wisner, Jacqueline Klopp, Kefa Otiso, Godwin Murunga, Amin Samir, Mahmood Mamdani, Dambisa Moyo, Cecilia Nyamweru, Thandika Mkandawire, Walter Rodney, and Francis Wegulo. In addition to research conducted by these individual scholars, there is substantial primary research that has been funded on urban development and other topics by organizations such as the Council for Development Research in Africa, Organization for Social Science Research in Eastern and Southern Africa, African Economic Research Consortium, Ford Foundation, and Rockefeller Foundation.

There are also contributions to planning and research by the ever-expanding research and professional networks and associations such as the African Centre for Studies in Transport, the Association of African Planning Schools, the Africa Academy of Management, Africa Studies Association, and the African Urban Research Initiative based at the University of Cape Town. In addition, research has been conducted on African urban development for master's and PhD degrees in universities within and outside Africa. Dissertations or theses prepared for these degrees end up in university libraries and other related depositories. Further, there are other research reports and papers published on African urban development. There is a telling joke to the effect that several useful research reports and publications on African urban development planning are lying on the shelves in university libraries, gathering dust, with hardly any researchers, decision-makers, and would-be interested readers ever looking at them, let alone mining the information they contain for planning and programmes.

There is a looming disconnect between publication of research findings and its use for policy guidance and action to solve societal problems. Our argument, therefore, is that to a large extent, relevant information exists but in disparate, scattered forms, and in that way, it cannot be made use of efficiently. To elaborate this claim, we conducted a thorough search and found no book that synthesizes the extensive and ever-growing body of knowledge on urban development planning in Africa; a book that would distil insights and advances coherent theories, research designs, planning approaches, and outcomes of planning that this research reveals about African urban settings. This situation presents a risk of unnecessary duplication of research and inadequate attention being given to extending research in new areas if the existing ones remain scattered in different organizations and publications, as happens to be the case now, and is not subjected to a critical review to unearth any new developments it contains.

Many readers may be familiar with Rodney's (1981) 'How Europe underdeveloped Africa' and Moyo's (2009) 'Dead aid'. These two books, based on mining existing information, show how knowledge harvesting can contribute to informative resources for research and policy. The two of us as editors of this book, have noted that every research and policy project on urban development planning in Africa starts from scratch to look for existing literature and resource persons. There is no comprehensive book to provide a base that could serve as the starting point. Apart from lack of a book or an annotated bibliography summarizing existing research, there is no comprehensive directory of urban development experts prepared and regularly updated by any of the academic institutions conducting research on this issue. Several other researchers we discussed these issues with reiterated these concerns and called for a book to synthesize existing knowledge. How then can we effectively harvest existing knowledge for urban development planning in Africa? An important action required is to take deliberate steps to mine this knowledge from available sources, both inside and outside Africa. The effectiveness of this deliberate action depends on nurturing a culture of searching, processing, preserving, packaging, and disseminating existing knowledge. We need to be proactive and strategic in our knowledge gathering efforts.

WHAT IS THE AIM OF THIS HANDBOOK?

This book is an important effort to harvest and make available for use the existing knowledge on urban development planning in Africa. This book provides insights into theories, methods, empirical findings, and planning approaches on selected topics in urban development planning in Africa based on a synthesis of existing knowledge. The book achieves this objective by addressing the following central questions:

1. What is the emerging trend in theories, concepts, and ideas in urban development planning research on Africa? Are there any new theories and insights transcending the old Western models which have been used over and over in spite of their apparent weaknesses? For example, have concepts of self-reliance, ordinary cities, ubuntuism, developmental state, post-coloniality, and informality been advanced as alternatives to conventional theories and conceptual models? Have these been rigorously tested in the studies of African urban development planning?

2. What developments and innovations in methods characterize the studies reviewed? Is there evidence of any dominant methods cutting across the reviewed studies? Is there any evidence that new methods have been explored?
3. What insights do the empirical findings from the research conducted in this book offer into the urban life and planning process in Africa?

Which Topics Have Been Included in This Handbook?

Several related concepts embrace the theme of urban development planning, including but not restricted to urban development, regional planning, and land use planning. The issues at the core of urban development planning suggest that it is and ought to be interdisciplinary engagement in nature and practice by professional planners as well as specific sectoral or technical experts and practitioners, and organizations. It is important to stress that in Africa, and perhaps elsewhere, urban development planning takes place within political, social, economic, and ecological contexts and at subnational and national levels (Box 1.1). It is not just a technical process but equally important, it is also a political and organizational process that involves decision-making, resource allocation, preparing plans, implementing and evaluating programmes.

The approach adopted in this book views African urban development planning as a system that consists of several closely related individual aspects in the context of an overall planning framework. It is this assemblage of several connected sectors, institutions, and processes that constitute a dynamic setting that has been studied over the years, generating a vast body of knowledge that requires a critical synthesis and evaluation to determine any emergent theories, planning models, research methods, and insights into the human and physical aspects of the urban environments. Equally important is the issue of how these components of the system have been individually and collectively planned and managed in urban areas in Africa.

Box 1.1: Key facts to consider for urban development planning in Africa
World population in 2019: 7.7 billion people, with 4.2 billion (55%) of this population residing in urban areas, a proportion that is expected to increase to 68% by 2050.

Sub-Saharan African population in 2019: 1066 million people, with 547 602 people (43%) residing in urban areas. Urban population in Africa is projeted to reach 59% by 2050.

Megacities (with 10 million or more residents) in Africa in 2018: Cairo, Kinshasa, and Lagos; Dar es Salaam and Luanda are each projected to grow beyond 10 million inhabitants by 2030.

94 cities in Africa are expected to have over 1 million people by 2030.
Source Mo Ibrahim Foundation (2015), United Nations (2018, 2019).

This view of urban development planning had implications on the scope of topics to include in this handbook. We included both conventional and relatively new topics in the proposal we submitted to Palgrave MacMillan. While two reviewers supported this approach, the third reviewer was sceptical of it, questioning why unconventional topics had been included. The reviewer recommended leaving out these topics to focus on the conventional or traditional ones such as planning approaches, master planning, and sectoral planning. As the book editors, we however challenged this suggestion based on our reading of the emerging literature that revealed diverse themes that were integral to urban development planning, for example, religion, recreation, and end of life services. Our argument was ultimately accepted by the publisher, leading to the adoption of the mix of conventional approach and what we consider 'innovative and unprecedented' inclusion of new topics in this handbook.

This development in topics in our view is a development which demonstrates that it is no longer the professional planner who has the monopoly of research ideas and practice of urban development planning; but indeed, other specialists who may not have been trained in urban and regional planning, and yet possess theoretical, empirical, and experiential knowledge critical in providing solutions to challenges faced in urban areas in Africa. Our view is therefore in line with a perspective of urban development planning as a system consisting of several related elements within an overall spatial planning framework (Newman & Kenworthy, 1999). As an ecosystem, urban centres are in a cyclic process of interaction among several elements in the physical and human environments consisting of soils, climate, vegetation, water bodies, rocks, industries, residential areas, commercial areas, recreational areas, farming, politics, governance, people from different cultures, health facilities, and educational institutions. Thus, a circular economy and ecosystem model of urban development planning provides a viable framework to examine this dynamic system (Bonato & Orsini, 2018; Girard & Nocca, 2019). Planning for this system seeks to create a liveable settlement that is in balance with nature and society. The challenge to planning is how to achieve this balance to ensure efficiency and quality of human life and ecology. This view suggests that different disciplines, people, and perspectives contribute to urban development research and practice.

Method

To achieve the above objective, we adopted a comprehensive literature review approach in preparing this book. The features of a comprehensive literature review that make it an appropriate approach for this book are: identification of the salient aspects to be examined; and critical evaluation, appraising and integrating the findings of all relevant, individual studies addressing a given set of research questions in a rigorous, transparent, and replicable way (Boland et al., 2017). The following are the key steps to follow when conducting a literature review. These steps were followed for each chapter in this book (Boland et al., 2017; Campbell Collaboration, 2018; Cochrane Library, 2018; Punch, 2014):

1. define the research or review questions;
2. develop a protocol for carrying out the review;
3. establish inclusion and exclusion criteria and a search strategy. The inclusion and exclusion criteria specify the relevance and acceptability of the literature to be reviewed, and may include population, key variables, research methods, cultural and linguistic range, time frame and publication types;
4. conduct a comprehensive search for both published and unpublished literature;
5. select relevant publications based on the inclusion and exclusion criteria;
6. extract information from the studies included using a tool developed or adopted;
7. appraise the information extracted using quality criteria;
8. analyse and synthesize the data or information extracted; and
9. interpret and communicate the findings to the relevant audience in a report and via other means.

The authors collected, synthesized and evaluated studies and prepared drafts of their chapters over a three-year period. The journey of preparing this book had high and low moments. Receiving news from Palgrave MacMillan that our book proposal had been accepted was a moment of celebration as was the launch of the book as well as setting up a WhatsApp forum, agreeing to contribute by several authors, and getting to work by the authors. We were not spared our share of low moments that included the passing on of two colleagues, Mary Khanyanji Khayesi and Joan Fairhurst, who were advancing well with preparing their chapters. COVID-19 also affected the pace of working and we had to request for an extension of 17 months to complete preparing the text. Additionally, there was withdrawal by a few authors due to other commitments. Further, laptops of three colleagues crashed, thus leading to loss of the information that had been gathered for a chapter.

As we journeyed on this intriguing knowledge synthesis venture, a few other colleagues showed interest in the book and were added to replace those who had withdrawn or joined others already working on their chapters. In some cases, the co-authorship partnership did not work very well with a few situations where the work was left to one person to do most of the work. We also witnessed one or two cases in which those who were added shifted the focus of the chapters from a rigorous literature review to a generic text. In two cases, two authors 'kicked out' their colleagues who were not providing any significant inputs. This experience made us understand deeply the division of labour in collaborative writing and how one person can easily do most of the work but end up including authors even when they have done almost nothing. We had to intervene in these situations to get things back on track in a fair and respectful manner.

Overall, it was a rich learning journey with a dedicated group of scholars who considered this synthesis as an important contribution to knowledge. We were touched by authors who were very determined to have their chapters included and undertook substantial corrections up to the last minute when we were almost cancelling their manuscripts. Indeed, they managed to achieve the quality required and we were happy to include their chapters. Nevertheless, we rejected chapters that did not meet the quality required even if the authors showed determination. We did not compromise on scientific quality.

A major lesson and inspiration to us was the dedication of authors to use their own resources—laptops, databases, offices, houses, networks, money, and e-mails—to gather evidence, synthesize studies selected for synthesis, write, revise, and finalize their chapters (Plate 1.1). We did not have external funding for this book project, but the authors were not deterred. Instead, they drew on their individual and collective resources, including sharing information with each other and contributing to a token for the technical editor, to prepare this book.

Another inspiring lesson was the role that the process of preparing book chapters played in triggering ideas for writing books. In one case, two authors synthesized substantial literature and produced a 150-page draft. We reviewed the material and recommended to them to focus on two aspects and use the rest of the material to prepare and submit a book manuscript to a publisher. In two other cases, the authors wanted to write more because they had assembled a lot of information, but we restricted them to no more than 10,000 words for each. Nevertheless, we encouraged them to consider preparing book manuscripts and submitting to a publisher.

A further lesson we learnt is the need to utilize the services of a professional scientific editor to thoroughly edit the manuscript before submission. In this regard, we secured the services of Felicia Yieke (Plate 1.2), who straightened the generally dense academic writing and identified several things like an omitted reference in the reference list which we somehow do not always see when writing. She ensured that each chapter and the entire text followed fully the writing guidance provided by Springer Nature and Palgrave Macmillan.

Plate 1.1 A determined author, leaving no stone unturned

What Do the Chapters Reveal?

Apart from this introduction, the book presents and discusses findings in 11 chapters. Each chapter assesses research designs, theories, and empirical findings. A summary of each chapter is thus presented.

Chapter 2 presents findings of planning cultures in African contexts. Using a planning culture framework, the chapter discusses the variety of ways in which planning occurs at different levels of government, scales of geography, and through varied historical influences. By looking at the historic colonial, postcolonial, and contemporary experiences of three African countries that share a British planning tradition, differences in planning culture emerge and can be more easily identified. Each of these countries has moved beyond their colonial past to construct a unique planning culture of their own making. At the same time, four case studies on housing within Nairobi, Kenya, are presented. The planning culture lens provides an approach for uncovering and understanding key drivers of planning and project conceptualization that suggest that planning practice is far more diverse and situational, even within the same city, than previously understood.

Plate 1.2 Felicia Yieke doing thorough editing of the handbook text

Chapter 3 examines urban political management and governance. It reveals that though African cities experience governance challenges, they also demonstrate great potential and creativity. The chapter assesses diverse theories on urban governance and management such as decentralization, good governance, right to the city theory, urban multiplex theory, and informality theory. The chapter points out that a more democratic approach through engaging the diverse stakeholders, including the urban gangs, political leaders, business leaders, women traders, and transport operators, has the potential of promoting locally generated solutions to the urban management challenges. The study demonstrates that residents have risen up to these challenges, not as mere spectators or subjects but as active participants. Studies focusing on dynamics of the informal sector bear witness to the residents' agency in tackling many of the challenges confronting them. The author recommends more case studies on specific urban centres in Africa. This will give researchers an opportunity not only to interrogate the complex challenges confronting these cities but also the strategies employed by the city authorities to surmount governance challenges and initiate adequate reforms. In addition, there is need for more multidisciplinary research in order to interrogate not only the emerging urban challenge dynamics, but also new theories that could help scholars and practitioners to come up with solutions to the complex dynamics in the urban centres in Africa in the face of rapid globalization.

Chapter 4 presents findings on urban agriculture. The evidence shows gender disparity in favour of women among the key players in the business. While low-income households engage in the activity for sustenance, their counterparts do so for leisure. In terms of literacy, lowly and highly educated female and male farmers respectively engage in urban agriculture. On the one hand, underprivileged farmers use family labour and affluent farmers on the other hand afford to hire skilled labour force. Very small plots of less than an acre usually located along main roads, river banks, public and private open spaces characterize urban plots. Also, farmers grow crops on land which does not belong to them and risk being chased away at any time or their crops slashed without notice. Urban farming activities are least recognized by law and thus there is no specific legislation enacted to govern urban agriculture. Consequently, local authorities, government, and other stakeholders cannot fund the business, hence most of the farmers lack inputs and other requirements to boost their yields. The enterprise faces intense competition with other urban land uses like housing and commercial enterprise among others. The availability of modern markets has furthermore created an illusion of access to high quality and safe agricultural products. In this regard, urban consumers are therefore willing to pay for safe food from supermarkets for reasons of disease avoidance. Thus, the low market for the produce, intense competition for land coupled with the shortage of funding cripple efforts by urban farmers to boost their outputs. From the literature, the challenges faced by urban farmers are aggravated by the fact that urban agriculture is not legally recognized in the context of urban and planning legislations. Given the role of urban agriculture to poor households in African cities, there is need for enactment of legislations that govern the business which is rapidly becoming a very crucial source of livelihoods for the hapless households in African cities.

Chapter 5 delves into findings related to financial resource management, examining the form, development, role, and outcomes of finance in urban development in Africa. The chapter shows that urban finance is at a relatively underdeveloped stage in Africa, and this has direct implications for the scope, nature, and outcomes of development. This state of affairs, the chapter reveals, is largely the consequence of policy and capacity limitations in strengthening urban finance. The chapter presents examples of instances of initiatives towards financing urban development with the objective of strong urban communities. The chapter points out that there are avenues through which African cities can pursue a variety of contemporary urban finance models such as the public–private partnerships and the sovereign wealth fund, towards greater urban development, and ultimately, overall national growth and development.

Chapter 6 examines evidence on trends and status of urban population growth and management strategies. The chapter reveals that from the 1960s to the late 1970s, African countries and cities favoured pro-natalist policies and were against the anti-natalist population policies adopted elsewhere.

The argument was that an increase in population triggers innovations and helps in the development of new technologies for easy resource exploitation. These policies coupled with improvements in medical facilities and medical care led to high child survival rates. Therefore, the African population in general and urban population is growing at a faster rate than other continents when they were at a similar level of development. Literature reveals that Africa's urban population accounts for 17.2% of the global urban population, and it has the highest (10%) rate of urbanization. The chapter demonstrates that rapid urban population growth triggered unemployment, accommodation shortages, the development of shanty towns, traffic congestion, pollution of all kinds, unemployment, and waste generation among many other urban challenges.

Chapter 7 presents evidence on managing poverty in African cities. The chapter shows that over 50% of the urban population in Africa lives in poverty, with varying inter- and intra-city poverty characteristics both at individual and community levels. Urban poverty is characterized by households' or individuals' combined lack of adequate resources thereby limiting their capacity to meet minimum basic needs. Further, it is manifested in increased morbidity and mortality, unsafe environments, social discrimination and exclusion, lack of participation in decision-making, and psychological/spiritual distress. The findings presented indicate that causes of urban poverty include both economic and non-economic factors such as vulnerable households' assets and low human capability elements; dictatorial governments that suffer from poor management and violation of human rights; and poor economic performance and increasing informalization of the urban economy. Further, the Structural Adjustment Programmes of the early 1990s; the ever increasing rural–urban migration; reliance on imports such as oil; inadequacy in urban planning; climate change; and natural hazards are also causes of urban poverty. The chapter shows how addressing urban poverty requires a contextualized multi-faceted approach, which may vary within and between cities. It also requires participation of all stakeholders, including the affected city or town residents, local and national governments, private sector and NGOs, and international organizations. Similarly, policies that aim to improve rural–urban dynamics remain critical in addressing urban poverty.

Chapter 8 discusses evidence on public transport services. The chapter shows that public transport services in African urban centres consist of large buses, mini-buses, trains, trams, taxis, bicycles, and motorcycles. The physical infrastructure is largely roadway with limited development of railway for intra-urban commuter train services in several cities. This chapter points out that several studies highlight the development, decline and inadequacy of the bus and train commuter services in African cities; a gap that has been filled over the years by the emergence and spread of mini-buses, bicycles, and motor-cycles. The bus rapid transit option is highlighted as a recent entry into the public transport services matrix. This mode is nevertheless at different stages of adoption and development in African cities.

Chapter 9 discusses findings on water management. The chapter highlights approaches and models that have been used in studying and planning for water systems and they include Integrated Urban Water Management (IUWM), the African Water Facility Approach (AWF), Sustainability Index for Integrated Urban Water Management (SIUWM), Community Self-Help and Partnership Models Participatory Approaches, and Sector Wide Approach (SWAP). Although these models exist, the chapter reveals that there is no single approach or model that can unravel the problems of water planning in urban areas. However, integrated models appear to work best in solving urban water management and planning challenges in Africa. Studies reveal that the urban poor in informal settlements are more affected when it comes to water access and availability and have had to use other alternatives, mostly informal and patchwork system of basic services to meet their demand for water. This situation has made water even more expensive especially now that people need to wash their hands frequently due to the Covid-19 pandemic hygiene requirements.

Chapter 10 presents findings on rural–urban linkages, pointing out that rural–urban relations consist of movements of people, resources, and information across the urban–rural continuum, with potential developmental effects on these two areas. The chapter reveals that rural–urban relations are complex and dynamic and cannot be restricted to the binary and dichotomous 'rural' and 'urban' areas. These relations are in constant flux depending on the socioeconomic and political environments in the various countries and parts of Africa, and elsewhere. Studies show that these relations also play an important role in shaping social and economic affairs of the regions in which they exist. These settlements, at various scales, play important roles and functions in facilitating the backward and forward links between the rural and urban areas with respect to resource movements and use. Urban centres, especially those at the lower end of the hierarchy such as market centres and small towns, mediate various linkages between rural and large urban settlements. Without this mediation, the regional spatial economy in various African countries and beyond would not function effectively. Behind the movement and transfer of goods and services between the two spheres are systems of organizations and production that involve coordinating labour, finance and management resources. Thus, these relations provide important insights into how regional and national economies function. The role or importance of rural–urban relations notwithstanding, the chapter highlights challenges that limit the effective functioning of the movement and transfer of resources between and within these two interdependent spaces; namely, poor transport infrastructure, lack of storage facilities for fragile produce, lack of value addition and therefore limited income earnings for the producers. Economic recession and structural adjustment programmes experienced in the 1980s and 1990s, and continuing in other forms, also negatively affected the effectiveness of rural–urban relations in Africa.

Chapter 11 is focused on recreation planning and management. The chapter reveals that the studies that have been synthesized approached recreation in urban Africa using diverse study designs, geographical scope and data collection methods that shed light on the state of recreation with implications for urban planning in Africa. Despite the diverse approaches, there is increasing interest as well as extensive research which reveal that recreational ecosystem services, such as urban parks, playgrounds, and other green spaces provide benefits both directly and indirectly to the user. Problems pertaining to recreation service delivery such as lack of adequate strategies, policies, the provision of recreation facilities, programming, financing, and human resources still exist in African countries, including South Africa, Kenya, Tanzania, Ethiopia, Zimbabwe, and Uganda. Coupled with the absence of policy or coordinated service delivery structures, is poor access to the recreation facilities due to limited investments in the recreational spaces required to enhance the well-being of urban residents. The lack of public investments has given rise to the call for public and private partnerships to meet the recreational needs of the people.

Chapter 12 presents findings on air quality, focusing on levels of air pollution by source and effects of air pollution on health and the economy. The chapter reveals that Africa lacks consistent monitoring of particulate matter, consequently leaving a vast majority of the population with no data of the quality of air they breathe and also lack of adequate regulatory and legislation frameworks to counter the currently rising air pollution trends in African cities. Evidence gathered points to increased concentration or levels of air pollutants. The authors present findings showing that Africa is home to some of the world's most polluted cities. Onitsha in Nigeria, the worst ranked city globally, recorded 30 times more than the WHO recommended levels of particulate matter (PM) concentration. Other cities that were highly polluted as per the reviews, included Cairo in Egypt; Capetown, Pretoria, Johannesburg and Durban in South Africa; Nairobi in Kenya; Algiers in Nigeria; Tunis in Tunisia; Harare in Zimbabwe; and Accra in Ghana. Findings from the few studies conducted in Africa and presented in this chapter have pointed out increased motorization, industrial emissions, poor waste management, and large-scale burning of biomass as key sources of air pollution in the urban areas. Long range transportation of pollutants across the continent has also played a significant role in increased PM concentration in the cities of Africa. Though particulate matter remains a major public health concern globally, its impact on population health in African countries remains unclear due to minimal systematic ambient air pollution (AAP) monitoring in this region, and lack of reliable primary AAP data for the vast majority of the populations. Nevertheless, the limited existing information indicates that the levels of exposure and pollutant concentrations exceed WHO guidelines. For example, in Morocco, recent epidemiological studies associated $PM_{2.5}$ with mortality related to five diseases; ischemic heart disease, stroke, chronic obstructive pulmonary disease, lung cancer, and Acute Respiratory Infections (ARIs).

Over 70% of the cases recorded originated from the major cities of Morocco (Casablanca, Rabat, Tangier, & Marrakesh). In 2014, over 6000 deaths were attributed to AAP, with an economic cost implication of US$1.14 billion, or 1.05% of the country's GDP.

References

Aberkane, I. J. (2015). *Economy of knowledge*. Fondation pour l'innovation politique.

Bonato, D., & Orsini, R. (2018). Urban circular economy: The new frontier for European cities' sustainable development. In W. W. Clark (Ed.), *Sustainable communities design handbook: Green engineering, architecture, and technology* (pp. 235–245). Butterworth-Heinemann/Elsevier.

Boland, A., Cherry, M. G., & Dickson, R. (2017). *Doing a systematic review: A student's guide*. Sage.

Campbell Collaboration. (2018). Campbell systematic reviews. Available from: https://campbellcollaboration.org/campbell-systematic-reviews.html (Accessed 22 December 2018).

Cochrane Library. (2018). About Cochrane reviews. Available from: https://www.cochranelibrary.com/about/about-cochrane-reviews (Accessed 22 December 2018).

Girard, F. L., & Nocca, F. (2019). Moving towards the circular economy/city model: Which tools for operationalizing this model? *Sustainability, 11*(22), 6253. MDPI AG. Retrieved from https://doi.org/10.3390/su11226253

Mo Ibrahim Foundation. (2015). African urban dynamics: Facts and figures (ibrahim.foundation/sites/default/files/2021-06/2015-facts-figures_african-urban-dynamics.pdf (Accessed 24th December 2021).

Moyo, D. (2009). *Dead aid: Why aid is not working and how there is a better way for Africa*. Douglas & McIntyre Publishers Inc.

Newman, P., & Kenworthy, J. (1999). *Sustainability and cities: Overcoming automobile dependence*. Island Press.

Powell, W. W., & Snellman, K. (2004). The knowledge economy. *Annual Review of Sociology, 30*, 199–220. https://doi.org/10.1146/annurev.soc.29.010202.100037

Punch, K. F. (2014). *Introduction to social research: Quantitative and qualitative approaches*. Sage.

Rodney, W. (1981). *How Europe underdeveloped Africa*. Howard University Press.

Serrat, O. (2017). Notions of knowledge management. In: Knowledge solutions. Springer, Singapore. https://doi.org/10.1007/978-981-10-0983-9_30

Tuoane, M., Madise, N. J., & Diamond, I. (2004). Provision of family planning services in Lesotho. *International family planning perspectives*, 77–86.

United Nations. (2018). *World urbanization prospects 2018*. United Nations.

United Nations. (2019). *World population prospects 2019*. United Nations.

CHAPTER 2

Planning Cultures

Andrea Garfinkel-Castro, Winnie V. Mitullah, and Michael A. Larice

Introduction

This chapter presents and discusses urban planning cultures in Africa through a synthesis of literature, practise analysis and case studies. Planning cultures are at once general and specific, reflecting values and ideologies that inform specific institutionalized norms about the practices of planning and what the expected work of planners is, nested within the national and social cultures of where it takes place (Friedmann, 2005a, 2005b; Keller et al., 1996; Sanyal, 2005a). On the one hand, planning culture is complex and illusive, with hidden layers and myriad outward manifestations; on the other hand, it can also simply be described as, 'the way the job gets done' (Khademian, 2002). While planning is practised globally and encompasses many sub-practises and areas of expertise, in this chapter, we focus on urban development planning in Africa and in African cities.

A. Garfinkel-Castro (✉)
Department of City and Metropolitan Planning, University of Utah, Salt Lake City, Utah, USA
e-mail: andrea.garfinkel.castro@gmail.com

W. V. Mitullah
Institute for Development Studies, University of Nairobi, Nairobi, Kenya

M. A. Larice
Salt Lake City, Utah, USA

We begin by describing the research design and the methods used in this three-part synthesis. This is then followed by first, a review of planning culture literature; second, an overview of planning practise at the national scale and third, a comparative case study analysis of differential municipal planning cultures with a focus on housing. We close with rationales for increasing the overall awareness of planning culture when assessing the processes and outcomes of planning practise.

RESULTS AND DISCUSSION

Research Design and Methods

Our discussion of planning culture in African cities is undertaken in three parts. Our literature review presents foundational and seminal scholarship, aimed at establishing a clear understanding of concept development and how scholars have built a small but growing body of knowledge around planning cultures. This conceptualization is followed by an applied modelling of planning culture in three African nations; Ghana, Tanzania and Eswatini (formerly Swaziland), presenting the broad strokes that are needed to contextualize local planning by first understanding the national context. A comparative case study of four planning cases in Nairobi, Kenya, presents planning cultures at the local level, demonstrating how planning cultures can share a national culture but be varied on-the-ground in practise.

As a nascent area of scholarship, the majority of theoretical literature on planning culture is reviewed in the first section, and identified using academic search engines complemented by scans of reference lists. Thirty studies specifically focused on planning culture were selected from the planning literature and augmented by social science and organizational scholarship, to present a balanced perspective of the cultural lens. The section on national planning cultures in Africa is drawn largely from author experience and practise in Africa, as well as from nearly two decades of teaching comparative planning theory and practise, including with a focus on Africa. A comparative approach is used to identify and describe the key driving forces behind the planning cultures of two African nations, noting the wide variety of planning approaches on a continent as vast as Africa, reinforced by supportive literature throughout the section. The case studies are informed by both published literature and documentary evidence drawn from project reports and evaluations. This is complemented by author background in housing studies and direct experience work on the low-income housing sector in Kenya.

What is Planning Culture?

Planning culture is the merging of two complex ideas, each with multiple defining qualities. As a starting point, the authors of this chapter offer this definition of planning:

> *In general, planning is the intentional ordering of means and actions to achieve desired ends through the filters of context, resources, stakeholders, influences and time; planning is both noun and verb, both product and process; planning is an activity performed naturally by humans in everyday decision-making, but is also a professional activity performed in a variety of organizational setting in both the private and public sectors.*

This overarching definition of planning captures planning in a broad sense; as a net, capturing and pulling into its scope a range of contextualizing filters, of being both action and outcome-oriented, practised in many settings. To more specifically reference urban development planning, we add that with respect to planning for nations, regions and cities, planning is the process of problem definition, analysis, strategic decision-making and collaborative decision implementation. Within cities, professional planning is widely accepted as an administrative process, the regulation and enforcement of development standards, infrastructure and development strategizing and visioning and plan-making; all at a variety of scales, from the citywide and community to the parcel and place scales. In some places, city planning can also incorporate social planning for the needs, health and quality of life for people, as well. Where professional planning lacks capacity, funding, authority or political will to effectively manage municipal land and services, ad hoc, unsanctioned and grassroots planning can fill failures and gaps, which can be at strategic odds with city officials, municipal government, legally adopted plans, regulations and professional standards.

Shaped by many actors—formal and informal, official and unofficial cities and other types of human settlements are true palimpsests, with traces of the past mingling with the present. Cities tend to outlive political regimes, wars, natural disasters and social transformation, adapting and carrying on by making room for new additions, styles and historic moments (Kostof, 1992). Cities are the outcomes of myriad decisions made over time, serving public and (or) private interests. A city's past lives on even as new planning ideas move in and take over, ushering in new development patterns and aesthetics, and sometimes, new social contracts; voluntary or otherwise. Though planning leaves its imprint on the built environment, cities reveal only a portion of planning's activities.

Across the world, planning has become a profession, with national legal frameworks and institutions leading to localized approaches and practices and formalized educational standards. Planning is also one among many professions that profess to serve both public and private interests, though the public interest is arguably paramount (Friedmann, 2005a). Just as with all professions, planning is steeped in a specific body of knowledge, expertise and skills, coalesced around shared sets of ethics and values (Noordegraaf, 2007). Therefore, it is not by chance but rather through rigorous training, stated expectations and shared commitments that planners learn to be planners; they are acculturated into the profession and its culture (Khademian, 2002). However, although planners are taught the ways in which they are expected to act in doing the job of planning, they must often intuit the underlying reasoning—the values and beliefs—behind the specific planning culture in which they practise (Schein, 2017). And, while planning has its own complex and unique culture, it does not exist in a vacuum. It reflects and responds to the sociocultural contexts in which it is embedded (Abram, 2016; Keller et al., 1996; Knieling & Othengrafen, 2009/2016; Sanyal, 2005a), including those of other professionals and their respective cultures, and is influenced by the agency of individuals and subunits embedded within the larger social culture (Gregory, 1983; Howard-Grenville et al., 2011).

In addition to planning as a formalized profession, there is a long history of informal planning practices—and, therefore, planning cultures—that date back to the earliest city—and settlement-building. Informal planning—the prastice of taking a proactive but unofficial role in shaping the socioeconomic and spatial arrangements of living is carried out by a wide range of actors, under many socioeconomic and political contexts, and in all types of geographies (urban, suburban and rural). Furthermore, there are few clear material distinctions between formal and informal, except as falling either within or without a legal framework, and has been a norm (rather than a deviation) for millennia (Perlman, 2004). Given its practise-based nature, it can arguably be stated that planning work—whether deemed formal or informal—follows the rubric of an organised culture (Friedmann, 2005a), and is recognized herein as an important dynamic in urban development across the African continent.

What is Culture?

Early definitions of culture were linked to human civilization and society. These late nineteenth century views emphasised behaviours, social mores and artefacts, as well as cross-generational sharing. By the early twentieth century, cultural scholars began to emphasize cultural relativism (the position that seeks to diminish cultural bias [ethnocentricity] by understanding cultures other than one's own through the lens of the other culture). Culture was still being studied primarily as behaviours and artefacts until Geertz in his seminal book, *The Interpretation of Cultures*, argued that culture is more akin to 'a set of control mechanisms—plans, recipes, rules, instructions—for the governing of behaviour' (Geertz, 1973/2017, p. 44). Indeed, behaviour is seen by some only as evidence for the presence of culture, but not as culture itself (Ramsey, 2012). However, the debate rages on. Swidler (2001), for example, argues that meaning and reason are overly subjective and reliant on conscious ends-means thinking, instead favouring action or practise-based models of culture which rely on 'routine activities…notable for their unconscious, automatic, un-thought character' and translate to either individual 'habits' or institutional and organizational settings (p. 57).

The evidence suggests that a definition of culture must include or centre on the cognitive mechanisms that consciously and unconsciously guide or shape behaviour. For the purposes of this chapter, the authors of this chapter synthesise the literature to provide this definition of cultures (in the plural sense):

Cultures consist of socially acquired, ever-evolving cognitive frameworks that guide individual and collective behaviours and resulting artefacts, and which include both knowable, stateable values and beliefs and unconscious, hidden biases and assumptions.

A number of naturalistic analogies are used to model culture, but the one most frequently used to convey a cultural framework is that of the iceberg (Dimitrov, 2012). The iceberg metaphor is frequently used as a visual model for culture, widely attributed to Edward T. Hall. And, although Hall refers to the model as an instructional mnemonic, he takes no claim for originating the concept (1959/1981, p. 61). Whomever first proposed the iceberg concept, it is a brilliant analogy for culture in many regards. The image suggests two layers or levels: one that is submerged below the surface, internal and hidden from view, symbolising underlying reasonings and informing values and beliefs; and a second that is visible above the surface, external, exposed and observable, symbolising material expressions, behaviours and manifestations. Although the number of divisions between visible and invisible aspects vary, culture is widely recognized as having two dominant and complementary aspects, often described in binary terms: visible/invisible, overt/covert, explicit/implicit, external/internal. Hall focused mainly on cross-cultural learning and transmission (aka, cultural competency) and cultural change or evolution, which led him to do work that focused on the relationship between the *why* as well as the *what* of behaviour (Hall, 1976/1989).

Defining (human) culture through the dual characteristics of cognitive processes and behaviour and its products remains firmly accepted, with the newer addition of subdividing the submerged aspects of culture. This tripartite approach currently dominates contemporary cultural research across a number of disciplines and foci, although the three aspects are described in varying terms. For instance, Edgar H. Schein, known for his substantial scholarship in organisational cultures, argues for a three-level model 'with the term "level" meaning the degree to which the cultural phenomenon is visible to you as participant or observer' (Schein, 2017, p. 17). According to Schein, only level one is visible to the observer, manifest in 'visible and feelable structures and processes; (and) observed behavior' (p. 18). The two invisible levels are subdivided by relative degree of consciousness to the participant. Invisible but conscious espoused beliefs and values include: 'ideals, goals, values, aspirations, ideologies, (and) rationalizations' (p. 18). Also invisible, but generally unconscious to the participant, are basic underlying assumptions: the 'taken-for-granted beliefs and values, (which) determine behavior, perception, thought, and feeling' (p. 18). Schein uses pyramid-building to demonstrate the difficulty in ensuring correct attribution between observed culture and underlying unspoken reasoning: '[t]he Egyptians and the Mayans both built highly visible pyramids, but the meaning of pyramids in each culture was very different—tombs in one, temples as well as tombs in the other' (p. 18).

In addition to the visible and invisible aspects of culture and regardless of how these aspects are understood, a universal characteristic of culture is ongoing change. Cultural change is a consequence of many factors, though precisely how cultures change continues to be a subject of considerable debate. Views about cultural change appear to be highly dependent on research approaches and disciplinary contexts (Gregory, 1983). For instance, Robert Wuthnow (1992), a sociologist, argues for 'multifactorial rather than unicausal explanations of cultural change…that translate broad societal changes into concrete episodes of innovative cultural production' (p. 273). He further argues that individuals do not carry out culture passively but 'produce (culture) collectively' (p. 274) and that in attempting to understand cultural change, attention should be paid to 'the institutional contexts in which it is produced, enacted, disseminated, and altered' (p. 274). Cultural change has also been described as adaptations made to changing ecological conditions (Varnum & Grossmann, 2017), language associated more with the life sciences than the social sciences. Swidler, who earlier was noted as favouring an action—or practise-based model of culture (Swidler, 2001), suggests that cultural practices (which she likens to a toolkit) serve cultural groups in two ways; to reinforce the status quo when social change is minimal, and as a catalyst for new and innovative practises during times of social change (Swidler, 1986). Under evolving conditions, ideologies are more forefront than practices; eventually, she argues, 'structural opportunities for action determine which among competing ideologies survive in the long run' (Swidler, 1986, p. 273).

Additional questions about cultural change include where the impetus for change is found and who can initiate change. It has been observed that individuals from within a cultural group will use their cultural resources to initiate change, without the benefit of a major push from an outside source, leading to new action and thought through incremental change (Howard-Grenville et al., 2011). This is a different model from that of the unified, cohesive group with a central figure at the helm who initiates change from the top-down (Schein, 2017). Modes of cultural change in organisations have also been explained using macro models linked to organisational paradigms: *integration* uses top-down grand narratives to coalesce members around new ideas (as with Schein's model); *differentiation* recognizes subcultures and supports them in initiating and directing change, though at the cost of organisation-wide cohesion; *ambiguity* is where levels of innovation and change are high, subgroup affiliation is flexible and in flux and change is the one constant (Meyerson & Martin, 1987).

A Model of Planning Culture

Just as planning and culture have multiple defining qualities that are complex and varied in their respective definitions and applications, so too is planning culture. And, just as both planning and culture are simultaneously broad and specific with qualities that elude clear boundaries, so too is planning culture. Finally, just as there is no one definition of either planning or culture, neither is there a single agree-upon definition of planning culture. In fact, it is argued that culture remains a fuzzy term within planning (Pallagst et al., 2021; Purkarthofer et al., 2021; Suitner, 2014). Fuzziness aside, planning scholars are increasingly turning to the cultural lens to better understand the interactive dynamics of planning practise across geographic, political, cultural and other socio-spatial boundaries, particularly since the first decade of the twenty-first century. For the purposes of this discussion, the authors of this chapter summarise the literature on planning cultures (in the plural sense) with the following definition:

Planning cultures are sets of learned principles and practises, institutionalised norms and values, and intuited biases and assumptions that support change in the built environment in accordance with rationalized ideas about how the built environment should look and function relative to specific social, economic, geographic, temporal and political contexts.

Planning culture is a relatively new concept in planning theory, and has been unevenly used as a conceptual lens across the various global regions. It could be argued, though, that without using the explicit term planning culture, planning theorists have been carrying the seeds of planning culture towards fruition (e.g., see Alexander, 2018; Friedmann, 2005a). The introduction of the term is credited to Keller et al. (1996), whose research in the early 1990s of four European countries provided the research model still widely used today—comparative case study. Sanyal's (2005b) edited volume, *Comparative Planning Cultures*, followed, about a decade later. This appears to be the first extensive attempt to study planning culture with several chapters on foundational theory and eleven case studies from Europe, North America and Asia. After a brief lull, the topic was picked up again in Europe, where increased cross-border and regional planning activities provided an excellent motivation and setting for comparative case studies (e.g., Abram, 2011/2016; Knieling & Othengrafen, 2009/2016; Othengrafen, 2012/2016). Comparative case studies continue to dominate scholarship on planning culture (e.g., Nunes Silva, 2015; Pallagst et al., 2021; Purkarthofer et al., 2021). Clarity on how to contextualise and frame planning cultures is still evolving, with planning culture (singular) emerging as something of a *meta-culture*: certain fundamental aspects structure the primary concept while infinite variations get expressed locally as distinct, on-the-ground cultures (Abram, 2011/2016; Friedmann, 2005a, 2005b; Keller et al., 1996; Sanyal, 2005a).

Research has consistently demonstrated that primary structuring factors occur at the national level, and include: national founding principles, ideologies and laws; professional planning standards and formal advanced education and ideas about 'the public' and 'the project of planning' (Abram, 2011/2016; Knieling & Othengrafen, 2009/2016; Sanyal, 2005a). These foundational ideas and principles can be difficult to identify as they are generally taken for granted 'common understandings' (Khademian, 2002, p. 3). Additionally, a half-century of neoliberal globalisation has brought sweeping economic and geopolitical change to virtually every region of the world, conflating local, national and global issues (Castells, 2005; Friedmann, 2005b). Planners everywhere are face-to-face with 'glocal' (simultaneously global and local) challenges, such as increasing urbanisation, greater population diversity with a concomitant rise in sectarianism and intergroup conflict, intensifying competition for resources, and extreme weather events. Within the framework of the meta-culture, planners' responses to these challenges both shape and are shaped by local planning cultures.

Complicating the study of planning culture is the fact that planners themselves will inevitably belong to multiple culture groups simultaneously—personal and professional, and some aspects of these cultures may conflict or be incongruent (Ghaziani & Baldassarri, 2011; Gregory, 1983). In planning culture research, this particular aspect of planning cultures—the individual cultural lens of the planner—has been largely overlooked or oversimplified (for examples of how the individual cultural lens has been incorporated, see Othengrafen, 2012/2016, pp. 57–58; Knieling & Othengrafen, 2009/2016, pp. 50–51).

Returning to planning culture as a tripartite model that occurs across all scales, we use the following to describe planning culture as comprised of these three fundamental tiers:

1. *Ideologies*: moral commitments contextualised and informed by national, local and individual values and beliefs.
2. *Institutions*: normative institutional commitments reflecting legal and constitutional frameworks, and professional standards and ethics.
3. *Practises*: actionable commitments expressed through planning processes and as outcomes of the specific activities undertaken by planners.

To summarize the scholarship on planning culture across decades, centuries and, in some cases, millennia, cities are socially constructed over time by myriad actors who work together in coordinated or prescribed, as well as informally and ad hoc ways. Urban development planners exhibit the characteristics of having a shared professional culture in the singular sense, in that their practise is learnt through overt methods such a formal education and training, as well as intuited. Planning cultures in the plural sense consist of practises, norms and ideas, and are shaped by and a reflection of complex and evolving contextualising social, temporal, environmental and spatial factors. Local planning cultures are embedded within national cultures, which structure local planning cultures but also allow for local variances to occur. Cultures are complex and often best understood in contrast, and with researchers often employing comparative case study to study planning cultures. And, while cultural change is ongoing, theories about mechanisms for change varies and is contested, with some suggesting that change depends on the cultural group's organisational form and structure, and the nature and drivers of the change that is afoot.

National Planning Cultures in Africa

The multi-variate differences in the context-based histories, ideologies, institutions and practises specific to Africa suggest a rich ground for the study of differential planning cultures. While several volumes of planning culture scholarship focus on disparate cases across the globe or on continent-specific groups of nations, surprisingly little of this text attempts a comparative synthesis, and even less of it is focused on Africa, save for Nunes Silva (2015). In understanding planning culture across this continent of many countries, each with its individual planning culture, it becomes our task to ask where planning cultures converge and diverge. For the purposes of this chapter, we suggest that there are similarities in planning cultures across the continent which may have much in common across the global south. Here we propose a few of the shared attributes that impact planning cultures:

1. The evolution from colonial to postcolonial experience has resulted in varying degrees of continuity with the older colonial planning traditions and institutions. Immediately after independence movements, many nations chose to continue with what was already in place to enable planning stability until such a time that new endogenously developed legislation and planning documents could be implemented (Home, 2015; Mabogunje, 1990). Or, conversely, when states had more combative separations, these ruptures resulted in discontinuities and the need for new institutions to be developed more quickly (Nunes Silva, 2015).
2. The rapid pace of change with high levels of uncertainty makes long-term general or comprehensive planning especially difficult. Consequently, most planning efforts in Africa now focus on relatively short and mid-term planning horizons or accept the reality that plans must be nimble or updated on a regular basis, requiring higher levels of professional planning capacity (Keeton & Nijhuis, 2019).
3. The locations of planning within government vary widely in African countries, beyond mere city planning. Planning continues to be highly centralised within some governments. Common also are municipal planning agencies with close relationships with the national government structure or with national planners seconded to local municipalities.

Many countries continue to carry out national and economic development plans. A variety of institutionally dependent planning efforts are associated with multi-lateral lending through a central government, often resulting from required structural adjustments (Lall et al., 2017). In many African countries, planning is so early in its emergence that it has required outside consulting to facilitate institutional establishment (Africa Renewal, 2012). Even though planning remains largely within national governments, decentralisation efforts are proceeding across the continent as planning capacity grows.

It is in the differences between nations where divergence in planning cultures can be most clearly recognised. This happens through the nearly unfathomable diversity that exists between and within African nations. Consider for a moment the vast differences in languages and cultural groups across the continent, where estimates range from 1250 to 3000+ distinct language groups and dialects within 55+ countries. The cultural values and attitudes that exist across these groups suggest different ways of communicating, social organisation, decision-making and dispute resolution, all of which are contributors to planning culture.

To understand both national and associated local planning cultures, one must first identify the driving forces that called each nation into being. Acknowledging that all local planning culture is embedded within a larger national setting, it becomes useful to understand what shaped the nation. The driving forces of nations include a host of elements that differentiate each planning culture. Historic rationales for the development of the nation include: past oppression and challenges; key economic drivers, land tenure systems and natural resources; the political economy; social characteristics (such as religion, language, ethnic and clan diversity), governance, rights, entitlements and legal systems, to name a few. Let us examine three different nations with differentiating national drivers to illustrate the possible divergence of planning culture experiences from country to country. Noting that planning cultures of the key colonising empires suggest significant regional differences (French, Portuguese, Italian, Spanish, Belgian, German, Dutch and British), we focus herein only on three Anglophone countries to reinforce this diversity of experience within a single colonial tradition.

Ghana: Planning Continuity and Decentralization in an Urban Development Regime

The early history of Ghana dates back to the 700s and a series of independent African empires that ruled periodically in various regions, with many of them involved in the Trans-Saharan trade. European settlement began in the late fifteenth century with the construction of the São Jorge de Mina Fort (now Elmina Castle) by the Portuguese to protect trading routes along the Gulf of Guinea and as one hub of the West African slave trade. The Portuguese were later supplanted by the Dutch in 1642 and later by the British in 1874. Over the several hundred years of European colonisation, more than 30 forts and trading posts were constructed along the coast. The later nation of Ghana was created from the British colony of the Gold Coast, the Northern Territories south of Burkina Faso and the eastern strip of Togoland. Economic progress from early twentieth century coffee and cacao production helped produce a relatively wealthy and well-educated local population compared to other West African countries. Ghanaian participation in World War II and strong African political organisation helped bolster calls for independence, which was gained in 1957, thus being the first sub-Saharan state to gain independence from colonial rule.

Planning culture in Ghana was firmly imprinted by Ghana's first Prime Minister and President, Kwame Nkrumah, who guided urban, educational and industrial development across the country. During his first years, he tried to tamp down the tribalism that was indicative of Ghana through most of its history. He helped to establish an urban development and planning mindset, that still remains to this day, including the adoption of a Seven Year Development Plan for National Reconstruction and Development. Planning in Ghana continues to utilise national development plans in several development sectors including housing, transportation, infrastructure, commerce and industry. These national plans help to guide funding decisions when local authorities petition for budget allocation.

Notable in Ghanaian planning is the continuity of the colonial planning institutions that carried over after independence. The Town and Country Planning Department established in 1945 continues to organise planning activity in the country. This central government department coordinated sectoral activity and national sector plans in a top-down and elite professional manner with little local input, which made planning particularly detached from real world conditions. Planning was oriented to large scale structure plans and local urban development schemes. Most planning was done within central government on behalf of local cities, towns, villages and rural areas. Distances and communication lags between central government and the local scene resulted in planning mismatch to local situations, lack of transparency, poor accountability, some amount of corruption and the relative disuse of planning documents (Home, 2015).

Planning education in Ghana began shortly after independence in 1958 at the Kumasi College of Arts, Science and Technology, which later became the Kwame Nkrumah University of Science and Technology (KNUST). Prior to decentralization of Ghanaian planning in 1988, planning practise was associated with top-down rational decision-making with questionable relevance and little opportunity for local inclusion. KNUST's Department of Planning now offers a variety of undergraduate and graduate degree programmes in settlement planning, urban development policy and urban management; including a Ph.D. programme. The KNUST programmes in planning now reflect and reinforce larger themes within Ghanaian planning culture, including the importance of context-based planning, community participation and interdisciplinary collaboration between the built-environment professions and government. In developing these programmes over time, curricular content has been closely linked to Ghana's specific issues and the needs of government in planning and managing the nation's urban development, without the need to rely on overseas planning programmes (Inkoom, 2009).

The demise of the Nkrumah administration was political in nature when Ghana devolved to a one-party state and quashed political dissent, which caused an opposite reaction as other parties jockeyed for voice. Nkrumah was overthrown in a military coup in 1966, followed by twenty+ years of political crisis, corruption and several additional coups, ending with the rise of Jerry Rawlings in a final coup in 1981. Rawlings promptly suspended the constitution and once again banned political parties. To inhibit additional political crises, the Rawlings administration began to dismantle the structures that led to corruption, installed conservative economic policies and began to decentralise government planning and decision-making in favour of local government control by way of 10 local districts, and governance through district assemblies. Through the early 1990s, a number of government reforms took place including a new constitution in 1992, a Civil Service Act in 1993 and the National Development Planning Commission and Systems Acts, both in 1994. All of these sought to coordinate central government, sectoral agencies, regional, metropolitan, municipal and district initiatives into a single hierarchical system focused on efficiency (Home, 2015). Inefficiency still exists within the back and forth of annual budget requests from local municipal and district councils to finance projects that are supported or unsupported within national planning documents that still function to justify expenditures.

The history of Ghanaian planning culture reflects the ongoing evolution from centralised and top-down planning practises to decentralised planning practises that incorporate greater levels of participation. It is facile to suggest that Ghana's planning decentralisation has been a success from an institutional standpoint, which it has been. And despite the presence of local planning education to provide context-relevant planning professionals, capacity issues continue to remain in service delivery, the absence of innovative planning and plan types, resource allocation from central government and disparate efforts at plan implementation and project sustainability. Planning culture in Ghana retains the heavy imprints of colonial institutions, Nkrumah's urban development mindset and decentralisation to local governments.

Tanzania: The Evolution of Planning Cultures Under Colonial, Socialist and Free-Market Regimes

The unique case of Tanzania demonstrates how planning culture has been influenced by the country's historic shift from colonial occupation to socialist practises to free-market forms of government. Located in East Africa, the area that is now Tanzania is the indigenous homeland of Bantu peoples speaking over 130 different languages and the later addition of Arab-Swahili speakers of Muslim practise largely along the Indian Ocean coast and nearby islands. The bulk of historic settlements are located along the coast, around the Great Lakes and in the mountainous north, largely due to the difficulty of establishing settlements in regions of tsetse fly prevalence.

The United Republic of Tanzania formed in 1964 from the mainland territory of Tanganyika and the island archipelago of Zanzibar, both of which were under British control at the time of union. Zanzibar was first colonised by the Portuguese and later Omani sultanates as a spice and slave trading colony from 1498 to 1698, respectively. The 1890 Heligoland-Zanzibar Treaty between Germany and Britain ceded Zanzibar to the British as a protectorate. Tanganyika, on the other hand, was a colonial possession of Oman for several hundred years, and later of Germany from the late nineteenth century until it came under British trusteeship following the World War I. At the Paris Peace Conference of 1919, German East Africa was carved up and allocated to Britain, Belgium and Portugal. The path to independence was circuitous with Tanganyika first gaining independence in 1961 and Zanzibar following in 1963.

Beginning in 1956, the British Town and Country Planning Ordinances became the de facto planning system for both Tanganyika and Zanzibar. Utilised throughout the Empire, these standardised land use laws were revised several times in Tanzania, but interestingly are still the model for land use planning in the country today. Mismatch continues to exist between the high level of regulation and administrative oversight required in contexts of urban informality and inadequate planning capacity. However, local planning capacity is now increasing, with several urban and regional planning degree programmes at Ardhi University and development courses at the University of Dodoma and the Open University of Tanzania.

This long history of colonial subjugation by four different empires greatly influenced the later political and government ideologies of Tanzania. With independence and union of the two territories, the need for social unification and nation building became the focus of the first President, Julius Nyerere. The 1967 Arusha Declaration established Nyerere's form of African socialism, called *Ujamaa* (meaning 'familyhood' or 'brotherhood'). To unify the diverse peoples of Tanzania, Nyerere opted to repress ethnic differences and socially engineer a new national identity through various laws and practises, including: a one-party government and the suppression of political opposition; universal economic and social equality for all peoples; democratic elections; various constitutional freedoms; the use of Swahili as a national lingua franca; delinking Tanzania from European dependence; internal self-reliance and freedom from victimisation thinking; free and compulsory education; and importantly, the uprooting and resettlement of people across the country through the use of agricultural cooperatives and villagisation schemes (Lall et al., 2017; von Freyhold, 1979). Through *Ujamaa*, the government assumed responsibility for economic production and became the largest employer. Importantly, a prime motivation of government was economic development and the use of five-year national development plans. Regular national planning became a doctrine of government.

While the hope of increased economic productivity eventually fell victim to the failure of collective socialism, many of the other social benefits materialised, including recognition of universal equality, education, personal freedoms, electoral democracy, agricultural modernisation, and most importantly, a continued spirit of self-reliance (Ergas, 1980; Samoff, 1981). The economic crisis of the late 1970s forced some retrenchment of Tanzanian delinking from international development assistance, resulting in heavy borrowing from the IMF to save the economy during the 1980s.

The move to a free-market economy and adoption of liberalisation policies in the 1990s was accompanied by increased involvement with western bi-lateral and multi-lateral aid agencies, supplementing aid from China, which continues (Jansson et al., 2009; Wang, 2020). Tanzania's liberalisation has increased the frequency of planning, but not necessarily its effectiveness (Burra & Kyessi, 2008). Although general plans are now required of all settlements greater than 30,000 residents, these documents are often developed with little local buy-in, sense of ownership or regular use by local officials, due in large part by their development by international consultants who 'parachute' in and deposit the documents prior to returning home. The mere presence of plans does not necessarily mean they will be utilised.

The country has judiciously begun to incorporate donor funding in urban development planning, where it helps to strengthen institutions and speed the pace of project delivery. Realising that blueprint master plans and regulatory land use planning were passive and inadequate forms of development implementation, planning strategies in the country have evolved to emphasise community participation, demand-based planning and resident initiative as a means of facilitating more effective development. A local government act adopted by the central government in 2007 began requiring participation in project development planning. This participation has largely been unenforced (Burra & Kyessi, 2008). Where participation has worked, it has come largely at the urging of donors as part of project funding agreements. Participation efforts have been best incorporated into lower-income slum upgrading projects, such as the one at Hanna Nassif, rather than moderate-income projects, such as the large Kariakoo project (Layson & Nankai, 2015).

Planning culture in Tanzania continues to show traces of each of its major historical phases. Colonial planning is still imprinted in practise through the continued and amended use of its originating Town and Country Planning structures. The socialist experiment of Ujamaa resulted in elevating social conditions across the newly independent Tanzania, but, perhaps more significantly, instilling confidence in self-reliance and eschewing a colonial victimisation mentality that has freed the nation to proactively face the future. Free-market movement is resulting in new global relationships to support government planning initiatives.

Eswatini: Building Local Government and Planning Capacity Through Structural Adjustment and World Bank Partnership

The newly renamed country of Eswatini (previously Swaziland, until 2018) provides an interesting case of how urban planning culture mirrors the nation's history and traditions, but also how the country is building local government and planning capacity through decentralisation and assistance from World Bank projects. Eswatini is a landlocked constitutional monarchy in south eastern Africa, bordered by Mozambique to the east and the Republic of South Africa on three sides. The kingdom's borders contain a single indigenous language group, which makes for a relatively peaceful place, with deep support for the monarchy, oral traditions and the chieftaincy system. But the country is also led by a statutory bicameral Parliament that includes a large civil service relative to the size of the country.

Urban development planning exists under the purview of several government ministries, including the Ministries of Finance, Economic Planning and Development, Tourism and Environmental Affairs and Public Works and Transportation. Physical Planning is administered through the Ministry of Housing and Urban Development in Mbabane, where it oversees Departments of Housing and Human Settlements, Urban Government, Emergency Services and the National Housing Board. The Ministry historically included planning functions for all cities, but these are now being decentralised to the larger cities as planning capacity is built. All other planning for the nation's human settlements and smaller cities remains with the central government. Several features impact planning culture in Eswatini.

First, planning for four different land tenure systems within the country each originate from different locations within government. Crown Land and Concession Land are administered by the statutory government through long-term leases and individual agreements. Freehold land is administered through the Deeds Office and the Ministry of Housing and Urban Development. And, Swazi Nation Land is administered through the monarchy and the chieftaincy system to provide land for Swazi residents in indigenous areas. Swazi Nation Land is the much-admired vestige of independence in 1968 from the British Protectorate that administered the Kingdom from 1903, after the Second Boer War, until independence. As freehold land comes on the market (outside of municipal boundaries), the King, on behalf of the Swazi people, acquires this land and contributes it to the growing land bank known as Swazi Nation Land; once consolidated, it can no longer be disenfranchised from the Swazi people by foreign interests. These varied land tenure systems make for a diverse set of planning agreements and supervising agencies, causing some degree of inefficiency and confusion.

Second, tensions have existed between many of these planning locations and ministerial agencies. Decision-making over permissions to settle peri-urban land is complicated due to both municipal and chieftaincy authorities administering the same land (De Groot, 2008). However, in upgrading peri-urban slums, this land has evolved and switched jurisdictions to the municipal government with the establishment of city infrastructure and services. Difficulties in planning these areas was uncovered by the World Bank-sponsored Swaziland Urban Development Project during the early- and mid-1990s. In 2006, the difficulty of dual jurisdictional oversight was settled after decades of land disputes by the nation's new constitution, which established a single local government institution over both city and peri-urban land. A second World Bank effort, the Local Government Project, continued to utilise structural adjustments as terms of loan negotiations to strengthen both central government and local municipal capacity building, with respect to planning, urban development and land administration (Lowsby & De Groot, 2007).

And third, capacity to administer physical planning remains relatively small, given the number of substantial upgrading and development projects that require a considerable amount of regulation, enforcement and oversight to manage them. Far too many steps in the development process existed for far too few planners to accommodate efficient decision-making. Planners have often been seconded to other government ministry positions as they moved up the seniority ladder, or otherwise got shifted to other agencies in fairly regular intra-ministry shakeups. Building capacity is made more difficult by the absence of professional degree programmes in planning and urban development in the Kingdom. Eswatini has relied on overseas planning programmes and bi-lateral educational grants for professional level education in the training of Swazi planners for programmes located primarily in the UK, Canada and the United States. This model of planning education is often mismatched to the urban contexts of Eswatini. With decentralisation of planning to the City Councils, the need to build capacity and scale up planning management continues to grow more necessary and urgent (Miles-Mafafo, 2001).

What emerges from this brief study of the planning culture in Eswatini is that of a nation with a strong ideological devotion to its monarchy and traditional land practices that are administered by both a chieftaincy system and a statutory government. But Swazi ideologies also include a commitment to government decentralisation and the strengthening of local municipal governance, including their planning functions. Since the development of its most recent constitution, Eswatini has moved towards local government and planning institutions that now have singular jurisdiction over all urban and peri-urban land. Planning culture in the Kingdom has also been impacted by some very ambitious goals, including the creation of cities without slums, adoption of policies for market-oriented urban upgrading, improving local quality of life across the informal sector and continuing structural adjustments with support from the World Bank and other international agencies. A dependence on and partnership with the World Bank and other development agencies is a key distinction of Swazi planning culture, one which leads their efforts to elevate their urban management practises to those on par with other middle-income countries of Africa.

The case studies of Ghana, Tanzania and Eswatini demonstrate several aspects of urban planning culture in Africa that are very different from the realities of planning culture in the global north, where a repressive colonial past might not have been a factor in the evolution of the country. Each of these Anglophone countries evolved through roughly similar colonial planning foundations, but with different outcomes. While each of them sought continuity to some degree with respect to British Town and Country Planning traditions, they also adapted these practises to the particularities of their own contexts. This suggests both a reticence to start afresh with land entitlements once these were already established, but also perhaps the absence of a suitable replacement planning system.

Secondly, in reforming their governments in the post-independence periods, their respective planning cultures reflect the direction of early leaders, ideologies and development contexts. Ghana utilised an urban development mindset to boost economic development, educational goals and continued participation in world agricultural markets. Tanzania adopted a socialist government ideology to socially engineer a new nation, blur ethnic differences, delink from future European dependency and become self-reliant without the yoke of colonial victimisation. Eswatini 'doubled down' with respect to its monarchy and chieftaincy traditions to ensure Swazis would never become disenfranchised from their land in the future. In evolving their planning systems into the late twentieth century, each of them relied on some degree of support in building capacity for planning; at times through the internal development of professional planning education tailored to their own particular needs; at other times through bi-lateral or multi-lateral assistance, and yet more recently through inclusive participatory practices. Decentralisation is playing a role in the continued evolution of planning culture in each case.

The three historical outlines presented above illustrate the ways that national contexts lead to unique and particular planning and development cultures. The planning cultures of these three nations are continuously differentiating to become more specific to their own independent identities. The contrast between them is to demonstrate a methodology by which a nation's planning culture can be associated with and traced back to its foundational ideologies and their contextualised histories, even as they evolve in real time. But just as important in illustrating the diversity of planning culture evolution between nations, no discussion of African planning culture is complete without discussing the great diversity of approaches to planning within individual cities themselves. And while we could have selected any metropolis within Africa to explore local planning culture diversity such as Johannesburg, Lagos, Cairo, Kinshasa or Algiers, we use Nairobi for this investigation. To drive home this point even further, we have chosen to illustrate the diversity of approaches to planning within a single development sector, that of informal settlement upgrading in four distinct experiences within Kenya's capital city.

Urban Planning Cultures in Nairobi, Kenya: Four Low-Income Housing Case Studies

The housing sector of most urban areas of Africa provides a good example of planning culture framed along Swidler's (1986) theory of shifts from status quo (settled periods), to evolving (unsettled) periods and back to status quo. Furthermore, as argued by Knieling and Othengrafen (2009/2016), planning that appears similar in practice and that have similar foundational roots can result in variations on the ground in response to the local cultural context. This is demonstrated in the housing case studies drawn from the City-County of Nairobi, Kenya, which all aim at addressing the housing conditions of low-income groups but use different planning approaches. These cases reveal that the different local culture(s) which inform planning drive the cases in different directions, leading to different outcomes.

Planning as a practice is part of human life, operational across sectors in all communities, irrespective of region and political orientation. The focus on housing projects in Nairobi is a vehicle for comparison and difference within a single nation. As a basic competitive need, housing attracts an array of actors with varied interests that have to be negotiated through planning. The Kenyan indigenous planning system was interrupted by colonial domination and pillared on segregated planning, like many others of former colonies. Colonial planning produced a few low-income housing projects for those employed by the colonial government, while others who were not employed were not catered for. The latter built their own shelters, which did not conform to any formal colonial standards and were viewed as slums by the colonial government. After independence, they were rebranded as squatter or informal settlements. These housing forms, although housing the majority of urban residents, had minimal services and infrastructure, attracting planning interventions and debates that continue to drive development of the sector as low-income housing improvement.

In spite of the many interventions by state-supported development partners, the low-income housing sector continues to have perennial shortcomings in its ability to produce housing that is well-matched to domestic budgets, places and households. This mismatch has been attributed to lack of land tenure, inappropriate planning informed by external planning and design cultures, lack of affordability, as well as ineffective involvement of those being planned for. The desire to address these issues has led to several low-income housing models being implemented, beginning in the 1970s with World Bank and USAID-funded sites and services housing schemes.

Those housing schemes did not fully achieve their intended objectives of housing low-income groups or the provision of infrastructure and services. A significant percentage of low-income households do not benefit from similar schemes developed under such programmes. Some sell their rights to others or rent out the units due to lack of affordability, while others are pushed out as settlements gentrify and become attractive to low-income housing investors.

Upgrading approaches remain common, taking different forms and supported by different stakeholders, as discussed in the case of collaboration between UN-HABITAT and the Kenya government, and the community-based collaboration between the Nairobi Catholic Diocese and Mathare 4A community. The other two cases are: the Dandora Site and Service Scheme, demonstrating a top-down approach led by the World Bank embedded in the framework of affordability and cost recovery; and a new consortium-based approach to the Mukuru Special Planning Area (SPA).

Case 1: Soweto East Kibera Slum Upgrading Programme: Mismatched Outcomes
The Soweto East Kibera Slum Upgrading Programme, initiated in 2004, falls under the Kenya Slum Upgrading Programme (KENSUP) and is a collaboration of the Kenya Government, UN-Habitat and other stakeholders. The programme is ambitious, with several objectives that include improving the lives and livelihoods of people working and living in slums through various initiatives and interventions. Upgrading activities include construction of low-cost housing, installation of social and physical infrastructure, introduction of income-generating activities, facilitating secure tenure, environmental and solid waste management, community and resource mobilisation, capacity-building among communities, and addressing cross-cutting issues such as HIV AIDS, alcohol, drug and substance abuse, and insecurity among others.

Soweto East has a population of 19,318 covering an area of 21.3 hectares, with the population spread out into four zones. It is part of the larger Kibera informal settlement, with a total area of 256 hectares accommodating 12 villages with most areas lack basic infrastructure and urban services (UN-Habitat, 2008). Although various publications give different population counts for Kibera, ranging from 500,000 to 1 million, the 2019 Kenya population census gives a population of 185,777 (GOK, 2019). Unemployment levels are high in the settlement and a majority rely on the informal sector for survival. The KENSUP aimed to improve the livelihoods of the residents by supporting small-scale community-based initiatives, water, sanitation and waste management, and providing basic services, infrastructure and capacity building.

To operationalise the upgrading project, institutional structures were established, including a Settlement Executive Committee (SEC), to act as a link between programme implementers and residents, a programme implementation unit, and an inter-agency coordination committee. The physical mapping and socioeconomic analysis of Soweto East, a draft Master Plan for Kibera, formation of housing cooperative societies, and the construction of 600 relocation houses in Lang'ata decanting site were undertaken. This resulted in the temporary relocation of 1200 households from Soweto East to a decanting site for 30 months, construction of 822 housing units and 245 market stalls in Soweto, and vetting and allocating of 691 units to beneficiaries.

The project was expected to be replicated in other villages in Kibera, but the outcome of the first section has already proven problematic. Many residents could neither afford to live in the decanting site nor in the redeveloped Soweto East. Families were not willing to share the unaffordable units in the decanting site while others did not favour relocation, which would have resulted in the loss of social networks and income. As for Soweto, some wanted to rent and not to own, while others had difficulty getting into cooperatives to enable the buying of houses, as envisaged by the developers of the project. While the project claimed to embrace a participatory planning approach, the outcome of community engagement, as designed, was not effective. Apart from the 17 members of SEC, there were hardly any effective lower-level structures for ensuring the effective participation of residents. Furthermore, the Ministry of Housing, holding the government's central role, is not known for participatory approaches and also seemed to have its own ideas about upgrading.

An evaluation revealed that there was inadequate involvement of the community in project identification, planning and implementation. The project was seen as an imposition from above; residents did not feel they had adequate information about the project, the housing costs, construction plans, or other details on the process of appropriating new houses on the rehabilitated site (Fernandez & Calas, 2011). This, in part, caused residents to reject, rent or sell the new houses allocated to them, with others opting to go back to the slums (Agayi & Serdaroğlu Sağ, 2020). While the Soweto East case is yet to be fully executed, the project reveals several challenges, including structure owners taking the government to court. A major gap also lies in the inadequate emphasis on income-generating activities, which has proven to be a necessary bedrock of any upgrading project, if the urban poor are to be adequately housed. The project opted to develop new houses for the community as opposed to improving housing, infrastructure and services, partly contributing to the failure of the project to fully achieve its goals.

Case 2: Mathare 4A Upgrading Project: Community-Based, Bottom-Up Partnership

Mathare 4A is one of the four villages that constitutes the Mathare Valley, which is one of the largest informal settlements in the City of Nairobi. The upgrading project covered 17 hectares with 6000 households and a population of 28,000, of which 92% were tenants paying rent to absentee structure owners. The upgrading project began in 1996 with a pilot phase led by the Catholic Diocese of Nairobi. Through the church, the project reclaimed government land that was to be held in trust for the area residents to avoid speculation and possible displacement of the poor. The church compensated the absentee structure owners for their rented structures and processed resident tenancy agreements, guaranteeing tenants the right to reside in the area and benefit from upgrading.

The project provided secure tenure, established the Amani Housing Trust (AHT) and provided infrastructure, utilities and acceptable housing with limited relocation to give way for infrastructure development. The exit of renters has been the case in most upgrading programmes. The project encouraged a maximum degree of self-sustainability through efficient rent collection, with surpluses used for improvement and maintenance of the neighbourhood. The rents were structured in a manner that did not exceed affordable levels and were comparable to those charged by private owners in poorer quality housing. The pilot phase included relocation of households into alternative housing with improved sanitation to give way for infrastructure and housing development. The houses were modest, constructed using affordable building materials composed of stabilized soil blocks for walls and corrugated galvanized iron sheet roofs. Average room sizes were 9–12 square meters. The project envisaged a gradual improvement of the shelter fabric financed from rent, and also created employment through use of appropriate construction materials.

The project had a different organisational structure compared to other upgrading programmes. It entailed a partnership of state, voluntary and private sector, with each partner playing its role, depending on their strength. The Government of Kenya and the Federal Republic of Germany represented the public sector, with the Kenya government giving land, allowing relaxed standards and approving architectural designs (Kigochie, 2001). Three private sector consultancy firms, Gitec, Key Plan, and Birdi Civil Engineering, were responsible for ensuring that upgraded units meet legal and safety guidelines while Wahere Construction was responsible for putting up the housing and physical infrastructure. Of the two non-governmental organisations (NGOs) involved (the Catholic Church and Appropriate Technology [Approtec]), the church was the implementer, manager, negotiator and bridge between the actors and the community. The church persuaded the German government to provide funding and the Kenya government to provide land and accept Grade 11 By-laws, allowing use of non-conventional materials (Otiso, 2003).

The project established a Consultative Advisory Board bringing all stakeholders together through the Muungano wa Wanavijiji Assembly, including the community. Residents organised and elected representatives to the Board, which also included local leaders, in particular, a Member of Parliament (MP) and a local government Councillor. Unfortunately, the two former Board members were aligned with structure owners who preferred owner-occupied housing, also known as asset creation, which, until the conceptualisation of Mathare 4A, were the only frameworks for housing the urban poor. The government and its development partners had abandoned the social housing developed during the 1960s and early 1970s, based on rental schemes developed by local authorities, and shifted to owner-occupied models. The latter model, although popular with international finance and government, does not serve well the urban poor, targeted by the projects.

Mathare 4A took a radical step through its planning and has been viewed as a successful upgrading project by accommodating the urban poor using a rental scheme held through a trust deed. The radical step was driven by the Catholic Diocese agency, led by its commitment to social justice and development. The church was familiar with the resident community, knew their challenges and was viewed as a neutral actor, committed to social justice and beyond manipulation by the elites who are a constant threat to efficient and effective upgrading. These shared planning principles overwhelmed the detractors who preferred owner occupation and even went to court to stop the project, though without success.

Case 3: Dandora Site and Service Scheme: Top-Down Control

Dandora Site and Service (DSS), operated as Dandora Community Development project, was the first major site and service scheme in Kenya under the World Bank's first urban development programme. The scheme, like many others in Africa, entailed publicly sponsored sub-divisions, providing a lot with minimal services and utilities for low-income owner-builders (Turner & Fichter, 1972). Turner popularized the concept of the participatory aided self-help approach, which is one of the planning means for housing the urban poor in a rapidly urbanizing world. It is viewed as a cost-effective approach and applies a progressive housing development approach (Buckley & Kalarickal, 2006). During the 1970s and 1980s, these projects were promoted across the African continent with different experiences. Overall, the schemes did not achieve their ultimate goal of housing the urban poor, largely due to a clash of planning cultures among different stakeholders.

DSS was a collaborative project between the Kenya Government, Nairobi City Council and the World Bank, aimed at meeting the needs of the urban poor. It was implemented from 1975 into the 1980s, with six phases providing residential plots, land for market purchase, infrastructure, utilities and community facilities. The house designs were of minimal dwellings consisting of a WC, storage, cooking space and two habitable rooms to be built to the requirements of the authorities within an 18 months period (UN-Habitat, 1984). The project had a top-down management structure administered through the Dandora Community Development Department (DCDD), later renamed Housing Development Department (HDD), and charged with implementation of the project and all other low-income housing.

The department was a requirement of the funding agency and had four units: management, technical, finance and community development. Apart from the latter, the other units had several foreign personnel supporting the project to ensure that planning guidelines were followed. The department which was supported by the Dandora Community Development Project Committee (DCDPC) comprised a city authority; ministries of Finance and Planning; Local Government, Housing and Social Services; the National Housing Corporation; and the Office of the President which was represented by the Provincial Commissioner for Nairobi. The DCDPC had the role of coordinating DCDD with other organisations and agencies involved in the project, although it was unclear how well community views were integrated during conceptualisation and at the top-level decision-making implementation organs of the project.

While the conceptualisation of the project embedded practices of progressive development, the planning culture between project managers and the authorities were not in sync. The Grade 11 By-laws used in the project were not acceptable to city authorities, with many insisting that Grade 1 By-laws be applied for sewerage, water supply, roads and ventilation. Additionally, project implementation criteria were too rigid for those being supported to own houses, contrary to principles central to progressive development. Furthermore, the criteria used by the World Bank for ownership qualification, which included affordability, cost recovery and replicability, were largely inappropriate. Even the minimum standards were unaffordable, resulting in many intended beneficiaries exiting the project. More affluent individuals replaced them, resulting in gentrification of the project as the years progressed, defeating the original plan to house a low-income group.

The self-help approach is anchored in lessons from informality, but the assumption that what occurs in informal progressive development can occur in controlled conditions of planning seems misplaced (Reimers, 1993) in low-income formal housing development. Planning culture in informal housing development is flexible, not coded, has internal synergy and hardly requires hard line protocols and supervision such as those of the formal system. This is the synergy that dictates many informal planning processes in Africa, an aspect which formal planning has yet to replicate.

Case 4: Mukuru Special Planning Area (SPA): Oversized Consortium-Based Participation
The Mukuru informal settlement in Nairobi City County covers a total area of 689 acres with a population of over 100,561 households, and is home to many informal enterprises and services (IIED & SDI-Kenya, 2020). The settlement developed organically on invaded private land, beginning with a business shed during the 1980s. The settlement grew into a large settlement through three forms of informal land acquisition; spontaneous, appropriation and speculation. These forms of land acquisition have generated five morphologically differentiated settlements, depending on the type of planning employed whether organic, moderately organic, moderately refined, refined or highly refined (CURI-UoN, 2014). While the informal planning and service provision vary across the hierarchy, all are contrary to the norms of formal development planning and service delivery. Thus, the planned in situ upgrading through special planning, as provided for in the Kenya Physical and Land Use Planning Act of 2019, is aimed at improving the settlement.

Mukuru was declared a Special Planning Area (SPA) in August 2017 through a Kenya Gazette after intense advocacy and action research by civil society organisations that included community groups. This looped the settlement into formal planning managed by the city authority in partnership with several actors. Embedded within the concept of an SPA is participatory planning, and Mukuru was the first test case. It reconfigures the planning process by going beyond the Planning Department of the City Government to incorporate all departments, as well as a multidisciplinary consortium of non-state actors, with community voices at the forefront of the planning process. The participatory approach isolated eight thematic areas of planning: housing infrastructure and commerce; education, youth affairs and culture; health services; land and institutional frameworks; water, sanitation and energy; finance; environment and natural resources; and coordination, community organisation and communication.

Each thematic area was led by a corresponding department of the city county government, which assisted in managing work plans and outputs. The consortiums were responsible for developing solutions that encompassed the community's vision, financing, legal and spatial dimensions. Proposed solutions of each consortium were consolidated through a series of planning studios completed in 2019. Consequently, partners, led by the University of California Berkeley, drafted the Mukuru Integrated Development Plan (IDP), which is yet to be ratified by the city authority. The co-produced draft plan provides for appropriate land use and upgrading plans integrating infrastructure and services, including community facilities such as markets and social halls (Makau et al., 2020).

The consortium-based participatory process of developing a physical development plan with both the community and the city authorities playing active roles has benefits. Through SPA, the statutory obligation of the city remains at the apex. This implies incorporating the settlement into the city's twenty-year vision and working with consortiums that range from academics and civil society groups to government officials, utility agencies and private firms. This appears to have the potential of facilitating improvement of housing, infrastructure and service delivery. However, the consortiums are dominated by external actors, and the city must be ready to take full charge once the planning phase is over.

Switzerland Caritas led the consortium developing water, sanitation and energy, while Stockholm Environment Institute led the environmental consortium. Other actors include University of California Berkeley; University of Nairobi, Department of Urban and Regional Planning; Strathmore University, Business School; and private sector entities; namely, Kenya Medical Association, New York-based global firm Sullivan and Cromwell LLC, and one of Kenya's legal firms, Pandya and Poonawala Advocates. The Muungano alliance, comprising of the Akiba Mashinani Trust and the local arm of Slum Dwellers International (SDI), SDI-Kenya, work closely with the local communities' organisation, *Muungano wa Wanavijiji* (Association of Residents). Backing these local efforts up are many other NGOs and private agencies that have and continue to provide services to the community.

Overall, this is a case of a progressive culture of planning that began informally, generating different forms of settlement and services, and then gradually embracing a participatory planning process whose full outcome is still to be achieved through ratification of the Integrated Development Plan (IDP). Often, there is an assumption that planning, in particular informal, has one culture, but as demonstrated in the three forms of land acquisition and the five morphologically differentiated settlements, informality has its own dynamics, which do not necessarily draw from a single culture of planning or development. Just as importantly, the participatory approach with its consortium of actors brought into play multiple planning cultures, resulting in the production of hybrid IDPs, anticipated to inform the planning of Mukuru in the years to come.

The four low-income housing projects in Nairobi, Kenya, illustrate four distinct planning cultures ranging from mismatched outcomes and top-down control to community-based and bottom-up to an oversized consortium of endogenous and exogenous actors. Each case looks at the overall planning approach and planning culture to consider how the development and planning actors related to the communities they were serving, the institutional frameworks in which they operated and the partnerships they created and navigated. For example, the UN-Habitat collaboration with the Kenyan government resulted in outcomes mismatched to the local community's needs and wants. The opaque approach taken left little room for planners to adequately engage with or inform the community. Rather than upgrading existing conditions without excessive displacement, decision-makers opted to create all new housing, which ultimately led to higher housing costs.

The Dandora Site and Service Scheme was similarly top-heavy, using top-down management methods whose overly bureaucratic approach was also poorly matched to the informal planning culture of the community. Conversely, at Mathare 4A, perhaps the most successful of the four projects presented, the strongest voice was that of the Catholic Church, who acted in an advocacy role. As an on-the-ground actor, the church knew the community and its needs well, and was also respected at all levels. The emphasis placed on ensuring affordability through sustainable cash-flows and incremental development further demonstrates the importance of practices that are well-matched to a community. And, the project of the Mukuru Special Planning Area demonstrates the interesting variations that can result from a diverse set of consortium actors engaging with an equally diverse context of informally developed settlement, but also exposes the risks of relying on an oversized collaboration, including unnecessary complexity and longer time frames.

On the surface, these four disparate cases appear to have no common cultural thread. Only by pulling back is it apparent that the consistent approach to planning in Kenya is one of international and institutional involvement. For instance, in the Kenya Slum Upgrading Programme, the least complex case, a Settlement Executive Committee was formed around actors representing the Kenya government and UN-Habitat, with the Ministry of Housing taking a central role. For the community-based Mathare 4A project, a Consultative Advisory Board was formed to bring all the stakeholders together, including the Kenya government, three international consultants, the Federal Republic of Germany and the Catholic Diocese of Nairobi. Dandora, with its top-down controlled approach, included the World Bank, the Kenya Government, the Nairobi City Council, the National Housing Corporation of Kenya and the Office of the President, all coalescing around the Dandora Community Development Project Committee that was formed specifically for this project. The most complex, however, is the Mukuru Special Planning Area project, credited with reconfiguring the planning process by going beyond the city planning department to include all city departments in a truly multidisciplinary effort. In addition to the city's actors, there were several international NGOs and advocacy groups, four universities (two international, two Kenyan) and multiple private sector firms. At the centre of this vast network of actors, was a consortium, charged with ensuring that community voices were at the forefront of the planning process.

The Kenyan government typically acts as a key or central figure in planning projects, and projects often have so many different actors that new committees, consortiums and advisory boards are a necessity for management. Planning in Kenya also relies heavily on non-Kenyan consultants and agencies for engineering, planning, funding and organszing. This support has, however, been a double-edged sword. Relationships between Kenyan and non-Kenyan actors often take on a paternalistic character, the result of deficit-based language that defines them as there to provide 'social protection' and 'welfare assistance'. Additional problems with over-reliance on outside actors are mismatched objectives and/or outcomes, cut-and-paste recommendations and plans, and under-development of endogenous planning capacity. These are key characteristics of Kenya's national, or foundational, planning culture. Analyses of planning cultures look at both the actors and their relationships as well as the contexts in which the planning activities take place to better understand the outcomes, whether positive, negative or both.

Each case offers lessons in advantages and disadvantages to a particular approach. Notably, those projects that took a genuinely participatory or advocacy approach resulted in housing that was better matched to the community and outcomes that were more in line with expectations.

Conclusion

In this chapter, we have suggested that urban planning culture occurs within varied institutional settings and at different geographical scales. For Africa, the variation of planning locations and different national contexts suggest a continental complexity that derives only in part from its long history of traditional, colonial, postcolonial and contemporary periods. These variations in planning locations point to broader notions of planning for the nation, the region and different government ministries and functions that claim new and different territories of planning and planning cultures. These broader notions, accompanied by variations in planning practice, help distinguish different African planning cultures, including variations in levels of unity in national focus and degree of diversity at the city scale.

We also wish to draw attention to global planning cultures at the macro scale. For instance, differentiating African planning cultures from the more narrowly defined city planning cultures of the global north are stronger linkages to development theory and practice. The reasons for this differentiation are often overlooked by academics of global north universities, and include: the great disparities of household wealth; the public health struggles of people with few social services; the growing size of the informal sector and its accompanying poor quality of life and the differentiating responsibilities of women and difficult educational futures for girls, to name but a few. This list is much longer, of course, implying that in Africa, there is a clear relationship between development theory, planning cultures and local planning practice. Thus, for Africa, planning cultures are synonymous with development cultures.

We began this chapter by discussing culture as a conceptual framework for understanding planning cultures, which we refer to as planning practices embedded within and contextualised by a nation and its founding principles, mediated by institutional norms. We referred to these contextualising and mediating factors as planning culture's three tiers. Using a planning culture lens, we presented variations in planning cultures in Africa at the national level by considering areas of convergence, noting some of the shared experiences and conditions that impact planning cultures on the continent, such as rapid paces of change, the need to evolve from colonial and postcolonial contexts, the need for planners to adapt to being embedded in diverse and evolving government structures and high rates of poverty and socioeconomic and political inequity. Across these areas of convergence, a primary driver of African planning cultures is that of temporality; namely, the colonial, postcolonial and contemporary periods. These three broad periods will eventually be encountered everywhere across the continent, but the specific timeframes vary, adding to the complexity of attempting generalizations about planning cultures in Africa.

We then presented variations in planning cultures in a single nation, Kenya, by considering four low-income housing case studies, revealing that seemingly disparate practices are nonetheless coalesced around a few central values, beliefs and frameworks, visible once the specific practices are peeled back and the underlying drivers of decision-making are discovered. Planning, in general, entails a wide range of activities, carried out by many formal and informal actors that have varying relationships and responsibilities to institutions and laws, embedded in places that often have long and complex histories. Understanding planning through a cultural lens, as planning culture, includes understanding both the immediate practice as well as the larger context in which it is embedded. In developing a framework for understanding planning cultures in Africa, a continent of infinite diversity and variation, we suggest that there is neither a single template for planning in Africa nor is there a single metric by which to measure the results of African planning.

We have found that the cultural lens provides an approach for understanding key drivers of planning decision-making that extend across multivariate planning practices. The cultural lens is a holistic lens that helps cull out extraneous or superficial elements of a practice. In the context of Africa, in particular, the cultural lens is a way to methodologically bring to bear the long history of indigenous and colonial socio-spatial reasoning on which planners draw. Rather than viewing planning efforts as simply pro- or anti-western, formal or informal, the cultural lens considers the inputs of endogenous as well as exogenous planning principles and how they may be at the root of mismatches or miscalculations. A cultural approach may also be used to reintroduce to planning practice indigenous values and principles, to self-consciously hybridise and evolve planning practices.

References

Abram, S. (2016). Culture? and planning? *Planning Theory & Practice, 17*(4), 654–657. https://doi.org/10.1080/14649357.2016.1230318

Abram, S. (2011/2016). *Culture and planning*. Routledge.

Agayi, C. O., & Serdaroğlu Sağ, N. (2020). An evaluation of urban regeneration efforts in Kibera, Kenya through slum upgrading. *IDA: International Design and Art Journal, 2*(2), 1–17.

Africa Renewal. (2012). *For sustainable cities, Africa needs planning: An interview with U.N. habitat's Joan Clos*. April 2012. https://www.un.org/africarenewal/magazine/april-2012/sustainable-cities-africa-needs-planning

Alexander, E. R. (2018). 70 years' planning theory: A critical review. In T. W. Sanchez (Ed.), *Planning knowledge and research* (pp. 7–23). Routledge.

Buckley, R. M., & Kalarickal, J. (2006). *Thirty years of world bank shelter lending*. elibrary.worldbank.org. https://doi.org/10.1596/978-0-8213-6577-9

Burra, M., & Kyessi, A. (2008). *Tanzania. International manual of planning practice*. ISoCaRP.

Castells, M. (2005). Space of flows, space of places: Materials for a theory of urbanism in the information age. In B. Sanyal (Ed.), *Comparative Planning Cultures* (pp. 45–63). Routledge.

CURI-UoN (Centre for Urban Research and Innovations-University of Nairobi and Muungano wa Wanavijiji). (2014). *Improving access to justice and basic services: Situation analysis*. University of Nairobi, Department of Urban and Regional Planning-CURI.

De Groot, D. G. (2008). *Project information document: Local government project appraisal report*. World Bank. Report No: AB3595.

Dimitrov, K. (2012). Natural analogies among organizational culture models. *Vanguard Scientific Instruments in Management*. Bulgaria Academic Simulation and Gaming Association, Sofia, 5(1), 99–125. https://doi.org/10.5281/zenodo.1434850, https://issuu.com/angelmarchev/docs/vsim_vol1_2012

Ergas, Z. (1980). Why did the Ujamaa village policy fail? Toward a global analysis. *The Journal of Modern African Studies, 18*(3), 387–410.

Friedmann, J. (2005a). Globalization and the emerging culture of planning. *Progress in Planning, 64,* 183–234.

Friedmann, J. (2005b). Planning cultures in transition. In B. Sanyal (Ed.), *Comparative planning cultures* (pp. 29–44). Routledge.

Fernandez, F. A. R., & Calas, B. (2011). The Kibera Soweto east project. *East African Review, 44,* 129–145.

Geertz, C. (1973/2017). *The interpretation of cultures: Selected essays.* Basic Books.

Ghaziani, A., & Baldassarri, D. (2011). Cultural anchors and the organization of differences: A multi-method XE "Method" analysis of LGBT Marches on Washington. *American Sociological Review, 76*(2), 179–206.

GOK. (2019). *Kenya population and housing census.* Kenya National Bureau of Statistics (KNBS).

Gregory, K. L. (1983). Native-View Paradigms: Multiple Cultures and Culture Conflicts within Organizations Administrative Sciences Quarterly, 28(3), 359–376.

Hall, E. T. (1976/1981). *Beyond culture.* Anchor Books.

Hall, E. T. (1959/1981). *The silent language.* Anchor Books.

Home, R. (2015). Colonial planning in anglophone Africa. In: Nunes Silva, C. (Ed.). (2015). *Urban planning in sub-Saharan Africa: Colonial and post-colonial planning cultures* (pp. 53–66). Routledge.

Howard-Grenville, J., Golden-Biddle, K., Irwin, J., & Mao, J. (2011). Liminality as cultural process for culture change. *Organizational Science, 22*(2), 522–539. https://doi.org/10.1287/orsc.1100.0554

IIED & SDI-Kenya (International Institute of Environment and Development & Slum Dwellers International-Kenya. (2020). *Achieving scale, social inclusion and multifaceted shelter solutions: Lessons from special planning area (SPA) in Mukuru, Nairobi.* IIED.

Inkoom, D. K. B. (2009). Planning education in Ghana. *Global report on human settlements.* Available at: http://staging.unhabitat.org/downloads/docs/GRHS2009CaseStudyChapter10Ghana.pdf

Jansson, J., Burke, C. & Hon, T. (2009). *Patterns of Chinese investment, aid and trade in Tanzania.* A briefing paper by the centre for Chinese studies. World Wide Fund for Nature. Stellenbosch, South Africa: University of Stellenbosch. October 2009.

Keeton, R. & Nijhuis, S. (2019). Spatial challenges in contemporary African New Towns and potentials for alternative planning strategies. *International Planning Studies, 24*(3–4). Visionary cities or spaces of uncertainty? Satellite cities and new towns in emerging economies, 218–234.

Keller, D. A., Koch, M., & Selle, K. (1996). 'Either/or' and 'and': First impressions of a journey into the planning cultures of four countries. *Planning Perspective, 11*(1), 41–54.

Khademian, A. M. (2002). *Working with culture: The way the job gets done in public programs.* QC Press.

Kigochie, P. W. (2001). Squatter rehabilitation projects that support home-based enterprises create jobs and housing: The case of Mathare 4A, Nairobi. *Cities, 18*(4), 223–233.

Knieling, J., & Othengrafen, F. (Eds.). (2009/2016). *Planning cultures in Europe: Decoding cultural phenomena in urban and regional planning*. Routledge/Ashgate Publishing.

Kostof, S. (1992). *The city assembled: The elements of urban form through history*. Thames & Hudson.

Lall, S. V., Henderson, J. V., & Venables, A. J. (2017). *Africa's cities: Opening doors to the world*. World Bank.

Layson, J. P., & Nankai, X. (2015). Public participation and satisfaction in urban regeneration projects in Tanzania: The case of Kariakoo, Dar es Salaam. *Urban Planning and Transport Research, 3*(1), 68–87.

Lowsby, J., & De Groot, D. (2007). *A brief history of urban development and upgrading in Swaziland*. Government of Swaziland/Cities Alliance.

Mabogunje, A. (1990). Urban planning and the post-colonial state in Africa: A research overview. *African Studies Review, 33*(2), 121–203.

Makau, J., Njoroge, P., Nyowino, N.K., & Sverdik, A. (2020). *Achieving scale, social inclusion, and multifaceted shelter solutions and lessons from Special Planning Area (SPA) in Mukuru, Nairobi: City Briefing*. Technical Report, International Institute for Environment and Development UK and Slum Dwellers International (SDI), Kenya.

Meyerson, D., & Martin, J. (1987). Cultural change: An integration of three different views. *Journal of Management Studies, 24*(6), 623–647.

Miles-Mafafo, M. (2001). Fantasies of development and housing provision for all? Revisiting Urbanization Issues in Swaziland. *Urban Forum*. 12, 107–118.

Noordegraaf, M. (2007). From 'Pure' to 'Hybrid' professionalism: Present-day professionalism in ambiguous public domains. *Administration & Society, 39*(6), 761–785.

Nunes Silva, C. (Ed.). (2015). *Urban planning in sub-Saharan Africa: Colonial and post-colonial planning cultures*. Routledge.

Othengrafen, F. (2012/2016). *Uncovering the unconscious dimensions of planning: Using culture as a tool to analyse spatial planning practices*. Routledge.

Otiso, K. M. (2003). State, voluntary and private sector partnerships for slum upgrading and basic service delivery in Nairobi City, Kenya. *Cities, 20*(4), 221–229.

Pallagst, K., Fleschurz, R., Nothof, S., & Uemura, T. (2021). Shrinking cities: Implications for planning cultures? *Urban Studies, 58*(1), 164–191.

Perlman, J. (2004). Marginality: From myth to reality in the *Favelas* of Rio de Janeiro, 1969–2002. In A. Roy & N. AlSayyad (Eds.), *Urban informality: Transnational perspectives from the Middle East, Latin America, and South Asia (Transnational perspective on space and place)* (pp. 105–146). Lexington Books.

Purkarthofer, E., Humer, A., & Mattila, H. (2021). Subnational and dynamic conceptualisations of planning culture: The culture of regional planning and regional planning culture in Finland. *Planning Theory & Practice*. https://doi.org/10.1080/14649357.2021.1896772

Ramsey, G. (2012). Culture in humans and other animals. *Biology & Philosophy, 28*, 457–479. https://doi.org/10.1007/s10539-012-9347-x

Reimers, C. A (1993). After sites and services: Planned progressive development strategies in low income housing during the 1990s. Massachusetts Institute of Technology, Department of Urban Studies and Planning, Master of Architecture Thesis.

Samoff, J. (1981). Crises and socialism in Tanzania. *The Journal of Modern African Studies, 19*(2), 279–306.

Sanyal, B. (2005a). Hybrid planning cultures: The search for the global commons. In B. Sanyal (Ed.), *Comparative planning cultures* (pp. 3–25). Routledge.

Sanyal, B. (Ed.). (2005b). *Comparative planning cultures*. Routledge.

Schein, E. H. (2017). *Organizational culture and leadership* (5th ed.). John Wiley & Sons.

Suitner, J. (2014). Cultures of image construction: Approaching planning cultures as a factor in urban image production. *European Spatial Research and Policy, 21*(1), 39–51. https://doi.org/10.2478/esrp-2014-0004

Swidler, A. (1986). Culture in action: Symbols and strategies. *American Sociological Review, 51*(2), 273–286.

Swidler, A. (2001). What anchors cultural practices. In T. R. Schatzki, K. K. Cetina, & E. von Savigny (Eds.), *The practice turn in contemporary theory* (pp. 74–92). Routledge.

Turner, J. F. C., & Fichter, R. (Eds.). (1972). *Freedom to build: Dweller control of the housing process*. Macmillan.

UN-Habitat. (1984). *Case study of the Dandora sites-and-services project*. UN-HABITAT.

UN-Habitat. (2008). *UN-HABITAT and the Kenya Urban upgrading programme: Strategy*.

Varnum, M. E. W., & Grossmann, I. (2017). Cultural change: The how and the why. *Perspectives on Psychological Science, 12*(6), 956–972. https://doi.org/10.1177/1745691617699971

Von Freyhold, M. (1979). *Ujamaa villages in Tanzania: Analysis of a social experiment*. Heinemann.

Wang, K. (2020, May 18). China, Tanzania stand together in hard times. *Global Times*.

Wuthnow, R. (1992). Cultural change and sociological theory. In H. Haferkamp & N. J. Smelser (Eds.), *Social change and modernity* (pp. 256–277). University of California Press.

CHAPTER 3

Political Management and Governance

Felix Kiruthu

INTRODUCTION

Cities are sites of major political, economic and social innovations as well as interactions (Myers, 2010). These interactions are not just confined within local societies given that cities also provide a platform for interaction with the rest of the world for trade and business, tourism and cultural interaction (Myers, 2010; Smit, 2018). As Smit (2018) has observed, with the rapid expansion of urbanization of the African continent, urban challenges which are characterized by the growth of slums and subsequent rising inequality have increased exponentially. In addition, since most of the urban growth in Africa is believed to arise from natural population growth, this is expected to translate into a strain on the already weak service delivery mechanisms (Resnick, 2014). Other attendant challenges include waste management, lack of access to adequate water supply, transport, electricity, unemployment, as well as housing. These challenges have a great bearing on both stewardship and governance of the urban spaces in Africa and at the same time, have implications for other aspects of administration, politics, socio-cultural, as well as economic activities in the continent, given the important role played by cities in the political economy.

F. Kiruthu (✉)
Department of Public Policy and Administration, Kenyatta University, Nairobi, Kenya
e-mail: kiruthu.felix@ku.ac.ke

© The Author(s), under exclusive license to Springer Nature Switzerland AG 2022
M. Khayesi and F. N. Wegulo (eds.), *The Palgrave Handbook of Urban Development Planning in Africa*, https://doi.org/10.1007/978-3-031-06089-2_3

This chapter presents evidence on African political management and urban governance and seeks to answer the following research questions: What theories have been used by authors to interrogate stewardship and governance in Africa? What are the main challenges confronting governance in African cities? To what extent have the city authorities in the continent attempted to tackle governance challenges? How can theory help in tackling the governance challenges encountered in the governance and management of African cities? This chapter, therefore, examines methods, theories and conceptual models as well as empirical findings of selected studies on this theme. The chapter highlights governance challenges and opportunities for urban centres in Africa.

Methods

The study identified a total of 65 studies that focus on urban governance in Africa in general. The researcher, however, focused mainly on 28 publications that are relevant to the theme at hand. The publications consist of books, book chapters and journal articles. Of the 28 publications, 10 focused on urban stewardship and governance. Majority of the selected studies examined, made reference to issues of governance either at the country or city level. Among the cities discussed are Accra, Lagos, Dakar, Nairobi, Kisumu and Harare. At the same time, some studies have focused on urbanization and sustainability in Africa concentrating on the continent in general, without paying attention to specific parts of the continent. Table 3.1 summarizes the different studies that were reviewed for the chapter.

Results and Discussion

Theorizing Governance and Management of African Cities

The case studies examined in this chapter specifically focused on various urban governance theories selected in the study. Governance of the urban phenomena has been viewed in diverse ways by scholars. These theories are interrogated in this section. Smit (2018) observes that while government is usually characterized by clear hierarchies between the state and societies, governance at the local level is characterized by the blurring of public–private boundaries, the rise of networks and increased role of actors, in addition to the local government actors. As already observed, the fast expansion of urbanization in Africa has presented a major challenge in the management of these multiple actors.

The World Bank and the donor community in general, view urban governance using theoretical approach of decentralization. Resnick (2014), for instance, has employed the theory of decentralization in his analysis of urban governance in the continent. He further observes that this same theory has been embraced in Africa by the Bretton Woods institutions for several decades and is taken as a key strategy for achieving good governance. He argues

Table 3.1 Summary of findings

Author(s)	Study focus/objectives	Geographical unit (city, country)	Theory	Method	Results
Aba and Owusu (2018)	Efforts of the Accra authorities towards decongestion of the city, mainly by the forceful removal of informal traders from the capital and the subsequent consequences on the urban metropolis	Accra	Right to the city theory	Analysis of media reports and review of literature	The decongestion approach adopted by the Accra authorities had harmful effects on the livelihoods of the poor segments of population, especially informal operators. Nevertheless, these operators have proved their ability to remain resilient through demonstrations and lobbying through trade unions in order to stop harassment by authorities
Awortwi (2004)	Relationship between policy expectations and outcomes of PPPs in relation to waste management in the three urban case studies in Ghana	Accra, Kumasi and Tema	Neo liberalism	Three case studies in Ghana: Accra, Kumasi and Tema	The research concludes that privatization of public service delivery without ensuring that the fundamentals are right, could have detrimental outcomes with regard to streamlining of urban waste management
Berg et al. (2013)	The study used a combination of oral interviews, as well as review of literature on community policing in respect to specific urban centres in both Nigeria and South Africa	Nigeria and South African cities	The study employed the concept of Plural social order	The chapter examined the empirical reality of state and non-state actors' efforts towards community policing in the urban, focusing on case studies of Nigeria and South Africa	The study findings indicate that in the two case studies, the Westphalian understanding of the state as the sole provider of security is contested, given the reality of the plural social orders. Consequently, the role of the police should be to align the non-state actors with accepted norms of security
Charlotte et al. (2020)	Urban sustainability in waste management, water and sanitation in the global south urban centres by national and international organizations	Continent wide	Multi-level governance framework	8 case studies on urban environmental governance in the global South	The focus on global actors to increase resilience of communities could compromise coordinated support from the national and regional governments. Hence, global agencies need to re-strategize to ensure sustainability of their initiatives after they exit

(continued)

Table 3.1 (continued)

Author(s)	Study focus/objectives	Geographical unit (city, country)	Theory	Method	Results
Dalberto et al. (2013)	The research used archival sources in addition to other historical sources, including colonial reports and newspapers as well as secondary data on the three different colonial towns	Kenya, Senegal and Guinea	The research employed Foucault's bio power by colonial authorities to indirectly influence subjects to submit to certain forms of behaviour	The chapter examines how colonial authorities used planning as an instrument of African control in three towns in East and West Africa; namely, Nairobi, Dakar and Conakry	State interventions aimed at regulating housing conditions and stabilizing urban centres created a wide gap between the well-off residents, mainly Europeans, vis-à-vis the native communities, in the three case studies
Dietz (2018)	Enhancing urban sustainability and inclusiveness in Africa	Continent wide	Urban sustainability	Review of websites on African urban design initiatives for sustainable cities supported by international agencies	Cities should pursue transformation, which encourages sustainable neighbourhoods that value natural and open spaces. Additionally, growth and sustainability were found to be interdependent, hence sustainability must be embedded in a city's development paradigm
Durand (2015)	To examine why a vast majority of households in West African cities cannot obtain secure tenure	West African countries	Concept of land delivery channel	Sources of data included desk studies on tenure policies, research and evaluation. Fieldwork included the use of interviews with stakeholders: residents, allottees, buyers and sellers of land, managers of property companies, surveyors, notaries, brokers, administration staff, councillors and decision makers at government levels	Policies that focus on titling and development of a formal market have largely failed with regard to West African urban centres. Therefore, it is necessary to devise a more relevant strategy to address the complex realities of West African cities, where formal ownership of land is beyond the reach of many residents

Author(s)	Study focus/objectives	Geographical unit (city, country)	Theory	Method	Results
Gbafiou et al. (2013)	To examine how political party politics impact on urban governance in Africa's major cities	Continent wide	Decentralization theory	Case studies of major cities in Africa through fieldwork, workshops and review of literature	Political party influence is an important reference point in the understanding of urban governance in Africa
Gramont (2015)	To examine the factors that led to the transformation of Lagos City in Nigeria from the 1980s	Lagos	Democratization theory	Field research in Lagos, including over 80 interviews with government officials and civil society representatives	Some reform initiatives, such as on tax and waste collection systems, served both political and megacity goals. Reforms were achieved through a combination of increased bureaucratic resources, managerial reforms, public outreach and cooperation with organized social groups
Grest et al. (2013)	To examine decentralization reforms in the management of waste in the four African cities	Accra, Addis Ababa, Maputo and Ouagadougou	Decentralization theory	The chapter examines case studies on urban waste management focusing on Accra, Addis Ababa, Maputo and Ouagadougou	Far from being limited to technical solutions such as the kind of technology employed, solid-waste management is first and foremost a question of politics
Groenewald et al. (2013)	This chapter focuses on local particularities of informal settlement in Southern Africa and the changes taking place over time	South Africa	Informality	The study examines both empirical data from respective cities as well as secondary data collected by the co-researchers	Informal settlements in the five case studies are very diverse in terms of tenure on security of housing. Nevertheless, all the five cities demonstrate inadequate settlement for residents in informal settlements with inevitable ramifications

(continued)

Table 3.1 (continued)

Author(s)	Study focus/objectives	Geographical unit (city, country)	Theory	Method	Results
Kamete (2012)	The research paper interrogates both city and government authorities' handling of the privileged affluent and the marginalized groups in Harare	Harare	Planning theory	The researchers utilized material from field research in Harare, Zimbabwe	The study findings indicate that in Harare, planning forms of control seem to be reserved for the privileged and affluent residents, while the same controls are used against the poor
Kinyanjui (2010)	The research paper examines the informal institutions and structures in the context of the urban socio-economic and political context in which these institutions operate in African urban centres	Nairobi and Thika	Informality	Fieldwork among informal sector sites in Nairobi and Thika in Kenya, in addition to secondary research	The key findings of the study are that informal institutions play an important role in Nairobi and other urban centres in Kenya. They provide social cohesion for members and coordinate the struggle for their rights, as well as social security
Lall and Venables (2017)	The study methodology entailed analysis of over 25 research papers produced as part of a research programme on Urbanization and Spatial Development in LDCs conducted by the World Bank, Oxford University and the London School of Economics	Cities in sub-Saharan Africa	Neo-liberal theory	The study examined urban challenges in different countries in Africa. One of the main concerns of the research is why cities in sub-Saharan Africa are experiencing rapid population growth but their economic growth has not kept pace	The study findings indicate that the main cause of urbanization challenges in Africa emanates from economic inefficiencies by leaders that have increased urban costs, characterized by low investment in residential, commercial, and industrial buildings and in infrastructure

Author(s)	Study focus/objectives	Geographical unit (city, country)	Theory	Method	Results
Meghan (2013)	The study sought to examine the operations of the informal modes of urban transportation in Nairobi, Kenya and their interactions with the socio-economic and political sphere	Nairobi	Informality	The researcher used interdisciplinary methods to gather data from people working and using the matatu sector. In addition, ethnographic data was collected as well as archival data on the public transport sector	The study findings indicate that mobility is a key factor among urban residents' experience. However, transportation can also be a space for leisure and fun for urban residents. Transportation also provides a key site of self-identification and sociability in the city
Myers (2010)	Review of literature on African urban centres, from all the regions of the continent, focusing on the relevant conceptual approach to capture the reality	Kinshasa, Douala, Johannesburg and Lagos	Multiplex theory of urbanization	The study surveys theory in the literature on African urban studies to identify key themes for future research, ranging from post coloniality to informality	The study concludes on the need to continue with research on all the seven themes in focus, with a view to resolving not only theoretical but also the pragmatic challenges experienced in African cities
Myers (2011)	The study adopts a comparative approach of different cities in all the regions of the African continent and addresses several themes including post-colonial challenges, informality and poor governance	Continent wide	Urban comparativism theory	The study sought to interrogate African urban concepts and experiences with a view to generating new ways of looking at theoretical and practical concerns in urban studies	The study findings show that though African cities are quite diverse, they share the same challenges such as colonial legacy of poverty, socio-spatial inequality, mal governance and struggles in coping with globalization. Theory should therefore assist in tackling practical challenges in the urban

(continued)

Table 3.1 (continued)

Author(s)	Study focus/objectives	Geographical unit (city, country)	Theory	Method	Results
Myers (2018)	The work entails a comparative analysis of different theories employed to analyse African urbanization	Zanzibar and Dakar	Urban comparativism theory, using the 'village in the city concept'	The study interrogates the 'Africa problem' in global urban theory by critiquing selected relevant urban thought, that focus on planetary urbanization using Eurocentric lens	The research proposes for a new urban comparative theory built from theories and conceptualizations that emerge from the global South that can be utilised to compare non-Western cities' urbanization processes. Hence, the notion of 'village in the city' derived from the Chinese urban thought
Mwaniki et al. (2015)	The researchers employed extensive literature review of published material and project document analysis. In addition, empirical practical experiences in the urban were utilized in the study	Nairobi	Inclusive urban governance	The research examines the past planning approaches employed by the Kenyan state and the Nairobi city planning authorities in housing provision	The research indicates that the rapid rate of urbanization in Nairobi has overwhelmed the planning systems in responding to expanding housing needs. This demonstrates the critical role of urban governance in addressing low-income housing and informality challenges in Nairobi's housing sector

Author(s)	Study focus/objectives	Geographical unit (city, country)	Theory	Method	Results
Pieterse (2018)	Research methodology involved analysis of policy formulation processes. The researcher tracked, and engaged these processes on the urban scale, with a view to evaluating their impact in regard to governing diverse spaces in Africa	Continent wide	Devolution theory of governance	The study examines why formal discourse at both the global and the African level, with reference to sustainable development, could provide new opportunities to actualize fresh politics on how urban areas are governed	The research findings indicate that urban governance policy discourses are now connecting urban investments and regulations with macroeconomic imperatives. This could lead to a greater awareness of urban governance within centres of state power and hence bring about transformative politics
Rapoport et al. (2019)	The study methodology entailed a review of the substantial body of work on leadership and city leadership in Africa, with a view to developing a practical theory of city leadership	Continent wide	Stakeholders' theory	The study examined city leadership globally, by analysing urban leadership and management in different regions in the African continent	The research results indicate that leadership in cities takes place through catalytic processes that bring together the agency of individuals and groups with relevant structures and tools. Some of these include council debates, public consultation, events, plan and strategy development, and negotiations with other levels of government

(continued)

Table 3.1 (continued)

Author(s)	Study focus/objectives	Geographical unit (city, country)	Theory	Method	Results
Resnick (2014)	The research entailed primary fieldwork that included oral interviews with a variety of knowledgeable stakeholders as well as officials from central government ministries, municipal authorities and members of the donor community on governance in African cities	Dakar	Decentralization theory	The researcher examined challenges of vertically divided authority in Dakar, Senegal, one of the three of Africa's traditionally more decentralized countries; the others being Uganda and South Africa	The research findings indicate that Africa's rapid urbanization continues and as its nascent democracies become more consolidated, the intersection between governance and service delivery will undoubtedly become more pronounced. Therefore, there is need to develop systems and policies to promote sustainable urban development
Satterthwaite (2017)	The methodology involved collection of data on country population and households as well as review of literature on urban centres in Africa	Sub-Saharan Africa	Sustainable development	The research examines both the scale of urban change and development challenges experienced in sub-Saharan Africa, as well as implications on risks for the residents	The study findings indicate that in spite of the smallest urban centres in the region having local governments, most of these urban authorities have little technical and funding capacity to mitigate risks and improve infrastructure and services

Author(s)	Study focus/objectives	Geographical unit (city, country)	Theory	Method	Results
Sebastian (2018)	The study was based on 11 months of field research involving collection of ethnographic data in the administrative district of Pikine in Dakar region of Senegal	Dakar	Negotiating multiple identities	The research examines strategies of young urban men to grapple with their inequality, marginalization and globalization in Dakar	The study findings indicate that in order to survive in the city, young men in Pikine demonstrate a great ability to adapt in order to cope with the difficult situation. They invent multiple identities, depending on the situation
Simone (2016)	The methodology involved analysis of separate articles examining struggles of urban dwellers in Cairo, Chicago and Manilla in the Philippines	Cairo	Urban multiplex theory	The study entails a series of articles focusing on how the city domains in Africa and elsewhere in the South, encapsulates a complex reality, where both positive energy and negative forces are unleashed	The findings from the research emphasize complexity of majority of city residents' life and struggles in Africa. They operate within a complex reality which they do not comprehend. The study illustrates that very often, residents just struggle to address the challenges they confront in order to keep alive

(continued)

Table 3.1 (continued)

Author(s)	Study focus/objectives	Geographical unit (city, country)	Theory	Method	Results
Stoll (2018)	The methodology entailed the analysis of social milieu in the city of Nairobi and Mombasa, focusing on the different social groups, including the youth, the elderly, professionals as well as the middle class	Nairobi and Mombasa	Social milieu analysis	The study examines the particularities of city life in Africa focusing on characteristic features and the specific actions of residents, using the case study of Nairobi	The literature on Nairobi and other Kenyan cities shows how elements of the environment determine the lifestyles of members of specific milieus or the city in general
Smit (2018)	The research methodology included fieldwork as well as a review of 101 peer reviewed articles on governance in Africa. The researcher drew on personal experience of working in a number of cities across the continent	Kisumu	The study used the theoretical paradigm of good governance	The chapter analyses the diversity of actors involved in urban governance in Africa, as well as the complexity of governance processes, using the Kenyan City of Kisumu	Research findings indicate that given the diversity of actors in urban governance, there is no coherence in the way issues are tackled. Urban governance is often fragmented, characterized by lack of coordination between the enforcement authorities and other actors

that decentralization has been associated with good governance in the urban regions for two reasons. First, decentralization and devolution for that matter, is believed to be critical in involving the local citizens in decision making, which is believed to increase accountability on the part of the administration to the citizenry. This implies that decisions on taxes and projects designed and implemented in cities must involve citizen participation. Moreover, this must be done in a transparent manner. Second, it is believed that decentralization translates into improved service delivery by virtue of designing service delivery to local preferences as well as needs.

Smit (2018) has noted that the World Bank's view of governance could be described as grounded on the need to enhance efficiency and accountability in service delivery. This has earned criticism from some Africanist urban scholars. They view this perspective as rather narrow, by virtue of focusing mainly on administrative and managerial interpretations of governance. On the other hand, the United Nations agencies have focused more on democratic practices, including civil and human rights, in their conception of good governance. For instance, the UN-Habitat (2014, p. 14) emphasizes that outcomes of good governance should result in ensuring that all residents have access to necessities of urban life, including shelter, security of tenure, safe water for drinking and other uses, sanitation, clean environment, health, education, nutrition, employment, public safety and mobility. It is our argument here that whereas these objectives sound good and reasonable in theory, it has been difficult to translate them into action in most African cities due to various factors.

In spite of misgivings raised in regard to the objectives of the global community such as the United Nations in regard to the promotion of rights for the marginalized groups in urban centres in the continent, Smit (2018) emphasizes the important role of using the governance lens in order to get a more nuanced understanding of the complex African urban phenomena. This is in recognition of the wide array of actors who are involved in the governance of African urban spaces, both formally and informally. These include government organizations, civil society organizations and the private sector. He observes that using the governance lens, therefore, is essentially about understanding the relations between these actors, which is intertwined inextricably with power and politics. However, in contrast to the formal sense of governance prescribed by the international organizations such as the UN and the World Bank, he observes that informal governance processes are sometimes even more important than formal governance processes in urban centres in the continent (2018, p. 60).

A similar approach has been adopted by Rapoport et al. (2019) who have advocated for the stakeholder theory and have observed that governance of cities has changed a great deal. They emphasize the fact that the term 'governance' is frequently used to describe the change from the traditional state-centred approach to governing cities, to the more inclusive sense of governance. They argue that while in academia governance can be defined in diverse approaches, all of these broadly imply the need to focus on informal horizontal networks over the formal vertical institutions. In other words, governance can no longer be defined or considered a top-down approach dominated by the state. Rather, given the complexity of the urban phenomena globally, other stakeholders must be roped in the governance of urban spaces in order to improve the living standard and quality of life in African cities.

Rapoport et al. (2019) have also observed that with the rising importance of these complex informal networks in urban governance, there has been a shift in the role of the state. Rather than provide services, the state has become a strategic enabler in service delivery in the urban. Its work has now shifted to formulating objectives as opposed to establishing rules for the players (2019, p. 16). Nevertheless, these scholars are quick to point out that no matter how important these informal networks are in city governance, they are in no way a substitute for government in terms of providing city leadership. This is an important observation as it helps to delineate city governance from city leadership. Non state actors provide an important role in governance, but government has an important role to play. Rapoport et al. therefore theorize city government as comprising the formal structures of either elected or appointed leaders such as the mayor, governor and the executives mandated to manage the city (2019, p. 17). On the other hand, they theorize city governance as the wider spectrum involving both public and private actors, both in the delivery of public services in the urban, but also in the management of the core services. In a nutshell, this understanding of city governance lays emphasis on the crucial role played by partnerships in the process of governing.

Whereas there is no doubt that the governance model supported by Rapoport et al. (2019) has a lot of merits that include increased capacity for innovation and efficiency arising from new ideas from diverse networks, it also has a number of drawbacks. First, it involves putting governance in the hands of unaccountable institutions and stakeholders such as business people, civil society and numerous other non-state actors. Secondly, whereas such networks offer flexibility and responsiveness to urban challenges, they can also be very difficult to control due to their diverse nature. Finally, quite often, such networks may not be durable and therefore are incapable of coordinating a comprehensive policy response over a long time.

The complexity of the term 'governance' in the literature on urban dynamics in Africa, has also been noted by Myers (2010). He observes that governance has come to be linked with decision making processes that are not limited to the setting of rules and regulations by the state, and is driven by the need to exercise power and settlement of conflicts that arise in the process. He notes that since the 1980s, there has been a steady rise in the discourse on good governance, viewed through the lens of democratization, privatization, de-concentration and liberalization. He further observes that advocates of neo-liberalism have advocated for privatization of service delivery and de-concentration of authority away from the state. This has inevitably created animosity and competition between the government, non-state actors, as well as the residents.

Another aspect of urban governance relates to the role of political parties. Gbaffou et al. (2013) have observed that although urban scholars interrogating urban dynamics in Africa have underlined the importance of party dynamics in African cities at the neighbourhood level, they have only recently begun to examine the articulation between patronage politics and urban governance. This in turn has implications on the challenges and opportunities experienced in urban centres in Africa. The notion of power play has therefore become critical in the interrogation of governance of African cities. Nevertheless, it must be noted that understanding the quest for resource accumulation and political domination by politicians is important. Accumulation of resources is an important enabler for politicians to capture and retain political power in cities. This could also explain the cut-throat competition for political control over urban centres, where economic opportunities such as prime plots, industries and other economic opportunities are in plenty.

A number of scholars have focused on the important role of theory in the understanding and tackling of Africa's urban challenges. Myers (2011, 2018) alongside other scholars have observed the futility of interrogating African urbanization from the perspective of selected urban thought such as theories based on globalization and world cities research group, which get inspiration from Lefebvre (1970). Such theories seem to indicate the presence of complete planetary urbanization, that imply a globalized picture of urbanization. Lefebvre who was a French Marxist philosopher and sociologist invented the right to the City Theory in response to the rise in capitalist urbanization. Myers therefore emphasizes that urbanization in Africa is characterized by a uniqueness which can be best understood from outside the Eurocentric network. This is important particularly in view of the fact that just as in other disciplines such as anthropology and political science, in urban studies, theorists and scholars often generalize events across Africa focusing more on the less palatable particularities, yet the continent is very diverse.

Similarly, Aba and Owusu (2018) have supported the views of Myers (2018) in regard to the importance of theory in interrogating urbanization in Africa. Noting the renewed attention from academics and grass roots activists who advocate for just urbanism (p. 214), they have used the case study of Ghana to illustrate the concept of the right to the city and inclusive urbanization. The two authors have used the theoretical lens of informality to point out the great contradiction between policy on one hand, and actions of the city government and national government on the other hand. What is clear is that the nexus between theory and actions of governments in Africa is a very important area of interrogation in regard to the African city. Notably, theory has been used in the past to advance activities of government that undermine stewardship in African urban centres in the name of good governance. Thus, the injustice carried out through such government actions especially against the marginalized groups can only be demonstrated by using theoretical tools that capture the complex reality of the African city.

Bekker and Fourchard (2013) on the other hand, have observed that in spite of the uniqueness characterizing different aspects of urbanization in Africa, scholars should not fall into the temptation like the one witnessed during the Apartheid era in South Africa. They note that regrettably, analysis of both the apartheid and post-apartheid urbanization in South Africa treated the region as exceptional in character when compared with the urban phenomena in the rest continent. The study is organized into eight chapters, with the introductory section, where the African urban phenomenon is introduced. The second part of the book constitutes four chapters and focuses mainly on urban public policies and informality in urban spaces in the continent. Informality, therefore, stands out as an important theoretical area of focus in understanding the complex interrelationships and means through which marginalized groups in many African urban centres are able to eke out a means of livelihood. Their argument is that informality should be viewed positively and should not be dismissed on the account of its character.

Simone (2016), in a series published under the title: *City of Potentialities: Race, Violence and Invention*, has examined the contradictory trajectories of urbanization in Africa focusing on both positive and negative dynamics in the continent's urban centres. He observes that whereas a lot of potential exists in terms of new innovations and creativity, there is a parallel existence of feelings of frustrations and desperation within urban spaces. Like Myers (2010, 2011, 2018), he argues that contemporary urban theory in the continent demonstrates that cities and urban regions are quite complex, multidimensional, differentiated, unique, unpredictable, emergent and relationally dense (Simone, 2016, p. 5). He therefore challenges scholars researching on urbanization in Africa to interrogate more specifically how this urban multiplex in Africa could be converted into a resource for imagining better urban centres. This could be potentially useful for both residents and African scholars in order to comprehend the dilemmas faced by residents as well as the activities needed in urban spaces with a view to survive in this challenging environment. Conclusively, Simone is of the view that this trajectory could help translate into tools and possibilities to counter the negative urban conditions experienced by both actors and interests. He alludes to a Multiplex theory that could be helpful in analysing the complexity of the African urban phenomenon.

Similarly, Myers (2010) has noted the great diversity of urban societies all over the continent. Consequently, he observes that one cannot speak of African urban areas as a homogeneous phenomenon, hence he calls for careful theoretical analysis of the urban phenomena in the continent. He observes correctly that smaller cities in the continent are also expanding and providing critical services to the residents. In this regard, these smaller urban cities deserve attention especially in the theorization of the urban spaces in the continent. Ultimately, he points out that as African societies urbanize, they do so in ways that challenge prevailing theories and models on urban dynamics. Consequently, Myers concludes that any attempt at treating urbanization in a specific part of the continent as exceptionally different from that of the rest of the continent should be discouraged as it runs the risk of confirming negative theoretical stereotypes that have been used in the past by Western scholars to describe African urbanization derogatively as dysfunctional, mainly due to its informal characteristics.

Pierterse (2018) whose work is based on his personal experience in conducting urban policy advocacy in Africa uses the lens of sustainable development in theorizing African urbanization. Borrowing from global debates at the UN Habitat and at the African Union level, he argues that sustainable development offers new opportunities to initiate fresh politics on how urban areas are governed. He argues that the UN derived Sustainable Development Goals (SDGs) recognize the importance of sustainable urbanization as a precondition for a greener and inclusive patterning of development in the continent. Nevertheless, Pieterse also emphasizes that the SDGs must be localized. This implies that for sustainable development to be actualized, they must be based on the grass roots support by municipalities and citizens' movements. This position resonates with the tenets of decentralization theory. It is only when communities can get the freedom to make decisions concerning their own welfare that local urban spaces can develop in a sustainable manner.

Rapoport et al. (2019) have made important observations on city governance which have implications on theorizing cities. They have observed that researching the processes of governing cities from a governance perspective calls for attention to two core issues, which have a bearing on urban theory. First, there is need to focus on the society and in particular the relationship between the society and the state. Secondly, a governance perspective emphasizes the role of networks and connections between the key stakeholders shaping the geography of governance. It is interesting that these arguments resonate well with the World Bank's advocacy for decentralization since the 1990s. As we have already seen, Resnick (2014) has observed that the World Bank, through the approach of decentralized governance, has also emphasized the importance of democratic participation in reforming urban governance in the continent.

On the other hand, Gramont (2015) has emphasized the role of democratic reforms, specifically in the transformation of Lagos from a chaotic city, which was taken to be the symbol of urban disorder, to a widely quoted example of effective city governance, in a span of only 15 years. He has observed that both domestic and international observers have acknowledged the important role of the Governor of Lagos State, Babatunde Fashola, who was first elected in 2007. Democratic governance stands out as an important theoretical approach in empowering social groups in African urban spaces. These reforms notably incentivized the citizens not only to pay taxes, but also to support democratic reforms that reproduced positive urban transformation.

Smit (2018) has echoed Gramont's (2015) theoretical argument. He observes that in order to comprehensively conceptualize the impacts of governance approaches in urban regions globally, we must focus on how urbanism, rather than urbanization, is governed. This, he observes, is helpful in that urbanism deals with a wider array of realities touching on complex interrelationships between development of built environments, multiple and complex identities, practices, struggles, as well as potentialities of urban social life in the continent. These observations resonate with Smit (2018), who notes that local governments in Africa are weak and disorganized. Moreover, they are described as having inadequately trained staff, in addition to being under-resourced, given the functions they are expected to perform. He notes that the work of local governments in the continent is made even more complicated by the position they occupy in the patronage system of political parties. Notably, African cities are often the bases of opposition political parties in the continent. This makes it difficult to understand the rationale behind some of the actions taken by both the city and national governments in the continent.

Aba and Owusu (2018) have, for instance, observed that the city authorities in Accra, Ghana, employ the term 'decongestion' as their approach of clearing parts of the city that are deemed undesirable. Ultimately, this approach results in adverse consequences on the street traders, slum dwellers and other informal operators. It is reported that in many instances, clearance of slums and street traders in many cities is done when it is politically correct to do so. For instance, politicians are known to have displaced people from slum areas where they are not popular during election seasons. This is done ostensibly in order to stop occupants from voting. Conversely, politicians who gain a lot of votes from such slum areas often stop urban clearance during the electioneering season so that they can get votes from the populations, only to turn against them as soon as the electioneering season is over. As Aba and Owusu have found out in the case of Ghana, the decongestion policy is like a two-edged sword. This is because it carries some political costs for leaders, both at the city and national levels. This explains why it tends to be suspended during election years and resumes soon after elections. Aba and Owusu conclude that one of the consequences of the removal of informal settlements and street operators from African cities, is the widening inequality between the richer population and the marginalized groups in African cities. This is antithetical to the right to the city theory, which has already been adopted by many African governments. The authors argue that the theory inevitably comes into conflict with both the city and national government elite, whose desire is to turn African cities into globally competitive spaces, with world class infrastructure, which can attract international investors such as multinational corporations and tourists, as well as highly qualified professionals.

Similarly, Kamete (2012) has noted that in Zimbabwe, the government has used the exigency for planning, in order to clear street operators and slum dwellers in urban centres. Noting that planning entails the exercise of power, he observes that three forms of power are exploited by the government through planning in specific socio-economic contexts in the case of Zimbabwe. Like in the case of Lagos and Accra, the privileged affluent groups have used the excuse for planning in order to violate the rights to the city of the marginalized communities. A case in point was the launching of an urban clean-up campaign in Harare on 19 May 2005 by the government authorities, which was given the term 'Murambatsvina' (Kamete, 2012, p. 6). The targets of this campaign were the informal urban traders and the low income neighbourhoods. These marginalized groups were branded the image of dirt and filth in order to justify the violent crackdown against them. This included conducting detentions and arrests of some of the operators by the government security forces.

In contrast to this violent operation in the low income neighbourhoods, there were double standards in the way the upmarket neighbourhoods were handled in Harare during the clean-up operation. Here, residents who utilized spaces without following the city regulations, were treated in a less violent manner. Eventually, the entire operation was stopped and the residents in these wealthy neighbourhoods were given a chance to regularize use of the space without going through painful evictions. Kamete observes that the Foucaldian concept of power was therefore employed by the government in the name of planning, in order to rid the city of the unwanted marginalized populations. It is this sense of Foucaldian power that is used by the powerful classes in order to take advantage of the prime spaces and the best urban infrastructural systems for themselves, often at the expense of the marginalized groups. Even in cities where national policies reflect the acceptance of the right to the city and inclusive urbanization, the notions of planning and decongestion seem to target those considered by the elite to be unwanted groups in cities. This ultimately narrows down to the eviction of informal urban settlers and street traders.

Political Management and Governance in Action

The studies discussed in the foregoing section are important in the understanding of political management and governance in Africa. The case studies in this chapter clearly indicate that urban governance in Africa encounters common problems, which could be tackled using the same governance framework but paying attention to the specific socio-cultural and economic context of each case. Smit (2018) has, for instance, noted that responsibility for key urban governance issues in Africa, in general, is often fragmented among the state and different stakeholders who have limited capacities. The private sector, such as the property development companies could play a key role in governance as they provide housing and other infrastructural services. International agencies, such as banks and donor agencies also provide some important services. In the Kisumu City of Kenya, for instance, the World Bank and the Agence Francaise de Development (AFD) have funded a number of development projects, including upgrading of informal settlements, as well as refurbishing and building new markets. Similarly, the civil society plays an important role in governance through networks such as religious associations, youth associations, as well as ethnicity-based networks. Smit calls for a more collaborative governance of the urban in order to boost co-production of these diverse stakeholders.

Similarly, Myers (2018) analysis of urban governance in the continent using the case study of Zanzibar and Dakar posits that urbanization in Africa presents new twists or dynamics that defy the Eurocentric framework. He alludes to the importance of political leaders paying attention to collaboration with citizens in land and housing development, as well as in urban governance in general. Such participative governance is often lacking and contributes to the problems bedevilling urban systems in Africa. Focusing on Ghana, Aba and Owusu (2018) point out the crucial importance of urban political managers paying attention to the specific context within which urban dynamics are taking place in the continent. Policies developed by political managers often prioritize modernization of cities, which contradict the reality of urban poverty, land scarcity and rising unemployment in the urban centres. Construction of super highways, new gated housing developments and malls are part and parcel of these modernization schemes. The injustice which results from government evictions of the less privileged urban residents in cities in the process of implementing such schemes is clearly demonstrated in different cities, including Harare (Kamete, 2012), Lagos (Gramont, 2015) and Accra (Aba & Owusu, 2018).

In the final analysis, lack of inclusive governance in the urban management is clearly demonstrated in almost all the urban case studies discussed. Gramont (2015) case study of Lagos clearly demonstrates some of the measures taken by political managers to address the challenges confronting the megacity. The return to democratic governance in the country in 1999 is believed to have impacted positively on Lagos City governance. This was perhaps demonstrated by the strong political relationship between urban political managers and the informal traders, better utilization of public funds in funding public sector projects in the city, as well services for city residents. These reforms took place mainly because there was increased bureaucratic political autonomy and resources, as well as cooperation with diverse social groups (2015, p. 4).

Challenges and Opportunities in the Governance of African Cities

Some of the challenges confronting African urban growth have been aptly summarized by many of the scholars already discussed. Some of these challenges include historical challenges that include those associated with colonial occupation and domination of Africa such as segregation in the development of urban centres and infrastructure; urban deprivation; poverty and inequality; and warfare, violence and disease.

Focusing on the challenges experienced in Lagos, which is undoubtedly the largest city in Africa with over 15 million inhabitants, Gramont (2015) observes that Lagos grapples with serious challenges including rapid population growth. The study observes that city government resources are draining away fast due to the emerging needs of the expanding population. Like elsewhere in the continent, in the light of the fast expansion of urban population, service delivery is taken over by self-help groups, and this results in several ramifications in regard to urban governance.

Given its huge population, Lagos also experiences challenges of an overburdened infrastructure, an enormous informal economy against a background of a long history of repressive military rule (Gramont, 2015, p. 4). Gramont's research points to the fact that there exists a significant relationship between existence of oppressive, undemocratic authorities and governance challenges in urban management. In the final analysis, cities like Lagos are polarized between a large, impoverished population of residents and a small group of the elite (Bekker & Fourchard, 2013). This situation often generates suspicion among the urban poor. Efforts to introduce reforms in such an environment attracts resistance especially from the poorer segments of the population. In the case of Lagos, bus operators were among the groups that resisted introduction of regulations fearing suffering losses by virtue of paying higher taxes to the government and city authorities. Moreover, some of the cartels who used to make money by charging for parking and security of passenger transport taxis and buses were fearful of losing their main source of income. Gramont (2015) observes that the so-called 'area boys'; namely, the local youth gangs, were at the forefront of resisting the new reforms aimed at transforming Lagos from the 1990s.

Governor Fashola's conception of a model megacity was therefore initially unpopular among the poor in Lagos. This is because the strategies aimed at streamlining waste collection and clearing informal settlements struck at the core of the livelihoods of the poor segments of the economy, who benefitted from the disorder in the city. Given that most informal operators have no rights to the land spaces on which they built their residences and for their informal businesses, most of them operate either on the roadside or public spaces. The state's focus on order and cleanliness inevitably leads to slum clearance and crackdown on street traders. The resistance to such clearance schemes is perhaps best understood against push factors that include rural landlessness, poverty and unemployment (Myers, 2010) among other factors that contribute to the phenomena of a large urban poor in the continent.

This situation of tension between city authorities and majority of urban residents often contributes to the prevalence of different forms of violence in African urban centres. However, more often than not, this violence operates alongside forms of non-violence advanced by the diverse civil society groups in the major urban centres. Urban violence has increased to such a huge scale to the extent that some cities in the continent that include Kinshasa, Douala, Johannesburg and Lagos (Myers, 2010) are characterized by piracy. Additionally, other forms of violence prevalent in African urban centres include violent conflict between different ethnic communities, gender-based violence as well as violence connected to abuse of alcohol and drugs. It is instructive to note that the ugly consequences of electoral-based violence in Africa are mostly felt in the major cities in the continent.

Gbaffou et al. (2013) have alluded to some of the factors that give rise to some of the violence experienced in African urban centres. Focusing on Cape Town and Lagos, they have observed the existence of mismatches between interests of local political leaders and the national political leadership. For instance, governance of Lagos has for several decades been undermined by the antagonism between the federal government and Lagos state leaders. The subsequent contestation over management and allocation of public resources has manifested in areas such as slum removal operations in the centre of Lagos as well as in battles over provision of road and railway infrastructure. This contest has taken place between the Lagos state and the federal government of Nigeria, all the way from the 1960s, to the 1980s. As already observed, control over the urban spaces is obviously contested between the two levels of government because of the lucrative economic opportunities and resources that reside in the major cities.

Potential for Transformation of African Cities

In spite of the highlighted challenges confronting rapid urbanization in Africa, a number of scholars have expressed optimism in the opportunities for positive transformation of African societies as a result of the expansion of urbanization in the continent. Bekker and Fourchard (2013) point out the fact that there have been two divergent approaches to the subject of African urban dynamics. On one hand, urbanization in Africa has been characterized as a process driven by poverty and desperation while on the other hand, it has been viewed as a process that engenders economic opportunities.

Gramont (2015) has pointed out the potential that lies in African urban spaces and notes that Nigeria's return to elected civilian rule in 1999 was a critical driver of reforms in Lagos. He further argues that indeed, Lagos' most significant institutional reforms took place during periods of relative political stability and continuity. This is an indicator that there is a window of opportunity to enhance reforms in the governance of urban centres in the continent. These will inevitably translate into huge benefits both at the state level and also for residents of these cities.

In regard to Lagos, governance transformation was driven by both the technocratic vision of a megacity on one hand and application of creative policy proposals on the other hand (Gbaffou et al., 2013; Gramont, 2015). These scholars have observed that in order to understand the transformation of Lagos, there is need to pay attention to several factors, including the importance of good leadership. However, attention should go beyond a focus on individual politicians in order to interrogate political, administrative, as well as social factors that could interfere with efficiency. They conclude that Governor Fashola who is credited with most of the reforms in Lagos and his predecessor, Governor Tinubu, had to balance pressures to deliver patronage to their supporters, with demands for improved public services in the city. Conclusively, the drivers of reforms in Lagos are summarized as constituting three factors; namely, a serious and persistent threat to elite interests, perceptions by the key actors that proposed reforms would benefit them, and finally, sufficient political stability to make change feasible. Simone (2016) and Myers (2018) have underscored the huge potential in African urban centres, which more often than not, is not well exploited.

Gramont observes that informal associations were instrumental in undertaking reforms in Lagos since 2007. In particular, the Lagos Men and Women Association that brings together smaller associations of traders who operate in the informal traditional markets were critical drivers in terms of encouraging city residents to support the City authorities. In this way, the state government was able to collect taxes from the informal traders. Similarly, Governor Fashola's administration also reached out to both the general public and various social organizations and appealed to them to encourage residents to change their waste disposal practices.

The business community was critical in supporting the city authorities through instituting tax reforms, as well as mobilizing residents to have respect for zoning regulations. Governor Fashola embraced the idea of tax collection through an out sourced professional company, which managed tax payment system in exchange for a commission. The link between effective tax collection and efficiency in the use of government revenue played an important role in winning over more people to pay taxes willingly. Support by the wealthy and influential urban elite has been demonstrated as one of the key enablers of reforms in Lagos.

Gramont (2015), Meagher (2007) and Kinyanjui (2010) have observed the important role played by the informal sector networks in Lagos, South Africa and Nairobi as well as other urban centres in Africa in terms of empowering urban residents. Citing ILO (2002), Meagher (2007) has noted that the informal economy was accounting for 60 percent of Africa's urban labour force, and creating over 90 percent of new jobs by the end of the last millennium. Similarly, the sector has been providing important economic activities beyond petty services to urban residents including complex informal manufacturing clusters, transport services, transnational trading networks as well as critical urban services such as housing, water supply using bowsers as well as sinking boreholes and providing waste collection services for the urban residents.

In addition to good leadership, potential for African urban reforms lies in tapping into the rich cultural dynamics in order to overcome the tremendous urban challenges confronting the continent (Pieterse, 2018). Citing the importance of notions of Pan Africanism and Ubuntu, for instance, he argues that these have great potential in empowering Africans in urban reforms. He notes that non-state cultural reference points such as religious affiliations and home town networks could be used to reform urban governance. In addition, social capital arising from such cultural affiliations has also been associated with many other economic and social developments. Ogino et al. (2008) have reported about the enormous positive impact brought about by Asian religious associations in Nairobi such as the Aga Khan community that has invested in hospitals, schools and banks among other facilities.

Conclusion

From the foregoing analysis of the urban governance and stewardship case studies in Africa, it has been demonstrated that urbanization in the continent is experiencing serious governance and management challenges, especially in the light of rapid urbanization process that is currently in progress. The chapter has identified a total of 65 studies that have focused on urban governance in Africa in general. It has however narrowed down the focus to 10 studies comprising books, book chapters and journal articles that specifically have examined urban stewardship and governance in Africa. Notably, various challenges have been experienced in these urban centres, but at the same time, great potential and creativity has also been witnessed. Among the challenges include the fast expansion of urban populations in cities such as Lagos, Accra, Nairobi, Johannesburg and Dakar, with the attendant challenges such as expansion of informal settlements, congestion, urban gangs and criminality, as well as unemployment.

The study interrogated research works that have employed diverse theories to analyse urban governance and management experiences in the continent including decentralization, good governance, right to the city theory, urban multiplex theory, as well as informality theory. The significance of each of these theories in examining the challenges and opportunities confronting authorities managing urban centres in Africa as well as the risks associated with some of these divergent theories in the analysis of African urbanization have been discussed.

From the studies looked at, it was noted that a more democratic approach through engaging the various stakeholders, including other initiatives such as the urban gangs, women traders and transport operators, has the potential of promoting locally generated solutions to the urban management challenges. This therefore calls for theoretical tools capable of analysing this complex African urban reality. The research has demonstrated that African urban residents have risen up to the challenges of this urban phenomenon, not as mere spectators or subjects but as active participants. Studies that have analysed the dynamics of the informal sector in all the urban centres discussed bear witness to the residents' agency in tackling many of the challenges confronting them.

From the foregoing analysis, it is clear that more case studies focusing on specific urban centres in Africa are required. This will give researchers an opportunity not only to interrogate the complex challenges confronting these cities, but also the strategies employed by the city authorities to surmount the challenges of governance and initiate adequate reforms in African urban centres. This also calls for more multidisciplinary research in order to interrogate not only the urban challenge dynamics, but also theories that could help scholars to come up with solutions to the complex dynamics in the urban centres in Africa in the face of rapid globalization.

REFERENCES

Aba, G. O., & Owusu, G. (2018). Accra's decongestion policy: Another face of urban clearance or bulldozing approach? In C. Ammann & T. Forster (Eds.), *African cities and the development conundrum* (Vol. 10). International Development Policy Institute.

Awortwi, N. (2004). Getting the fundamentals wrong: Woes of public–private partnerships in solid waste collection in three Ghanaian cities. *Public Administration and Development Journal, 24*, 213–224.

Bekker, S., & Fourchard, L. (Eds.). (2013). *Politics and policies governing cities in Africa*. Human Research Council.

Berg, J., Akinyele, R., Fourchard, L., Waal, V. D. M., & Williams, M. (2013). Contested social orders: Negotiating urban security in Nigeria and South Africa. In S. Bekker & L. Fourchard (Eds.), *Politics and policies governing cities in Africa*. Human Research Council.

Charlotte et al. (2020). *Governing sustainability in secondary cities of global South*. A paper published in Stockholm Environment Institute.

Dalberto, S., Charton, H., & George, D. (2013). Urban planning, housing and the making of responsible citizens in the late colonial period: Dakar, Nairobi & Conakry. In S. Bekker & L. Fourchard (Eds.), *Politics and policies governing cities in Africa*. Human Research Council.

Dietz, T. (2018). Online representation of sustainable city initiatives in Africa: How inclusive? In C. Ammann & T. Forster (Eds.), *African cities and the development conundrum* (Vol. 10). International Development Policy Institute.

Durand, A., (2015). Tenure security and exclusion processes in per-urban areas and rural Hinterlands of West African cities. In P. Katharina & S. Oliver (Eds.), *Governing access to essential resources*. Columbia University Press.

Gbaffou et al. (2013). Exploring the role of party politics in the governance of African cities. In S. Bekker & L. Fourchard (Eds.), *Politics and Policies governing cities in Africa*. Human Sciences Research Council.

Gramont, G. D. (2015). Lagos: Unlocking the politics of reform. *Carnegie Endowment for International Peace*.

Grest, J., Baudouin, A., Bjerkli, C., & Quénot-Suarez, H. (2013). The politics of solid-waste management in Accra, Addis Ababa, Maputo and Ouagadougou: Different cities, similar issues. In S. Bekker & L. Fourchard (Eds.), *Politics and policies governing cities in Africa*. Human Research Council.

Groenewald, L., Huchzermeyer, M., Kornienko, K., Tredoux, M., Rubin, M., & Raposo, I. (2013). Breaking down the binary: Meanings of informal settlement in southern African cities. In S. Bekker & L. Fourchard (Eds.), *Politics and policies governing cities in Africa*. Human Research Council.

ILO. (2002). *Decent work and informal economy*.

Kamete, A. (2012, February). Integrating planning power on an African city, time for reorientation? *Planning Theory, 11*(1), 66–88.

Kinyanjui, M. N. (2010). Social relations and associations in the informal sector in Kenya. *Social Policy and Development Programme Paper Number 43, January 2010*. United Nations Research Institute for Social Development (UNRISD).

Lall, V. S., & Venables, A. (2017). *Africa's cities: Opening doors to the world*. The World Bank.

Lefebvre, H. (1970). *The urban revolution*. Gallimard Press.

Meagher, K. (2007). *Afrika Spectrum, 42*(3), 405–418. GIGA Institute of African Affairs.

Meghan, F. E. (2013). *Moving targets: Meanings of mobility in metropolitan Nairobi*. Ph.D. dissertation, Washington University of St. Louis.

Mwaniki et al. (2015). *Urbanization, informality and housing challengein Nairobi: A case of urban governance failure?*

Myers, G. A. (2010). *Seven themes in African urban dynamics* (Discussion Paper 50). Nordiska, Afrikainstitute.

Myers, G. A. (2011). *African cities: Alternative visions of urban theory and practice*. Zed Books.

Myers, G. A. (2018). The African problem of global urban theory. In C. Ammann & T. Forster (Eds.), *African cities and the development conundrum* (Vol. 10). International Development Policy Institute.

Ogino, F., Kiruthu, F., & Akala, W. J. (2008). *A critical analysis of the social and economic impact of Asian diaspora in Kenya*. In T. Falola & N. Afolabi (Eds.), *Trans-Atlantic migration: The paradoxes of exile*. Routledge.

Pieterse, E. (2018). The politics of governing African urban spaces. In C. Ammann & T. Forster (Eds.), *African cities and the development conundrum* (Vol. 10). International Development Policy Institute.

Rapoport, E., Acuto, M., & Grcheva, L. (2019). *Exploring city leadership catalysts of action*. UCL.

Resnick, D. (2014). Urban governance and service delivery in African cities: The role of politics and policies. In *Development Policy Review, July 2014*.

Satterthwaite, D. (2017). The impact of urban development on risk in sub-Saharan Africa's cities with a focus on small and intermediate urban centres. *International Journal of Disaster Risk Reduction, 26*, 16–23.

Sebastian, P. (2018). Urban identities and belonging: Young men's discourses about Pikine. In C. Amman & T. Forster (Eds.), *African cities and the development conundrum* (Vol. 10). International Development Policy Institute.

Simone, A. (2016). City of potentialities: Race, violence and invention. *Theory, Culture & Society, 33*(7–8), 5–29.

Smit, W. (2018). Urban governance in Africa: An overview. In C. Ammann & T. Forster (Eds.), *African cities and the development conundrum* (Vol. 10). International Development Policy Institute.

Stoll, F. (2018). The city's ways of life: Local influences on middle income milieus in Nairobi. In C. Ammann & T. Forster (Eds.), *African cities and the development conundrum* (Vol. 10). International Development Policy Institute.

UN-Habitat. (2014). *The state of African cities 2014: Re-imagining sustainable urban transitions*. UN-Habitat.

CHAPTER 4

Agriculture

Reniko Gondo and Joseph E. Mbaiwa

Introduction

Urban agriculture (UA) is understood as activities that make use of natural resources and recycles urban wastes to produce crops and animals (Olufemi, 2019). UA is also defined as the cultivation of crops within metropolitan centres as opposed to rural areas (Adedayo, 2012; Dossa et al., 2011; Mupeta et al., 2020). In this sense, UA includes a range of activities encompassing vegetables, fruits, grains and raising fish, bees, chickens, goats and pigs inter alia (Mbiba, 1999). Other authors view UA as the production, processing and distribution of a variety of foods including vegetables and animal products within a city with the intention of home consumption or income generation (Theresa & Pride, 2017; van Averbeke, 2007). Similarly, some authors prefer to outline the features of UA than to give a definite definition. In this category, there are authors like Rudolph et al. (2021), Adedayo (2012) and Mupeta et al. (2020) who outline the characteristics of UA as an activity practised within the boundary and periphery of a city.

The idea of UA may look contradictory to urbanisation that tends to be associated with non-farming activities. However, UA in African cities continues to attract research and policy attention, partly because it is a livelihood option

R. Gondo (✉) · J. E. Mbaiwa
Okavango Research Institute, University of Botswana, Maun, Botswana
e-mail: rgondo@ub.ac.bw

J. E. Mbaiwa
e-mail: jmbaiwa@ub.ac.bw

for a growing majority of inhabitants (Popoola et al., 2020). The 2008–2009 food crisis in Africa and its impact on political instability could have been the main driver which compelled researchers and policymakers to pay attention to it. There is an increase in the number of people affected by hunger and poverty in developing countries. For instance, Rudolph et al. (2021) reveal that in 2008, about 800 million people were hunger and poverty-stricken with the figure surging to about 1 billion in 2009.

Despite a global rise in food production over the same period, the situation has not changed much, especially in Africa where estimates show that a population of about 350 million were suffering from hunger (Rudolph et al., 2021). An increase in the world population projected to hit 9 billion by the year 2050 will negatively impact food production capacity with attendant effects on hunger and poverty if appropriate measures are not put in place to address this phenomenon. Strategies to boost food production across all levels, including urban areas are therefore imperative. Data shows that urban areas in developing countries will host 63 percent of the population by the year 2050 (United Nations World Statistics Pocketbook, 2020). In Africa, over half of the population will reside in urban areas (Gómez-Villarino & Ruiz-Garcia, 2021). Sanchi and Muhammad (2021), among other researchers, have demonstrated that UA is a potential and proven strategy through which access to, and distribution of food in an urban area can be enhanced. It is therefore not surprising that in 2019, over 800 million people globally were engaged in UA (UN Food and Agriculture Organization [UNFAO], 2019).

UA has been considered a key strategy to mitigate the increasing food insecurity, especially of low-income urban residents. This chapter presents and discusses UA in terms of study designs, theories underpinning UA studies in Africa, and factors driving UA as well as socio-economic characteristics of urban farmers. Also discussed in this chapter is the location of urban plots and land rights. Noted also in this chapter is that there is no clear policy and legislation is governing UA in Africa and yet UA is a source of livelihoods. The last issue of concern in this chapter is the challenges encountered in UA in general. While the main research objective of this chapter is to assess UA in African cities in terms of methodology, and key findings from previous studies conducted offer a summary of the key findings, the specific objectives of this chapter are to: determine trends in UA in African cities; assess the nature and role of UA and analyse the empirical findings from UA studies.

METHODS

A total of 450 publications that satisfied search criteria were retrieved and reviewed. The studies were drawn from diverse sources ranging from journal articles, reports of postgraduate research reports (theses), book chapters and conference proceedings. A total of 35 studies were selected and included in the final analysis. The selection of the criteria for these studies emphasises those articles with a focus on African cities only. Studies that analyse UA but without a focus on African cities were excluded in the final analysis. Only book chapters and journal articles were included in the final analysis, thus postgraduate studies, commentaries and letters to the editors were also excluded. Once all the relevant studies were retrieved in hard copies, each was scrutinised and relevant information was extracted and summarised in a data extraction matrix (Table 4.1). The variables extracted included author(s) and publication date, the focus of study, a geographical unit of the selected study, sample size, theories, research design and main findings were derived from each of the studies.

Results and Discussion

Study Designs

Of the 35 studies reviewed, one was conducted in Botswana (Hovorka, 2005), one in Malawi (Mkwambisi et al., 2011), seven in Nigeria (Adedayo, 2012; Anosike & Fasona, 2004; Etim et al., 2006; Olufemi, 2019; Popoola et al., 2020; Sanchi & Muhammad, 2021; Taiwo, 2014), three in Tanzania (Flynn, 2001; Mlozi, 1997; Schmidt et al., 2015), six in Zimbabwe (Chaminuka & Dube, 2017; Hungwe, 2006; Jongwe, 2014; Kutiwa et al., 2010; Mbiba, 1999; Mubvami et al. (2006), three in Ghana (Armar-Klemesu, 2000; Ayerakwa, 2017; Bolang & Osumanu, 2019), two in Kenya (Lado, 1990; Mireri et al., 2007), five in South Africa (Kanosvamhira, 2019; Malan, 2015; Martin et al., 2002; Rudolph et al., 2021; van Averbeke, 2007), three in Zambia (Mupeta et al., 2020; Theresa & Pride, 2017; Thornton et al., 2010), one in Sierra Leone (Cissé et al., 2005), one in Mali (Dossa et al., 2011) and one in Burkina Faso (Dossa et al., 2011).

In terms of year of publication, one was published in 1990 (Lado, 1990), one in 1997 (Mlozi, 1997), one in 1999, one in 2000 (Armar-Klemesu, 2000), one in 2001, one in 2002, two in 2005 (Cissé et al., 2005; Hovorka, 2005), 3 in 2006 (Etim et al., 2006; Hungwe, 2006; Mubvami et al., 2006), two in 2007 (Mireri et al., 2007; van Averbeke, 2007), three in 2010 (Kutiwa et al., 2010; Thornton et al., 2010), three in 2011 (Dossa et al., 2011; Dossa et al., 2011; Mkwambisi et al., 2011), one in 2012 (Adedayo, 2012), three in 2014 (Frayne et al., 2014; Jongwe, 2014; Taiwo, 2014), two in 2015 (Malan, 2015; Schmidt et al., 2015), three in 2017 (Ayerakwa, 2017; Chaminuka & Dube, 2017; Theresa & Pride, 2017), three in 2019 (Bolang & Osumanu, 2019; Kanosvamhira, 2019; Olufemi, 2019), two in 2020 (Mupeta et al., 2020; Popoola et al., 2020) and two in 2021 (Rudolph et al., 2021; Sanchi & Muhammad, 2021).

While 31 studies gathered and analysed evidence on UA without basing their designs on a theoretical model, only four studies were underpinned in a model or theoretical framework. The four studies are Taiwo (2014) which is used in the Von Thunen locational factor theory and Olufemi (2019) who utilised Longwe's framework. While Lado (1990) used open spaces and the

Table 4.1 Summary of research on urban agriculture in African cities

Author	Geographical unit	Study focus	Sample size	Data collection techniques	Theory	Research design	Results
Kutiwa et al. (2010)	Harare, Zimbabwe	Quantitative analysis and contribution of UA to food security at the household level	59	Field observation Key informant interviews Household structured questionnaire	Access, availability and utilisation conceptual framework	Cross-sectional study	1. UA is the surviving strategy for the poor urban residence with the propensity to reduce poverty and improve the food security of urban poor households 2. UA is not classified as an urban activity 3. Urban Planning does not cater for UA 4. UA is only recognised by Harare and Nyanga Declarations by Ministers of local governments of Eastern and Southern Africa 5. Declarations encouraged local Authorities to support UA
Mulwami et al. (2006)	Harare, Zimbabwe	Urban planning for agriculture	—	Field observation Key informant interviews Household structured questionnaire	Urban planning models	Literature review	1. Policymakers and town planners need to recognise UA as a form of livelihood for the urban poor 2. Urban development master plans do not recognise UA as a Land-use activity in Africa 3. City development plans fail to recognise UA 4. City planners need to demarcate zones for UA
Taiwo (2014)	Osogbo, Nigeria	Factors shaping locational choice behaviour of urban farmers	300	FGDs, questionnaire survey	Location factor theory		1. Key locational factors: • Cultivation close to water sources • Cultivation close to farmer's residence • Availability of labour and market • Fertile soils attract farming

Author	Geographical unit	Study focus	Sample size	Data collection techniques	Theory	Research design	Results
Mireri et al. (2007)	Kisumu municipality, Kenya	Environmental risks threatening sustainable urban agriculture in Kisumu municipality	194	Structured questionnaires			1. Lack of access to basic infrastructure and services such as water, sanitation and solid waste management impacts negatively on UA and leads to pollution of farms 2. The urban policy environment does not recognise UA as urban land use
Appeaning (2010)	Accra, Ghana	Remote sensing technology and its role in integrated monitoring techniques for urban farmlands		Collection of: • GPS • Georeferencing area of interest • Digitising • Scanning		Remote sensing and field survey	Technology advancement provides data to monitor and manage UA
Ayerakwa (2017)	Bono and Tamale, Ghana	The contribution of UA to meet food security	2004	Key informant interviews Household questionnaires			1. Urban agriculture should not be treated in isolation from other mechanisms that households employ to meet their food and nutrition needs 2. The contribution of urban agriculture to household food security should be viewed in the context of understanding the values that households involved in urban agriculture place on produce, considering how produce is utilised

(continued)

Table 4.1 (continued)

Author	Geographical unit	Study focus	Sample size	Data collection techniques	Theory	Research design	Results
Hungwe (2006)	Gweru, Zimbabwe	Understanding of urban agriculture as food access or survival strategy	250	Questionnaire		Cross-sectional survey	1. The poor engaged in urban agriculture to ensure food availability while the affluent engage in UA as a hobby since agriculture has some cultural value 2. The poor engaged in illegal open space farming while the rich had bigger yards and therefore could afford to farm within them 3. Whether or not UA improves household food security and diet is dependent on the original reason for engaging in the activity
Hovorka (2005)	Gaborone, Botswana	Potential role of commercial urban agriculture in addressing food security and economic growth	109	Key informant interviews Household questionnaire		Survey	1. Productivity levels in UA stem from gender differential in socio-economic disparities between male and female urban farmers 2. Socio-economic gender differences have a major impact on women's access to productive resources, including capital, labour and land
Flynn (2001)	Mwanza, Tanzania	Factors influencing urban farming		Literature review	Open space concept	Literature review	1. UA enterprise utilises any open spaces in the city 2. Rapid urbanisation and rise in demand for urban food leads to UA

Author	Geographical unit	Study focus	Sample size	Data collection techniques	Theory	Research design	Results
Anosike and Fasona (2004)	Lagos, Nigeria	Gender analysis of opportunities and constraints in providing food in Lagos	100	Key informant interview Field observation Household questionnaire surveys		Field survey	1. Urban farms, especially those headed by women, are often located in unsafe and insecure areas on the edges of the cities, which lack basic services such as water and electricity 2. Women depend on the assistance of hired and family members (children), which makes the product expensive and unprofitable, and in addition, affects the quantity of time the children can spend at school
Lado (1990)	Nairobi, Kenya	Open spaces and the garden city concept	250			Field survey	1. Cultivation is conducted in all public or private vacant spaces 2. UA is conducted by city dwellers who have more than 5 years of living in the city 3. Mostly those employed in low-paying jobs are involved in UA 4. Usually, one household has several small plots scattered across the city
van Averbeke (2007)	Pretoria, South Africa	Material benefits UA				Field survey	1. Family obtains fresh food 2. Increase cash income 3. Save on food expenditure 4. Enjoy working in the garden 5. Apply knowledge of farming

(continued)

Table 4.1 (continued)

Author	Geographical unit	Study focus	Sample size	Data collection techniques	Theory	Research design	Results
Mbiba (1999)	Harare, Zimbabwe	Urban agriculture and policy/legislation		Field observations Household questionnaire surveys Key informant interviews		Field survey	1. UA is an on-plot, off-plot and peri-urban activity; on-plot crop production is allowed but livestock rearing is illegal 2. The activities are legal in designated areas and illegal in some areas 3. UA provides food for home consumption 4. Low levels of fertiliser application 5. Increases chances of environmental degradation (floods, run-off, soil erosion) 6. Women provide the bulk of labour and management 7. Policymakers do not regard UA as a viable solution to food security and unemployment 8. Municipality Act provides for urban food production but gives local authorities the discretion to determine the desirability and extent of the activity at any point in time 9. No loans, subsidies and credit facilities or extension services to urban farmers 10. Policymakers regard UA as in contradiction of urban legislation

Author	Geographical unit	Study focus	Sample size	Data collection techniques	Theory	Research design	Results
Chaminuka and Dube (2017)	Mkoba, Gweru, Zimbabwe	Suburban agriculture practices	26	Interviews FGDs		Field survey	1. UA confirmed the growing of vegetables and poultry production 2. UA restricted to residential properties 3. Deals with food insecurity and job creation 4. Most urban poor are involved 5. No specific legislation outlines how UA should be conducted 6. A legislation environment prohibits the practice of UA
Malan (2015)	Johannesburg, South Africa	Significance of policy vis-à-vis assessment of urban agriculture		Interviews FGDs		Review	1. UA succeeds with the strengthening of farmers' organisations 2. Linkages of urban farmers with the retailer are vital 3. Farmer's training is crucial for the success of UA 4. The City council needs to put in place a policy that enhances UA
Rudolph et al. (2021)	Johannesburg, South Africa	Prevalence of food insecurity in greater Johannesburg metropole	1000	Household questionnaire		Field survey	1. Food insecurity varies in terms of seasons 2. Supermarkets are common food sources 3. High food insecurity in high-density residential areas 4. Coping strategies for supply include UA, reducing food portions, size and borrowing from family members 5. Food sources include formal and informal retail

(continued)

Table 4.1 (continued)

Author	Geographical unit	Study focus	Sample size	Data collection techniques	Theory	Research design	Results
Mupeta et al. (2020)	Lusaka, Zambia	Impact of urban agriculture on household income in Zambia	2682	Questionnaire survey		Field survey	1. UR contributes to increased household income 2. Farming households had higher incomes than non-farming households 3. Policymakers need to create an enabling environment for UA 4. UA has the potential to reduce poverty, enhance the standard of living and improve household food security
Sanchi and Muhammad (2021)	Southern Kebbi State, Nigeria	Gender participation in agricultural productivity	120				1. UA is an activity for both males and females 2. Women labour is highest in UA 3. Competition and power of ownership of land led to shrinkage of farmland 4. Lack of government support and credit facilities constrain UA
Etim et al. (2006)	Akwa Ibom State (Oyo), Nigeria	Factors determining urban farming outputs	100				1. The majority of urban farmers are women 2. Farmers own many small plots of less than 1 ha 3. UA ensures sustained food supply in urban households 4. UA is a means of augmenting family income

Author	Geographical unit	Study focus	Sample size	Data collection techniques	Theory	Research design	Results
Olufemi (2019)	Nigeria, Lagos	Role of urban agriculture in empowering urban women farmers as well as meeting their practical and strategic gender needs	255			Field survey	1. More women than men are involved in UA
2. Women are deprived of access to land
3. Income generated from UA reduces household expenditure
4. UA is a veritable source of food, income and poverty alleviation
5. Majority of the women (86 percent) were either married or widowed
6. Women farmers use farming not only as a means of livelihood but also as an empowerment tool for decision making
7. Urban female farmers should take part in policy formulation
Bolang and Osumanu (2019)	Wa Municipality, Ghana	Participation of formal sector employees in UA and their contributions to the food supply	364			A cross-sectional survey,	1. There are very few civil servants involved in UA
2. Those involved in UA have very many, small scattered farms
3. Common crops grown are maize, vegetables, and legumes
4. Males are dominant in UA
5. Factors such as gender, age, household size, availability of credit facilities and formal workload determine who participates in UA
6. Policy options need to be targeted at training formal urban farmers to build their capacity

(continued)

Table 4.1 (continued)

Author	Geographical unit	Study focus	Sample size	Data collection techniques	Theory	Research design	Results
Adedayo (2012)	Lagos, Nigeria	Poultry waste management and utilisation technique in urban vegetable farms		Questionnaire		Cross-sectional survey	1. Poultry waste is an important soil ameliorating resource for UA 2. Application of manure is done without protective clothing 3. Exotic vegetables require more poultry manure than local vegetables 4. The use of poultry manure reduces the burden of inorganic fertilisers
Popoola et al. (2020)	Ibadan, Nigeria	Urban farmers' perception of climate variability and its effect on urban food production	244			Cross-sectional survey	1. 48 percent of urban residents depend on farming as a main source of livelihood 2. Large households of 10 people needed as a source of labour 3. The majority of females (55 percent) were younger than 45 years with youthful strength 4. UA was practised with people of varying marital status 5. 62 percent of the urban farmers received extension services 6. A variety of difficulties affect urban farmers and climate is among them 7. Urban farmers need to be provided with both formal and informal training, retraining and extension services to broaden their knowledge

Author	Geographical unit	Study focus	Sample size	Data collection techniques	Theory	Research design	Results
Kunoswanhira et al. (2019)	Cape Town, South Africa	Coordination of activities among key supporting organisations in UA				Literature review	1. Limited coordination amongst organisations that support urban farmers 2. There are many agendas amongst organisations that support urban farmers 3. There is duplication of efforts amongst urban key stakeholders in urban agriculture 4. Urban farmers need to be included in all stakeholders' dialogue 5. Need for the farmer-driven organisation at the local level
Schmidt et al. (2015)	Dar es Salaam, Tanzania	Associations between UA and urbanisation	562			Field survey	1. Crops mostly grown are vegetables 2. There are shortages of spaces 3. Most farmers grow crops for home consumption and sale 4. Rapid urbanisation impedes UA
Martin et al. (2002)	South Africa	Role of UA			Sustainable livelihoods		1. Characteristics of poverty are dynamism 2. Poor individuals are not permanently poor 3. Poor families go hungry, eating less frequently 4. Non-essentials (e.g., rice, tea, sugar) are dropped from the budget
Cissé et al. (2005)	Sierra Leone	Institutional aspects of UA				Literature review	1. Urban farmers are constantly harassed by municipal policy 2. The lack of organisations to represent urban farmers 3. UA is regarded as irrelevant 4. There is no clear policy to support UA

(continued)

Table 4.1 (continued)

Author	Geographical unit	Study focus	Sample size	Data collection techniques	Theory	Research design	Results
Dossa et al. (2011)	Kano, Nigeria; Bobo Dioulasso, Burkina Faso Sikasso, Mali	Relationship between household socio-economic status and participation in UA	700			Field survey	1. The number of households participating in UA is more significant than those not participating 2. People who recently migrated to cities are the ones engaged in UA 3. UA constitute a livelihood strategy across all socio-economic grouping of the three cities 4. There is a high number of people involved in UA in West Africa
Mlozi (1997)	Dar es Salaam	Factors encouraging livestock production in peri-urban environments				Field survey	1. UA hurts the population, e.g. domestic animals spread diseases such as zoonoses 2. Animal dung produces odour 3. The raising of animals in urban areas results in air pollution 4. The city council do not enforce by-laws 5. Cattle are raised in UA

Author	Geographical unit	Study focus	Sample size	Data collection techniques	Theory	Research design	Results
Mkwambisi et al. (2011)	Malawi	UA for poverty reduction, employability creation and food security	330	Interviews FGDs		Field survey	1. Urban households on average produce 228 kg of cereals per year enough to feed themselves 2. More educated wealthier and male-headed households harvest more than their poorer, less educated and female-headed counterparts 3. Elite households harvest more due to access to large plots of land and better technology 4. Best technology is not available to all urban farmers in Malawi urban farmers 5. Maize is the main food crop 6. Other products of UA include poultry, cattle and vegetables 7. Access to land, land ownership, use of inputs and participation in livelihoods activities UA favours educated, middle- and upper-income families

(continued)

Table 4.1 (continued)

Author	Geographical unit	Study focus	Sample size	Data collection techniques	Theory	Research design	Results
Frayne et al. (2014)		Role of UA in alleviating food insecurity	6453	A household questionnaire survey		Field survey	1. The benefits of UA as a broad urban development and food security strategy are unclear 2. UA has limited poverty alleviation benefits under current modes of practices and regulations 3. Economic, political and historical circumstances determine participation in UA at the household level 4. No evidence to support UA as an effective household food security strategy 5. Participation in UA is determined by the household level of income, land ownership, with wealthier households participating much more than their poorer households' counterparts 6. UA requires complex preconditions, inputs, extension services, financial access, land, marketing infrastructure and knowledge for urban farmers to benefit from farming

Author	Geographical unit	Study focus	Sample size	Data collection techniques	Theory	Research design	Results
Thornton et al. (2010)	Zambia	Institutional responses to UA		Literature review and policy documents studies			1. Women farmers need support for them to do well in UA 2. Both farmers and local authorities lack sufficient financial resources to support local farmers 3. Structural adjustment, recessions and poor performance of the economy worsen the socio-economic conditions and thus trigger UA 4. The state does not have adequate resources to respond to poverty and unemployment 5. UA has a critical role to play at the household level 6. Major types of UA are backyard gardens, animal and crop farming 7. Small proportions of urban farmers are engaged in animal husbandry
Theresa, and Pride (2017)	Zambia	Benefits of UA		Literature review			1. UA: • Provides avenue for individuals to access past experiences in farming • Creates spaces for recreation to household • Reduces poverty and beautifies the city • Saves participants' money • Provides resources of income • Improves food access and security

(continued)

Table 4.1 (continued)

Author	Geographical unit	Study focus	Sample size	Data collection techniques	Theory	Research design	Results
Armar-Klemesu (2000)	Ghana	UA for food security		Literature review			1. Factors influencing urban dwellers food access are: • Macro-economic policies • Employment • Market and food prices 2. Constraints of UA are: • Prohibitive urban policies and regulations • Limited access to productive resources and insecure land tenure • Lack of support services • Lack of organisations amongst urban farmers
Jongwe (2014)	Zimbabwe	Assessment of the extent to which urban household food insecurity is mitigated by UA activities	150	Structured and unstructured questionnaires Interviews		Field survey	1. Age, gender and employment status determine participation in UA 2. Bigger families are more involved in UA than smaller families 3. Risks of food insecurity drive UA 4. Households size affects food provision in urban areas 5. Major crops grown in urban areas include maize and vegetables

garden city concept in his study, Martin et al. (2002) used sustainable livelihoods theoretical frameworks to analyse the impact of UA at the household level. The two groups of studies generated meaningful findings bordering UA in Africa. While the findings are of significance in the mainstreaming of UA into urban planning, there is an avenue as well for increased urban agricultural productivity. Thus, from these two groups of studies, a comprehensive land use plan which incorporates food production and socio-economic structures for urban centres is paramount.

Sample Size

Sample size measures the number of individuals or household members used in a survey. A study sample size is calculated using a formula. Of the 35 studies, 22 of them indicated a sample size while 13 did not reveal the sample size because their studies were based on a review of related literature. Two studies (Chaminuka & Dube, 2017; Kutiwa et al., 2010) had a sample of less than 100. While Kutiwa et al. (2010) used a sample of 59 households, Chaminuka and Dube used a sample of 26 households. These were the least number of samples in the reviewed articles. The highest (6453 households) sample size was noted in the study by Frayne et al. (2014) which used data gathered from four countries.

Theories

Four main theories were adopted in the studies. These were the Von Thunen locational theory utilised by Taiwo (2014), Longwe framework (Olufemi, 2019), sustainable livelihood (Martin et al., 2002) and Flynn's (2001) open space concept. For the locational model adopted by Taiwo (2014), the model has unique applicability and is independent of scale and can apply very well in developing countries. However, it is noteworthy that the model has no relevance in modern economic situations, especially with the modification in transport and new technological achievements, thus the needs of the past centuries seem obsolete. The use of refrigeration can now preserve perishable products for a longer time and so can be transported over long distances. With the introduction of air freight, the world has now shrunk into one big farm. Thus, no such concentric pattern is visible. On the other hand, the Longwe framework emphasises the fact that women and men have equal control over factors of production and the distribution of benefits influences dominance or subordination. Women, therefore, have access to resources such as land, labour and benefits on an equal basis with men. However, it is important to note that in Africa unless there is a reform on customary law and practices which disadvantage women, access to resources in UA will continue to be gender skewed in favour of men rather than women.

Based on Taiwo (2014), Von Thunen's agricultural location theory is concerned with the process of location and allocation of land as well as the spatial distribution of agricultural land use. The theory posits that transport cost and land use are the major determinants of agricultural production. The physical distance between farm and market, transport costs, market prices, yield and production cost, therefore, determine urban agricultural rent. Based on his model, agricultural activities are organised in a concentric manner around the city with the inner ring being a zone of intensive farming. Perishable products such as milk and vegetables that must get to the market quickly occupied the inner ring. Thus, Taiwo (2014) in his study in Lagos, Nigeria corresponds the inner zone with the activities of urban farmers in the city.

Olufemi (2019) utilises the Longwe framework to assess the extent to which UA supports urban female farmers' empowerment. The study was aimed at showing the varying levels of empowerment of the female farmers based on the notion of five different levels; namely, welfare, access, conscientization, participation and control at the highest level. Applying Longwe's levels of equality, Olufemi (2019) has shown how financially empowered urban women can support their households on a daily basis.

The livelihoods framework (Martin et al., 2002) assists in conceptualising the interrelationships between the different dimensions of people's lives and helps to reveal the complexity of urban livelihoods and poverty. It is holistic and cross-sectoral, encouraging interdisciplinary thinking. It puts people, including women and children, at the centre of the analysis and explores access to and control over different kinds of assets, which include human and social assets as well as natural, financial and physical. It is useful in the analysis of multifaceted urban livelihoods, and situations of poverty and vulnerability. However, low levels of food security are still experienced within the urban areas in Africa. With the Sustainable Livelihood Approach as a theoretical framework, the studies accentuate other livelihood outcomes of UA such as improving health, improving self-esteem and improving food security.

The open space concepts as utilised by Flynn (2001) originated from the city gardens idea by Howard (1902) who advocated for an urban area with land uses separated from one another by a strip of open spaces with only grass. For instance, residential areas are separated from commercial and industrial by a strip of open space with only grass. Also, the use of the neighbourhood principle to separate local interaction from traffic, the aesthetic functional conversion of the main roads into wide boulevards with grassed paths, grass stripes along streams and drainage fall in the same open space concept. The use of this theory shows that urban open spaces have the potential to be utilised as urban farming land, where hapless inhabitants could be the main actors to manage UA to provide their food.

Factors Driving Urban Agriculture

Literature has shown that several underlying factors contributed to the rising importance of UA in African cities; among the drivers include the adoption of neoliberal economic policies such as structural adjustment programmes

(ESAPs) of the 1980s and 1990s. The introduction of ESAPs alongside economic recessions in most African countries led to food price increases and high unemployment levels (Malan, 2015; Popoola et al., 2020; Schmidt et al., 2015). In the early 1980s, only 25 percent of urban households in Kampala were involved in UA and this increased to over 70 percent by the beginning of the 1990s (Mbiba, 1999). Rapid urbanisation attributed to both rural–urban migration and natural increases resulted in adverse economic and social repercussions on the development of urban economies in Africa (Mbiba, 1999; Sanchi & Muhammad, 2021).

The consequences of unprecedented urbanisation were noted to be high unemployment levels, increased food shortages as well as high food prices. The aforementioned attributes threatened the food security of the urban population in Africa whose food access was dominated by purchases from supermarkets. Increased food prices negatively eroded the urbanites' purchasing power, and especially so for the low-income households.

Socio-Economic Characteristics of Urban Farmers

Research has shown that in terms of the gender of urban farmers, particularly in the high-income category, male farmers are involved in farming whereas in the low-income category, it is females who are usually involved. For instance, Hungwe (2006) and Hovorka (2005) found that in Gweru and Gaborone, more poor women were the majority in urban cultivation and only affluent males participate in UA.

In terms of literacy and food production, it has been shown that high-income urban farmers use people with low levels of illiteracy that results in high crop production (Martin et al., 2002; Theresa & Pride, 2017). On the other hand, in low-income farmers, there is also high levels of illiteracy that results in low crop yields. For high-income urban farmers (UF), the plot size is almost half a hectare (ha) and for low-income UF, the plot is usually less than 0.01 ha. While on the one hand, high-income farmers practice UA as a hobby and personal consumption, on the other hand, low-income farmers regard UA as a household food security and income.

For high-income farmers, the labour supply is mostly permanent and skilled and only use casual and unskilled labour in the crop sector (Malan, 2015). The low-income farmers mostly use temporal and unskilled labour and at times use skilled labour on livestock only. Literature for Gweru and Harare in Zimbabwe has also shown that the season for supplying labour in UA is all year round for both low and high-income farmers (Hungwe, 2006; Mbiba, 1999).

Location and Land Rights

In terms of the exact location of UA, literature has shown that in some locations, farmers enjoy conditions that are more secure and conducive to cultivation than others due to a more favourable mix of soil type, the extent of public or private vacant lands, absence of harassment by city authorities, land use competition and other factors (Lado, 1990; Mupeta et al., 2020; Theresa & Pride, 2017). The most common locations for UA in the reviewed studies include the private residential land (Taiwo, 2014), alongside major roads. For instance, Hungwe (2006) found several small plots along riverbanks and on open spaces in Gweru, Zimbabwe. This stem from the fact that valuable agriculture sites are those with water access because profits are highest in the dry season when supply is limited.

On the issue of land tenure, one of the most intriguing aspects of UA in reviewed studies is the issues of usufruct arrangements agreed upon by farmers and owners of urban spaces. From the reviewed literature, the use of public land is more prominent in African cities than the use of private residential areas perhaps owing to the small sizes of such residential areas. From the literature, there is no intention on the side of city authorities to legalise UA or urban farmers obtaining formal permission to use land or pay an official rent. Farmers simply decide to occupy and use vacant land in the city. Thus, urban farmers feel more vulnerable and insecure.

Lack of Legislation on Urban Agriculture in African Cities

A common denominator among UA in Africa is the absence of legislation governing the activity. Urban policymakers are reluctant to engage in pro-UA legislation. Thus, during the colonial era, UA was considered illegal; an attitude that continues to perpetuate in some independent African countries up to the present day (Kutiwa et al., 2010; Mlozi, 1997). Accordingly, UA is illegal in Gweru, Zimbabwe (Hungwe, 2006) and Sierra Leone as well (Cissé et al., 2005). The absence of specific legislation, therefore, constraints government to support UA by extending credit facilities to urban households in Kebbi city in Nigeria (Sanchi & Muhammad, 2021). The illegal status of UA in modern cities has led to a general decline in the abilities of urbanites to feed themselves (Appeaning, 2010; Popoola et al., 2020).

The factors that significantly challenge the ability of the urban poor to cope include rapid urbanisation; the dearth of arable land and policies that furnish cheap imported food for urban populations, thus providing little incentive for local food production for urban markets (Kutiwa et al., 2010; Olufemi, 2019). In this regard, urban food security issues in African cities have underscored the significance of UA in the development community as a component of sustainable urban development.

A selection of some cities in Africa revealed a mixed policy on UA. Studies reviewed showed that several factors influenced UA policies in African cities. For instance, in Kampala, the political upheaval and economic decline of the 1970s created a conducive environment for urban farming as a way of surviving (Kutiwa et al., 2010; Mkwambisi et al., 2011). With a few exceptions such as dairying farming, urban farming activities in Kenyan cities continue to be harassed or ignored, particularly in large urban areas such as Mombasa and Nairobi (Frayne et al., 2014; Lado, 1990). Based on the Local Government Act, UA can either be permitted or restricted by local authority by-laws. Only Nairobi by-laws prohibit cultivation in undesignated areas such as public streets maintainable by the city. In short, municipalities of Kenyan towns and cities such as Kakamega, Mombasa and Nairobi have a laissez-faire attitude towards UA (Lado, 1990), whereas Kisumu authorities actively prevent urban farming except on private land (Bolang & Osumanu, 2019; Lado, 1990).

In Harare, Zimbabwe (Chaminuka and Dube, 2017) as well as in Lusaka, Zambia (Mupeta et al., 2020), studies have shown that the nature of the enforcement of legislation on UA discourages UA in these cities. To ensure that cultivation is not done within the undesignated points, there is airdrop of information leaflets stating that cultivation within 30 metres of any water source is illegal. There is also supervision of agricultural activities by the municipal police. Periodic destruction of the crops growing in contravention of the relevant legislation under the auspices of the city authorities was also noted in the literature (Hungwe, 2006; Jongwe, 2014; Mbiba, 1999). However, the enforcement of legislation either through the destruction of crops or levying of fines has been mollified to some extent by the opportunities for residents to form cooperatives and as such, apply for permission to use designated urban land for the cultivation of crops. Literature has noted that the procedures for this, are lengthy and cumbersome and as such, few groups have applied. Even when some groups have obtained permission, bureaucratic confusion has resulted in unfortunate incidents where crops grown legally were slashed and cooperatives have to request financial compensation running into thousands of dollars to make up for the costs of lost inputs. Yet in Dar es Salaam, UA is recognised by the Local Government Act (section 80) of 1992 which specifically allowed but regulated urban crop and livestock production. From 1992 onwards, the Sustainable Dar es Salaam programme supported by the UN and aimed at building the capacity of local government identified UA as a major concern. Thus, in Tanzania, UA was built into laws and institutions.

Literature has shown that UA is an intricate issue for policymakers and it involves several policy goals. However, from literature, there are two key goals; namely, hunger and poverty alleviation and ecological urban management (Flynn, 2001; Mlozi, 1997). Ideally, UA policies should identify their priority which should be clear and strategies targeted to achieve specific outcomes which should be monitored accordingly. The clarity of purpose is needed especially if and when trade-offs have to be made. For instance, the opportunities for developing a vibrant agriculture sector in and around urban centres seem obvious from literature. However, given the figures outlined in literature and terms of the Sustainable Development Goals, the alleviation of hunger and poverty among poor urban households would seem to be priority policy goals in African cities.

In the absence of other adequate employment opportunities, UA looks promising and as argued by Mupeta et al. (2020), allowing urban farming is a requirement of the right to food. That is, the minimum obligation of central and local governments under international human rights instruments is not to prevent people from providing themselves with food essential to their survival, and to protect them against others who would stop them (Mlozi, 1997). Of course, governments may go further; promoting and fulfilling the Right to Food by ensuring marginalised groups have the means to provide themselves with food—mainly land—and by providing extension services so that food is produced healthily. From the literature, a significant number of countries are moving in this direction, as they formulate UA policies. For instance, Hungwe (2006) notes that despite urban planning failing to cater for UA in Harare, the authorities are urged through the Harare and Nyanga Declarations to recognise UA as a viable business entity for the poor.

A useful policy guideline that supports UA emerged from urban farmers in Kampala was adopted following the directive by the declaration by the ministers of local government for Eastern and Southern Africa (Kutiwa et al., 2010) for UA to be recognised. The application of policy in Dar es Salaam which allows for virtually unregulated backyard farming (for the better-off) and open space farming (for the poor) deserves careful monitoring in implementation for its effects (Mlozi, 1997). Ongoing experiments in Nakuru involving the allocation of space in high-density neighbourhoods for urban farming—and using excess livestock wastes there—likewise deserve attention. Key policy implementation strategies were suggested in literature. These include Hungwe's (2006) study which encourages Gweru city authorities to promote backyard farming and avail parcels of land to poor households as well as women-headed households. In Lusaka, Zambia, Thornton et al. (2010) recommend providing extension and other support services to urban farmers in and around Lusaka.

Source of Livelihoods for the Urban Poor

Despite some controversial UA policies, there seems to be no doubt that UA is one of the livelihoods strategies for poor households in urban areas. Popoola et al. (2020) found that 48 percent of the population of Ibadan city in Nigeria depend on UA as a source of livelihood. It provides one important solution to the problems of food security confronting the African cities; thus, it can play a significant role if policies are better targeted at the poor and marginalised households.

Challenges of Urban Agriculture in African Cities

The reviews identified a number of challenges that face urban farmers. The reviews found that an increase in urban population exerts pressure on land which also increases the opportunity costs of land in urban areas. In this regard, UA faces intense competition with other urban land use such as housing, commercial enterprise. In cities with rapid urbanisation, undeveloped land for agricultural use may not be available or may be difficult to identify

(Schmidt et al., 2015; Taiwo, 2014). Urbanisation displaces farming activity by replacing farming with more economically lucrative land uses or preventing new farming from starting by erecting buildings and structures that effectively preclude farming. Agriculture usually cannot provide economic returns such as an industry or housing.

With high demand on land, UA face short tenure contracts or other aspects of tenure insecurity (Schmidt, 2015; Thornton et al., 2010). Increasing opportunity costs of land also implies that UA as a viable business venture needs to be increasingly profitable to secure its position in cities. Literature has also shown that access to water has increasingly become scarce and costly, thus reducing the competitiveness of UA in cities (Thornton et al., 2010). To curb the problem of water scarcity and related high costs, literature revealed that some farmers use wastewater for irrigation as well as low-cost fertilisers which may lead to the spread of diseases among consumers of their products. Thus, these problems are likely to intensify given the rate of urbanisation in Africa which is exacerbated by increasing population and lack of proper infrastructure for freshwater harvesting (Martin et al., 2002; Theresa & Pride, 2017).

Also highlighted in the surveyed literature is the unsafe handling and transportation practices of the products. The use of poor-quality water, pesticides and fertilisers contaminate the products, and this raises concerns about public health (Theresa & Pride, 2017). Another challenge is the existence of modern supermarkets which are perceived by consumers as offering high quality and hygiene products. Thus, the availability of modern markets has created an illusion of access to high quality and safe agricultural products. Consumers are willing to pay for safe food for reasons of disease avoidance. Furthermore, food handling conditions in supermarkets are perceived by consumers as providing safer and high-quality products than those from UA farmers (Malan, 2015; Martin et al., 2002; Popoola et al., 2020; Schmidt et al., 2015; Theresa & Pride, 2017). All these issues put pressure on products by urban farmers which end up with no market.

Summary of Key Findings

UA, the growing of crops and keeping of small animals, has its origins from the adoption of neoliberal policies as well as global economic recessions. Consequently, high unemployment and high food prices were experienced. The high food prices negatively affected the urbanites purchasing power and the low-income households were hit hard. The key players in UA are women in the low-income brackets and males in the high-income brackets. While low-income households engage in UA for sustenance, high-income urban farmers do so for leisure. In terms of literacy, highly educated male and lowly educated female farmers engage in UA. While on the one hand, poor farmers use family labour, high-income farmers on the other hand afford to hire a skilled labour force.

UA is commonly characterised by very small plots of less than a hectare usually found along main roads, riverbanks and any other open spaces within the urban centres. Farmers grow crops on land which does not belong to them and risk being chased away at any time or their crops slashed without notice. UA is not recognised by law and thus there is no legislation governing the activity. The consequence of this is that government and other stakeholders cannot fund the business and thus most of the farmers lack inputs and other requirements. UA also face intense competition with other urban land use such as housing and commercial enterprise.

Urbanisation displaces farming activities and replaces them with more economically viable land uses such as industry. The availability of modern markets has created an illusion of access to high quality and safe agricultural products. Consumers are willing to pay for safe food for reasons of disease avoidance. This result in a low market for UA produce. The key characteristic of urban poverty is dynamism whereby the poor households are not permanently poor. To perpetuate food availability, poor households remove certain foodstuffs from their diet. Thus, foods like rice, tea among others usually are removed from the diet of poor urban households as they are regarded as non-essential.

A number of challenges faced by urban farmers emanate from the fact that UA is regarded as an illegal activity in the context of urban and planning legislation in African cities. While directives and declarations on UA are being formulated in recent years to encourage UA, the bottom line is that there is no law to govern UA in African cities in as much as the reviewed articles are concerned.

Conclusion

The chapter has synthesised 35 studies on UA in African cities. The most crucial issues raised in the literature related to UA include food security as a driver of UA and the socio-economic characteristics of urban farmers. On this issue, poor women and affluent male farmers are the main players in UA. In terms of the importance of UA, it was noted that it is a surviving strategy for the poor majority of urban dwellers and that the activity has the propensity to reduce poverty and improve the food security of urban poor households. However, it is noteworthy that there is limited legislation to practically no legislation governing UA in the majority of African cities. Thus, UA remains an illegal activity. There is, therefore, a need for recognition of the diversity of UA and developing a policy within this field. From literature, legal access to land beside the backyard was found to be a constraining factor. Poor access to water and problems of electricity supply and theft were also common challenges in UA. In this regard, a policy to help guarantee land access either by allowing community gardens or providing leasehold rights to current urban farmed land could go a long way to offering urban farmers practical assistance and a sense of security. One area in which policy has to be formulated by local authorities in African cities is the issue of limited finances. There is a need for policy and systems that will allow for the financing of urban farmers.

REFERENCES

Adedayo, V. (2012). Poultry waste management techniques in urban agriculture and its implications: A case of metropolitan Lagos, Nigeria. *Asian Journal of Agricultural Sciences*, 4(4), 258–263.

Anosike, V., & Fasona, M. (2004). Gender dimensions of urban commercial farming in Lagos, Nigeria. *Urban Agriculture Magazine*, 12, 27–28.

Appeaning, A. K. (2010). Urban and peri-urban agriculture in developing countries was studied using remote sensing and in situ methods. *Remote Sensing*, 2(2), 497–513.

Armar-Klemesu, M. (2000). Urban agriculture and food security, nutrition and health. *Growing cities, growing food: Urban agriculture on the policy agenda*, 99–118.

Ayerakwa, H. M. (2017). Planting to feed the city. *Agricultural production, food security and multi-spatial livelihoods among urban households in Ghana*. Published Ph.D. thesis, Lund University.

Bolang, P. D., & Osumanu, I. K. (2019). Formal sector workers' participation in urban agriculture in Ghana: Perspectives from the Wa Municipality. *Heliyon*, 5(8), e02230.

Chaminuka, N., & Dube, E. (2017). Urban agriculture as a food security strategy for urban dwellers: A case study of Mkoba residents in the city of Gweru, Zimbabwe. *PEOPLE: International Journal of Social Sciences*, 26–45.

Cissé, O., Gueye, N. F. D., & Sy, M. (2005). Institutional and legal aspects of urban agriculture in French-speaking West Africa: From Marginalization to legitimization. *Environment and Urbanization*, 17(2), 143–154.

Dossa, L. H., Abdulkadir, A., Amadou, H., Sangare, S., & Schlecht, E. (2011). Exploring the diversity of urban and peri-urban agricultural systems in Sudano-Sahelian West Africa: An attempt towards a regional typology. *Landscape and Urban Planning*, 102(3), 197–206.

Dossa, L. H., Buerkert, A., & Schlecht, E. (2011). Cross-location analysis of the impact of household socioeconomic status on participation in urban and peri-urban agriculture in West Africa. *Human Ecology*, 39(5), 569–581.

Etim, N. A., Azeez, A. A., & Asa, U. A. (2006). Determinants of urban and peri-urban farming in Akwa Ibom State, Nigeria. *Global Journal of Agricultural Sciences*, 5(1), 13–16.

Flynn, K. C. (2001). Urban agriculture in Mwanza, Tanzania. *Africa: Journal of the International African Institute*, 71(4).

Frayne, B., McCordic, C., & Shilomboleni, H. (2014). Growing out of poverty: Does urban agriculture contribute to household food security in Southern African cities? *Urban Forum*, 25(2), 177–189. Springer Netherlands.

Gómez-Villarino, M. T., & Ruiz-Garcia, L. (2021). Adaptive design model for the integration of urban agriculture in the sustainable development of cities: A case study in northern Spain. *Sustainable Cities and Society*, 65, 102595.

Hovorka, A. J. (2005). The (re) production of gendered positionality in Botswana's commercial urban agriculture sector. *Annals of the Association of American Geographers, 95*(2), 294–313.

Howard, E. (1902). *Garden cities of tomorrow.* Swan Sonnenschein & Co.

Hungwe, C. (2006). Urban agriculture as a survival strategy: An analysis of the activities of Bulawayo and Gweru urban farmers, Zimbabwe. *Urban Agriculture Notes, 2.*

Jongwe, A. (2014). Synergies between urban agriculture and urban household food security in Gweru City, Zimbabwe. *Journal of Development and Agricultural Economics, 6*(2), 59–66.

Kanosvamhira, T. P. (2019). The organisation of urban agriculture in Cape Town, South Africa: A social capital perspective. *Development Southern Africa, 36*(3), 283–294.

Kutiwa, S., Boon, E., & Devuyst, D. (2010). Urban agriculture in low-income households of Harare: An adaptive response to economic crisis. *Journal of Human Ecology, 32*(2), 85–96.

Lado, C. (1990). Informal urban agriculture in Nairobi, Kenya: Problem or resource in the development and land use planning. *Land Use Policy, 7*(3), 257–266.

Malan, N. (2015). Urban farmers and urban agriculture in Johannesburg: Responding to the food resilience strategy. *Agrekon, 54*(2), 51–75.

Martin, A., Oudwater, N., & Gündel, S. (2002). Methodologies for situation analysis in urban agriculture. In *e-Conference on Appropriate Methodologies for Urban Agriculture: Research, Policy Development, Planning, Implementation and Evaluation* (pp. 4–16).

Mbiba, B. (1999). *Urban agriculture in Harare: Between suspicion and repression.* The University of Sheffield.

Mireri, C., Atekyereza, P., Kyessi, A., & Mushi, N. (2007). Environmental risks of urban agriculture in the Lake Victoria drainage basin: A case of Kisumu municipality, Kenya. *Habitat International, 31*(3–4), 375–386.

Mkwambisi, D. D., Fraser, E. D., & Dougill, A. J. (2011). Urban agriculture and poverty reduction: Evaluating how food production in cities contributes to food security, employment and income in Malawi. *Journal of International Development, 23*(2), 181–203.

Mlozi, M. R. (1997). Urban agriculture: Ethnicity, cattle raising and some environmental implications in the city of Dar es Salaam, Tanzania. *African Studies Review, 40*(3), 1–28.

Mubvami, T., Mushamba, S., & De Zeeuw, H. (2006). Integration of agriculture in urban land use planning. *Cities Farming for the Future: Urban Agriculture for Green and Productive Cities. RUAF, IIRR and IDRC, Silang, the Philippines*, 54–74.

Mupeta, M., Kuntashula, E., & Kalinda, T. (2020). Impact of urban agriculture on household income in Zambia: An economic analysis. *Asian Journal of Agriculture and Rural Development, 10*(2), 550–562.

Olufemi, D. B. (2019). The role of urban agriculture in empowering urban women farmers in the city of Lagos. *Afro Asian Journal of Social Sciences, X*(10.4).

Popoola, A., Wahab, B., Hangwelani, M., Chipungu, L., & Adeleye, B. (2020). Urban food production and climate variability in Ibadan, Nigeria. *Bangladesh e-Journal of Sociology, 17*(1).

Rudolph, M., Kroll, F., Muchesa, E., Paiker, M., & Fatti, P. (2021). Food security in urban cities: A case study conducted in Johannesburg, South Africa. *Journal of Food Security, 9*(2), 46–55.

Sanchi, Y. J. A. I. D., & Muhammad, M. A. (2021). Effectiveness of gender participation in agricultural productivity in Zuru Southern Guinea Savannah of Nigeria. *International Journal of Agricultural Extension and Rural Development Studies, 8*(1), 1–8.

Schmidt, S., Magigi, W., & Godfrey, B. (2015). The organization of urban agriculture: Farmer associations and urbanization in Tanzania. *Cities, 42*, 153–159.

Taiwo, O. J. (2014). Determinants of peri-urban and urban agricultural locational choice behaviour in Lagos, Nigeria. *Land Use Policy, 39*, 320–330.

Theresa, K., & Pride, C. (2017). The social, economic and health impacts of urban agriculture in Zambia. *Asian Journal of Advances in Agricultural Research*, 1–8.

Thornton, A., Nel, E., & Hampwaye, G. (2010). Cultivating Kaunda's plan for self-sufficiency: Is urban agriculture finally beginning to receive support in Zambia? *Development Southern Africa, 27*(4), 613–625.

UN Food and Agriculture Organization (UNFAO). (2019, 2020). Retrieved October 15, 2021, from http://www.fao.org/home/en

United Nations World Statistics Pocketbook. 2020 Edition, Series v No. 44, New York.

van Averbeke, W. (2007). Urban farming in the informal settlements of Atteridgeville, Pretoria, South Africa. *Water Sa, 33*(3).

CHAPTER 5

Financial Resources

Raphael Ngolo and Rodney Asilla

INTRODUCTION

The push towards political and administrative decentralisation in recent years has meant that an increasing number of functions are now vested at the local level (UCLG, 2007). A key assumption in the debate is that decentralisation leads to accountable and responsive governance. However, this has not led to increased financial resources at local and urban levels; finance has not followed function (Kamiya & Zhang, 2017). Local authorities have to do more with less. The ever-increasing demand for urban infrastructure and services due to rapid urban transition has led to a frayed social contract (Smoke, 2015).

Infrastructure development is central to Africa's efforts to meet the Sustainable Development Goals (SDGs) as it encompasses many of the goals such as access to energy, health services, education, clean water and sanitation (Economist Intelligence Unit, 2019). Saghir and Santoro (2018) argue that for sub-Saharan Africa, a net positive correlation exists between economic growth and the productivity of its urban areas. They suggest that the region is already suffering the consequences of a lack of investment in urban infrastructure such as the decline in productivity, weak investment and negative

R. Ngolo (✉)
Independent Researcher, Mombasa, Kenya
e-mail: mwadori@gmail.com

R. Asilla
Languages, Literature and Linguistics, Egerton University, Nakuru, Kenya
e-mail: rodney.asilla@gmail.com

per capita income growth. Floater et al. (2017) frame the problem more succinctly; that urban infrastructure investments or lack thereof will not only dictate urban form, but also lock in economic, climate and social benefits or costs for generations. Therefore, cities will need to manage urbanisation and pay particular attention to efficient urban design as well as financing and governance mechanisms if the desired development outcomes are to be realised.

This chapter, therefore, seeks to provide a comprehensive review of research on financing urban development in Africa, with a specific focus on two areas of urban finance. First, it looks at the nature of urban finance in Africa. This looks at the form, characteristics and functioning of urban finance. Secondly, this review also interrogates the implications of this urban finance on development: the relationship between urban finance and development in Africa.

Methods

This study made use of literature on urban financing that was accessed from electronic databases such as Elsevier, JSTOR, Research Gate, Taylor & Francis Online and SSRN. Also included in this study are articles from organisational databases such as the world Bank, United Nations, UN-Habitat, Japanese International Cooperation Agency (JICA), The UK's Department for International Development (DFID), International Institute for Environment and Development (IIED), Korean Institute for International Economic Policy (KIEP), Brookings Institution, Chr. Michelsen Institute (CMI), and the Centre for Strategic and International Studies (CSIS). Additionally, the study included literature from academic institutions such as Georgia State University, Obafemi Awolowo University, Federal Polytechnic Ede, South African Institute of International Affairs (SAIIA), and the University of Cape Town.

Keywords used during the search for literature were financing urban development in Africa, financing local development in Africa, fiscal decentralisation and urban development in Africa. The search yielded 73 publications out of which 25 were selected for the topic at hand. From the selected studies, relevant information was extracted and summarised in a data extraction matrix. The variables included the Name of the Author, Geographical unit, Data Collection method, Theoretical framework, study focus and findings.

Results and Discussion

Study Design

As seen in the data extraction matrix (Table 5.1), majority of the studies (8) focused on specific African cities (Berrisford et al., 2018; Cirolia, 2020; Dabara et al., 2015; Gorelick, 2018; Khatleli et al., 2020; Muhammad & Abubakar, 2019; Mutua & Wamalwa, 2017; Simpson et al., 2019). Another eight studies (8) focused on specific countries (Adam Smith International, 2018; Brun &

Table 5.1 Summary of the research on financing urban development programmes in Africa

Author, Year	Geographical unit	Data collection method	Theoretical framework	Study focus	Results
Turok and McGranahan (2013)	Africa	Review of Documents	Agglomeration Economics	The relationship between urbanisation and economic growth	There is no simple linear relationship between urbanisation and economic growth. Benefits of urbanisation can only be realised with supportive policies, markets and infrastructural investments
Lall et al. (2017)	Africa	Review of Documents	Socio-economic Development	Analyses the link between urban form, population growth, production of globally tradeable goods and services, capital density and socio-economic well-being of African cities	Africa's cities are costly, crowded and disconnected leading to low capital density, urban sprawl, disconnected from global markets and pushed into a low development trap
Hommann and Lall (2019)	Sub-Saharan Africa	Review of Documents	Socio-economic Development	Examines key criteria necessary to transition African cities to liveable status	Three key criteria to liveability are identified: Empowering land markets, strengthening urban planning and regulation and infrastructure investment
Paulais (2012)	Africa	Review of Documents	Policy Reform	Looks at the known frameworks for financing urbanisation with respect to Africa's exceptional rate of urban growth	There exist irreconcilable gaps between the sheer amount of capital investment required and the capacity of the local government to finance, organise and support urban growth
Platz et al. (2017)	Least Developed Countries (LDCs)	Review of Documents and Expert Groups	Sustainable Development	An overview of the multi-dimensional challenges local-level entities in LDCs face in their quest to finance sustainable development from political, institutional and economic perspectives	3 key areas were identified as being pivotal to sustainable development: recognition of critical role of local authorities; meaningful intergovernmental collaboration and inclusion of local communities in decision-making

(continued)

Table 5.1 (continued)

Author, Year	Geographical unit	Data collection method	Theoretical framework	Study focus	Results
Berrisford et al. (2018)	Sub-Saharan Africa Addis Ababa, Harare, Nairobi and 29 Large-Scale Urban Projects	Review of Documents, Case Studies and Interviews	Policy Reform	The paper examines the potential of land-based financing in helping to bridge the growing urban fiscal gap experienced by African cities in attempting to address infrastructure and service needs	Some African cities have deployed some form of land-based financing methods albeit to a limited and inconsistent extent. More extensive and progressive use should be encouraged
Nixon et al. (2015)	Low-Income Countries	Expert Interviews and Review of Documents	Policy Reform	Analyses the most effective interventions for City governments in low-income countries to increase their access to both public and private financial resources	The key to increasing access to finance lies in strengthening key fundamentals: improving intergovernmental coordination; coherent decentralisation and improving the administration of core revenues
Gorelick (2018)	Sub-Saharan Africa (SSA) Johannesburg, Douala, Dakar and Kampala	Review of Documents	Policy Reform	Challenges and opportunities faced by SSA municipalities in their attempts to mobilise financing for capital-intensive projects	Bleak short-term outlook for SSA municipality access to municipal bonds. Successful attempts noted in jurisdictions with full autonomy or with paternalistic central authorities
Franzsen and McCluskey (2017)	Africa	Review of Documents	Sustainable Development	A review of developments in policies, laws and administrative practices pertaining to property taxation in African countries	Inappropriate policies, lax administration and enforcement impede property tax development in Africa. The solution in large part entails going beyond public finance policy and into politics, governance, culture and the general economic setting
Dabara et al. (2015)	Abuja, Lagos and Port Harcourt, Nigeria	Review of Documents	Sustainable Urban Development	Evaluates infrastructure development strategies and their effect on urban development in Nigeria	There is a widening infrastructure gap in the major urban centres of Lagos, Abuja and Port Harcourt owing to their reliance on federal funds. Public–Private Partnerships (PPPS) have the potential to bridge the gap. However, political uncertainty and the fear of policy reversals by succeeding governments deter the certainty required for long-term infrastructure financing

Author, Year	Geographical unit	Data collection method	Theoretical framework	Study focus	Results
Masaki (2018)	Tanzania Urban and Rural Municipalities	Statistical Data Review of Documents	Fiscal Decentralisation	Analyses the impact of intergovernmental transfers on local revenue generation	Intergovernmental transfers facilitate rather than undermine local revenues but the positive impact is less pronounced in urban than in rural areas
Park et al. (2017)	Africa	Review of Documents	Policy Reform	Determining the demand for, and cost of infrastructure in key sectors (roads, power, water and sanitation) for the years 2016–2030	Infrastructural needs were highest in power, roads, water and sanitation in that order. The importance of African cities in driving economic growth was confirmed with dependence on cities higher in lower-income countries. Average yearly infrastructure spend was estimated to be US$60.5 Billion per year
Ogbuagu and Ujunwa (2008)	Nigeria	Review of Documents	Sustainable Development	Examined the financing challenges faced by local governments in Nigeria and evaluates their ability to access finance from Capital Markets	Greater fiscal autonomy and revitalization of the Urban Development Bank of Nigeria are key factors that support local governments' access to capital market finance
Fjeldstad et al. (2017)	Africa	Review of Documents	Sustainable Development	Examining the political and administrative constraints affecting the development of effective property tax systems	Substantial improvement in the collection of this tax is possible even in environments with low tax collection capacity. The major constraints to improved property tax systems is political rather than technical
Simpson et al. (2019)	Cape Town, South Africa	Review of Documents Interviews	Climate Adaptation and Resilience	Examines the public and private adaptation actions that played out during the City's drought and the resulting 'shock' in the municipality's budget	The actions of the different actors were divergent and uncoordinated which inevitably have an impact on the City's fiscal ability and its resilience going forward. The City's future resilience depends on its finance system exhibiting short-term coping and long-term adaptation if the municipal water service is to be safeguarded

(continued)

Table 5.1 (continued)

Author, Year	Geographical unit	Data collection method	Theoretical framework	Study focus	Results
Brun and El Khdari (2016)	Morocco	Statistical Data Review of Documents	Fiscal Decentralisation	Assesses the fiscal incentive effects of conditional and unconditional transfers on Moroccan Municipalities	The incentive effect of unconditional transfers is significant while that of conditional transfers is less robust
Taiwo (2020)	Nigeria	Statistical data Review of Documents	Fiscal Decentralisation	Tests the relationship between fiscal transfers to state governments in Nigeria and local revenue growth	Fiscal transfers to state governments in Nigeria act as a disincentive to local revenue generation as it 'crowds-out' local revenue growth, which makes state governments heavily dependent on fiscal transfers
Brun and Sanogo (2017)	Ivory Coast	Statistical data Review of Documents	Fiscal Decentralisation	Examines the relationship between fiscal transfers and local revenue mobilisation during and after a period of civil conflict	A positive incentive effect of fiscal transfers on local revenue mobilisation was realised. The positive effect was larger on tax revenue than non-tax revenue
Mogues et al. (2009)	Ghana	Statistical data Review of Documents	Fiscal Decentralisation	Tests the relationship between transfers to Ghana's 110 district governments and their own revenue growth performance	Fiscal transfers to district governments were a disincentive to internal revenue generation. In addition, a distinction between expenditure type and its effect on revenue growth is noted, with higher past spending on recurrent expenditure associated with higher own-source revenues as opposed to capital expenditure
Cirolia (2020)	Africa SA Metropolitan Municipalities, Nairobi, Mombasa, Addis Ababa, Luanda, Dakar, Lagos, Abuja, Kigali	Review of Documents Interviews Case studies	Fiscal Sustainability and Sustainable Urban Development	Historically examined the African urban experience in relation to decentralisation with its contestations and its effect on service delivery in the continent's urban areas	Hybrid service-delivery models have emerged due to fractured fiscal authority of urban authorities and fragmented network infrastructure. There is a need to discard conventional approaches to financing urban infrastructure in favour of models that take into account the local context

Author, Year	Geographical unit	Data collection method	Theoretical framework	Study focus	Results
Muhammad and Abubakar (2019)	Abuja, Nigeria	Review of Documents	Sustainable Development	Reviewed the successes and challenges faced during the implementation of the mass housing programme in Abuja under the PPP model	The mass housing programme recorded dismal performance with 12 percent of houses delivered at the project's end. The lack of genuine private partners, transparency in the procurement process and limited public sector capacity are the main challenges that explain the poor performance
Khatleli et al. (2020)	SADC Region Dar es Salaam, Gauteng Province, Windhoek, Dolphin Coast Borough, Durban, Mbombela	Review of Documents	Sustainable Development	Assess the footprint of PPP infrastructure projects in the SADC region and identify best-practice urban infrastructure projects with respect to design, financing, implementation and socio-economic impact	The six urban infrastructure projects identified in the study have diverse structures with regard to financing, implementation and legal frameworks in which they operate. Despite challenges to implementation and operation, these urban infrastructure projects deliver socio-economic and environmental benefits to the cities involved
Adam Smith International (2018)	Kenya All Counties	Review of Documents Questionnaires	Fiscal Sustainability	Estimating the revenue potential of Kenya's county governments and conducting a legal and policy review	Kenya's counties have a huge unrealized own-source revenue potential that is approximately 5 times their current collection. In addition, there is a clear disconnect between revenue collection and policy objectives
GLTN-UN-Habitat (2016)	Tanzania	Review of Documents	Sustainable Development	Analysed the framework for the efficient application of land-based revenue systems in the country	Evidence of inconsistent application of land-based revenue systems with as Dar es Salaam alone accounts for 70 percent of all land rents. Dismal performance is observed as the size of land-based revenues falls far short of 1 percent of GDP (best practice)
Mutua and Wamalwa (2017)	Nairobi City County	Review of Documents, Interviews	Fiscal Sustainability	A review of the challenges and opportunities of enhancing local revenue mobilisation in Nairobi City County	Evidence of lack of a comprehensive policy and legislation guiding revenue collection, e.g. with regard to land rates, low capacity for collection and enforcement with costs of these disregarded, low compliance levels due to lack of taxpayer education and the mismatch between service delivery versus fees/charges paid

El Khdari, 2016; Brun & Sanogo, 2017; GLTN-UN-Habitat, 2016; Masaki, 2018; Mogues et al., 2009; Ogbuagu & Ujunwa, 2008; Taiwo, 2020). Six (6) studies focused on the African continent as a whole (Fjeldstad et al., 2017; Franzsen & McCluskey, 2017; Lall et al., 2017; Park et al., 2017; Paulais, 2012; Turok & McGranahan, 2013). The remaining three (3) studies had regional focus (Hommann & Lall, 2019-sub-Saharan Africa; Platz et al., 2017-Least Developed Countries; Nixon et al., 2015-Low Income Countries).

Results and Discussion
Empirical Findings

Own-Source Revenues

Own-Source revenues (OSR) refers to taxes and charges that local governments are able to raise directly. The capacity to raise own-source revenue is a key determinant to the quality of service delivery and infrastructure that local governments provide their citizens (Germán & Glass, 2017; Smoke, 2015). The rapid pace of urbanisation in Africa underscores the need for a sound urban revenues system to meet the enormous pressure to provide services and infrastructure. The dependence of local authorities in developing countries on fiscal transfers is well documented in literature. However, the relative inconsistency and unpredictability of the size, frequency and the political contests surrounding fiscal transfers makes managing transfers hugely problematic for local authorities. This lack of direct control over a critical pillar in financing urban local authorities inevitably leads to the need to mobilise Own-Source revenues to complement fiscal transfers over which they have no direct control.

Smoke (2015) posits that local authorities have inherent advantages in service delivery while central/national authorities enjoy inherent advantages in revenue generation. This is a reflection of the inadequacies of the benefit theory of subnational government taxation. The theory emphasises the need for subnational governments having the necessary powers to raise revenue to meet responsibilities that confer local benefits. In practice, however, most urban governments in developing countries will not obtain such tax powers and there are cost efficiencies in tax collection for higher-level governments, hence laying the foundation for local authorities' reliance on fiscal transfers (Bahl & Linn, 2014; McLure & Martinez-Vazquez, 2000).

There are various handbooks and studies that offer normative approaches to the design and implementation of effective instruments that will lead to improved capacity of local authorities to generate own-source revenues. The focus is on enhancing the mobilisation of non-tax own-source revenues since in practice, local governments in the developing world and Africa in particular, are constrained in their ability to raise tax revenue. Table 5.2 details some of the common instruments used by local authorities the world over to raise non-tax own-source revenue.

Table 5.2 Examples of non-tax own-source revenues

Revenue source	General characteristics
Utility and User Charges	Charges for sewer, water, publicly provided electricity and other similar services (paid by a citizen, organization, or institution) where the benefits accrue to specific individuals and payment for the service varies according to consumption
User Fees	Fees for voluntary services such as entry to public museums, marriage licences, tolls, motor vehicle registration, permits, and others paid by a citizen, organisation or institution. Cost is typically set at specific market prices, and subsidies are at times offered to certain users
Fines	A penalty assessed on a citizen, organisation or institution because of a violation of law, or a civil or criminal infraction
Surcharges	An additional sum added to a particular, pre-existing charge, such as a tax, fee, fine or penalty paid by a citizen, organisation or institution
Special Assessments	Compulsory payments, in the form of development fees or betterments, imposed on the owners of real property for specific benefits generated from public investments. Costs imposed are typically aligned with the benefits received
Payments in-lieu of Taxes (PILOTS)	Voluntary payments made by private non-profits and other tax-exempt entities to compensate a local government for the loss of tax revenue due to the nature of the ownership or use of a particular piece of real property
Royalties	Payments arising from the assignment of the right to harvest and exploit naturally occurring resources (oil, gas, minerals, etc.) by citizens, institutions, or organisations. Royalties may be structured via agreement or in the form of a lease
Rents & Land-use Fees	Payments arising from the right to use and occupy government property or land by citizens, institutions, or organisations. Often structured pursuant to a lease or other agreement providing for the payment of fees for specific land-use rights

Source Adapted from Finance for City Leaders Handbook (Kamiya & Zhang, 2017)

The revenue performance of urban authorities in developing nations is reputedly weak. For example, property taxation, a key component in raising OSR accounts for just 0.5 percent of GDP in developing nations as compared to over 2 percent in OECD countries (Smoke, 2015). Consensus is that the capacity to grow own-source revenues is heavily influenced by the degree of political, administrative and fiscal autonomy within a specific country context (Germán & Glass, 2017; Nixon et al., 2015; Platz et al., 2017). Four key factors from the studies aforementioned have been identified as being key to explaining the seemingly lacklustre performance of developing countries. These are: Restrictions on taxing powers and tax bases imposed by higher-level authorities on local governments; disincentives resulting from poorly designed fiscal transfers programme; limited local capacity to collect revenue and deliver services and weakening compliance to local taxes and charges due to lack of accountability and/or poor credibility of the local authority.

In a study commissioned by the World Bank on behalf of the Kenya National Treasury, Adam Smith International (2018) set out to estimate the own-source revenue potential and tax-gap analysis of Kenyan counties. The analysis covered the common sources of OSR, which are land and property rates, parking fees, market fees, lease rents, hospital/health service charges, business permits, trade/building permits, advertisement and billboard fees, liquor licenses and cess. The study adopted a two-pronged approach to its methodology: Estimating revenue potential (by County and by revenue stream) fulfilled through frontier analysis and A legal and policy review.

The study revealed a huge untapped revenue potential. Short-term projections of OSR potential were in the region of Kenya Shillings 55–66 billion up from 35 billion in 2018. Administrative capacity improvements and legal reforms in the long-term could further enhance OSR potential to the range 125–172 billion representing a total tax gap of between 35–94 percent for the different sources of revenue. According to the study, Property taxes outweigh all other sources, with the potential to raise up to 66 billion under conservative assumptions. These findings mirror the conclusions of Hobdari et al. (2018) where they note that although Kenya's devolution largely follows international best practice regarding the distribution of responsibilities between the two levels of government, the 'big bang' approach to devolution resulted in administrative and intergovernmental relationship challenges giving rise to poor OSR collections (0.5 percent of GDP) and higher taxes and charges. Higher taxes and charges have a negative impact on investment and disproportionately affect the poor. In addition, the lack of taxpayer education and the mismatch between service delivery and high charges has contributed to poor OSR collection (Mutua & Wamalwa, 2017).

A common characteristic of local government OSR systems in Africa is the numerous numbers of revenue instruments. It is clear that all efforts are geared towards raising as much revenue as possible without due consideration for economic distortions that may result therefrom. Complicated tax systems are costly to local economies in Africa as they encourage corruption, inhibit economic growth and by their very design, end up disproportionately affecting the poor thereby inadvertently harming the same local authorities that they are designed to support (Boschmann, 2009; Mutua & Wamalwa, 2017).

Mutua and Wamalwa (2017), in assessing the challenges and opportunities of improving the collection of local revenue in Nairobi County, find that the challenges are similar to those faced by most cities in Africa and indeed the developing world. The lack of a comprehensive policy and legislation guiding revenue mobilisation ensures that the city underperforms with respect to high potential revenue instruments like property taxes, entertainment licences and trade licences. The authors note that the city operates at 45–50 percent capacity to collect and enforce revenue collection, and that there is little regard for their costs. Also noted was the low level of tax compliance by the city's inhabitants for which the authors attributed to the lack of taxpayer engagement through education campaigns and the mismatch between the quality of services delivered by the county and the fees/charges paid.

While there is consensus that local authorities require meaningful fiscal autonomy to improve revenues, some evidence assessed suggests capacity development should play a central role if OSR improvements are to be realised. Fjeldstad (2006), in considering the question of fiscal autonomy versus capacity development in Tanzania, concluded that it was unrealistic to expect that fiscal autonomy would result in improved OSR, efficiency and responsiveness of local authorities in Tanzania. This was inevitable as for many years, public financial management improvement efforts focused solely on central authorities. Comprehensive local government reforms in Tanzania over the years has led to the simplification of local government revenue collection by abolishing numerous taxes and charges that were unsustainable to collect, simplifying rates and collection procedures with the expectation of future revenue growth. This is consistent with the findings of studies by Adam Smith International (2018) and Mutua & Wamalwa (2017) who demonstrated the potential of capacity development to improve own-source revenues for subnational governments and urban centres.

Land-Based Financing and Property Taxes
Hobdari et al. (2018) defines a good local tax as one whose base is immobile and has a stable and predictable yield. By such a criterion, taxes on property, income, user fees and charges qualify as good local taxes. Property tax in particular, is widely touted as being key to improving own-source revenues. The administrative cost of collecting this tax is low as property is immovable and easily identifiable even within the context of limited capacity of a local authority. Property taxes are also less economically distortionary than income tax, being that it is a tax on wealth and therefore will not inhibit productive activities in the economy.

Despite the clear advantages that property taxes offer, evidence suggests that it is notoriously difficult to administer. Developed nations enjoy better performance relative to their counterparts in the developing world. For example, in the United States, property taxes are the main source of revenue for local governments. The use of complicated instruments such as Tax Increment Financing (TIF) is a testament to the strong administrative capacity of local governments in that country (Walters & Gauntner, 2017). Property taxes in the highly urbanised, high-income countries register in the range 1.5–2 percent of GDP compared to the African average of 0.5 percent of GDP. Franzsen and McCluskey puts the number even lower, at 0.38 percent of GDP.

Morocco, Mauritius and South Africa are notable exceptions, where property taxes exceed 1 percent of GDP (Fjeldstad et al., 2017; GLTN-UN Habitat, 2016).

Property Taxes
Property tax is administered in diverse ways in Africa. Key differences emerge when their tax administration practices are analysed along linguistic lines. In francophone West Africa, for example, Fjeldstad et al. (2017) found that property tax systems are in embryonic stage and tax collection responsibility is likely to be vested in central authorities. In Anglophone countries, local authorities are responsible for property tax administration, having inherited these responsibilities from the colonial administrations. They have greater experience and hence record better performance relative to their West African francophone counterparts. Franzsen and McCluskey (2017) posit that the poor performance by Francophone countries is due to the highly centralised property tax administration, poor properties data capture, poor billing and collection, weak enforcement and generous exemptions.

In assessing property taxes in East African countries (Kenya, Uganda & Tanzania) all of which share a common British colonial legacy, Boschmann (2009) notes distinct approaches to tax policy with respect to tax base, assessment basis and tax rates. The study finds that the primary obstacle to improving property tax collection is limited administrative capacity as opposed to effective tax policy. All countries in the study experienced common problems related to limited tax base coverage, outdated valuation rolls and low collection rates due to lax enforcement.

In concluding, while all three studies by Fieldstad et al. (2017), Franzsen and McCluskey (2017), and Boschmann (2009) assessed revealed deficits in the technical aspects of local administration such as weak assessment, valuation, cadastral systems and enforcement mechanisms, they all identify political will as the major constraint to unlocking significant property tax revenues for urban authorities in Africa.

Land-Based Financing
According to Floater et al. (2014), land plays a dual purpose in urban development: it directs the shape of urban form and infrastructure and is an important revenue-raising instrument. Taxation on land is premised on the idea that land values appreciate without effort by its owners and mostly in response to factors such as government investments in public infrastructure, land-use policy changes and population growth. Local governments should recover, at least in part, some of the public investment costs through land taxes (McLure & Martinez-Vazquez, 2000; Walters & Gauntner, 2017).

Land value capture is prominent in urban finance literature and is primarily based on economic efficiency. Being a tax on wealth and not on production, imposing taxes on land does not inhibit productive activity. Land value capture is a good source of urban finance because land is visible and immovable hence easier to administer; land taxes funding local investments are appropriate in terms of the benefit principle and local authorities own/control large swathes of land that may potentially generate revenue from sales and leases. Sales and leases are particularly suited for funding initial investments in infrastructure.

Some notable drawbacks emerge such as:

(a) Land is a finite resource. Land sales are therefore unsustainable in the long-term;
(b) Administration—Land taxation requires strong and effective local administrations. Local authorities in LDCs historically have low capacity and experience to administer such taxes. Land is the subject of control by different levels of government making collaboration difficult, more so in developing countries with historically dismal intergovernmental relations;
(c) Taxpayer resistance—Land taxation is subject to sustained resistance from the public owing to high rates charged and a perceived mismatch between tax levied and benefits accruing, thereby leading to a lack of political buy-in especially in developing nations.
(d) Valuation—Differences in valuation methods encourages administrative discretion. This subjectivity exposes local governments to possible losses in taxable value when assessed value for tax purposes is below value realised in the open market.

A case study on land-based revenues in Tanzania conducted by GLTN and UN-Habitat (2016) for the financial years 2006/2007 to 2012/2013 provides a useful perspective. During the period under review, total domestic taxes in Tanzania grew from 7.7 to 10.6 percent of GDP while total combined land-based taxes (for both central & local levels of government) remained almost unchanged, growing from 0.112 to 0.136 percent of GDP over the same period. This falls short of the 64-nation average recorded in the GLTN report (2016) of 0.75 percent of GDP as well as the international best practice at 1 percent of GDP. It is evident that Tanzania has the potential to improve land-based revenues multiple times.

The importance of Dar es Salaam and Arusha cannot be overstated. While consisting of less than 14 percent of the country's population, they account for a combined 74 percent of national direct and indirect taxes with Dar es Salaam alone contributing 70 percent of all land rents thus highlighting the enormous burden imposed on taxpayers from the two regions. Strong economic growth, increased migration into urban areas, a vibrant real estate market and strong tax administration in urban areas are key factors that explain the large urban taxpaying footprint. This also affirms the findings by Saghir and Santoro (2018) on the importance of the productivity of urban centres to sub-Saharan economies and the inconsistent application of land-based taxation (Berrisford et al., 2018; Franzsen & McCluskey, 2017).

A study by Berrisford et al. (2018) draws on three case studies (Addis Ababa, Harare & Nairobi) and a rapid assessment of 29 ongoing urban projects in several African countries to examine the applicability and potential of land-based financing in Sub-Saharan cities. The study examined the experiences of each city against three conditions that form the basis for the existence of a good land-based financing model. These conditions are; a strong legal and fiscal framework, competent local administration and demand for urban land.

The study revealed that Addis Ababa meets all the set conditions with the added advantage that all land is state-owned. In addition, the presence of a credible land lease system ensures that Addis Ababa has experienced extraordinary urban renewal. There is scope to believe that the instruments employed in its land-based financing model have the potential to generate greater revenues. Prices at lease auctions can be as much as 7 times higher than at land allocations yet it is severely underused, for a paltry 10 percent of the land. Additionally, property taxes contribution to Addis Ababa's revenues remains very low due to the city's low capacity to collect. In this city, development can proceed on serviced land only even within the context of the government's limited ability to service land. This introduces unnecessary supply-side constraints that results in very high land prices and formation of informal settlements in un-serviced areas. The state's approach to the welfare of project-displaced persons is politically costly. Addis Ababa has achieved tremendous success in urban renewal based on the strength of state ownership of land and the city authority's control over land allocation. Therefore, this model has limited application outside Ethiopia.

Harare misses the mark with respect to the set conditions. Access to finance is limited due to the ongoing economic downturn, which in turn limits both demand and supply since developers and buyers face financing difficulties. Devolution is a highly contested space where the capacity of local authorities is undermined when service provision and collection of revenue is shifted to agencies of the central authorities. The land-based financing instruments Harare uses include in-kind contributions, development charge, land sales and property taxes. The city relies heavily on property taxes, with the instrument generating approximately 40 percent of total revenue but a notable drawback is that the funds are not ring-fenced to provide capital for long-term infrastructure investments and is used to fund operations.

Nairobi has some of the prerequisites for land-based financing in place. The urban land market is vibrant with increasing demand and responsive supply. The advent of devolution in 2013 established clear legal and fiscal rules that strengthens the position of city authorities. The city employs land-based financing instruments that are similar to Harare's. Property taxes are vital and account for roughly 25 percent of the city's revenue. Land-based finances are not ring-fenced and are often used to finance recurrent expenditure. Land is highly contested and politicised. The influence exerted by the complex nexus of landholding elites, city officials and politicians ensure that the process of capturing urban land values because of large-scale public infrastructure investment lacks transparency. This has also made certain that little has been done to curb the rampant speculation in the urban land market. The absence of systematic regulations to guide In-kind contributions gives rise to the subjectivity of officials' discretion.

A rapid assessment of 29 ongoing large-scale projects in 22 of the largest cities in sub-Saharan Africa was conducted to determine the extent to which land-based financing was applied. Each project was rated on −5 to 5 scale with −5 score indicating significant subsidisation of the developer while a 5 score was indicative of a developer contributing to social and community infrastructure in addition to the immediate infrastructure needs of their developments. A zero score indicates the absence of land-based financing. The study yielded interesting results; No project obtained a 5 score. Projects in most countries (18 of 29) used some form of land-based finance while in two projects (in Zimbabwe and Mozambique), no land-based finance instrument was used. The remaining projects (Ivory Coast, Rwanda, Uganda, Benin, Cameroon and Angola) registered negative scores thus indicating that the developers enjoyed some form of subsidisation from the authorities. The overarching implication is that developers view in-kind contributions as a means to afford their own developments with key infrastructure needs with little if any consideration for the progressive aspects of in-kind contributions such as developer contributions to social and community infrastructure.

In conclusion, the evidence presented shows that African cities use land-based finance instruments in some form or other but its full potential is yet to be realised due to limited and inconsistent application in the cases covered. Addis Ababa has used its land lease systems to fund an ambitious urban renewal programme while Harare and Nairobi pale in comparison, partly due to a lack of ring-fenced funds raised solely for infrastructure investment. For African cities to realise the full potential of land-based financing instruments, they need to navigate a complex interplay between growing urban infrastructure needs, social contracts, fiscal sustainability, urban governance structures and political economy pressure to develop the most appropriate configuration for each city.

Borrowing and External Financing
Municipal Bonds and Public–Private Partnerships
Cities in the developing world have a constrained fiscal role, largely imposed by central authorities as is evidenced by the mismatch between functions allocated and finance required to fulfil them. Therefore, local authorities have had to do more with less and as a result, infrastructure development has suffered (Smoke, 2015). Infrastructure development is central to Africa's efforts to meet the SDGs as it encompasses many of the goals such as; access to energy, health services, education, clean water and sanitation (Economist Intelligence Unit, 2019).

In this section, we examine literature that highlights the experience of local authorities in Africa in attempting to tap into the municipal bonds market and Public–Private Partnerships (PPPs) to finance urban development.

Municipal Bonds
Cities in developing countries have had limited access to bond financing compared to those in developed nations, which typically have investment-grade credit ratings that opens access to the financial markets through the issuance of municipal bonds. The fortunes of cities in the developing world pale in comparison: up to 93 percent of low and lower-middle-income countries have sovereign credit ratings that are below investment grade. The close correlation between local credit ratings of cities and that of their respective countries makes their access to debt finance harder, as potential investors prefer financing infrastructure projects in high-income countries instead. As a result, these cities have had to make do with costly commercial bank loans. However, Dakar and Kampala have shown that opportunities for debt-finance still exist for well-managed cities in low-income countries. These cities have registered investment-grade ratings in their local markets, which is a testament to their financial maturity, even though Senegal and Uganda have below investment-grade sovereign credit ratings (Floater et al., 2017).

In the first study analysed, Gorelick (2018) examined the challenges faced by African local governments in accessing finance to initiate capital-intensive projects. The study involved combing through literature to identify key challenges or gaps in the African experience with developing the municipal bonds market. The challenges are as follows:

(a) The failure to create an enabling environment and legal framework for investment. The long-term nature of capital projects means that project execution and debt service will extend beyond electoral cycles. A sound legal framework provides certainty that debt service obligations will be honoured. Capital Flows require certainty that is often lacking or inadequate in most sub-Saharan Africa countries and the nascent nature of capital markets means that intermediaries and the tools required to facilitate transactions and mitigate risk are not yet fully developed.
(b) The mismatch between investment needs and available finance. Theoretically, credit rating agencies help to develop bond markets by bridging the information asymmetry between the lender and borrower. In Africa, however, the success of international credit rating agencies is mixed and local rating agencies are still growing.
(c) Lack of creditworthy local governments and bankable projects. Local authorities need to commit to provide information on their pipeline of bankable projects, financial activities and demonstrate proper management of financed projects over the life of the loan/bond and generation of strong revenue streams for debt service.

To underscore the effect of challenges identified already identified, Gorelick reviewed case studies on four African cities that have attempted to source debt finance for long-term, capital-intensive and revenue generating projects. These four cities are Johannesburg, Douala, Dakar and Kampala.

In the case of Johannesburg, bond issuance was a means to diversify its funding sources as the city had exhausted its credit limits with Banks. South African municipalities' right to borrow is constitutionally enshrined and operationalised through the Municipal Finance Management Act (MFMA) of 2004, which stipulates that long-term debt is for purposes of capital expenditure and offers no safety net in form of guarantees from central authorities. This granted significant latitude for Johannesburg and other municipalities to access municipal bond market financing.

The city of Douala experiences the lowest level of decentralisation of all cities considered under this study. All local government debts accrue to and are guaranteed by national authorities. This explicit guarantee made it cheaper to access funds through a municipal bond issuance even with lingering questions regarding the City's ability to pay. Post bond issuance, the emergence of financial and regulatory impropriety allegations during the bond transaction, while not affecting the city's ability to meet its debt obligations, significantly hamper the likelihood of future municipal bond issuance in the country.

In Senegal, legislation empowers local authorities to enter into debt arrangements for capital investments. The City of Dakar has a strong demonstrable history of creditworthiness, having borrowed from concessional and commercial lenders in the past without guarantees from national authorities. Dakar's municipal bond proposition was particularly appealing given Senegal's political stability, macroeconomic soundness and a strong domestic demand for bonds. National authorities called off the bond issue on the eve of the launch, underscoring the lack of autonomy of the municipal government and insufficient collaboration with national authorities (Sarr, 2019).

The City of Kampala is run by the Kampala Capital City Authority (KCCA), an entity that reports to national authorities unlike all other subnational governments in Uganda. Interestingly, KCCA finds its borrowing activities hamstrung by law relative to other local governments thus confined to a maximum 10 percent of internal revenues with all others at 25 percent. The potential for a successful bond issuance in the future is contingent on comprehensive legislative reforms on subnational borrowing.

In yet another study, Ogbuagu and Ujunwa (2008) take a historical approach to reviewing the process of decentralisation in Nigeria. They note that decentralisation gained prominence with the local government reforms of 1976, which gave them recognition as the third tier of government. Conflict with the other levels of government was observed; state governments are known to have 'hijacked' allocations to local governments, necessitating the adoption of direct transfers from federal to local level. Even as local governments enjoyed increased allocation over the years, they have had minimal impact on the ground, a development attributed to poor management capacity and corruption. The dependency of local authorities on federal funds is well established which is further compounded by their inability to grow local revenues over time. Generally, local government finances are fiscally unsustainable given the rapid pace of urban transition and the rising demand for services and infrastructure, hence the need to diversify their sources of finance to include access to long-term finance through municipal bonds. The authors posit that bond financing has a net positive effect; as a *sine qua non*, local authorities must reform their operational and administrative processes, streamline tax collection and strengthen governance practices. Further, the authors urge the revitalization of the Urban Development Bank of Nigeria, an entity tasked with the mandate of facilitating local governments in the bond issuance transaction.

In conclusion, the findings by Gorelick (2018) suggest that success in the municipal bond market occurs in countries whose laws grant full autonomy to municipal governments (such as South Africa) and those that take on a paternalistic view (like Cameroon). While the fundamentals of demonstrating the ability to pay and having bankable projects are key to any bond issuance, the success of municipal bond issuance is contingent on strong intergovernmental collaboration and supportive regulatory and political environment. From the case studies examined, it is evident that access to municipal bond markets is not just a technical finance issue but also a matter under the heavy influence of politico-economic factors prevalent in each country. The findings by Ogbuagu and Ujunwa (2008) highlight the potential for bond financing in revolutionising infrastructure financing in urban Nigeria given the immense challenges posed by rapid urban transition. The success factors for accessing the municipal bond market mirror those in Gorelick's study. They predict that bond financing will have a net positive effect on financial management and governance practices and identify the Urban Development Bank of Nigeria as a key institution in helping urban authorities access the bond market.

Public–Private Partnerships
Public–Private Partnerships (PPPs) have been widely cited as a credible alternative to financing urban infrastructure and a means to long-term efficiency in service delivery (Bahl & Linn, 2014; Platz et al., 2017; World Bank, 2013a). While there is a clear compelling case for using PPPs in public infrastructure development projects, it is manifestly difficult to mobilise private finance, large infrastructure needs and healthy appetite from potential investors notwithstanding. In their report on Bridging Local Infrastructure Gaps, McKinsey Global Institute (2016) argues that the presence of a pipeline of bankable infrastructure projects is the key ingredient to unlocking the participation of private capital in public infrastructure projects. In their African Economic Outlook report, the AfDB (2018) also takes note of the low PPP numbers globally and points out that Africa attracts fewer PPP deals than other developing regions. Sub-Saharan African countries managed PPP deals worth US$ 3.3 Billion in 2016, a tiny 5 percent of global PPP investment. A weak record

of full cost recovery, the unwillingness of local authorities to support tariff levels, the public sector picking up the tab at the failure of a private operator (Bahl & Linn, 2014), ownership issues (World Bank, 2013a), as well as concerns surrounding privatisation and neoliberal efforts (Miraftab, 2004) are among the downsides of PPP arrangements highlighted in literature. In this section, we assess literature focusing on the viability of Public–Private Partnerships (PPPs) in financing urban development in Africa.

Dabara et al. (2015) take stock of the current level of Nigeria's basic infrastructure against the rapid pace of urban growth in the large urban areas of Abuja, Lagos and Port Harcourt. They acknowledge the weaknesses of the current infrastructure-financing model, where the federal government of Nigeria shoulders the burden of financing, implementing and maintaining large infrastructure projects. They find that severe budget constraints and the high demand for services occasioned by the rapid urban transition resulted in inadequate financing for the development and maintenance of basic infrastructure. They assessed the potential for PPPs, given the relative ease of applying user charges and the steady cashflows that contribute to its commercial viability. The authors conclude that in theory, PPPs show great potential to ease the burden on federal finances but there are notable hurdles; namely, a lack of refinancing facilities, the paucity of bankable projects, uncertain political and economic environment, and the fear of policy reversals as infrastructure projects may outlive electoral cycles.

Muhammad and Abubakar (2019) investigate PPPs arrangements in delivering housing projects in Nigeria's capital, Abuja. Using qualitative content analysis on secondary data, they review the successes and challenges faced during the implementation of an ambitious mass housing programme in Abuja initiated by the Federal Capital Territory (FCTA) in the year 2000. Under the model, FCTA would provide land and primary infrastructure (for example roads, sewer lines and drainages) while private developers construct housing units for sale to citizens. The mass housing programme was to deliver 35,659 units in three phases stretching from the year 2000–2011. Their assessment of this programme uncovers a dismal performance record, where only 4158 units were completed as at the end of phase III of the project in 2011, reflecting an 11.7 percent success rate. In addition, 29 out of 356 developers completed their projects by the year 2011, with only 7 developers completing their projects within the 3 year stipulated project timeline. The authors posit that a number of key bottlenecks greatly contributed to the poor performance of the mass housing scheme. These were identified as: inadequate public sector capacity especially for planning, monitoring and supervising the project; lack of genuine commitment by partners; inadequate access to finance; lack of competent private partners and the lack of transparency and competitiveness in the procurement process.

Khatleli et al. (2020) take stock of the growing utilisation of PPPs to finance infrastructure projects in Africa with special focus on 10 best-practice infrastructure projects across the Southern African Development Community (SADC) region spanning the water and sanitation, transport and energy sectors. From their analysis, it is clear that for the SADC region, South Africa is the model/template for PPP systems across the region and as a result, has a well-developed PPP market with a healthy pipeline for infrastructure projects in its portfolio. Out of the 10 projects highlighted in the study, we narrow our focus on six projects that have a strictly urban footprint to provide a brief highlight of the implementation of PPP projects in the SADC region. These projects are the Gautrain project, the Dar es Salaam Bus Rapid Transit (BRT) system, the New Goreangab Water Treatment Plant, the Durban Water Recycling project, the Dolphin Coast Water and Sanitation Concession and the Mbombela Water and Sanitation Concession.

The Gautrain project was mooted in response to crippling traffic congestion along the highway that links Pretoria to Johannesburg, with the expectation that the project could absorb up to a fifth of private vehicle drivers thereby easing traffic flow. The Gautrain PPP is a Design-Finance-Build-Operate-Transfer (DFBOT) concession agreement between the Gauteng Provincial Government and the Bombela Consortium to finance, construct and operate the R26billion rail transport project. In this risk-sharing method, the private operator borrowed 88.7 percent of the total project outlay from the provincial government and financed the remainder (11.3 percent) from its own sources. The provincial government would earn interest on the loan advanced to the Bombela consortium as the consortium earns the right to proceeds during the lifetime of the PPP arrangement. Notable challenges to the implementation of this project include disruptions caused by industrial action by employees of the operator, theft of cabling along the tracks and disputes pitting the provincial government against the private consortium with respect to construction standards. Overall, the authors found that the project had a positive socio-economic impact such as; reduced pollution, strong growth in the province's economy, job creation to the tune of 121,800 jobs during its 6-year construction period, and a R5 billion revenue growth over 6 years for the provincial government.

The Dar es Salaam bus rapid transit (BRT) system began operations in May 2016 with the completion of the €134 million Phase 1 of the project. This phase of the project consisted of 140 buses carrying 300,000 passengers per day operating on a dedicated bus lane separate from all other traffic in the city. The authors posit that the Dar es salaam BRT is an ideal model for developing countries because of the low cost of implementation as compared to the costly metro and light rail methods but provides the same capacity and speed. Project implementation was beset by delays occasioned by factors such as conflict between the City Council and Dar es Salaam Rapid Transit Agency (DART), compensation and resettlement issues, cost overruns, inadequate engineering designs and weak supervision. Notable benefits of the BRT include a 50 percent reduction in wait times at terminals, 60 percent reduction in duration of travel, 25 percent cost savings relative to the 'daladala' privately run vans/minibus alternative, and the low fares charged which encourage use by low and medium-income earners.

The New Goreangab Water Treatment Plant came into being when the City of Windhoek signed a performance management agreement with Windhoek Goreangab Operating Company (WINGOC) to improve the production capacity and water treatment processes of the Goreangab plant. The PPP is based on the Operations and Maintenance model. The new plant is a Direct Potable Recycling (DPR) plant that converts sewage to drinking water and is currently servicing 35 percent of the city's water needs. Public acceptance for the idea of turning sewage to drinking water was a significant challenge but a public sensitisation campaign allowed for public acceptance of the project.

The Durban Water Recycling Project entailed the construction of a R74m sewage-to-clean-water recycling plant capable of treating 47.5 million litres of domestic and industrial water for sale to industrial consumers and drinking water for about 300,000 people. Based on a 20-year Build Own Operate and Transfer (BOOT) contract between the city and Durban Water recycling (private operator), the project has delivered credible economic and environmental benefits such as lower tariffs for consumers, delayed capital investment for water supply infrastructure and the extension of the life of the city's water catchment resources and the like.

The Dolphin Coast water and sanitation concession is a 30-year R 130 million concession agreement signed between the borough of Dolphin coast and Siza water company (SWC) in 1999 to provide water and sewerage services. Under the agreement, the SWC is expected to meet prescribed service levels while taking full risks in developing and maintaining infrastructure, providing the service and tariff collection. As part of the PPP terms, the concessionaire was mandated to prefer locals for employment and to institute a social investment programme for the benefit of the local community.

The Mbombela water and sanitation concession is a 30-year R189 million PPP project between the Mbombela local municipality and the Greater Nelspruit Utility Corporation. User charges form the basis for the PPP revenues. The concession has enjoyed considerable success in the sense that every household in the concession area has some access to water. The concessionaire has exhibited good management and operational capabilities that has seen it receive excellent ratings for water and effluent quality while maintaining tariffs at levels that are similar or lower than in comparable municipalities. Notable challenges include weak contract management on the part of the municipality. Various renegotiations of the concession agreement have seen the concessionaire limit its risk and responsibility for all investment in infrastructure.

In conclusion, Dabara et al. (2015) identified the need for the application of PPPs in Abuja, Lagos and Port Harcourt. The rapid urban transition and the challenge it poses makes it necessary to shift from a funding to a financing approach through the involvement of private capital. Muhammad and Abubakar (2019) enumerated Abuja's negative experience with PPPs in its mass housing project. They explain the technical and political challenges that led to the failure of the project. Khatleli et al. (2020) examined the experiences of ten projects in the SADC region, out of which we chose six that have an urban component to highlight as best-practice urban PPP projects in the region. These projects are mainly in the water and sanitation as well as transport sectors. While they have diverse financing, legal and operational structures, the said projects have delivered tangible socio-economic and environmental benefits to their urban constituents.

Fiscal Transfers

Fiscal transfers are instruments that were borne out of the process of political, administrative and fiscal decentralisation. The pace towards decentralisation was driven by the demand for greater regional autonomy owing to ethnic/cultural differences, economic disparities between regions and the desire for responsive governance Morales et al. (2017). Eaton et al. (2011) suggest that decentralisation is not a simple mechanical process; it is one in which the process and outcome is determined by political and institutional dynamics. Hence, the tension between the different levels of government is inevitable; this is the norm in state formation.

Fiscal decentralisation refers to the shifting of taxing and spending power from central authorities to authorities at the subnational levels. The ideal fiscally decentralised system has two key components, which are powers to tax, and the existence of a healthy tax base. It is widely held that local authorities in the developed world are fiscally better empowered relative to their counterparts in the developing world, where some local authorities exist as units of the central authorities with limited autonomy or experience frustration from central authorities (Bahl & Linn, 2014; Smoke, 2015). Central authorities in developing nations in particular, are notoriously resistant and unwilling to relinquish power to lower level authorities, an impediment that damages the premise of fiscal decentralisation even in the presence of an appropriate legal framework to guide decentralisation (Boschmann, 2009).

Table 5.3 highlights the limited fiscal autonomy that local authorities in developing nations face compared to their counterparts in the developed world, with the revenue side of the equation particularly constrained.

Fiscal decentralisation is based on general normative theories proposed in the seminal work by Musgrave (1959) and Oates (1972). Musgrave (1959) suggested a conceptual separation of government functions in three ways, the first two of which are ideally suited to central authorities and the last one (resource allocation) suited to local authorities. The first one is the macroeconomic stabilisation function, which ensures the achievement of price stability and high employment. The second one is the income redistribution function, which aspires to achieve an equitable distribution of income, and the third one is the resource allocation function that ensures that the resources are used efficiently.

Table 5.3 The comparative fiscal role of local governments

Regions	Local government share of Total Public Sector (percent)	
	Revenue	Expenditure
Northern Europe	52	52
Europe	25	25
Asia–Pacific	33	33
Middle East and West Asia	10.1	10.8
Eurasia	N/A	N/A
Latin America	23	19
Africa	17	15

Source Gold V Report (UCLG, 2019)

Conclusions by Oates (1972) were based on the 'home rule' principle which suggests that voters at local levels take control of expenditure and revenue assignment at that level on the condition that efficiency considerations (such as economies of scale and externalities) are met, failure to which control of service provision and financing should be handled at higher levels of government. In summary, Both Musgrave and Oates provide a useful normative framework through which functions and the fiscal instruments for fulfilling those functions are assigned to authorities in their different levels.

The Role of Fiscal Transfers

Intergovernmental/fiscal transfers are a critical component in financing service provision and infrastructure needs in local authorities. An enduring expectation is that urban/city/town authorities are able to fund their service provision and infrastructure needs. This is a realistic expectation as cities and towns are magnets of economic activity with higher incomes, which means that they have a greater capacity to raise local revenue (Bahl & Linn, 2014). However, this is not always the case and fiscal/intergovernmental transfers are an important source of finance available to local authorities in both the developed and developing world alike.

Fiscal transfers are the focus of a vast array of literature that provide normative and/or positive frameworks on pertinent issues such as the principles of revenue and expenditure assignments, fiscal autonomy and intergovernmental relations, fiscal transfers and dependency (Boadway & Shah, 2007; McLure & Martinez-Vazquez, 2000; Platz et al., 2017). First Generation Fiscal Federalism (FGFF) literature takes a normative approach to public finance goals, which were allocation efficiency, equity in distribution and stabilisation. This type of literature provides the textbook approach that guides policymakers on the basic building blocks for the existence of a healthy fiscal decentralisation system. Some practitioners view this approach as timeworn and incongruent with reality due to the assumption of the existence of benevolent policy makers in local authorities. On the other hand, Second Generation Fiscal Federalism (SGFF) literature takes on a much more nuanced approach by recognising the influence of fiscal and political incentives facing local officials thus complementing the First Generation Fiscal Federalism (FGFF) literature (Oates, 2005; Weingast, 2013).

From literature (McLure & Martinez-Vazquez, 2000; Steffensen, 2010; Smoke, 2015) available, the textbook approach to the design of a healthy fiscal transfer system should meet a set of objectives, which are as follows:

(a) Correcting vertical imbalances—closing the fiscal gap between expenditure assignment and revenue assignments;
(b) Correcting horizontal imbalances/Equalisation—Ensuring that local authorities have a similar ability to provide basic services to the citizens;
(c) Correcting for externalities—Grants may be used to compensate Local governments for services they provide that affect areas beyond their jurisdictions and
(d) Ensuring efficiency in local government revenue mobilisation, financial management and utilisation of funds.

In assessing the design, function and outcomes of fiscal transfers, three key classifications relating to the design and function of fiscal transfers emerge. These are the determination of the size of transfer pool (like share of revenue or gross domestic product [GDP]); the conditionalities imposed on the use of funds (such as conditional or unconditional); and the method of allocation of resources (like ad hoc, formula-based, or reimbursement basis).

Dependence on Fiscal Transfers

A common argument in the fiscal transfers debate is the assertion that while transfers are essential for financing the provision of public services at local level, they may become a disincentive to local revenue generation, thus undermining the fiscal autonomy of the same local authorities (Morales et al., 2017; Smoke, 2015; UCLG, 2007; UN-Habitat, 2015). The degree to which cities and other urban centres are dependent on fiscal transfers varies widely across the world, with the differences being a reflection of the taxing powers assigned to the local authorities. In Africa, South African cities on average finance nearly 70 percent of their budgets from own-source revenues owing to the significant taxing powers available to them whereas in Tanzania, fiscal transfers account for almost 90 percent of budgets of local authorities (Nixon et al., 2015). The evidence assessed in this study paints a mixed picture; some studies affirm that fiscal transfers create dependence and 'crowd-out' local revenue (Mogues et al., 2009; Taiwo, 2020) while others discount this hypothesis, instead supporting a 'crowding-in' effect of fiscal transfers on local revenue mobilisation (Brun & El Khdari, 2016; Brun & Sanogo, 2017; Masaki, 2018).

Taiwo (2020) tested the relationship between fiscal transfers to state governments in Nigeria and the growth of local revenues using public finance data from 2007–2013. The study found that Nigeria's states are dependent on fiscal transfers to the tune of 75–95 percent of their budgets. It also found that fiscal transfers crowd-out local revenue is established, where a 1 percent increase in fiscal transfers is associated with a 0.64 percent decline in local revenue generation. The analysis also unearthed political economic manoeuvres on the part of state officials as local revenues plummeted during election years. Taiwo posits that the revenue-sharing arrangements, political economy issues and the lack of clear benefits from taxpaying may have contributed to the lack of effort to raise local revenue.

Mogues et al. (2009) considered this question with respect to the district governments in Ghana. They analysed public finance and other data from Ghana's 110 districts for the period 1994–2004 to examine the impact of fiscal transfers on the districts' own-source revenues. They found that districts that receive large transfers had lower levels of own-source revenues and subsequently experienced slower growth of local revenue. In addition, their results showed that higher past spending on recurrent expenditure was associated with higher own-source revenue generation than capital spending. This is due to the practice of linking fiscal transfers to capital expenditure and recurrent expenditure to own-source revenues. This confirms that in Ghana, fiscal transfers crowd-out local revenue generation, effectively negating equity and efficiency benefits associated with decentralisation. They attribute this result to the mismatch between the policy goals of external financiers versus local priorities. They aver that increasing the discretionary component of fiscal transfers and aligning external policy goals with local priorities will increase the fiscal autonomy of the districts.

Brun and El Khdari (2016) empirically tested the incentive effect of two types of transfers disbursed to Moroccan municipalities; unconditional transfers (formula allocated) and conditional transfers (allocated on ad hoc basis) on the local revenue effort of Moroccan Municipalities. The study yielded the existence of a positive incentive effect on both types of transfers, with unconditional transfers being particularly robust; meaning that unconditional transfers create a positive incentive to grow local revenues.

Masaki (2018) empirically tested the relationship between intergovernmental transfers and local tax revenues in Tanzania using district-level quarterly local revenue data for financial years 2010/2011 to 2012/2013. The findings confirmed a 'crowding in' effect. This means that intergovernmental transfers have a net positive effect on local revenue mobilisation efforts of Tanzanian municipalities with the condition that the positive effect is less significant in urban than in rural municipalities, where fiscal capacity is weaker and the political cost of tax enforcement is low.

Brun and Sanogo (2017) performed statistical analysis to test the incentive effect of fiscal transfers on local revenue mobilisation with fiscal data on 115 municipalities from the Ivory Coast for the period 2001–2014. The period in focus presented an opportunity to test the incentive effect during a time of conflict and post-conflict, which Ivory Coast suffered from 2001 to 2008. Their analysis yielded a positive incentive effect of fiscal transfers on local revenue mobilisation on both tax and non-tax revenues with the incentive effect larger on tax revenues as opposed to non-tax revenues. During the conflict, a 10 percent increase in fiscal transfers translated to 3.3 percent increase in local revenue while during the post-conflict, a 10 percent increase in fiscal transfers yielded a 5.9 percent increase in local revenue.

African Decentralisation and Service Delivery
An enduring narrative emerging out of a wide array of development discourse is that African cities are sites of deficit saddled with weak governance, poor service delivery and infrastructure-financing gaps (Lall et al., 2017; Platz et al., 2017). Using information sourced from secondary literature and interviews, Cirolia (2020) historically traced the African urban experience from postcolonial to contemporary times. While being careful not to minimise the depth of the challenges faced by African cities, Cirolia asserts that the deficit narrative fails to take into account the heterogeneous nature of service delivery in Africa's urban landscape. In addition, the study identified the unevenness and contested nature of decentralisation on the continent with sustained resistance by central authorities to devolving power with the South African experience being a notable exception thereby confirming conclusions in existing literature (JICA-RI, 2013; Nixon et al., 2015; Smoke, 2015). Finally, the study established the sustained attraction to financing large infrastructure projects on the part of the lenders and central authorities. This has led to uncoordinated infrastructure investments in African cities and continuing fragmentation of urban infrastructure on the continent. Faced with fractured fiscal authority and fragmented networked infrastructure, a multitude of hybrid service delivery responses emerged to fill in the gaps. Examples include; the proliferation of household septic tanks in response to the lack of centralised sewage systems and the emergence of minibuses, motorcycles and *tuktuks* in response to the lack of an efficient public transport system (Berrisford et al., 2018). Consequently, financing such cities must discard the conventional model of simply calculating the cost of the infrastructure gap and instead take into consideration the material differences of the African context, and build financing models that reflect actual conditions on the ground.

In conclusion, this section has dealt with various aspects in fiscal decentralisation, beginning with its theoretical underpinnings and the general framework for creating a healthy fiscal transfer system. Also considered in the study was the issue of dependency on transfers, and the different outcomes on local revenue mobilisation realised in each situation. Lastly, the contested nature of decentralisation on the continent and its effect on local fiscal authority and service delivery was examined to bring out the unique African perspective.

Sovereign Wealth Funds

Sovereign wealth funds represent a viable option for financing urban infrastructure in Africa, especially for countries that have significant energy and mineral wealth (World Bank, 2013b). The number of African Sovereign Wealth Funds (hereinafter referred to as SWFs) grew rapidly on the buck of the commodities boom (year 2000–2014) where several African countries experienced huge windfalls from commodity exports. Recent discoveries of mineral deposits in Kenya, Uganda, Tanzania and Guinea are likely to lead to formation of more SWFs. The World Bank and the IMF have long advocated for the formation of SWFs in natural resource-rich countries for the simple reason that they represent the best way to manage and invest the vast windfalls from commodity exports (Hove, 2016; Lipsky, 2008; Triki & Faye, 2011).

Vast foreign currency inflows into developing countries with weak banking and financial institutions quickly fall victim to an insidious economic phenomenon called Dutch Disease; aptly named as the Dutch realised that while the oil economy flourished in the early sixties, everything else slumped thereby leading to job losses. These currency inflows cause a rapid appreciation of the local currency leading to imports becoming cheaper relative to local products, and effectively killing off all sectors not connected to the extraction of natural resources. Burgis (2015) posits that the debilitating effects of Dutch disease are visible in many resource-rich African countries today such as Angola, Nigeria and the Democratic Republic of Congo (DRC), where the share of manufacturing to GDP continues to drop. This has stifled the opportunity to create mass employment through industrial development. In Nigeria, for example, Burgis traces the hegemony of Northern Nigeria's crime lords, the breakdown of institutions and the collapse of the textiles industry directly to the discovery of oil in the Niger delta. Shaxson (2018) frames this simply as the Resource Curse, which is a paradox of poverty from plenty. For natural resource-rich countries, a pattern of slow economic growth, endemic corruption, authoritarian politics, greater conflict and poverty emerges relative to their resource-starved peers.

The size and scope of African SWFs pales in comparison to the global tally; about a half of African SWFs were established during the past decade. This is evidence of the nascent nature of SWFs in the continent. Africa is home to an estimated 12–20 SWFs with combined assets of US$ 89–159 Billion versus a 2015 global tally of US$ 7.2 Trillion. Libya and Algeria each account for US$ 55 Billion in assets under management, with Angola and Botswana coming second with a combined total of US$ 10 Billion in 2015, accounting for a large proportion of the African tally. Globally, 57 percent of assets under management of SWFs are derived from oil and gas against Africa's 83 percent highlighting the importance of oil and gas export revenues as the primary source of funding for these SWFs (Ajambo et al., 2020; Chen, 2019; Hove, 2016). The variation in the Africa tally for assets under management is due to differences in the definition of an SWF. According to the 'Santiago Principles', a set of generally accepted principles and practices for the SWF industry, the

International Working Group of Sovereign Wealth Funds (IWG, 2008) affirms the expanded definition of SWFs as it includes commodity export revenues (traditional/conservative/restrictive) alongside Balance of Payments (BOP) surpluses, official foreign currency operations, fiscal surpluses and proceeds from privatisations (expanded definition).

Kamiya and Ma (2019) make the case for SWF investment in urban infrastructure in emerging markets. Paulais (2012) reckons that African economic growth makes it an attractive destination for SWFs since post-2008; these funds have shifted away from banking sector assets to infrastructure and industrial assets to seek better returns on their investment. Farid and Pozhidaev (2017) explain that in Africa, private capital (which includes SWFs and other institutional investors control assets (USD 1.5 trillion) that dwarf government revenues and official development assistance (ODA). They reckon that private capital will likely play a key role in financing municipal infrastructure as the capital markets in Africa mature in terms of scope and sophistication which mirrors the assertions in the Infrastructure Consortium for Africa (ICA) report (2018). Clark et al. (2017) note that over half of the world SWFs invest in real estate, which is an asset class that is closely linked to urban development.

Traditionally, SWFs have five key functions or goals (Ajambo et al., 2020) in as far as stabilisation funds, saving funds, reserve funds, development funds and pension funds are concerned. Stabilisation funds are set up to insulate home economies from commodity price volatility and external shocks, essentially to smooth out boom/bust cycles. Saving funds are set up to facilitate intergenerational wealth sharing through long-term financial investments to provide for future generations even when the natural resource is depleted. Reserve funds allow earning high returns from reserves even though they are still classified as such. Development funds are set up to finance government projects that have significant positive socio-economic outcomes. Finally, there are pension reserve funds without explicit pension liabilities (Table 5.4).

Generally, African SWFs tend to have multiple mandates as opposed to singular mandates even when it is not explicitly stated. The SWFs include Botswana's Pula Fund, Libyan Investment Authority (LIA), Fundo Soberano de Angola (FSDEA), Nigerian Sovereign Investment Authority (NSIA), Ghana Petroleum Fund, Rwanda's Agaciro Development Fund (AGDF), and Senegal's Fonds Souverain d'Investissements Stratégiques (FONSIS). A recent survey of the leadership of African SWFs conducted by the International Forum of Sovereign Wealth Funds (IFSWF) and Franklin Templeton (2021) further underscores the nature of multiple mandates as a recurring theme in Africa. A majority of those surveyed (62.5 percent) pointed to having more than one policy mandate, with singular mandates such as savings for future generations and development funds accounting for 25 percent and 12.5 percent respectively. Multiple mandates may reflect the most efficient use of scarce resources for African governments hence their relative prevalence; however, the survey unearthed some notable challenges to this model. SWFs

Table 5.4 Some of Africa's sovereign wealth funds

Country	Name of SWF	Capitalisation (US$ Billion)	Type of fund	Source of funds
Libya	Libyan Investment Authority	67.00	Development	Oil
Algeria	Fonds de Regulation des Recettes	56.70	Future Generations	Oil
Botswana	Pula Fund	6.90	Future Generations	Minerals
Nigeria	Nigeria Sovereign Investment Authority	1.40	Stabilisation	Oil
Ghana	Ghana Petroleum Funds	0.49	Future Generations	Oil
Senegal	Fonds Souverain d'Investissements Stratégiques	1.00	Development	Non-Commodity
Rwanda	Agaciro Development Fund	0.21	Development	Non-Commodity
Gabon	Gabon Sovereign Wealth Fund	0.40	Future Generations	Oil
D.R.C	Fonds de Stabilisation de Recettes Budgetaries	1.39	Stabilisation	Oil and Minerals
Equatorial Guinea	Future Funds for Generations	0.08	Future Generations	Oil
Sao Tome	National Oil Account	0.01	Stabilisation	Oil

Source Ajambo et al. (2020), Hove (2016)

reported struggling with prioritising each mandate given the shifting political realities, challenging macroeconomic environments further exacerbated by Covid-19 and the different skillsets and structures needed to deliver them. The stabilisation motive is also visible in literature. Hove (2016) explains that Mauritania used US$ 45 million from its SWF to fund an economic stimulus programme in 2009. Algeria also used resources from its SWF to plug fiscal deficits and repay public debt, essentially confirming the insulating nature of stabilisation funds on government budgets in the face of external shocks and volatile commodity prices.

Botswana's Pula Fund stands out as a best practice in terms of clarity in mandates/objectives, fund management, transparency and governance structures. It is noteworthy that Botswana is a founding member of the IFSWF and signatory to its 'Santiago Principles'. A great deal of scholarship identifies key African SWFs which have excelled in investment in key thematic areas some of which are crucial for the attainment of the sustainable development goals (SDGs), effectively encompassing aspects of urban development as well

(Chen, 2019; IFSWF & Franklin Templeton, 2021; Markowitz, 2020). These SWFs are from Angola, Ghana, Morocco, Nigeria and Senegal. In our analysis, the investment activities of these SWFs can be grouped into three (3) key thematic areas; climate-friendly investing, social impact investing and domestic infrastructure financing which are discussed.

Climate-Friendly Investing
Senegal's FONSIS has a wealth of experience investing on solar power projects in Senegal and thanks to its efforts, Senegal ranks among the leading solar power producers in West Africa. These investments line up with the attainment of SDGs and tackling the urban challenge as Senegal's population may likely double by the year 2050 with half of its population expected to live in urban areas.

Morocco's Ithmar Capital created the Green Growth Infrastructure Facility (GGIF), a Pan-African Fund whose focus is on green infrastructure projects in Solar and Hydropower as well as low carbon transportation. Its partnerships with the Ghana Infrastructure Investment Fund (GIIF) and Senegal's FONSIS deepens the impact of such green growth projects across Africa.

Social Impact Investing
The Nigeria Sovereign Investment Authority (NSIA) is bound by law to provide up to a maximum asset allocation of 10 percent of its infrastructure fund towards social infrastructure projects in underserved communities in Nigeria. This has seen the NSIA channel support to Fund for Agricultural Finance in Nigeria (FAFIN) that invests in Nigerian companies in the agricultural value chain that meet strict environmental, social and corporate governance (ESG) principles and healthcare investments targeting the tertiary healthcare segment and pharmaceuticals.

Angola's FSDEA is a great example of an African SWF incorporating impact investments into its portfolio of projects. FSDEA maintains a maximum asset allocation of 7.5 percent dedicated to social development projects and socially responsible investments. On this mandate, FSDEA invests in agriculture, education, electricity, healthcare, technical and vocational skills development and water projects. Partnerships with Non-Governmental Organisations (NGOs) involved in social development work in Angola are key to the success of its programmes.

Domestic Infrastructure Financing
Most SWFs from Africa are now investing in local infrastructure as a mandate, highlighting the importance attached to such funds by governments. However, this was not always the case as a few studies have demonstrated the external investment preference of African SWFs (Amoako-Tuffour, 2016; Diallo et al., 2016; Triki & Faye, 2011). Examples of African SWFs investing in domestic infrastructure are discussed in this section.

Angola's Fundo Soberano de Angola (FSDEA), Ghana Infrastructure Investment Fund (GIIF) and Nigeria Infrastructure Fund (NIF) feature prominently in SWF literature. While the NIF and GIIF have a strictly local infrastructure development focus, half of FSDEA's endowment is focused on diversified investments in sub-Saharan African countries and emerging markets. This makes it one of the most externally focused SWFs in Africa. FSDEA footprint in domestic infrastructure projects includes an outlay of US$ 1.1 Billion spent in the five years between 2012 and 2016. FSDEA's investment strategy maintains an asset allocation limit/ceiling of 30 percent solely for infrastructure investments.

Ghana's GIIF has been a key enabler for the country's digital transformation with its involvement in the Western Corridor project, which involved laying 880 kms of Fibre Optic cables to support broadband internet services in the western parts of Ghana with an investment outlay of US$ 51million in a public–private partnership. The GIIF has also become an important catalyst in attracting foreign capital to invest in local development projects; a key example being the US$ 85 million facility from the French Development Agency (AFD).

Nigeria's NIF is heavily involved in the country's infrastructure development. Notable projects conducted by the NIF and its co-investment partners include the Abuja-Kano Highway, the second Niger Bridge, development of export-oriented special economic zones, a US$ 1.5 billion fertiliser plant, and a US$ 200 million infrastructure credit facility that is expected to deepen the local corporate and infrastructure bond markets.

In conclusion, this section has considered the idea of SWFs and the vast resources that are under their management to finance urban infrastructure in Africa. While African SWFs are small compared to global peers, they are financing critical social and economic infrastructure that will underpin the achievement of SDGs as well as urban and national development goals into the future.

Urban Finance in the Context of Climate Emergencies
Simpson et al. (2019) make the case for building financial and administrative resilience to respond to projected severe climatic events. They examine the actions and processes that Cape Town authorities instituted in response to the 2015–2018 drought. Substantial new investments in diversifying the city's water supply and expanding water storage was needed but the responsibility to finance such requirements was disputed among the local, regional and national governments. The drought severely affected the city's fiscal position, with revenue from water and sanitation services revenues dipping an estimated 24.8 percent and 30.8 percent respectively. This drop was attributed to demand management measures and heavy consumption households seeking alternative supplies through off-grid technologies. This intervention by households securing private supply of essential services is not just detrimental to the city's fiscal position going forward but also reduces the scope for cross-subsidisation

of essential services, disproportionally affecting the poorest communities. The city authorities responded by mandating connection to the water and electricity grid as a back-up for those who had sought alternative supply. This attracted a monthly fixed charge which is independent of consumption.

In conclusion, climate change has made the use of historical rainfall records and conventional planning techniques ineffective. Cape Town's experience during the 3-year drought exposes the difficulties of managing the effects of climate change on a city's fiscal position while attempting to meet service obligations to its citizens. Simpson et al. (2019) argue that Cape Town's experience reinforces the need for urban authorities to develop innovative fiscal systems that exhibit both short-term coping and long-term adaptation-resilient cities that will not only bounce back but also bounce forward.

Conclusion

This chapter has reviewed literature on the form, development, role and outcomes of finance in urban development in Africa. From the literature reviewed, it can be inferred that urban finance is at a relatively underdeveloped stage in Africa, and this has direct implications on the scope, nature and outcomes of development. This is largely the consequence of policy and capacity limitations in strengthening urban finance. That said, there are instances of initiatives towards financing urban development with the objective of strong urban communities. It is imperative that African governments realise the role that strong urban profiles play in the growth and development of countries and hence act towards realising this. There are avenues through which they may pursue a variety of contemporary urban finance models such as the Public–Private Partnerships and the Sovereign Wealth Fund, towards greater urban development, and consequently, overall national growth and development.

References

Adam Smith International. (2018). *Own-source revenue potential and tax gap study of Kenya's county governments.* Adam Smith International. https://documents1.worldbank.org/curated/en/280021585886703203/pdf/Own-Source-Revenue-Potential-and-Tax-Gap-Study-of-Kenya-s-County-Governments-Final-Report.pdf

African Development Bank (AfDB). (2018). Financing Africa's infrastructure: New strategies, mechanisms, and instruments (Chapter 4). In African Development Bank (Ed.), *African economic outlook 2018* (pp. 95–124). African Development Bank Group.

Ajambo, E., Pang, S., & Fernandez, C. (2020). *Africa's sovereign wealth funds are a source of development finance.* United Nations (U.N.) Namibia.

Amoako-Tuffour, J. (2016). *Should countries invest resource revenues abroad when demands for public infrastructure are pressing at home? The dilemma of sovereign wealth funds in sub-Saharan Africa.* African Centre for Economic Transformation (ACET).

Bahl, R. W., & Linn, J. F. (2014). *Governing and financing cities in the developing world*. Lincoln Institute of Land Policy.

Berrisford, S., Cirolia, L. R., & Palmer, I. (2018). Land-based financing in sub-Saharan African cities. *Environment and Urbanization, 30*(1), 35–52. https://doi.org/10.1177/0956247817753525

Boadway, R., & Shah, A. (2007). *Intergovernmental fiscal transfers: Principles and practice*. World Bank.

Boschmann, N. (2009). *Fiscal decentralization and options for donor harmonisation*. Development Partners Working Group on Local Governance and Decentralization (DPWG-LGD).

Brun, J.-F., & El Khdari, M. (2016). *The incentive effects of conditional and unconditional transfers on local own revenue generation: Empirical Evidence from Moroccan municipalities*. CERDI.

Brun, J.-F., & Sanogo, T. (2017). *Effect of central transfers on municipalities' own revenue mobilization: Do conflict and local revenue management matter?* CERDI. http://cerdi.org/production/show/id/1888/type_production_id/1

Burgis, T. (2015). *The looting machine: Warlords, tycoons, smugglers and the systematic theft of Africa's wealth*. William Collins.

Chen, J. (2019). Financing the sustainable development goals: The role of African sovereign wealth funds. *The Journal of International Law & Politics, 51*, 1259–1292.

Cirolia, L. R. (2020). Fractured fiscal authority and fragmented infrastructures: Financing. *Habitat International*. https://doi.org/10.1016/j.habitatint.2020.102233

Clark, G., Moonen, T., & Carr, D. (2017). The role of real estate development in urbanizing cities. In M. Kamiya, & L.-Y. Zhang (Eds.), *Finance for city leaders handbook: Improving municipal finance to deliver better services* (pp. 216–237). United Nations Human Settlements Programme (UN-Habitat).

Colenbrander, S., & Barau, A. (2019). Planning and financing urban development in the context of the climate crisis. *International Journal of Urban Sustainable Development, 11*(3), 237–244. https://doi.org/10.1080/19463138.2019.1673529

Dabara, D. I., Ankeli, A. I., Guyimu, J., Oladimeji, E. J., & Oyediran, O. (2015). Infrastructure financing and urban development in Nigeria. *Conference of the International Journal of Arts & Sciences, 8*(1), 79–86. http://ssrn.com/abstract=2784497

Diallo, B., Tchana, F. T., & Zeufack, A. G. (2016). *Sovereign wealth funds and long-term investments in sub-Saharan Africa*. The World Bank.

Eaton, K., Kaiser, K., & Smoke, P. J. (2011). *The political economy of decentralization reforms: Implications for aid effectiveness*. World Bank.

Farid, M., & Pozhidaev, D. (2017). Improving capital markets for municipal finance in least developed countries. In M. Kamiya & L.-Y. Zhang (Eds.), *Finance for city leaders handbook: Improving municipal finance to deliver better services* (pp. 238–253). United Nations Human Settlements Programme (UN Habitat).

Fjeldstad, O.-H. (2006). *Local revenue mobilization in urban settings in Africa*. Chr. Michelsen Institute.

Fjeldstad, O.-H., Ali, M., & Goodfellow, T. (2017, March). *Taxing the urban boom: Property taxation in Africa*. Chr. Michelsen Institute.

Floater, G., Dowling, D., Chan, D., Ulterino, M., Braunstein, J., McMinn, T., & Ahmad, E. (2017). *Global review of finance for sustainable urban infrastructure*.

Coalition for Urban Transitions. http://newclimateeconomy.net/content/cities-working-papers

Floater, G., Rode, P., Friedel, B., & Robert, A. (2014). *Steering urban growth: Governance, policy and finance*. London School of Economics and Political Science.

Franzsen, R., & McCluskey, W. (2017). *Property tax in Africa: Status, challenges, and prospects*. Lincoln Institute of Land Policy.

Germán, L., & Glass, E. (2017). Non-tax own-source municipal revenues. In M. Kamiya & Z. Le-Yin (Eds.), *Finance for city leaders handbook: Improving municipal finance to deliver better services* (2nd ed., pp. 66–80). United Nations Human Settlements Programme (UN-Habitat).

Global Land Tool Network (GLTN) & United Nations Human Settlements Programme (UN Habitat). (2016). *Leveraging land: Land-based finance for local governments*. United Nations Human Settlements Programme (UN-Habitat).

Gorelick, J. (2018). Supporting the future of municipal bonds in sub-Saharan Africa: The centrality of enabling environments and regulatory frameworks. *Environment & Urbanization, 30*(1), 103–122. https://doi.org/10.1177/0956247817741853

Hobdari, N., Nguyen, V., Dell'Erba, S., & Ruggiero, E. (2018). *Lessons for effective fiscal decentralization in sub-Saharan Africa*. International Monetary Fund.

Hommann, K., & Lall, S. V. (2019). *Which way to livable and productive cities? A road map for sub-Saharan Africa*. World Bank.

Hove, S. (2016). *Sovereign wealth funds and infrastructure development in Africa*. Quantum Global Research Lab.

Infrastructure Consortium for Africa (ICA). (2018). *Infrastructure financing trends in Africa—2018*. The Infrastructure Consortium for Africa Secretariat.

International Forum of Sovereign Wealth Funds (IFSWF) & Franklin Templeton. (2021). *Investing for growth and prosperity: In Africa sovereign wealth funds focus on G, S and E*. International Forum of Sovereign Wealth Funds (IFSWF).

International Working Group of Sovereign Wealth Funds (IWG). (2008). *Sovereign wealth funds: Generally accepted principles and practices "Santiago Principles"*. International Working Group of Sovereign Wealth Funds. https://www.ifswf.org/sites/default/files/santiagoprinciples_0_0.pdf

JICA-RI. (2013). Chapter 6: Urbanization. In JICA-RI (Ed.), *Development challenges in Africa towards 2050* (pp. 102–116). JICA Research Institute (JICA-RI).

Kamiya, M., & Ma, W. (2019). *Sovereign investment funds could be the answer to the SDGs*. World Economic Forum. https://www.weforum.org/agenda/2019/12/sovereign-wealth-funds-sdgs/

Kamiya, M., & Zhang, L.-Y. (Eds) (2017). *Finance for city leaders handbook: Improving municipal finance to deliver better services* (2nd ed.). United Nations Human Settlements Programme (UN-Habitat).

Khatleli, N., Shipalana, P., Markowitz, C., & Parshotam, A. (2020). *Best practices on PPP infrastructure development in SADC countries*. South African Institute of International Affairs (SAIIA).

Lall, S. V., Henderson, J. V., & Venables, A. J. (2017). *Africa's cities: Opening doors to the world*. World Bank.

Lipsky, J. (2008, September 3). Sovereign wealth funds: Their role and significance. In *Sovereign funds: Responsibility with our future*. International Monetary Fund (IMF).

Markowitz, C. (2020). *Sovereign wealth funds in Africa: Taking stock and looking forward*. South African Institute of International Affairs (SAIIA).

McLure, C. & Martinez-Vazquez, J. (2000). *The assignment of revenues and expenditures in intergovernmental fiscal relations*. ResearchGate. https://www.researchgate.net/publication/252586054_The_Assignment_of_Revenues_and_Expenditures_in_Intergovernmental_Fiscal_Relations

Masaki, T. (2018). *The impact of intergovernmental transfers on local revenue generation in sub-Saharan Africa: Evidence from Tanzania*. Elsevier Ltd. https://doi.org/10.1016/j.worlddev.2018.01.026

McKinsey Global Institute. (2016). *Bridging global infrastructure gaps*. McKinsey & Company.

Miraftab, F. (2004). Public-private partnerships: The Trojan horse of neoliberal development? *Journal of Planning Education and Research, 24*(1), 89–101. https://doi.org/10.1177/0739456X04267173

Mogues, T., Benin, S., & Cudjoe, G. (2009). *Do external grants to district governments discourage own-revenue generation? A look at local public finance dynamics in Ghana*. International Food Policy Research Institute (IFPRI).

Morales, A., Letelier, L., & Platz, D. (2017). Decentralization and local government financing. In M. Kamiya, & L.-Y. Zhang (Eds.), *Finance for city leaders handbook: Improving municipal finance to deliver better services* (pp. 46–63). United Nations Human Settlements Programme (UN Habitat).

Muhammad, Z., & Abubakar, I. R. (2019). *Transformative urbanization through public-private partnership in Abuja, Nigeria*. IGI Global.

Musgrave, R. A. (1959). *The theory of public finance: A study in public economy*. McGraw-Hill.

Mutua, J., & Wamalwa, N. (2017). *Enhancing mobilization of own source revenue in Nairobi city county: Issues & opportunities*. Institute of Economic Affairs.

Nixon, H., Chambers, V., Hadley, S., & Hart, T. (2015). *Urban finance: Rapid evidence assessment*. Overseas Development Institute.

Oates, W. E. (1972). *Fiscal federalism*. Harcourt Brace Jovanovich.

Oates, W. E. (2005). Toward a second-generation theory of fiscal federalism. *International Tax and Public Finance, 12*, 349–373.

Ogbuagu, E., & Ujunwa, A. (2008). Broadening local government financing in Nigeria: The capital market option. *Journal of Banking, Finance and Development*, 28–37.

Park, Y.-H., Bang, H. K., Cheong, J.-W., Lee, B., & Kim, Y. (2017). An analysis of urbanization in Africa and its implications for Korea: Future demands for urban infrastructure. *World Economy Brief, 7*(11). https://ssrn.com/abstract=2971746

Paulais, T. (2012). *Financing Africa's cities: The imperative of local investment*. Agence Française de Développement and the World Bank.

Platz, D., Hilger, T., Intini, V., & Santoro, S. (2017). *Financing sustainable urban development in the least developed countries*. United Nations.

Saghir, J., & Santoro, J. (2018). *Urbanization in sub-Saharan Africa: Meeting challenges by bridging stakeholders*. Center for Strategic & International Studies.

Sarr, K. D. (2019). *Boosting urban development in Africa through new mechanisms of financing*. Urbanet.

Shaxson, N. (2018). *The finance curse: How global finance is making us all poorer*. The Bodley Head.

Simpson, N., Simpson, K., Shearing, C., & Cirolia, L. (2019). Municipal finance and resilience lessons for urban infrastructure management: A case study from the Cape

Town drought. *International Journal of Urban Sustainable Development.* https://doi.org/10.1080/19463138.2019.1673529

Smoke, P. (2015). *Financing urban and local development:The missing link in sustainable development finance.* The Global Taskforce of Local and Regional Governments. United Cities and Local Governments.

Steffensen, J. (2010). *Fiscal decentralisation and sector funding principles and practices: Grant allocation principles.* Danish International Development Agency (DANIDA).

Taiwo, K. (2020). *Intergovernmental transfers and own revenues of subnational governments in Nigeria.* Munich Personal RePEc Archive (MPRA). https://mpra.ub.uni-muenchen.de/104374/

The Economist Intelligence Unit. (2019). *The critical role of infrastructure for the sustainable development goals.* The Economist Intelligence Unit Limited.

Triki, T., & Faye, I. (2011). *Africa's quest for development: Can sovereign wealth funds help?* African Development Bank (AfDB).

Turok, I., & McGranahan, G. (2013). Urbanization and economic growth: The arguments and evidence for Africa and Asia. *Environment and Urbanization, 25*(2), 465–482. https://doi.org/10.1177/0956247813490908

UN-Habitat. (2015). *The challenge of local government financing in developing countries.* United Nations Human Settlements Programme (UN-HABITAT).

United Cities and Local Governments (UCLG). (2007). *UCLG support paper on local finance: Background paper to the UCLG policy paper on local finance.* United Cities and Local Governments.

United Cities and Local Governments (UCLG). (2019). *The localization of the global agendas: How local action is transforming territories and communities.* United Cities and Local Governments.

Walters, L., & Gauntner, L. P. (2017). Sharing the wealth: Private land value and public benefit. In M. Kamiya, & L.-Y. Zhang (Eds.), *Finance for city leaders handbook: Improving municipal finance to deliver better services* (pp. 192–215). United Nations Human Settlements Programme (UN Habitat).

Weingast, B. R. (2013). *Second generation fiscal federalism: Political aspects of decentralization and economic development.* Elsevier Limited. https://doi.org/10.1016/j.worlddev.2013.01.003

World Bank. (2013a). *Planning, connecting, and financing cities—Now: Priorities for city leaders.* World Bank. https://doi.org/10.1596/978-0-8213-9839-5

World Bank. (2013b). *Harnessing urbanization to end poverty and boost prosperity in Africa: An action agenda for transformation.* Sustainable Development Series. World Bank.

CHAPTER 6

Population Planning and Management

Reniko Gondo

INTRODUCTION

This chapter presents and discusses evidence on trends and status of urban population growth and management strategies, critically assessing the specific theories, research designs, planning approaches and outcomes that have been studied in Africa. Many regions of the world including Africa are experiencing a surge in population growth leading to urbanisation. Whereas Africa's population accounts for 17.2 percent of the global population (Boadi et al., 2005), it is worth noting that the continent has the highest (10 percent) rate of population growth and urbanisation in the world (Dodman et al., 2017).

Population growth and urbanisation in Africa are unique because an upsurge in the phenomena is not accompanied by employment opportunities as has been the case in other continents (Boadi et al., 2005). It is the only continent where more than 10 percent of the urban labour force comprising mostly the youths roam the streets (Beauchemin & Schoumaker, 2005). Statistics reveal that several of the cities in Africa are growing at an average of 4.8 percent per annum (Bower & Buckley, 2020); this increase in urban population although slow is higher than anywhere else in the world. Estimates show that by the beginning of the twentieth century, 95 percent of the African population was living in rural areas (Dodman et al., 2017). Accordingly, Africa was the least urbanised continent in the world (Dodman et al., 2017). In

R. Gondo (✉)
Okavango Research Institute, University of Botswana, Maun, Botswana
e-mail: rgondo@ub.ac.bw

© The Author(s), under exclusive license to Springer Nature Switzerland AG 2022
M. Khayesi and F. N. Wegulo (eds.), *The Palgrave Handbook of Urban Development Planning in Africa*, https://doi.org/10.1007/978-3-031-06089-2_6

the 1960s, about 18.8 percent of the African population were urbanites. This percentage doubled between 1990 and 2010 to over 40 percent (Bower & Buckley, 2020; Linard et al., 2013). It is noteworthy that much of such growth is taking place only in large cities.

Projections indicate that by the end of the year 2050, two thirds of the African population will be living in cities (Linard et al., 2013; Mosha et al., 2013). While it is part of the African Union Agenda 2063 to ensure that Africa is urbanised by the year 2063, poor economic performances, corruption in the distribution and utilisation of resources, civil wars among other factors work against the capability of African governments in general and city authorities, in particular, to provide adequate infrastructure and services to urban residents (Geyer & Geyer, 2015).

In light of rapid population growth, planning and management are the only solutions to achieve sustainable cities. Controlling population growth cities and governments at large, should be able to promote optimum population which can open opportunities for investment and economic growth over a long time (Frank & McNicholl, 1987). Thus, population planning and management are crucial approaches to achieve this. In this regard, urban authorities must influence population dynamics by making them an integral part of national policies and planning processes (Jolly, 1994; Turok & Borel-Saladin, 2014).

Population planning entails the enactment of policies and strategies aimed at limiting the growth of a population, especially in densely populated areas such as cities (Casterline & Agyei-Mensah, 2017). Simply put, population planning is the practice of intentionally controlling the growth of a human population to a manageable level. Urban population planning and management are crucial for local authorities to achieve sustainable development. This is because it helps in formulating medium to long-term objectives that reconcile a collective view (Frank & McNicoll, 1987).

Population planning and management make most of the city budgets by informing infrastructure and services investment and balancing demands for growth with the need to protect the environment. It also distributes economic development within a given area to reach social objectives and creates a framework for collaboration among local governments, the private sector and the public at large (Casterline & Agyei-Mensah, 2017; Robinson, 2015). However, three key factors explain the lack of population planning and management in African cities. First, the absence of up to date information and data about city residents makes proper population planning and management difficult (Frank & McNicholl, 1987; Robinson, 2015). Secondly, lack of finance as a result of weak fiscal systems hinders the process of population planning and management (Robinson, 2015). Thirdly, land registry management is absent (Robinson, 2015). The three are inextricably linked with each strengthening the other. This is because without information, it is impossible to have a land registry system, and without an up to date land recordings, it is impossible to collect taxes needed to finance population planning and management programmes. Lack of information about the city and its residents is detrimental to population planning and management.

Theories and Conceptual Models

There is a myriad of conceptual models to explain population growth (Jolly, 1994) and people's mobility propensity (Bodo, 2019; Byerlee, 1974). In general, two groups of theories on population are discussed in this chapter. These are population growth (Classic and neo-classic) and migration (theory of self-generated urbanisation, modernisation and dependency) theories. While population growth theories focus on the relationship between population increase and its impact on resources consumption, migration theories deal with the movement of people from rural to urban areas.

Based on neo-classic theory, the output of a well-functioning market keeps up with population growth. Thus, population growth is a necessity for the development of innovation to exploit resources. Boserup was also of this opinion that an increase in population is necessary as it helps to boast production through innovations (Jolly, 1994). Thus, demand for resources leads to the development of new technologies. The classic theories argue that high population growth is the panacea to environmental degradation. Based on Malthus, the population grows at geometric progression and food supply at an arithmetic rate. Thus, food output cannot keep pace with population growth. Owing to the reason that population growth will outstrip the food supply, Malthus advocated for fertility control to curb rapid population growth.

On the migration theories, there is consensus that migration is a function of micro-level economic incentives and disincentives existing between rural and urban areas (Byerlee, 1974). It is envisaged that peoples' movement is predicated on the benefits they seek to realise from the movement (Byerlee, 1974). Thus, migration involves a cost–benefit analysis kind of decision-making matrix. Based on Byerlee (1974) and Amrevurayire and Ojeh (2016), migrants are not immediately absorbed into the urban labour market but there is a lag time before securing a job.

The views of Byerlee (1974) as well as Amrevurayire and Ojeh (2016) oversimplify migration processes especially by assuming that the rural–urban movement would eventually cease with a rise in unemployment in urban areas and a decline in labour supply from the rural areas. The theory ignores the high natural increase which is the norm in rural economies throughout Africa (Crentsil & Owusu, 2018; Potts, 2006). The self-generated theory visualises urbanisation as a consequence of surplus yields generation in rural areas that are capable of sustaining the livelihoods of people in the non-agrarian economy (Bodo, 2019). Its weakness lies in the emphasis that rural to urban migration is the cause of urbanisation, yet other factors are contributing to rural–urban migration. The dependency model simply says the capitalist tendency existing in society creates an imbalance in the exchange of goods and services. Consequently, rural areas become peripheral and depend on the urban areas.

Methods

This chapter is based on a review of literature in which 400 publications fulfilling search criteria were downloaded, retrieved and reviewed. The studies were drawn from diverse sources such as journal papers, working papers, reports, book chapters and conference papers. In selecting these studies, only those with the main focus on urban population planning, management and migration in one or more of the African cities were included in the final analysis. Studies that examined population migration and management outside Africa and all those articles which focused on population migration and management of people to cities outside Africa were excluded from the analysis.

In the final analysis, only 32 articles including journal and book chapters relevant to the search criteria were retrieved in hard copies, each was scrutinised, and relevant information was extracted, summarised and presented (Table 6.1). The following information was extracted: name(s) of author(s); date of publication; study focus, sample size, geographic unit, study design, data collection tools, the theoretical or conceptual model used and the main arguments or findings of the study.

Research Designs

Out of the 32 articles reviewed, 20 were published between 2014 and 2021 (Abdel et al., 2020; Abimaje et al., 2014; Adama, 2020; Adedire, 2020; Adeleke & Olaleye, 2020; Ajakaiye et al., 2015; Amrevurayire & Ojeh, 2016; Bashingi et al., 2020; Bodo, 2019; Bower & Buckley, 2020; Casterline & Agyei-Mensah, 2017; Crankshaw & Borel-Saladin, 2019; Dakyaga et al., 2021; Dodman et al., 2017; Geyer & Geyer, 2015; Kherbache, 2020; Nzau & Trillo, 2020; Sahiledengle et al., 2018; Turok & Borel-Saladin, 2014; Yiran et al., 2020). The rest were published between 1974 and 2013 (Akeju, 2007; Beauchemin & Schoumaker, 2005; Boadi et al., 2005; Byerlee, 1974; Frank & McNicoll, 1987; Hope, 2012; Jolly, 1994; Lucas, 1992; Mosha et al., 2013; Potts, 2006; Tuoane et al, 2004).

In terms of geographical unit, 10 studies were conducted in West Africa (Abimaje et al., 2014; Adama, 2020; Adedire, 2020; Adeleke & Olaleye, 2020; Ajakaiye et al., 2015; Akeju, 2007; Amrevurayire & Ojeh, 2016; Bodo, 2019; Crentsil & Owusu, 2018; Yiran et al., 2020). Seven were conducted in East and Central Africa (Dakyagaet al., 2021; Frank & McNicoll, 1998; Hope, 2012; Mosha et al., 2013; Nzau, & Trillo, 2020; Sahiledengle et al., 2018; Yiran et al., 2020). There were 11 studies from southern Africa (Bashingi et al., 2020; Casterline & Agyei-Mensah, 2017; Crankshaw & Borel-Saladin, 2019;

Dodman et al., 2017; Geyer & Geyer, 2015; Jolly, 1994; Lucas, 1992; Potts, 2006; Tuoane et al., 2004; Turok & Borel-Saladin, 2014). Further, 4 were from North Africa (Abdel et al., 2020; Beauchemin & Schoumaker, 2005; Boadi et al., 2005; Byerlee, 1974). In this regard, an almost equal number of studies were drawn from North and Southern Africa with East and West Africa contributing twelve of the studies reviewed in this chapter. In general, issues of urban population planning and migration contained in this chapter represent the issues of concern bordering population and urbanisation in Africa.

Out of the 32 studies, 8 focused on population growth through natural increase (Ajakaiye et al., 2015; Casterline & Agyei-Mensah, 2017; Frank & McNicoll, 1987; Geyer & Geyer, 2015; Jolly, 1994; Lucas, 1992; Mosha et al., 2013; Tuoane et al., 2004). Ten of the studies focused on housing (Abimaje et al, 2014; Adama, 2020; Abdel et al., 2020; Adedire, 2020; Adeleke & Olaleye, 2020; Akeju, 2017; Bower & Buckley, 2020; Geyer & Geyer,2015; Nzau & Trillo, 2020; Potts, 2006). Further, 14 studies focussed on issues bordering traffic congestion (Bashingi et al., 2020); sanitation management (Sahiledengle et al., 2018); and the rest of the 14 were dealing with other urban challenges like electricity among others. Data reveal that housing issues ranging from house renting, construction, managing informal settlements and slums were the most common issues of concern.

In terms of sample size, 15 studies had a sample ranging from 124 households (Adeleke & Olaleye, 2020) to 4258 (Beauchemin & Schoumaker, 2015). In terms of study designs (see Table 6.1), 12 used mixed methods approaches (Abdel et al, 2020; Abimaje et al., 2014; Adama, 2020; Adedire, 2020; Adeleke & Olaleye, 2020; Ajakaiye et al., 2015; Akeju, 2007; Bashingi et al., 2020; Dakyagaet al., 2021; Kherbache, 2020; Nzau & Trillo, 2020; Potts, 2006). Thirteen studies were based on desktop study and reviewed literature (Adeleke & Olaleye, 2020; Boadi et al., 2005; Bodo, 2019; Byerlee, 1974; Crankshaw & Borel-Saladin, 2019; Dodman et al., 2017; Frank & McNicoll, 1987; Geyer & Geyer, 2015; Hope, 2012; Jolly, 1994; Lucas, 1992; Turok & Borel-Saladin, 2014; Yiran et al., 2020). Three of the studies were based on cross-sectional study (Beauchemin & Schoumaker, 2005; Casterline & Agyei-Mensah, 2017; Sahiledengle et al., 2018), two used the case

Table 6.1 Summary of research designs on urban population and planning in African cities

Study design	Number of studies
Desktop	13
Cross-sectional	3
Case study	2
Survey	2
Mixed methods	12

study design (Amrevurayire & Ojeh, 2016; Tuoane et al., 2004) and also two used a survey (Crentsil & Owusu, 2018; Mosha et al., 2013). The most common study designs were, therefore, the mixed methods (Table 6.2).

Results and Discussion

Natural Increase

One of the emerging issues of the African population is the natural increase. The improvements in medical health care coupled with robust disease control together with the desire for many children lead to population growth (Casterline & Agyei-Mensah, 2017). In Africa, natural increase accounted for about 30 percent and migration constitutes 70 percent of urban growth between 1960 and 1990 (Lucas, 1992; Tuoane et al., 2004). The government pronatalist policies adopted in the 1970s triggered a high birth rate.

Besides government policies, the culture which values many children for labour and as a sign of virility among others also triggered high population growth (Casterline & Agyei-Mensah, 2017; Robinson, 2015). Males usually determine the size of a family in most African communities (Casterline & Agyei-Mensah, 2017). Thus, it is noteworthy that male involvement in family planning issues is crucial to curb population growth in cities. However, on the one hand, males show little interest in participating in family planning programmes (Tuoane et al., 2004), and on the other hand, females are constrained by cultural norms to actively participate in family planning programmes (Casterline & Agyei-Mensah, 2017). Given this scenario, the only solution to deal with the natural increase effectively is the enactment of policies by the government to control and manage both natural increase and rural–urban migration. For instance, family planning programmes in the city of Harare, Maseru and Windhoek are a case in point (Lucas, 1992; Robinson, 2015).

Measures to reduce fertility include improving the health of women and children by preventing maternal and infant mortality. There has been increased distribution of family planning facilities to reduce childbearing. From the 1980s onwards, population control measures took centre stage. Family planning measures were integrated into maternal and childcare services in Lusaka, Gaborone, Windhoek and Blantyre (Lucas, 1992; Robinson, 2015).

Rural–Urban Migration

The key issue in population planning and management in African cities is rural–urban migration. Increased rural–urban migration in African countries is due to deteriorating livelihoods in rural areas and the attraction of urban areas. Thus, the rural poor migrate from rural to urban areas in the hope of getting a job (Beauchemin & Schoumaker, 2005). To curb the rural–urban

Table 6.2 Summary of research on population and planning in African cities

Author(s) & publication year	Study focus	Sample size	Geographic unit	Theories	Study design	Data collection techniques	Results
Jolly (1994)	Population growth theories	10 countries	Southern Africa	Neoclassical and Classical population theory	Desktop study	Literature review	• Neo-Classic and classic economic theories • Neo-classic theory argue that population increase leads to substitute of land by labour • Population growth is vital as it leads to new technology being devised • Fertility need not be controlled Proponents include Boserup • Classic economic theory Rapid population growth leads to a decline in natural resources Population growth will lead to a reduction in the food supply • The best approach is to reduce fertility Thomas Robert Malthus is the key proponent of reduction in population growth

(continued)

Table 6.2 (continued)

Author(s) & publication year	Study focus	Sample size	Geographic unit	Theories	Study design	Data collection techniques	Results
Lucas (1992)	Population growth control	8 countries	Southern Africa • South Africa • Lesotho • Malawi • Namibia • Zambia • Zimbabwe	Neoclassical	Desktop study	Literature review	• Pronatalist population policies were dominant • Low cautiousness in population control measures • Children in great demand • Very short birth space • Fertility levels highest in the world From 1980s, the onwards population control concerns form part of national development agendas • National population policies target to reduce fertility from an average of 7.2 children per woman to 6 • Integration of modern family planning into maternal and child health programmes • National governments start promoting population decline programmes
Casterline and Agyei-Mensah (2017)	Fertility control in SSA	8 countries	Southern Africa	Neo-classic Classical theory (Boserup)	Cross-sectional study	• Questionnaires • Document studies	• High demand for children in SSA • High fertility; highest in the world • Children are a source of labour and security • Low contraceptive use • Cultural norms • Low access to family planning facilities

Author(s) & publication year	Study focus	Sample size	Geographic unit	Theories	Study design	Data collection techniques	Results
Frank and McNicoll (1987)	Population growth and control	45 published articles	Kenya	Classical theory (Malthus)	Desktop study	• Literature review -Databases search	• High fertility rate in Kenya • 8 children per woman (1950–1960) • Lack of access to family planning methods • Use of traditional family planning methods • Lack of knowledge of effective family planning modern methods • Low efficacy of customary methods of family planning • Government Policy • Reduction of fertility through family planning programmes • Population reduction policies are ineffective due to cultural norms which prefer traditional to modern methods of reducing fertility • Population doubling period delayed to 20 years

(continued)

Table 6.2 (continued)

Author(s) & publication year	Study focus	Sample size	Geographic unit	Theories	Study design	Data collection techniques	Results
Boadi et al. (2005)	Urbanisation in Africa	4 Countries	Northern Africa	Migration theories	Desktop study	Databases search	**Urban growth trends** • Africa was the least urbanised continent in the 1960s with an urban population of only 18.8 percent • Majority of Africa's population until the 1960s have been living in rural areas • An urban growth rate of 4.87 percent being faster than in any other continent in the world • Much of the growth in population is taking place in large cities • Sub-Saharan Africa has the highest rate of urbanisation **Causes of Growth** • Natural increase • Decline in death rates • Cultural beliefs • Rural–urban migration • Economic Crisis **Strategies to curb Urban growth**
Tuoane et al. (2004)	Provision of family planning services	500 Households	Maseru		Case study	Questionnaire Interview FGD	• Population control goal is to achieve replacement-level fertility in Maseru • Population control yield positive results on infrastructure and service provision

Author(s) & publication year	Study focus	Sample size	Geographic unit	Theories	Study design	Data collection techniques	Results
Amrevurayire and Ojeh (2016)	Rural–urban migration control measures	216 Households	Ughievwen (Nigeria)	Theory of Urban Bias	Case study	Questionnaires	• Migration to urban centres decreases with age • Levels of infrastructure development of a region determine the magnitude of migration • Excessive drain of youth from the rural populace • Establishment of higher educational centres • Industrialization of the area • Decentralisation of government parastatals to the area • Youth and women empowerment
Beauchemin and Schoumaker (2005)	Rural–urban migration control measures	4258 Households	Ouagadougou and Bobo Dioulasso	Theory of Urban Bias	**Cross-Sectional Study**	Questionnaire FGD Interview	• Demilitarisation of the area • Rapid increase in the population of the two cities • Increase in unemployment • Control of rural–urban migration • Provision of economic opportunities in rural and small towns • Rural development (including road upgrading, water supply, improvement of rural health centres, furnishing rural schools)

(continued)

Table 6.2 (continued)

Author(s) & publication year	Study focus	Sample size	Geographic unit	Theories	Study design	Data collection techniques	Results
Mosha et al. (2013)	Family planning decision	100 households	Mwanza		Survey	FGD Interview	• Males determine the number of children at the household level • Males' involvement in family planning is crucial • Males show little interest in participating in family planning programmes • Cultural norms prevent women from being active in family planning issues
Adama (2020)	Upgrading of low-quality housing	450 Households	Lagos		Mixed methods	Focus group Discussions Interview	• A conflict of interests exists between city planners and poor people in the Makoko area • The eviction of slum dwellers in the Makoko area was halted due to protests by the residents
Abdel et al. (2020)	Establishment of housing affordability Finding ways to ease accommodation problems in light of urbanisation	350 households	Cairo	Sustainable Green Transportation	Mixed methods	Interview Questionnaires	• 56 percent of the population in the city could not afford to build their own house • 68 percent of the civil servants can't afford to build their own home • Urbanisation has created an accommodation crisis

Author(s) & publication year	Study focus	Sample size	Geographic unit	Theories	Study design	Data collection techniques	Results
Abimaje et al. (2014)	Housing affordability	20 Households	Ida		Mixed methods	Questionnaires	The majority of the people cannot afford to build their accommodation due to low salaries
Adedire (2020)	Causes and effects of urbanisation on housing	386 Households	Lagos		Mixed methods	Interview Questionnaire Survey	• Residential land use increases from 622.23 hectares in 1980 to 17,972.62 hectares in 2002 • There is a development of new towns outside Lagos due to population growth
Adeleke and Olaleye (2020)	Housing Affordability capability of low-income civil servants in Lagos State, Nigeria	124 Households	Lagos	Rule of thumb ratio paradigm	Mixed methods	Mixed methods	• 50 percent of the respondents were male and female • 71.5 percent were married, 22.8 percent were single • The majority of the respondents (57.7 percent) were young adults. The average monthly income was N30,002 • Average monthly rents of N2950
Ajakaiye et al. (2015)	The paradox of high economic growth alongside rising poverty	450 Household	Lagos	Economic growth sustainability model	Mixed method	Questionnaire survey	Economic growth in most west African countries is sustained by resources reallocation rather than productivity

(continued)

Table 6.2 (continued)

Author(s) & publication year	Study focus	Sample size	Geographic unit	Theories	Study design	Data collection techniques	Results
Akeju (2007)	Housing provision	350 households	Abuja	Theory of Self-Generated	Mixed method	Quantitative and Secondary data	• Lack of primary infrastructure such as roads, water, electricity hinders housing provision • Restriction on the importation of cement hinder housing construction
Bashingi et al. (2020)	Traffic congestion	200 households	Gaborone		Mixed methods	questionnaire survey	High car ownership results in an increase in traffic
Bodo (2019)	Theories of urbanisation in African cities	98 Sample documents articles inclusive of Policy documents, Development strategy, journal articles and policy briefs	Akwa Ibo	Theory of Self-Generated Urbanisation modernisation Theory Dependency/World-System Theory Theory of Urban Bias	Desktop study	Literature Review	Poor government policies that encourage the concentration of basic social amenities and employment opportunities in only the cities
Bower et al. (2020)	Housing policy and development strategies in Rwanda	112 sample documents inclusive of Policy documents, Development strategy, journal articles and policy briefs	Kigali	Urban sustainability	Document studies	Literature review	Low-income city dwellers cannot afford housing provision
Byerlee (1974)	Impact of rural–urban migration	46 Documents reviewed comprising Policy documents and journal articles	Algiers	Theory of Urban Bias	Desktop study	Literature review	• Rural to urban migration reduce the imbalance between rural and urban income • Migration affects social welfare by changing the pattern of income distribution

Author(s) & publication year	Study focus	Sample size	Geographic unit	Theories	Study design	Data collection techniques	Results
Dakyaga et al. (2021)	Water Provision	35 household heads 3 key informants	Dar es Salaam	Governance for sustainability	Mixed methods	Face to face interview Questionnaire	• Many actors exist in the water supply within informal urban water space
Dodman et al. (2017)	Impact of urbanisation	102 documents comprising Journal articles, Conference papers and Policy documents	Southern Africa	Theory of Urban Bias	Desktop study		• African cities are expanding rapidly • Migrants are connected to their rural hinterlands • infrastructure is inadequate in small industrial sectors • A large informal sector
Hope (2012)	Influences of urbanisation	68 Articles Journal articles	Kenya	Smart city concept	Desktop study	Literature review	• Drivers of urbanisation in Kenya are natural population increase and rural–urban migration
Kherbache (2020)	Water demand management	123 Households	Algiers	Theory of Urban Bias	Mixed methods	Questionnaire survey	• Water policy is characterised by a lack of institutional coordination and many multi-level governance gaps
Nzau and Trillo (2020)	Accommodation improvement Strategies	156 Households	Nairobi	Theory of Urban Bias	Mixed methods	Questionnaire Survey	• Housing backlog can be reduced if government allows market forces to take centre stage

(continued)

Table 6.2 (continued)

Author(s) & publication year	Study focus	Sample size	Geographic unit	Theories	Study design	Data collection techniques	Results
Potts (2006)	Housing challenges	450 Households	Harare	Theory of Urban Bias	Mixed methods	Questionnaires Observation Interviews	• About 650,000–700,000 people lost the basis of their livelihoods
Sahiledengle et al. (2018)	Sanitation practices	392 Households	Addis Ababa,	Sustainable cities	cross-sectional study design	Questionnaire Interview	• The sanitation practice of slum dwellers was very low and unhygienic
Turok and Borel-Saladin (2014)	Urbanisation and living condition	54 Articles Comprising Journal, Policy documents Grey literature	South Africa	sustainable urbanisation	Desktop study	Literature review	• Population trends coincide with employment growth patterns over the last decade, producing a better match than before • Provision of urban infrastructure kept pace with population growth in the cities • The provision of affordable housing has not kept pace with household growth, so more people than ever are living in shacks

Author(s) & publication year	Study focus	Sample size	Geographic unit	Theories	Study design	Data collection techniques	Results
Yiran et al. (2020)	The direction of urban sprawl in SSA	85 Articles Comprising Journal, Policy documents Grey literature	Nigeria Kenya South Africa & Ghana	Theory of Urban Bias	Desktop study	Literature Review	• Neo-liberalisation is the major cause of urbanisation • Non-enforcement of planning regulations • Inadequate planning schemes and non-enforcement of regulations leads to unsustainable residential development Water and air pollution Vegetation destruction and consumption of green/open spaces
Crentsil and Owusu (2018)	Decongestion of city space	650 Households	Accra	Decongestion policy	Survey	Questionnaire Interviews	• There is an unbalanced and skewed distribution of the urban population in favour of large cities • A high concentration of population in Accra due to migrants' belief that urban centres offer better economic opportunities • High concentration of population in Accra resulted in the conversion of rural settlements into the urban agglomeration
Geyer & Geyer (2015)	Population and urbanisation patterns	108 documents Comprising Journal articles, Conference papers and Policy documents	South Africa	Theory of Urban Bias	Desktop study	Literature review	• migration patterns in South Africa are far more complex • The population is declining in large and increasing in small cities • Migration to small and large cities is increasing

(continued)

Table 6.2 (continued)

Author(s) & publication year	Study focus	Sample size	Geographic unit	Theories	Study design	Data collection techniques	Results
Crankshaw and Borel-Saladin (2019)	Drivers of urbanisation	65 Articles Comprising Journal, Policy documents Grey literature	Lusaka	Theory of Urban Bias	Desktop research	Literature review	• Urbanisation in Zambia is rapid in major cities • Migration is triggered by economic challenges • Change in urban population is attributed to natural increase that rural–urban migration • Between 1990 and 2000 rate of natural increase was 2.0 • Between 2000 and 2010 natural increases was 2.1

migration into Ouagadougou and Bobo Dioulasso in Burkina Faso, Beauchemin and Schoumaker (2005) show that there were provisions of economic opportunities in both rural and small towns.

Massive rural development programmes that include road upgrading, water supply, improvement of rural health centres and rural schools were the major population management strategies to control urbanisation in Burkina Faso. Migration is selective and rural–urban migration is not an exception. There is an excessive drain of youth from the rural populace; and it has been shown that migration to urban centres decreases with age. Measures taken to control population movement from rural to urban centres include the establishment of higher educational centres, decentralisation of government parastatals to the rural area as well as youth and women empowerment.

Housing and Policies

Rural–urban migration, driven by the desire to improve lives, is an African problem that is there to stay. Projections are that the phenomenon is likely to increase (Dodman et al., 2017). The main issue of concern in African cities is housing. The introduction of the World Bank (WB) and International Monetary Fund (IMF) backed Economic Structural Adjustment Programmes (ESAP) in the early 1990s resulted in services becoming expensive and housing was not an exception among African cities. For instance, there are housing challenges in Kigali (Bower & Buckley, 2020), Harare (Potts, 2006), Lagos (Ajakaiye et al., 2015; Akeju, 2007; Bodo, 2019), Akwa, Ibo (Bodo, 2019), Algiers (Kherbache, 2020), and Nairobi (Nzau & Trillo, 2020) among others. Informal settlements and slums are also a problem in Dar es Salem (Dakyaga et al., 2021).

There are several policies to control or deal with the issue of accommodation challenges. While some implemented policies ensure that sufficient and affordable accommodation is provided in the city, others were adopted to force people to leave urban to rural areas. For instance, in Kigali, the city authority adopted a housing construction policy to accommodate the poor residents (Bower & Buckley, 2020). It is noteworthy that Kigali has the least informal settlements and is the only African city with the least affordable formal housing in Africa (Bower & Buckley, 2020).

In Harare, the Harare municipality with the grace of the central government adopted a policy dubbed *Operation Murambatsvina* that was meant to purportedly restore order in the city (Potts, 2006), even though the reasons were more political. Although too draconian, *Operation Murambatsvina* forcibly destroyed unregistered structures within the central business district, and unplanned and informal settlements were not spared. All houses constructed that were found to have contravened council by-laws were demolished. The operation is believed to have destroyed between 650,000 to 700,000 illegal structures in Harare alone. Several people lost their homes in the process. A similar scenario took place in the 1980s in Dar es Salem where informal settlements were also destroyed.

Like in Harare, Dar es Salem informal settlements were a feature of the colonial era which intensified with the gaining of political independence. While in both cases the colonial masters could afford to control the urban population by restricting people to enter and live in the city, the independent governments have either no resources or lack the political will to do so. With the gaining of independence, informal settlements in African cities surged seventeen times (Hope, 2012). It is surprising to note that while the shanty towns were increasing, Town Planning Departments noted the increase in such illegal structures and took no action. Lagos and Accra city authorities also adopted a housing demolition policy dubbed 'decongestion' (Crentsil & Owusu, 2018). The policy was implemented to reduce the population living in urban areas. Bulldozers demolished all structures within areas perceived undesirable. While the policy succeeded in clearing unwanted housing, its weakness lies in the fact that it failed to put in place a solution to the informal settlements. Clearing housing units belonging to people with low incomes in the name of cleaning the town is tantamount to saying that people with low incomes have no rights at all.

Potable Water Scarcity

A similar issue of concern in African cities is scarcity of potable water. These challenges require innovative ideas and should not be left to city administrators to deal with them alone. For instance, in Algiers, the public programme funding policy was backed by the central government in collaboration with the local government who managed to permanently deal with water scarcity.

Despite water scarcity challenges in cities like Tunis, Casablanca and Cairo, water tariffs are very low in this part of Africa. Kherbache (2020) believes this is just a political gimmick to ensure minimal protests against the government. Nevertheless, any ploy that benefits the residents and leaves them satisfied with service delivery is a welcome development. The other related challenge of North African cities includes water leakages due to ageing pipes in cities like Tunis, Casablanca and Cairo. While Cairo relies on River Nile for water supply, pollution is rampant and water treatment is very expensive for the city (Boadi et al., 2005).

Traffic Congestion

Traffic congestion together with high levels of energy consumption in the transport sector is also a concern in the reviewed articles. An instance of these problems was reported in Gaborone (Bashingi et al., 2020), Dar es Salaam (Dodman et al., 2017), Harare (Potts, 2006), and Nairobi (Hope, 2012; Nzau & Trillo, 2020). To alleviate such problems, several policies in the transport industries were adopted.

Whereas banning cars older than 20 years in the city of Casablanca and Tunis (Hope, 2012) was adopted, encouragement of the use of public transport to ease congestions is also a policy in the transport industry. For instance, the 30-km train in Casablanca has to a greater extent reduced traffic congestion in the city (Abdel et al., 2020). The use of public rather than private transport has the propensity for reducing energy consumption as well as reducing air pollution.

Waste Generation and Management

Waste generation and management are other issues of concern in African cities. In light of this challenge, a waste recycling and reuse policy was implemented in Cairo. It is noteworthy that a public–private partnership policy in Alexandria significantly reduced wastes in the city. In Tunis, the landfill policy resulted in more landfills built to improve waste management. Besides reducing wastes in the city, a landfill created employment among the youths who engage in recycling and energy generation as part of the zero-waste policy in Tunis (Kherbache, 2020).

Summary of Key Findings

The key findings in this chapter reveal that in the 1960s and 1970s, African governments adopted pronatalist population policies. Coupled with a culture that prefers a high birth rate, population growth in Africa increased tremendously. This is because cultural values mostly demand many children. Birth control uptake was very low and, in some instances, not available at all. In the late 1970s, the fertility averaging was on average 7.2 children per woman in most countries. Only traditional family planning methods were mostly used, and these were not robust enough to curb high fertility. Males dominated more in decisions on the number and size of a family. Males showed low interest in discussing family planning issues.

Literature for the 1990s shows a trend towards a desire for a low population. This is because during that period, national governments became conscious of the negative impact of high population growth. High rural–urban migration, accommodation shortage and high unemployment became a daily challenge for cities like Dar es salaam, Harare, Cairo and Maseru among others. With high rural–urban migration and urban areas failing to absorb the migrants, development of shanty settlements became a daily problem. The cities' reaction to the development of slums ranged from slum clearance to slum upgrading, which they did by providing services and infrastructure.

With these challenges, city planners as well as the national government became conscious of the need to control population growth by adopting anti-natalist population policies. Thus, family planning and population control measures took centre stage. Integration of traditional and modern child spacing into maternal and child health programmes was promoted by the governments. While the government programmes of family planning and population growth to a greater extent managed to reduce fertility to lower levels, the high birth rate cultural inertia continues to persist. As such, fertility in Africa continues to be the highest in the world.

Conclusion

The chapter reviewed the literature on urban growth population planning and management issues in selected African cities. Literature from North, West, East and southern Africa were reviewed. Available information shows that Africa's urban population accounts for 17.2 percent of the global urban population, and it has the highest (10 percent) rate of growth in urbanisation. The uniqueness of African urbanisation lies in the upsurge in the phenomenon but within a weak supportive environment. Moreover, rapid urban population growth has not been accompanied by growth in employment opportunities as the case was/is in other continents. Literature drawn from diverse sources and different parts of the continent brings to light several challenges that arise from this scenario; exacerbation of informal settlements, inadequate infrastructure and traffic congestion among others. These challenges call for decisive and appropriate responses and actions by national governments and local authorities. Focusing on strategies and actions that address the major driver (s) of the challenges facing urban population expansion issues amidst weak socio-economic environments and structures in African cities will go a long way in alleviating these problems now, and in the future.

References

Abdel, W., Ahmed, M. M., & Abd El Monem, N. (2020). Sustainable and green transportation for better quality of life case study greater Cairo-Egypt. *HBRC Journal, 16*(1), 17–37.

Abimaje, J., Akingbohungbe, D. O., & Baba, A. N. (2014). Housing affordability in Nigerian towns: A case of Idah, Nigeria. *International Journal of Civil Engineering, Construction and Estate Management, 1*(2), 31–38.

Adama, O. (2020). Slum upgrading in the era of world-class city construction: The case of Lagos, Nigeria. *International Journal of Urban Sustainable Development, 12*(2), 219–235.

Adedire, F. M. (2020). Disparity in peri-urbanisation process in Lagos, Nigeria. In *Landscape architecture-processes and practices towards sustainable development*. IntechOpen.

Adeleke, F. G., & Olaleye, A. (2020). Housing affordability among low income civil servants in Lagos State, Nigeria. *African Journal for the Psychological Studies of Social Issues, 23*(1), 1–13.

Ajakaiye, O., Jerome, A. T., Nabena, D., & Alaba, O. A. (2015). *Understanding the relationship between growth and employment in Nigeria* (No. 2015/124) (WIDER Working Paper).

Akeju, A. A. (2007). Challenges to providing affordable housing in Nigeria. In *Proceedings of 2nd Emerging Urban Africa International Conference on Housing Finance in Nigeria* (pp. 17–19).

Amrevurayire, E. O., & Ojeh, V. N. (2016). Consequences of rural-urban migration on the source region of Ughievwen clan Delta State Nigeria. *European Journal of Geography, 7*(3), 42–57.

Bashingi, N., Mostafa, M., & Das, D. K. (2020). The state of congestion in the developing world; The case of Gaborone, Botswana. *Transportation Research Procedia, 45*, 434–442.

Beauchemin, C., & Schoumaker, B. (2005). Migration to cities in Burkina Faso: Does the level of development in sending areas matter? *World Development, 33*(7), 1129–1152.

Boadi, K., Kuitunen, M., Raheem, K., & Hanninen, K. (2005). Urbanization without development: Environmental and health implications in African cities. *Environment, Development and Sustainability, 7*(4), 465–500.

Bodo, T. (2019). Rapid urbanisation: Theories, causes, consequences and coping strategies. *Annals of Geographical Studies, 2*(3), 32–45.

Bower, J., & Buckley, R. (2020). *Housing policies in Rwanda: Riding the urbanisation whirlwind* (C-38433-RWA-1).

Byerlee, D. (1974). Rural-urban migration in Africa: Theory, policy and research implications. *International Migration Review, 8*(4), 543–566.

Casterline, J. B., & Agyei-Mensah, S. (2017). Fertility desires and the course of fertility decline in sub-Saharan Africa. *Population and Development Review, 43*, 84–111.

Crankshaw, O., & Borel-Saladin, J. (2019). Causes of urbanisation and counter-urbanisation in Zambia: Natural population increase or migration. *Urban Studies, 56*(10), 2005–2020.

Crentsil, A. O., & Owusu, G. (2018). Accra's decongestion policy: Another face of urban clearance or bulldozing approach? In *African Cities and the Development Conundrum* (pp. 213–228). Brill Nijhoff.

Dakyaga, F., Ahmed, A., & Sillim, M. L. (2021, March). Governing ourselves for sustainability: Everyday ingenuities in the governance of water infrastructure in the informal settlements of Dar es Salaam. In *Urban forum* (Vol. 32, No. 1, pp. 111–129). Springer Netherlands.

Dodman, D., Leck, H., Rusca, M., & Colenbrander, S. (2017). African urbanisation and urbanism: Implications for risk accumulation and reduction. *International Journal of Disaster Risk Reduction, 26*, 7–15.

Frank, O., & McNicoll, G. (1987). An interpretation of fertility and population policy in Kenya. *Population and Development Review*, 209–243.

Geyer, H. S. Jr., & Geyer, H. S. Sr. (2015). Disaggregated population migration trends in South Africa between 1996 and 2011: A differential urbanisation approach. *Urban Forum, 26*(1), 1–13. Springer Netherlands.

Hope, K. R., Sr. (2012). Urbanisation in Kenya. *African Journal of Economic and Sustainable Development, 1*(1), 4–26.

Jolly, C. L. (1994). Four theories of population change and the environment. *Population and Environment, 16*(1), 61–90.

Kherbache, N. (2020, March). Water policy in Algeria: Limits of supply model and perspectives of water demand management (WDM). *Desalination and Water Treatment, 180*, 141–155.

Linard, C., Tatem, A. J., & Gilbert, M. (2013). Modelling spatial patterns of urban growth in Africa. *Applied Geography, 44*, 23–32. https://doi.org/10.1016/j.apgeog.2013.07.009

Lucas, D. (1992). Fertility and family planning in Southern and Central Africa. *Studies in Family Planning, 23*(3), 145–158.

Mosha, I., Ruben, R., & Kakoko, D. (2013). Family planning decisions, perceptions and gender dynamics among couples in Mwanza, Tanzania: A qualitative study. *BMC Public Health, 13*(1), 1–13.

Nzau, B., & Trillo, C. (2020). Affordable housing provision in informal settlements through land value capture and inclusionary housing. *Sustainability, 12*(15), 5975.

Potts, D. (2006). 'Restoring order'? Operation Murambatsvina and the urban crisis in Zimbabwe. *Journal of Southern African Studies, 32*(2), 273–291.

Robinson, R. S. (2015). Population policy in sub-Saharan Africa: A case of both normative and coercive ties to the world polity. *Population Research and Policy Review, 34*(2), 201–221.

Sahiledengle, B., Alemseged, F., & Belachew, T. (2018). Sanitation practice and associated factors among slum dwellers residing in urban slums of Addis Ababa, Ethiopia: A community based cross-sectional study. *Journal of Public Health and Epidemiology, 10*(10), 370–379.

Tuoane, M., Madise, N. J., & Diamond, I. (2004). Provision of family planning services in Lesotho. *International Family Planning Perspectives*, 77–86.

Turok, I., & Borel-Saladin, J. (2014). Is urbanisation in South Africa on a sustainable trajectory? *Development Southern Africa, 31*(5), 675–691.

Yiran, G. A. B., Ablo, A. D., Asem, F. E., & Owusu, G. (2020). Urban sprawl in sub-Saharan Africa: A review of the literature in selected countries. *Ghana Journal of Geography, 12*(1), 1–28.

CHAPTER 7

Managing Poverty

Humphreys W. Obulinji

INTRODUCTION

Urban poverty is a critical element of urban lives in African cities and towns that needs to be addressed. Over 50 percent of urban dwellers in sub-Saharan Africa live in slums and only 40 percent of the urban population has access to improved sanitation facilities, a rate that has not changed since 1990 (Barofsky et al., 2016). The breadth and depth of the problem is growing geometrically and is exemplified in a number of ways, as depicted by the kind of life majority of the urban people live.

In 2018, more than 55 percent of the global population lived in urban areas, and the United Nations estimates that this will rise to 68 percent by 2050. While over a half of the population in sub-Saharan Africa remain rural, rapid urbanization and population growth in this region means that they will account for 90 percent of urban growth over the next 30 years. Between now and 2050, the sub-Saharan Africa region is expected to transition from having 'rural majority' populations to 'urban majority'. Moreover, the number of sub-Saharan Africa countries that have more urban than rural residents will double (United Nations Population Division, 2018). Urban poverty and its management, therefore, remains an important subject of concern that both national and urban planning needs to address.

H. W. Obulinji (✉)
Department of Geography, Egerton University, Nakuru, Kenya
e-mail: humphreys.obulinji@egerton.ac.ke

This chapter presents the dynamics of poverty in African cities based on a review of empirical studies, highlighting insights into the scope of poverty; measurement and analytical methods; factors contributing to poor urban households' livelihoods; and approaches to managing urban poverty.

METHODS

This chapter is based on a thematic analysis of publications from 1980 to date. This period was considered critical so as to explain neo-Fabian and neo-Liberal approaches to city development in Africa; that is, a change from the provision of most basic services to the urban residents by national governments in the 1980s to privatization of the same in the early 1990s to date (Shah, 2013; World Bank, 2002). Further, this period marked a change in the stable and good performance of the manufacturing sector that is mostly associated with urban centres and employing majority of the urban labour force, to the deteriorating growth that was evidenced in the 1990s to date. This was as a result of liberalization policy, coupled with reduced external support to developing countries among other factors. Both scenarios had a significant impact on urban economies that degenerated in mass unemployment levels in the manufacturing sector (Shah, 2013; World Bank, 2002). Table 7.1 summarizes the inclusion and exclusion criteria for studies.

Journal papers, published books, book chapters and policy briefs on urban poverty in Africa were accessed from electronic databases such as Research4life, Google scholar and Elsevier Additionally, the study also reviewed literature from organizational databases such as Microsoft Access, My SQL and Microsoft SQL Server. Keywords used in the search for literature were the nature of urban poverty; characteristics of urban poverty; trends in urban poverty; causes of urban poverty; models of urban poverty; measurement and analysis of urban poverty; vulnerability and sustainability of urban households' livelihoods; and policies and strategies in addressing urban poverty. This process yielded a total of 16 relevant publications for final review out of a total of 210 articles.

Theoretical Framework

Selection of studies to be reviewed in this chapter was informed by the Household Livelihoods Framework (Fig. 7.1). The framework portrays dynamic and complex relationships in measurement, analysis, planning and management of urban poverty (DFID, 2000). At the centre of the framework are socio-economic and physical assets on which rural and urban households or individuals draw to build their livelihoods (Carney, 1998, 1999). However, access to, and use of these assets are influenced by policies, institutions, processes, available basic infrastructure and the households' internal

Table 7.1 Criteria for inclusion and exclusion of studies

Criteria	Excluded	Included	Justification
Date of Publication	Articles published prior to 1980	Articles published between 1980 and December 2020	It is assumed that most urban centres were still small in size and population, with low urban unemployment levels. Most basic services were provided by the government and were affordable or subsidized before the liberalization of the same took place in the early 1990s
Language of Publication	Articles not published in English	Articles published in English	Articles readable and understandable by the author
Main Theme of Publication	Articles on poverty but not focusing on urban poverty in Africa	Articles that focused on urban poverty in Africa	The chapter looks at urban poverty in Africa
Availability of Article	Articles not subscribed to, by Egerton University within the review period (July 2020–March 2021)	Articles subscribed to, by Egerton University within the review period (July 2020–March 2021)	Subscription costs for accessing the required information could not enable the Author to access a wider range of data bases
Study Area	Articles that did not focus on urban poverty in Africa	Articles that focused on urban poverty in Africa with reference to the objectives of the chapter	Publications have to focus on Africa
Type of Article	None	Grey literature and peer-reviewed articles	Urban Poverty is a broad and dynamic area of study

and external vulnerability contexts. A synergy of these factors affects households' livelihood strategies and opportunities adopted. According to Rakodi (1999), individual households may adopt same or different strategies that vary over space and time.

Analysing vulnerability also involves looking at households' resilience by being able to mobilize assets to exploit opportunities and recover from shocks (Moser, 1998). According to Scoones (1998), an urban livelihood is sustainable when it can cope with, and recover from stresses and shocks, maintain or enhance its capabilities and assets, while not undermining the natural resource

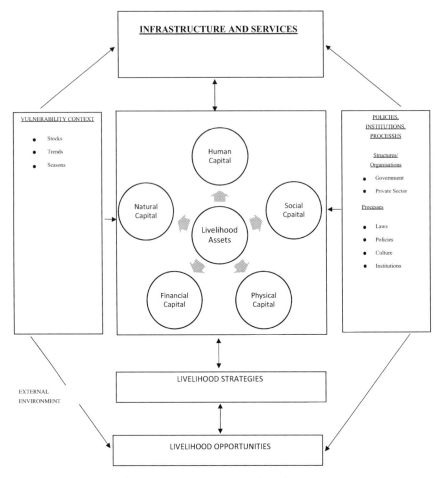

Fig. 7.1 Livelihoods framework (*Source* DFID, 2000)

base. Carney (1998) notes that households' livelihoods sustainability is critical and core to the livelihood framework. Irrespective of the livelihood options adopted at all levels, ecological sustainability is critical in ensuring the availability of physical capital in the long run. Further, de Haan et al. (2000) note that the concept of social sustainability is achieved when social exclusion is minimized and social equity maximized; for instance, through social change or redistribution of wealth and power that is aimed at achieving lasting poverty reduction in urban areas. Furthermore, stability and continued existence of policies, institutions and processes are critical in ensuring poverty reduction. Finally, proponents of the livelihood framework argue that in addressing poverty, it is appropriate to start with an analysis of strengths (assets) as opposed to the needs of households (DFID, 2000).

RESULTS AND DISCUSSION

Results of the synthesis of literature are presented in Table 7.2 and discussed in this section.

Thematic data on poverty is critical for an in-depth understanding of the problem and also appropriate for policy intervention measures. Apart from the use of surveys and review of documents, World Bank (2004), Awinia-Mushi (2013), Lubaale (2014) and Abu-Salia et al. (2015) recommend the use of mixed-method that involves a questionnaire survey of households and community; key informants; case study approach; focus groups discussions; use of both qualitative and quantitative research method; structured and unstructured qualitative in-depth interviews and discussions; working interviews as well as participant and non-participant observation. The mixed-method approach ensured complementarity between the different methods used in data collection. This improved the quality, clarity and accuracy of data collected. It also brought out the variations in perception and needs of the poor as regards addressing their plight.

In addition, Lubaale (2014) used extensive document reviews and extensive review of urban planning and political science literature, and also noted that triangulation can be used to confirm data from different sources, thus improving the quality of data collected. Awinia-Mushi (2013) notes that the case study method requires the researcher's prior knowledge of the poverty situation and may not be used for generalization purposes but can serve to give insights into poverty. The case study method can also provide room for a detailed analysis of poverty in a given spatial area.

The qualitative approach is good in understanding contextual poverty, which is critical in effective and specific poverty redressal while the quantitative approach generates poverty data that can be useful in evaluation, assessment, comparison and monitoring. Structured and unstructured qualitative in-depth discussion helps a researcher to gather data on specific variables as well as collect additional data not set out in the initial conceptualization of the study. Triangulation serves to confirm the accuracy of data collected by comparing similar data but from different though related sources thus improving the accuracy of data collected.

Baker and Nina (2004) observe that urban poverty is a complex phenomenon that varies in inter and intra-city perception, including variables selected for analysis. Apart from the study by the World Bank (2004) in Conakry City, most studies are aggregated and focus on a few areas of the city, which should not be the case. There is a need, as suggested by the World Bank (2004), to disaggregate urban poverty and study specific aspects of it in the overall urban context if research findings are to be accurate and relevant to policy intervention and planning. Disaggregation allows several correlations to be made in achieving specific study objectives, for instance, the linkage between crime and inequality. due to the varied dynamics of urban poverty, large samples will tend to be representative of the population.

Table 7.2 Summary of review of empirical research studies on urban poverty in Africa

Author(s)	Study focus	Geographical unit	Methods	Theory	Results
Awinia-Mushi (2013)	Association between human capability development, housing, health conditions, and poverty levels	Dar es Salaam, Tanzania	A case study. Secondary documentary survey method, qualitative structured questionnaire method, unstructured qualitative in-depth discussions and non-participant observation	Human capability approach	1. A positive correlation between low human capability development levels and poverty in housing and health conditions exist 2. Lack of human capability elements such as formal education, vocational skills and lack of participation in urban informal sector activities, credit services and productive assets reduces effectiveness of households to minimize housing and health problems 3. Poor housing conditions such as overcrowding, unfinished houses and poor sanitation have adverse effects on health conditions among households 4. There is a vicious cycle between low levels of income and human capability development, holding poor households under a capability deprivation trap

Author(s)	Study focus	Geographical unit	Methods	Theory	Results
Awumbila (2014)	Linkages between urbanization, rural–urban migration and poverty in African Cities	20 African Cities (Ouagadougou, Niamey, Mogadishu, Yamoussoukro, Dar es Salaam, Lusaka, Kampala, Lilongwe, Nairobi, Antananarivo, Abuja, Huambo, Kigali, Onitsha, Port Harcourt, Luanda, Mombasa, Conakry, Enugu and Kananga)	Review of Documents	Policy	1. Rural–urban migration will continue to play a significant role in urbanization in Africa, where the rate is twice that of the global average 2. Development challenges of the twenty-first century will mainly be met in urban areas, where 95 percent of the world's population will be residing by 2050 3. Given significant shortfalls in urban institutional capacities, poverty is likely to become even more widespread. Hence, managing urban growth will require the establishment of realistic and sustainable national urban development policies, enhanced urban management capacities and significant improvements in access to urban livelihood opportunities, rather than implementing policies aimed at discouraging rural–urban migration. Fortunately, Sustainable Development Goal no. 11 commits to 'make cities and human settlements inclusive, safe, resilient and sustainable by 2030'. This provides an opportunity to change the negative perception of 'cities as vessels of problems' to cities as 'accelerators and facilitators of sustainable urbanization and development'

(continued)

Table 7.2 (continued)

Author(s)	Study focus	Geographical unit	Methods	Theory	Results
Abu-Salia et al. (2015)	Conditions under which urban slum dwellers can maximize the prospects and potentials of their livelihood systems to minimize the challenges of poverty	The Wa Municipality, Ghana	Empirical in nature and use of mixed methods (household questionnaire survey, in-depth interviews, participant observation and working interviews) that formed a basis for participatory method	Policy reform	1. Existence of diversity in social and economic capital, which are resources and sources of resilience among slum dwellers should not be looked at as a problem but used to address poverty instead of relying on state urban interventions 2. With liberalization of markets, welfare issues are a matter of individual responsibility since the state is unable to provide services to the poor due to reducing revenue resources 3. Neither the market nor communities have solutions to the diverse urban problem outside state reformed instruments of planning, where a mismatch exists with the actual needs of the poor. Hence, the need to rethink the planning approach and make it relevant through participatory urban planning

Author(s)	Study focus	Geographical unit	Methods	Theory	Results
Baker and Nina (2004)	Urban Poverty in selected cities in developing countries (eight from Africa), focusing on specifics of methodology (approaches) and data rather than specific outcomes and analysis	Cities in selected Developing Countries, including Abuja, Accra, Johannesburg, Harare, Lagos, Luanda, Lusaka and Maseru in Africa	Household and community survey, Questionnaire (Qualitative and Quantitative data), GIS, use of secondary data, Case studies and Participatory Assessment	Policy Reform	1. Urban poverty is a complex phenomenon that varies in inter and intra-city perception, including variables selected for analysis 2. There is a need to disaggregate urban poverty and study specific aspects of it if research findings are to be accurate and relevant to policy intervention and planning 3. Use of both qualitative and quantitative primary and secondary data, coupled with correlated analysis is critical in the study of urban poverty 4. Poverty studies must be done in partnership with local stakeholders to ensure capacity building and making data collected public for use and monitoring changes in poverty indices 5. Challenges in the study of urban poverty are evident in delayed publication of the findings, timing of surveys, dynamism in city socio-economic environment, gaps in households' data collection, spatial coverage of city varied poverty dynamics, and omission in coverage of some sub-groups of the populations 6. Response levels are comparatively low because most household members are either unavailable or busy
Chirisa and Matamanda (2016)	To propose an agenda and framework for the formulation of policies and strategic plans aimed at provision of adequate and sustainable housing in urban areas beyond 2015	Africa	Population-A few selected Countries Sampling-None Study Design-Documentary Review Data Collection-Secondary Sources	None	1. Urban poverty is due to unemployment, high cost of goods and services as well as rent 2. Africa suffers a deficit and poor housing 3. Development of sustainable housing is hinged on smart partnerships between local authorities and private sectors, where the former provides land and the latter provides finance and expertise. But this must accommodate the plight and needs of the urban social strata

(continued)

Table 7.2 (continued)

Author(s)	Study focus	Geographical unit	Methods	Theory	Results
Crush (2017)	Urban food systems: poverty, income and services	Nairobi, Kenya	Review of Documents	Policy Reform	1. Sixty-three percent of Nairobi's slum populations live below the poverty line 2. Income distribution varies spatially and is connected to housing distribution and land tenure 3. Living conditions in the slums is 'appalling, characterized by non-existent public services, poor housing and sanitary conditions, yet rents are high, absorbing a sizeable fraction of the household budget' 4. Widespread unhygienic conditions (water-borne disease, parasites refuse, and poor drainage are common features), inaccessibility and low use of power, reliance on carbon fuels is a health risk and frequent cause of domestic fires. Lack of piped, clean water that is reliable is evident. School attendance is high, though underserved with quality education

Author(s)	Study focus	Geographical unit	Methods	Theory	Results
Iyenda (2007)	Methodological procedures in researching and measurement of urban poverty	Sub-Saharan Africa, with specific reference to DRC (Kinshasa)	Inductive and deductive techniques as well as qualitative and quantitative methods	None	1. Income (consumption and expenditure), access to health care and education, good and sufficient food, living conditions, safety and human rights are key indicators of poverty 2. Income (GNI and GNP, as crude measures, and others not captured in formal economic statistics such as subsistence production, domestic labour, informal work and other un-remunerated households and social tasks), poverty line, budget standards and household expenditure are key in measurements of poverty 3. Western concepts of urban poverty do not fit with the Congolese reality 4. Income poverty and high unemployment throughout Kinshasa have denied people access to decent homes, quality health services and low-quality education. Poor transport situation, lack of a clean urban environment, insecurity, and human rights abuses are also common characteristics of poverty-stricken areas of Kinshasa 5. Half of the poor households surveyed receive their total or complimentary incomes from the informal sector economy or self-employed, where real incomes are low and declining 6. Improvement in gender equity and participation in decision-making at the household has helped address poverty as more females become actively productive in income generating activities
Lubaale (2014)	Challenges faced by public institutions in urban planning in poverty reduction in urban Kenya	Nairobi-Viwandani, Kenya	Qualitative research, including FGDs, in-depth and semi-structured interviews, and key informants, all triangulated	Rational Choice Theory and Institutionalism	Political power and vested interests virtually overlook planning legal framework, destroy planning institutions, deny public participation in decision-making for self-gain and do not provide for accountability by public officers

(continued)

176 H. W. OBULINJI

Table 7.2 (continued)

Author(s)	Study focus	Geographical unit	Methods	Theory	Results
Potts (1995)	Increase in urban–rural flows in African urbanization processes during the era of the debt crisis and structural adjustment programmes, and the implications for urban policy in addressing poverty	African Cities in Zambia, Uganda and Tanzania	Surveys and review of documents	Policy	1. African Cities suffered poor economic performance during the debt crisis in the 1980s and from the Structural Adjustments Programmes of the 1990s, reducing significantly growth in urban economies, governments' provision of essential services and real incomes of the urban poor 2. Evidences of reverse-migration exist, though with some net in-migration registered that is still higher than urban economic growth 3. Lack of accurate data on economic performances and demographic statistics as evidenced from census data, surveys and analyses that have misguided and had significant biases in urban planning affecting efforts to address urban poverty
Rogerson (1996)	Urban poverty and the informal economy in South Africa's economic heartland	South Africa, the Pretoria-Witwatersrand-Vereeniging region (which includes Johannesburg)	Review of documents and survey	Policy reform	1. The demise of formal sector, leading to high unemployment levels (29–48 percent) 2. Lack of proper shelter, water and sanitation 3. Poor infrastructure and social facilities 4. Engagement in illegal activities such as crime, prostitution, etc

Author(s)	Study focus	Geographical unit	Methods	Theory	Results
Rogerson (1998)	Urban agriculture and urban poverty alleviation	South Africa	Review of documents	Policy	5. The spatial distribution of urban poverty is uneven with small towns, secondary cities and informal shack lands emerging as the major problem areas for policy attention 6. Urban agriculture, with reducing urban employment and new urban policy initiatives introduced since 1994 offer a window of opportunity for promoting urban agriculture as a potential policy tool for strengthening the asset base of South Africa's urban poor. However, there is limited promotional work by South African governments (at all levels; national, provincial and local) to promote urban agriculture as a specific tool for poverty redressal
Stren (1992)	A review of major publications in the African urban fields, including the role of management of African Cities and informalization of aspects of urban life in urban poverty issues in the late 1980s and early 1990s. Other areas covered in the review are urban agriculture, housing development, and the supplementary role of NGOs in service provision	Africa	Review of Documents	Policy	A review of literature indicates that the focus of urban research was on the growing concern with the poor management of African Cities, and the increasing informalization of the many aspects of urban life that were found to be the causes of increasing urban poverty
Turyahabwa (2012)	Definition and contextualization of poverty in Kampala, Uganda	Kampala, Uganda	Interviewing using a semi-structured questionnaire	Policy	Two distinct individual and community-level definitions of urban poverty were evident

(continued)

Table 7.2 (continued)

Author(s)	Study focus	Geographical unit	Methods	Theory	Results
Tacoli (2013)	Link between urban poverty, food security and climate change	African Cities	Empirical	Policy	1. In the context of climate change, food insecurity is seen primarily as a problem of insufficient production rather than of insufficient consumption, and urban food security is often neglected 2. Food insecurity is deeply connected to poverty. As low-income and middle-income countries urbanize rapidly, both poverty and food insecurity will concentrate in urban areas 3. Low incomes are the primary cause of urban food insecurity, but poor living conditions, local environmental hazards (exacerbated by climate change) and limited access to markets also contribute to urban poverty
World Bank (2004)	Poverty and how urban mobility impacts livelihoods of poor households' access to basic services	Conakry, Guinea	Household and individual quantitative survey involving structured and semi-directed qualitative interviews	Policy Reform	1. The poor households stay in the outer-most districts, far away from the CBD where rents are lower. They suffer from inadequate and poorly developed transport systems that are also congested. Fare is high due to distance from the CBD and they walk long relatively distances before accessing means of transport 2. Because of poor and expensive transport services, the poor encounter many difficulties in accessing basic services, i.e., commuting to work, getting access to (good) schools, accessing quality health services, food markets, and water supply

Author(s)	Study focus	Geographical unit	Methods	Theory	Results
Zeleke et al. (2008)	Nature, characteristics and determinants of poverty along the Addis Ababa-Bahir Dar gradient	Ethiopia (Addis Ababa-Bahir Dar area)	Empirical household survey	Policy-RUD model	1. RUD analysis shows a symbiotic relationship that is mutualistic in the flow of resources between the city of Addis Ababa and its rural and peri-urban areas in development process 2. Significant differences along the gradient exist in households' socio-demographic characteristics, poverty levels, determinants of poverty, and perceived poverty levels

Further, Baker and Nina (2004) note that initial and follow-up surveys, in partnership with local governments and other stakeholders, are necessary for capacity building and replication. Making data collected public and timely is essential in monitoring changes in poverty indices and overall effective intervention and management of poverty. Moreover, the timing of surveys is critical due to the fact that cities are dynamic and indices of poverty are likely to change rapidly; for instance, they may change as a result of human or natural hazards. Additionally, it is important to design tools that take a shorter time to collect data from town respondents because most of them are busy and have no time. In poverty-related studies, Baker and Nina (2004) note that response levels are likely to be low because most of the selected respondents are difficult to find at home unless you make several follow-ups at different times of the day. Furthermore, sub-groups that may not have permanent residence such as street children, pavement dwellers and the like may be missed out, thus requiring specially designed data collection instruments and approaches for the study. These are some of the challenges that may be encountered in urban poverty studies.

Study Designs

Different methods have been used in the study of urban poverty. For instance, in the analysis of the coverage of urban research in Africa from the early 1980s to 1992, Stren (1992) relied purely on a review of research documents conducted by local and international foundations and agencies. Studies by Rogerson (1996, 1998), Awumbila (2014), Crush (2017), and Chirisa and Matamanda (2016) relied on both surveys and review of documents as methods of accessing data. They note that poverty is too broad, and a researcher may be required to examine a number of poverty variables at the household. To cut down on resources required, a researcher may opt to rely more on documented information and supplement it with both qualitative and quantitative primary data through household and community level surveys in achieving the objectives of the study. This view is also supported by Baker and Nina (2004). Moreover, it may be aggregated, requiring one to supplement documented data with primary sources for clarity of issues under investigation.

Iyenda (2007) recommends inductive and deductive techniques as well as qualitative and quantitative methods in researching urban poverty. Qualitative methods, which includes indirect observation, interviews, questionnaire and participant observations, help collect detailed contextualized data. Probability sampling that includes simple random, systematic, stratified and cluster sampling are relevant in achieving representative results depending on the characteristics of the urban population under study (Iyenda, 2007). Indeed, it is evident from the studies reviewed that qualitative methods yield detailed and contextualized findings, which are reminiscent of the spatial and temporal variations in urban poverty dynamics. However, the World Bank (2004) in its study of the City of Conakry observes that for sampling to be representative and generate accurate findings, respondents need to be contacted and interviewed at their place of occupation and in selected pedestrian areas where foot traffic is heavy. The aim is to represent the different situations in which the poor live, instead of giving a statistical summary representation of the poor as a whole. Nevertheless, it is evident from the studies reviewed, except that of the World Bank (2004), that they did not adopt this approach in the collection of data on poverty issues.

Measurement and Analytical Methods of Urban Poverty

Measuring urban poverty presents a number of challenges due to its multidimensional nature. Baker and Nina (2004) define Urban Poverty Analysis (UPA) as a process of gathering, analysing, and presenting information on the extent, location and conditions of poverty in a given city. From UPA, a city poverty profile and baseline can be developed which policymakers and other stakeholders can use in the management of urban poverty. Further, they note that while there is no single approach to conducting urban poverty assessments, there are some common good practices that may facilitate the exercise.

However, before any analysis is done, it is also prudent to identify specific characteristics that are more pronounced to the poor in urban areas. These include but are not limited to the following:

- Commoditization (reliance on the cash economy);
- Overcrowded living conditions (slums);
- Environmental hazard (stemming from density and hazardous location of settlements and exposure to multiple pollutants);
- Social fragmentation (lack of community and inter-household mechanisms for social security, relative to those in rural areas);
- Crime and violence;
- Traffic crashes; and
- Natural disasters.

Studies reviewed in this chapter adopted five approaches either singly or in a triangulated way in the analysis of poverty dynamics. The five approaches discussed in this section are; income or consumption measures, unsatisfied basic needs index, asset indicators, vulnerability and participatory methods.

1. Income or Consumption Measures

Income or consumption measures are based on data that assess whether an individual or household can afford a basic basket of goods (food, housing water, clothing, transport, etc.) in a given period of time (Iyenda, 2007). Consumption was the generally preferred measure compared to income because incomes tend to fluctuate over time and there is the problem of under-reporting of income earned from the private and informal sectors. Money metric measures can be adjusted to account for the higher cost of living in urban areas when measuring poverty. Similarly, quantifying actual income levels may either be difficult to access data or value all goods and services produced and rendered by a household. Income was also pegged on the global poverty line to determine whether a given household or individual is poor.

2. Unsatisfied Basic Needs Index

The unsatisfied basic needs index approach was used in defining a minimum threshold for several dimensions of poverty classifying those households who do not have access to these basic needs. They included characteristics such as literacy, school attendance, piped water, sewage, adequate housing, overcrowding, and some kind of caloric and nutritional requirements. If a household is deficient in one of the categories, they were classified as having unsatisfied basic needs.

3. Asset Indicators

The asset indicators approach was used to a range of variables on the ownership of household assets are used to construct an indicator of households' socio-economic status. The assets included owning a car, refrigerator, television, dwelling characteristics (type of roof, flooring, toilet), and access to basic services such as clean potable water and electricity. Asset indicators were directly used to infer on income levels and household capability levels.

4. Vulnerability

The vulnerability approach defines vulnerability as a dynamic concept referring to the risk that a household or individual will experience an episode of income or health poverty over time, and the probability of being exposed to a number of other risks (violence, crime, natural disasters, being pulled out of school, etc.). For instance, Awinia-Mushi (2013) measured vulnerability using indicators that make it possible to assess a household's risk exposure over time through panel data that include physical assets, income levels, number of income sources (diversification levels), nature of the occupation, human capital, links to networks, participation in the formal safety net and access to credit markets.

5. Participatory Methods

Participatory methods rely on qualitative approaches as recommended by the World Bank (2004) so as to capture aspects of urban poverty that may not be identified through pre-coded surveys. Through tools such as focus group discussions, case studies and individual open-ended interviews, interviewing an individual in their operational environments, it was possible, for instance, for Turyahabwa (2012) to determine the perceptions of poverty, identify priority needs and concerns, and gain insight on the effectiveness of programmes and policies from the perspective of the beneficiaries.

Even though there are global standards in the measurement and analysis of poverty, Iyenda (2007) recommends that researchers contextualize the measurement and analysis of poverty. He identifies income (consumption and expenditure), access to health care and education, good and sufficient food, living conditions, safety and human rights as key global indicators of poverty. Income (Gross National Income and Gross National Product, as crude measures, and others not captured in formal economic statistics such as subsistence production, domestic labour, informal work and other un-remunerated households and social tasks), poverty line, budget standards and household expenditure are identified as key measures of poverty (Iyenda, 2007). Further, no single approach is satisfactory in the measurement and analysis of urban poverty dynamics. Employing more than two approaches in a triangulated way is likely to yield better results than relying on a single method.

Theories of Urban Poverty

It is evident from the review of literature that only studies by Zeleke et al. (2008), Awinia-Mushi (2013), and Lubaale (2014) used the Rural–Urban Dynamics Model, Human Capability Model and Rational Choice Theory and Institutionalism, respectively, to inform their studies on urban poverty. The three theoretical frameworks revolve around different thematic areas espoused by the Livelihood Framework developed by DFID (2000) in informing discussions on poverty related issues. Despite other studies reviewed not having used any theoretical framework(s), their focus and discussions on issues of urban poverty are partly within the confines of the Livelihood Framework.

Awinia-Mushi (2013) used the human capability model, comprehensively defined by Sen (1999), in the study on urban poverty, inequalities and human capability development in Dar es Salaam. The model defines capabilities as the range of freedom or entitlements that a person can access that makes one able to do or not to do a certain range of things. The concept of entitlement is, therefore, central to the human capability approach. An entitlement is defined as a guarantee of access to benefits based on established rights, legislation or policy instruments (Sen, 1999). Entitlements are further defined as a certain set of commodities, endowments or provisions that a person has access to or commands that include among others: access to good levels of education; health; credit services; and productive assets (Clark, 2010). This discussion on entitlements becomes particularly relevant in relation to urbanization and capability deprivation in developing countries.

Further, the human capability model pays special attention to the way non-income factors influence the relative capabilities of different social economic groups to function in ways that achieve wellbeing (Clark, 2010; Sen, 2004). These include factors such as social-structural arrangements, relative access to endowments, economic facilities, political freedom, and freedom of movement and association. Others include occupational choice, social inequalities, demographic distribution of skills and physical health and distribution of ownership of assets (Bourguignon et al., 2005; Clark, 2010; Sen, 2004).

An important distinction of the human capability model as a theoretical framework is that it evaluates poverty by taking into consideration non-income dimensions of wellbeing (Sen, 1999). The model is a departure from a traditional economic utilitarian approach which evaluates wellbeing from the standpoint of relative access to income or consumption (Clark, 2010). Furthermore, the capability model pays special attention to the centrality of social inequalities in human development. Bourguignon et al. (2005) draw a link between urban poverty and social inequalities by arguing that disruptions in flow of incomes of urban households translate into immediate disruption in the capabilities of its members to survive. The application of this model to poverty studies offers a contribution to the ongoing scholarly discourse on sustainable urbanization in the twenty-first century. But the model fails to capture the role of other factors that affect urban poverty as espoused by the livelihood framework, consequently making it not comprehensive in addressing urban poverty issues. In spite of this, the model in understanding and addressing urban poverty focuses on the strengths of the households or individuals rather than on their needs.

Lubaale (2014) used the rational choice theory and institutionalism by North (1990) to examine the challenges faced by public institutions in addressing urban poverty. The theory is framed by four main ideas (power, poverty reduction, urban planning, and institutions) that interplay to determine and influence the success of institutions charged with planning and resources utilization in poverty reduction. The theory, out of the many variables that interplay to understand the dynamics and management of urban poverty as depicted by the Livelihood Framework, singles out the critical role of political power and vested interests in virtually overlooking planning legal framework. This destroys planning institutions, denies the public meaningful participation in decision-making, and ensures self-gain, thus making public officers not accountable. The role of politics and governance in influencing livelihoods is well espoused in the livelihood framework and has factors that cannot be underestimated in any urban poverty redressal.

Zeleke et al. (2008) incorporated the rural–urban dynamics model in carrying out a transect analysis of the nature, characteristics and determinants of poverty along the Addis Ababa-Bahir Dar gradient. An understanding of the existing rural–urban dynamics is critical in designing policies and strategies that will ensure a symbiotic relationship that is mutual in the development process and poverty reduction in both the rural and urban areas. It is evident from their empirical findings that addressing urban poverty will require policies that focus on both the core and the periphery. This model provides a deviation from the traditional thinking within the Livelihood Framework that poverty can be effectively managed from the confines of statistically defined administrative district/county or national boundaries by invoking a new perspective of spatial linkages in planning for effective urban poverty redressal. Critical analysis of spatial linkages, which may be at micro, macro or even global levels are key in the formulation of policies and planning geared towards effective urban poverty management.

Nature, Characteristics and Levels of Urban Poverty

Poverty has traditionally been isolated on the sole basis of economic resources available to the household. However, a consensus has gradually emerged regarding the multidimensional character of poverty in many works and papers produced by international institutions and researchers. Yet, there is no single definition of poverty (World Bank, 2004). Even though this is the case, in very general terms, the World Bank (2004) defines poverty as a combined lack of various resources (economic, social, cultural, etc.) limiting an individual's or household's capacity to meet minimum nutritional standards, participate in the daily life of society, and ensure economic and social reproduction.

In a related perspective, the United Nations (1995) points out that 'Overall, poverty occurs when there is lack of income, education, housing and basic services; acute hunger and malnutrition; increased morbidity and mortality from illness and unsafe environments; and social discrimination as well as exclusion. Further, it is also characterized by lack of participation in decision-making in civil, social and cultural life; loss of livelihoods as a result of economic recession; sudden poverty as a result of disaster or conflict; the poverty of low-wage workers; and the utter destitution of people who fall outside family support systems, social institutions and safety nets' (United Nations).

Despite the above definitions, a number of authors conceptualize urban poverty in different ways. Turyahabwa (2012) observed two distinct definitions of urban poverty in Kampala, Uganda from the individual and community perceptions. Five sub-themes were identified under individual level that included a lack of basics needs; low income/low purchasing power; social exclusion/failure to fulfil social roles; poor human capital; and psychological/spiritual distress. At the community level, urban poverty was conceptualized to mean 'lack of employment and income', 'few people have purchasing power', and 'scarcity of goods and services'. Kasente (1999) in the same spatial setting, observes that a poor community is characterized by no roads, poor houses, no cash crops; no cattle, and the members of that community use poor methods of farming.

Turyahabwa's findings draw us to a perspective of poverty that is often not considered by the individualistic approaches; the community level. Focus on only one particular level of analysis may lead to important gaps in understanding and managing urban poverty. Different aspects of poverty and deprivation are evident at different levels of social organization. For example, the lack of street-lighting or access to markets may apply predominantly at the level of the community while food security and income may apply to the household level, or even at an intra-household level due to differentiation based on age, gender, or relationship to the household head (Turyahabwa, 2012). Analysis of poverty at different levels allows any inter-linkages between them to be explored. Understanding the community perspective of poverty has a number of benefits. It permits an understanding of differences within the community; community-level poverty and changes in provision and access to produced capital such as water and electricity; collective action and social capital; political capital; relations between different groups in the community, for example, clans; and potential community-level transformation and beyond (Turyahabwa, 2012).

Many households in Africa's cities and urban areas are unable to meet their basic needs due to high levels of unemployment, high cost of goods and services such as rent. According to Nahinga (2017), 71 percent of urban populations in sub-Saharan Africa are poor and live in slums. Despite the high levels, the spatial distribution of urban poverty is uneven with small towns, secondary cities and informal shack lands emerging as the major problem areas for policy attention (Nahinga, 2017). Crush (2017) observes that in Kenya, 63 percent of the population in Nairobi live in slums, where income distribution among households vary spatially and is connected to housing distribution and land tenure. Living conditions in the slums are appalling and are characterized by non-existent public services, poor housing and sanitary conditions. This notwithstanding, the rents are high and absorb a sizeable fraction of the household budget. Widespread unhygienic conditions (water-borne disease, parasites refuse, and poor drainage are common features), inaccessibility and low use of power are also evident. The majority of households rely on carbon fuels, which is a health risk and a frequent cause of domestic fires. The households also lack piped, clean water. Further, school attendance is high, though underserved with low-quality education in low-income residential areas. Moreover, poor households are engaged in illegal activities such as crime, prostitution and the like (Crush, 2017).

Rogerson (1998) observes similar prevailing conditions and characteristics in cities and towns in South Africa. Therefore, a synthesis of the above definitions shows that poverty is dynamic and varies in urban spatial structure and perception both at the individual and community levels. Understanding what constitutes urban poverty is, therefore, critical in its effective management.

Causes of Urban Poverty

Causes of urban poverty are many and diverse, including economic and non-economic factors. Stren (1992) observes that rapid urbanization, poor management of African Cities and the increasing informalization of many facets of urban life were the causes of increasing urban poverty in the 1980s and early 1990s. According to the World Bank (1990) African Cities on average registered an annual growth rate of 6.2 percent, thus contributing significantly to informalization of urban life. Potts (1995) observes that the causes of urban poverty stem from poor economic performance of economies of developing countries, especially during the economic downturn of the 1980s and the Structural Adjustment Programmes of the 1990s. Both periods were associated with a reduction in real incomes of the urban poor; employment opportunities; and government revenues that is essential in meeting the cost of service provisions in urban centres.

The liberalization process was also characterized by increasing costs of services to urban residents. During both periods, prices of commodities shot up due to rising petroleum prices that are associated with imported inflation. Further, Potts (1995) observes that evidence of reverse-migration exists, though with some net in-migration registered that is still higher than the growth in urban economies. This has had a net effect of reduced employment opportunities for the growing labour force in urban areas. Similarly, Iyenda (2007) also observed this in Kinshasa, where high unemployment levels among city residents denied them access to income, health care, adequate food, education, good living conditions and a clean environment.

Further, Iyenda (2007) attributes increasing poverty among the residents of Kinshasa to government dictatorial tendencies, poor economic management and lack of respect for human rights. Moreover, Rogerson (1996) found out that in South Africa, the poor economic performance led to the demise of the informal sector, which resulted in high unemployment levels of between 29 and 48 percent. Consequently, the majority of the urban poor engaged in illegal activities such as crime and prostitution in order to earn a living. Also, Potts (1995) avers that lack of accurate data on economic performances and demographic statistics, as evidenced from census data, surveys and other analyses, have misguided and had significant biases in urban planning, thereby affecting efforts to address urban poverty. Rogerson (1996) notes that lack of accurate demographic statistics affected government efforts in South Africa to plan and provide adequate shelter, water and sanitation, infrastructure and social facilities to the urban residents.

Awinia-Mushi (2013) observes that social inequalities exist in urban informal settlements and that a positive correlation exists between low human capability development levels and poverty in housing and health conditions. Lack of human capability elements (such as formal education, vocational skills and lack of participation in urban informal sector activities, credit services and productive assets) is a factor in hindering the effectiveness of households to reduce housing and health problems. Poor housing conditions (overcrowding, unfinished houses, lack of solid waste disposal mechanisms and poor sanitation) have adverse effects on health conditions among households. Thus, a vicious cycle between low levels of income and human capability development holds poor households under a capability deprivation trap.

According to Tacoli (2013), there is a link between urban poverty, food security and climate change. In the context of climate change, food insecurity is seen primarily as a problem of insufficient production rather than of insufficient consumption. Further, urban food security is often neglected. Food insecurity is deeply connected to poverty. As low- and middle-income countries urbanize rapidly, both poverty and food insecurity will concentrate in urban areas. Low incomes are the primary cause of urban food insecurity although poor living conditions, local environmental hazards and limited access to markets also contribute to the same and are also exacerbated by climate change.

Zeleke et al. (2008) observe that vulnerability of households to poverty is directly linked to their level of income; socio-economic and demographic characteristics; level and type of assets owned and livelihood diversity; and housing quality. Also, access to and use of services, including health, accessibility by road or other modes, telephone, markets for goods and services are critical determinants of households' vulnerability to poverty.

Strategies for Addressing Urban Poverty

Urban poverty is a broad and dynamic facet of the urban economy (Turyahabwa, 2012; UN, 1995; World Bank, 2004). Addressing urban poverty, therefore, requires a multifaceted approach, which may vary from one city to the other depending on the context. It is critical for urban planners and other stakeholders involved, including local and national governments to contextualize and understand in-depth the dynamics and courses (both economic and non-economic) of urban poverty. This will facilitate the designing of effective policies and strategies to address the very poor who are left out by current poverty intervention programmes in urban areas and cities in Africa (Turyahabwa, 2012). For instance, Rogerson (1998) notes that, by reducing urban employment, the new urban policy initiatives introduced in 1994 offer a window of opportunity for promoting urban agriculture as a potential policy tool for strengthening the asset base of South Africa's urban poor. This finding is shared by Zeleke et al. (2008) in a study done in Addis Ababa. Despite this, there is limited promotional work by the South African government (at all levels-national, provincial and local) to promote urban agriculture as a specific tool for poverty redressal.

Rogerson (1996) further recommends the development of the survivalist segment of the informal sector, which is multifaceted in nature, to complement other strategies aimed at reducing poverty levels within a reconstruction and development programme for the Pretoria-Witwatersrand-Vereeniging (PWV) region. However, to achieve this, it requires the enactment of an appropriate supportive policy framework to develop the urban informal sector. Additionally, Rogerson proposes a raft of measures that can be taken so as to address urban poverty in South Africa cities. These measures include food-based programmes for the poor; gainful employment generation programmes for the poor; promotion of community empowerment; formation of social groups among women; skill training to the poor; housing programmes; and development of social infrastructure (education, health and transport). Achievement of these proposals requires sound policy formulations and resources on the part of the government.

From a different perspective, Chirisa and Matamanda (2016) recommend the development of good housing as a critical strategy in addressing urban poverty. The development of sustainable housing is hinged on smart partnerships between local authorities and private sector, where the former provides land while the latter provides finance and expertise. However, this strategy must accommodate the plight and needs of the urban social strata. Further, they suggest housing policies and strategies that include in-situ upgrading of informal settlements, a view supported by Awumbila (2014). Furthermore, they recommend the regulation of the real market, and engagement of the poor in decision-making so as to ensure development of sustainable housing units. However, they note that most housing programmes have failed to be cost-effective in addressing the plight of the urban poor.

World Bank (2004) suggests some measures based on the mobility of the poor, who in most cases stay in the outer-most districts of the cities, that will help address urban poverty. For instance, there is need to do the following: come up with a transport policy that focuses on the development of efficient modes of transport and public transport supply that will help cut down on the high proportion of incomes spent on mobility by the poor; ensure equal spatial distribution of transport network in the city; and improve conditions for both motor and pedestrian traffic. Such a policy will in effect reduce the distance walked to access transport services and cut down on high cost of transport for commuters to work, school and even those seeking medical services and markets, as was observed in Conakry, Guinea. It will also improve the reach to, or availability of basic services and ensure high circulation and incomes, especially for merchants, which is good for overall economic growth and development process.

Further, Awumbila (2014) has suggested the need to strengthen inclusion to ensure that the poor and vulnerable groups are not left behind in governance structures and decision-making process and development of urban policies, so as to make decisions that are rational and effective in addressing their needs. There is also need to promote pro-poor social programmes and investment in public goods and services for the poorest or most vulnerable groups. This will not only drastically reduce urban poverty levels, but also bridge the urban income divide. Moreover, measures need to be put in place to address housing needs and improving access to basic social and health services for the poor people in urban slums.

Focusing on an urban planning approach that takes into account rural–urban linkages is also inevitable. In fact, Zeleke et al. (2008) observe that such an approach created a functional economic relationship between Addis Ababa and its hinterland. This in essence promotes cities that can offer sustained livelihoods to rural migrants as well as to those living on the urban periphery. Further, Zeleke et al. (2008) observe that addressing poverty along the urban–rural gradient will require development of policies that are geared towards strengthening rural–urban dynamics. Also, different but a mix-up of policies and strategies that focus on household socio-economic and demographic characteristics, housing, public investments in health, transport and market infrastructures are inevitable as they drastically cut down the cost of living for the poor. Furthermore, Awumbila (2014) suggests that addressing the negative external social and environmental costs that come with ill-managed urbanization will also help in reducing poverty. Moreover, diversifying economic activities through the creation of new economic hubs oriented towards sustainable and value-added production and exportation in areas of origin will also be of great importance in addressing poverty. Similarly, there is a need to ensure that migration remains part of the solution in policies and programmes aimed at addressing the challenges of urbanization.

To improve livelihoods, Awinia-Mushi (2013) recommends the need for urban policy planning and poverty reduction strategies to factor in social inequalities and human capabilities analyses. This is a view shared by proponents of livelihood framework, including DFID (2000) who argue that it is appropriate to start with an analysis of strengths as opposed to needs of urban households. Further, they observe that starting with needs can restrict policy issues that may enhance household opportunities based on their assets or none. Hence, according to Awinia-Mushi (2013), there is a need for the adoption of key measures to develop, repair and sustain human capabilities such as access to participation in the urban informal sector; credit services to the urban poor; education and upgrading skills through vocational training; and assets and social protection against cyclic vulnerabilities that are brought about by adjustments measures. For instance, informal sector activities were found to generate or supplement households' incomes. Credit provision enabled individuals to start or expand their businesses. Training enabled individuals to venture into different occupational activities that were in line with the skills attained. Such measures are, therefore, important in protecting, repairing and promoting households' capabilities which have been attained.

To address urban poverty, Stren (1992) has also recommended the need to improve urban management and address the informalization of many aspects of urban life such as the informal sector and urban agriculture by incorporating them in urban policy agenda. Other critical areas that need consideration are gender issues, urban history, housing and planning and the environment. These facets represent a growing interest among researchers, both African and European, in the 'problems' faced by African cities and possible rational responses to these problems.

Further, Stren (1992) notes that every African country perceives its urban problems somewhat differently from its neighbours, and the cycle of research ideas generated by external forces, however benign and constructive these ideas may be, cannot as effectively translate local needs into useful and effective policy proposals as when this research is driven by national institutions and local scholars. For instance, how can a Eurocentric paradigm of urban management be synchronized and effectively accommodate important and creative development possibilities such as the informal sector, as African cities respond directly to the needs of their low-income populations? Local actors are likely to understand contextualized urban issues and therefore come up with effective policies. Iyenda (2007) supports the issue of contextualizing indicators, measurements, skills, knowledge, and cultures in resolving poverty. Further, he proposes the need to promote employment in the formal sector to ensure sustained and higher incomes, which enables the disadvantaged to access their basic need. Also, he observes that the promotion of gender equity and related issues at the household level is critical in addressing urban poverty, as evidenced in his study.

Lubaale (2014) notes that the legal framework and political governance aspects are critical in addressing poverty issues. He asserts that institutional and law reforms are necessary and should be cognizant of the insidious power of the political class and governance structures in urban centres and consequently address it. It should also give the citizenry vested sovereign power to participate in the decision-making process and hold institutions and public servants accountable in the implementation of poverty reduction strategies. From a different perspective, Tacoli (2013) points out that improving access to affordable food by the urban poor will require boosting their capacity to adapt to climate change impacts, and their access to secure incomes as well as to both formal and informal food markets.

Conclusion

This chapter sought to review empirical literature on the dynamics of poverty in African cities. It has highlighted insights into the scope of poverty; measurement and analytical methods; factors contributing to poor urban household livelihoods and approaches to managing urban poverty. The search for literature within the scope of the review yielded no articles between 1980 and 1990. A majority of the literature accessed and reviewed was conducted after the year 2000. Most of the research works conducted between 1980 and 1990 were accessed focused on poverty in developing countries in general and more so, on rural areas, where it is assumed that poverty is relatively more rampant than in urban areas. Further, access to a number of databases was constrained by the cost involved, thus limiting the researcher's ability to review articles on poverty from a range of databases. With the increasing urban poverty levels, there is a need for researchers, local and international institutions to shift their attention to urban poverty, particularly in Africa and other developing regions. This will help generate current data and information that is critical for effective planning.

Given that urban poverty is dynamic and varied in socio-economic and spatio-temporal aspects, there is a need to carry out thematic studies that focus on disaggregated poverty aspects using a mixed-methods approach that ensures complementarity, accuracy and quality of data collected. The mixed-methods approach will also reduce data collection costs, with empirical individual, household and community surveys complementing documented data. The use of probability sampling, large samples and data collection tools that are shorter generate quality and representative results. Making timely surveys and findings to stakeholders is also critical in the monitoring, evaluation and management of poverty. Incorporation of all local stakeholders in poverty research is critical and recommended for capacity building. Further, some sub-groups such as street families and those without permanent residence may require specially designed data collection instruments and approaches for study. These are some of the challenges that may be encountered in urban poverty studies. Moreover, measurement and analysis of urban poverty dynamics will require the use of two or more approaches, if better outcomes are to be achieved.

Urban poverty is characterized by households' or individuals' combined lack of various adequate resources thereby limiting their capacity to meet minimum basic needs. Further, it is characterized by increased morbidity and mortality, unsafe environments, social discrimination and exclusion, lack of participation in decision-making and psychological/spiritual distress. Over 50 percent of urban population in Africa live in poverty, with the conceptualization of urban poverty varying spatially both at individual and community levels. Thus, understanding what constitutes urban poverty at different levels is, therefore, critical in its effective management.

The causes of urban poverty are quite diverse and include both economic and non-economic factors such as vulnerable households' assets and low human capability elements; dictatorial governments that suffer from poor management and violation of human right; and poor economic performance and increasing informalization of the urban economy. Further, the Structural Adjustment Programmes of the early 1990s; the ever-increasing rural–urban migration; reliance on imports such as oil; data inadequacy in urban planning; climate change; and natural hazards are also causes of urban poverty.

Addressing urban poverty requires a contextualized multifaceted approach, which may vary within and between cities. It also requires the participation of all stakeholders, including the affected city or town residents, local and national governments, private sector and NGOs, and international organizations. Further, there is a need to enact an effective, appropriate and supportive local policy framework that incorporates the poor in the decision-making process and development of urban policy and planning; and addresses social inequalities. Such a policy framework should also strengthen core–periphery dynamics, address instability in the physical environment and economic markets and reduce vulnerability among households. Besides, it should aim at promoting households' capabilities and enhance access to resources and opportunities. Moreover, law reforms that address the insidious power of the political class and urban governance structures, urban history and gender issues are also critical. Investment in programmes that accommodates the needs of the urban social strata such as housing, transport, health, water will also help address urban poverty. Also, urban environmental conservation efforts emanating from ill-managed urbanization, creation of new economic hubs, promotion of urban agriculture and informal sector and formalization of both subsectors, by incorporating them in the urban policy agenda are also essential in addressing urban poverty.

REFERENCES

Abu-Salia, R., Osmannu, I. K., & Ahmed, A. (2015). Coping with the challenges of urbanization in low income areas: An analysis of the livelihood systems of slum dwellers of the Wa municipality, Ghana. *Current Urban Studies, 3,* 105–118. Published Online June 2015 in http://dx.doi.org/10.4236/cus.2015.32010

Awinia-Mushi, C. (2013). *Examining urban poverty, inequalities and human capability development in the context of adjustment: The case of Vingunguti and Buguruni settlements, Dar-es-Salaam.* Unpublished PhD Thesis in Development Studies, The Open University of Tanzania.

Awumbila, M. (2014). *World migration report 2015: Linkages between urbanization, rural-urban migration and poverty outcomes in Africa.* International Organization for Migration (IOM).

Baker, J., & Nina, S. (2004). *Analysing urban poverty: A summary of methods and approaches* (World Bank Policy Research Working Paper 3399). World Bank.

Barofsky, J., Siba, E., & Grabinsky, J. (2016). *Can rapid urbanization in Africa reduce poverty? Causes, opportunities, and policy recommendations.* https://www.brookings.edu/blog/africa-in-focus/2016/09/07/can-rapid-urbanization-in-africa-reduce-poverty-causes-opportunities-and-policy-recommendations/. Accessed 22 May 2021.

Bourguignon, F., Ferreira, H. G., & Lustig, M. (Eds.). (2005). *The microeconomics of income distribution dynamics in East Asia and Latin America.* World Bank and Oxford University Press.

Carney, D. (1998, July). Implementing the sustainable rural livelihoods approach. In D. Carney (Ed.), *Sustainable livelihoods: What contribution can we make?* Papers presented at the DFID's Natural Resource Advisers' Conference.

Carney, D. (1999). *Approaches to sustainable livelihood for the rural poor* (Working Paper ODI Poverty Briefing 2). Overseas Development Institute, London.

Chirisa, I., & Matamanda, A. (2016). *Addressing urban poverty in Africa in the post-2015 period: Perspectives for adequate and sustainable housing.* https://www.researchgate.net/publication/304215418_Addressing_Urban_Poverty_in_Africa_in_the_Post-2015_Period_Perspectives_for_Adequate_and_Sustainable_Housing/stats. Accessed 25 Jan 2021.

Clark, D. (2010). *The capability approach: Its development, critiques and recent advances.* Global Poverty Research Group.

Crush, J. (Ed.). (2017). *The urban food system of Nairobi, Kenya: Hungry cities report No. 6* (pp. 25–28). Hungry Cities Partnership. https://profiles.uonbi.ac.ke/samowuor/files/2017_urban_food_systems_of_nairobi.pdf. Accessed 25 Jan 2021.

De Haan, A., Lipton, M., Maxwell, S., & Martin, F. (2000). *Poverty monitoring in Sub-Sahara Africa.* Background paper for the SPA Poverty Status Report 2000.

DFID. (2000). *Sustainable livelihoods guidance sheets.* Department for International Development. https://www.google.com/search?q=dfid+and+livelihoods+Framework&oq=dfid+and+livelihoods+Framework&aqs=chrome..69i57j0i22i30l3.17723j0j7&sourceid=chrome&ie=UTF-8. Accessed 1 Apr 2021.

Iyenda, G. (2007). Researching urban poverty in Sub-Saharan Africa. *Development in Practice, 17*(1), 27–38.

Kasente, D. (1999). *The role of financial services towards reducing vulnerability of poor individuals and households—The impact of microfinance in poverty alleviation.* Micro-Safe. Africa and Uganda Women's Finance Trust.

Lubaale, G. N. K. (2014). *The challenges of planning for poverty reduction in urban Kenya: The case of Nairobi's Local Authorities Service Delivery Plans (LASDAP) (2005–2007) planning approach in the Viwandani Ward.* Unpublished PhD Thesis Submitted to the Faculty of Engineering and the Built Environment, University of the Witwatersrand, Johannesburg, South Africa.

Moser, C. (1998). The asset vulnerability framework: Reassessing urban poverty reduction strategies. *World Development, 26*(1), 1–19.

Nahinga, D. (2017). *5 facts about urbanization in Africa and arising threats and opportunities.* Retrieved March 28, 2021, from https://ub.co.ke/index.php/2017/03/30/5-facts-urbanization-africa-arising-threats-opportunities/

North, D. C. (1990). *Institutions, institutional change and economic performance.* Cambridge University Press.

Potts, D. (1995). Shall we go home? Increasing urban poverty in African cities and migration processes. *The Geographical Journal, 161*(3), 245–264.

Rakodi, C. (1999). A capital assets framework for analysing household livelihood strategies: Implications for policy. *Development Policy Review, 17*(3), 315–342.

Rogerson, C. M. (1996). Urban poverty and the informal economy in South Africa's economic heartland. *Environment and Urbanization, 8*(1), 167–179. https://doi.org/10.1177/095624789600800115. Accessed 25 Jan 2021.

Rogerson, C. M. (1998). Urban agriculture and urban poverty alleviation: South African debates. *Agrekon, 37*(2), 171–188. https://core.ac.uk/download/pdf/6553743.pdf. Accessed 25 Jan 2021.

Scoones, I. (1998). *Sustainable rural livelihoods: A framework for analysis* (Working Paper, vol. 72). Institute for Development Studies, Sussex.

Sen, A. (1999). *Development as freedom.* Oxford University Press.

Sen, A. (2004). *Why health equity.* Wiley.

Shah, A. (2013). Structural adjustment—A major cause of poverty. Retrieved March 21, 2021, from https://www.globalissues.org/article/3/structural-adjustment-a-major-cause-of-poverty

Stren, R. E. (1992). African urban research since the late 1980s: Responses to poverty and urban growth. *Urban Studies, 29*(314), 533–555. Retrieved April 3, 2021, from https://journals.sagepub.com/doi/10.1080/00420989220080561

Tacoli, C. (2013). *Urban poverty, food security and climate change.* IIED (International Institute for Environment and Development) Briefing.

Turyahabwa, J. (2012). Definitions of urban poverty by lay persons in Uganda and its implications for effective anti-poverty interventions. *Poverty and Public Policy, 4*(2), Article 5. https://doi.org/10.1515/1944-2858.5

United Nations. (1995). *The Copenhagen Declaration and Programme of Action: World Summit for Social Development 6–12 March 1995.* United Nations Department of Publications.

United Nations Population Division. (2018). *World urbanization prospects: 2018 revision.* UNPD.

World Bank. (1990). *World Development report 1990: Special issue on poverty.* Oxford University Press for the World Bank.

World Bank. (2002). *The policy roots of economic crisis and poverty: A multi-country participatory assessment of structural adjustment*. Prepared by the Structural Adjustment Participatory Review International Network (SAPRIN). Retrieved June 15, 2021, from https://documents1.worldbank.org/curated/en/553081468326959937/pdf/647580WP0v200B0PUBLIC00Policy0roots.pdf

World Bank. (2004, September). *Poverty and urban mobility in Conakry: Final Report Prepared by STRASS, International Solidarity on Transport and Research in Sub-Saharan Africa*. World Bank.

Zeleke, G., Alemu, D., Bewuket, W., Alemu, B., Assefa, Y., & Trutmann, P. (2008). *Poverty gradient along the rural-urban transect in Ethiopia: The case of Addis Ababa-Bahir Dar Gradient* (Working Paper Series on Rural-Urban-Linkage Theme of the Global Mountain Programme [GMP] Working Paper 2).

CHAPTER 8

Public Transport Services

Meleckidzedeck Khayesi

INTRODUCTION

Planning for public transport services is important in ensuring improved accessibility to places and activities for the urban population in Africa. Public transport services in African urban centres consist of large buses, mini-buses, trains, trams, taxis, bicycles, and motorcycles. The physical infrastructure is largely roadway with limited development of railway for intra-urban commuter train services in several cities. This chapter presents and discusses results of a synthesis of literature on public transport services, assessing theories, research designs, planning approaches, and service provision. The chapter answers two questions: What are the dominant research designs and theories in research on public transport services in African cities? What does research reveal about the state of planning and provision of public transport services in African cities?

METHODS

An extensive search for information was conducted to gather and synthesize studies for this chapter. I started off by identifying and selecting publications from my personal library. I have gathered publications on this topic over the years for research, teaching, and policy work. I followed this source by a search for additional literature from databases like Google Scholar using the following

M. Khayesi (✉)
Geneva, Switzerland
e-mail: mkhayesi@yahoo.com

key words; 'public transport', 'Africa', 'urban', 'cities', 'bus', 'train', 'bus rapid transit', 'matatu', 'tram', and 'ridership'. In addition to published and unpublished scientific research, there is information on public transport in African cities on YouTube videos, websites, and blogs. I kept an eye on any relevant publications on tables of contents and links from alerts that I have created for journals and research groups. I tracked publications shared on this topic on social media, online platforms, and list serves I belong to.

Enquiry with colleagues about publications on this topic also generated useful resources. In the process of this iterative search for literature, I identified recent literature review reports and studies on paratransit, public transport, and motorcycle transport services in African and global cities. I also found and drew upon bibliographies and/or reviews on informal public transport (Institute for Transportation and Development Policy and Volvo Research and Educational Foundations, 2021; Xie & Wagner, 2010), and transport in Africa in general (Pirie, 2018). This reinforcing process generated over 500 publications, which I scrutinized for relevance to the theme of this chapter, yielding 14 core publications for review for this chapter.

The approach, just described, to selecting the final 14 publications for synthesis was based on the need to focus on pivotal and key studies. I identified these key publications and sought to determine how other studies build on them, either extending or deviating from the themes and approaches in the pivotal studies. I looked up literature review sections in several studies to identify recurring themes as well as authors or studies cited to guide my selection. For example, several studies on paratransit transport in African cities cite Cervero (2000) as providing a comprehensive assessment of informal public transport in the developing world, including Africa. A study by Rizzo (2002, 2017) is also frequently cited on mini-bus transport in Dar es Salaam. An edited book on paratransit by Behrens et al. (2016) not only presents empirical findings but also highlights key developments in research on this topic.

I read each selected key study and extracted information on the study focus, theories, methods, and findings. I then looked for subsequent studies that extended or deviated from these anchoring studies and discussed their findings. The information was organized using a table that enabled interpretation and synthesis of the studies reviewed. Results from this synthesis are presented in the next section.

Results and Discussion

Results of two or three key studies that anchor an emergent theme are first presented, following by results from other studies that either advance or deviate from these key studies (Table 8.1).

Table 8.1 Results of anchoring studies on public transport services

Author(s) and publication year	Focus	Theories	Methods	Results
Institute for Transport Policy and Development and Volvo Research and Educational Foundations. (2021)	Current state of knowledge and ongoing activities in paratransit and shared mobility services with attention paid to service impacts, transportation management, and paratransit improvement	None stated	A literature review of over 100 publications covering several cities in the world and in Africa. Consultations with 13 experts	1. Findings reconfirm Cervero's study (2000) about the important role that paratransit and shared mobility services play in urban transport in different parts of the world 2. The study highlights issues related to the impacts of these services, management practices, and policy actions to improve them, which have been covered in several studies 3. This study also identifies gaps in knowledge, for example, employment and economic impacts of these transport services, government capacity requirements for effective management of public transport systems, effective business models for paratransit service, and use of government subsidies to spur service improvements

(continued)

Table 8.1 (continued)

Author(s) and publication year	Focus	Theories	Methods	Results
Olvera et al. (2020)	How can we objectify the massive and lasting development of a 'motorcycle taxi model' in the cities of SSA? How does this model function in practice?	None stated	A review of 334 studies covering several African cities and field work in Lomé, Togo	1. The 334 studies are found or located in 14 countries. Nigeria accounts for almost half the references, and only four other countries; Kenya, Uganda, Benin, and Cameroon that account for more than 5 percent each. The 9 other countries together provide only about 15 percent of all the references 2. There has been a change in the issues covered in the studies. Substantial attention was initially given to drivers, neglecting an analysis of the industry as a whole. Road safety aspects have steadily increased in coverage, for example, between 12 and 16 percent of the documents during the period from 2007 to 2016 dealt with development issues, governance and the economics of the industry. Environmental and security issues receive marginal coverage 3. Two main centres are identified in the origin and spread of motorcycle taxis: West Africa, with Nigeria being a key driver; and East Africa with the Uganda–Kenya border being a key origin 4. Factors underlying the spread: proximity; landlockedness; type of economy inherited from the colonial period; cheap imports of motorcycles from China and India; and the role of international bodies 5. Field work in Lomé identified main features governing the functioning of motorcycle taxis as the ambivalent approach or attitude of the state; the heterogeneous characteristics of the players; and the strong and multifaceted linkages of motorcycle taxis with formal activities

Author(s) and publication year	Focus	Theories	Methods	Results
Klopp and Cavoli (2019)	Can collaborative mapping projects help encourage official transportation planning to be more inclusive of these important mini-bus systems and engage with them in new, more data-driven ways?	None explicitly stated though concepts of big transport projects and exclusion of paratransit systems are highlighted	Participatory mapping of paratransit routes and stops using geo-location enabled cell phones and Global Positioning System in Nairobi (Kenya) and Maputo (Maputo). Comparative analysis	Inclusive, collaborative mapping can help render these mini-buses more visible in planning and provoke more grounded and inclusive 'planning conversations' on multimodal integration, passenger information, and mini-bus upgrading
Klopp et al. (2019)	How bus rapid transit projects shape the formation of metropolitan governance and impinge on the future of the currently dominant mini-bus systems	Political economy	Review of literature. Case studies of Lagos, Johannesburg, and Nairobi	1. Very little independent analysis on the success and failures and overall impacts of bus rapid transit in Africa. Thus, there is a knowledge gap with regard to rigorous evaluation and analysis of bus rapid transit projects, their political economy dynamics and related institutional effects in Africa and elsewhere. Rizzo is one of the few political economy critiques of bus rapid transit, which he has characterized as a tool of neoliberalism, a vehicle for banks, construction companies, and private transport service operators to access Africa's private transport market 2. There is poor integration between bus rapid transport and popular paratransit or mini-bus service because of the focus of the bus transit project to displace these popular transport services. As a result, bus rapid transit stations and terminals are not aligned with stops, stands, and stations of other modes as has been found in Dar es Salaam

(continued)

Table 8.1 (continued)

Author(s) and publication year	Focus	Theories	Methods	Results
				3. There is little discussion in existing studies about the politics of subsidies and financing of operations and maintenance of bus rapid transit systems. The focus is these studies are on planning, implementation, and the technical performance of bus rapid transit systems that are in operation. It is mainly in South Africa where there is growing discussion about fairness of subsidies and bus rapid transit systems
Ehebrech et al. (2018)	A comprehensive summary research on the role played by motor-taxi services in providing public transport options in Sub-Saharan Africa	None stated	A review of 100 studies	A detailed summary of findings on supply and demand aspects of motorcycle taxi service; actors, organization and politics; service regulation; and negative externalities
Behrens et al. (2016)	An overview of the development, operations and decline of large-scale bus and tram services in African cities included in an introductory chapter to an edited book	None stated	Review of selected publications covering several African cities	1. Large-scale monopolistic bus services existed in several African cities in the first half of the twentieth century due to constrained road capacity and limited financial resources from the governments, leading to their nationalization in the 1960s. Fares were regulated 2. This model faced a lot of pressure in the second half of the twentieth century due to constrained road capacity and limited financial resources from the governments, leading to their nationalization in the 1960s. Fares were regulated 3. Many of these state-owned bus companies were able to operate without government subsidies in the initial stage of nationalization 4. These companies faced financial challenges due to growing operating deficits and stagnation in subsidy budgets, resulting in a 'steady decline in both the quantity and quality of service'

Author(s) and publication year	Focus	Theories	Methods	Results
Bruun et al. (2016)	Historical development and state of public transport systems in Cape Town, Dar es Salaam and Nairobi	None stated	Historical trends and patterns in Cape Town, Dar es Salaam and Nairobi Comparative analysis Secondary sources	1. Initial public transport service dominated by either a bus and or a commuter system gave way to a mix of bus, commuter train and paratransit systems as the three cities of Cape Town, Dar es Salaam and Nairobi went through colonial, independence, and post-independence periods 2. The three cities of Cape Town, Dar es Salaam and Nairobi share certain common characteristics such as predominance of paratransit in public transport modes, slow public transport systems with an average commute time of more than 50 min, and pursuit of efforts to reform the public transport systems in the three cities over the years 3. The three cities of Cape Town, Dar es Salaam, and Nairobi also reveal significant differences in several characteristics: public transport fares in cape town are 10 times higher than in Dar es Salaam and Nairobi; 85 percent of the population in Cape Town is within 1 km of public transport facility compared with Nairobi with a figure of 73 percent; and average percent of household income spent on public transport is higher in Dar es Salaam (17 percent) compared with Cape Town (5–10 percent) and Nairobi (10–15 percent)

(continued)

Table 8.1 (continued)

Author(s) and publication year	Focus	Theories	Methods	Results
Schalekamp et al. (2016)	Approaches to paratransit reform	None stated	Case studies of Cape Town, Johannesburg, Dar es Salaam, Lagos, Port Elizabeth, Accra, and Dakar Secondary sources to identify trends and experiences in paratransit reform	1. Four approaches to paratransit reform: comprehensive bus rapid transit implementation and paratransit incorporation into operating companies; a stepped process entailing paratransit operational improvements and paratransit corporatization, with the aim of their becoming the operators of future conventional large bus, or even bus rapid transit, services; regulating competition in the paratransit market through franchising or concessioning agreements; and incrementally upgrading existing paratransit services without altering ownership or competition regulation mechanisms 2. Paratransit reform efforts have stalled or been delayed due to several reasons, including overemphasis on infrastructure and inadequate consideration of established operator interests
Wood (2015)	Adoption and spread of bus rapid transit in South African cities	Policy circulation and recursive policy adoption	Synthesis of selected studies in cities like Cape Town and Johannesburg. Temporal trend and narrative analysis	1. Bus rapid transit adoption was gradual, repetitive, and at times delayed and not a rapid process 2. Starting with a published discussion of bus rapid transit in a conference report in 1973, the process witnessed a failed attempt to introduce bus rapid transit in Cape Town in 2003, introduction of bus rapid transit in Johannesburg in 2009, Cape Town in 2011 and several South African cities in the 2010s
Agyemang (2015)	Reasons for the failure of first bus rapid transit pilot in the greater Accra metropolitan area, Ghana	None stated	Study conducted in the Greater Accra Metropolitan Area; interviews; surveys; in-depth interviews; traffic observations and counts; thematic narratives	1. Bus rapid transit pilot operated on a 20-km highway from 2005 to 2007 2. Reasons for failure were: recurring traffic congestion, passengers' inadequate comfort and personal security, resistance from existing public transport operators, lack of legal status for a bus rapid transit system, and limited advertisement for the pilot

Author(s) and publication year	Focus	Theories	Methods	Results
Khayesi et al. (2015)	Informal public transport in Kenya	Entrepreneurial process model, political economy, and logic of practice.	Synthesis of existing publications by the authors and others covering cities like Nairobi and Eldoret as well as rural areas. Interviews	1. Informal public transport or matatu sector is a self-organizing industry with a distinctive culture and strategy 2. Matatu industry is embedded into the political economy of Kenya 3. Matatu industry is key in movement of people and goods in both urban and rural areas of Kenya, accounting for 29 percent of daily trips in Nairobi in the 2000s
Cervero (2000)	Market, organizational and regulatory characteristics of informal transport in the developing world including case studies from cities in Egypt, Ghana, Kenya, Niger, Nigeria, and South Africa	No theory explicitly stated though concepts from institutional, entrepreneurship as well as transport demand and supply models	Synthesis of information in existing publications covering several cities in the world	1. Diverse informal transport services in African cities and rural areas: two-wheeled bike taxis, motorcycle taxis, mini-buses, and tracks 2. Informal mini-bus is essential in urban and rural public transport services 3. Unregulated operating environments 4. Poor and non-existent public bus services 5. Several challenges, crowded buses, long queues at bus and mini-bus terminals, poor vehicle maintenance, and road traffic crashes
Kanyama and Cars (2009)	Devise an effective framework for institutional coordination in planning for public transportation in Dar es Salaam and Nairobi	Sustainable public transportation, partnership, governance, institutional development, and analysis, stakeholder analysis, coordination models, and intellectual capital	A comparative case study based on review of documents and interviews conducted in Dar es Salaam and Nairobi	1. Factors that hinder institutional coordination in planning for public transportation in both Dar es Salaam and Nairobi include: lack of vision for cities, lack of effective city and public transport plans, lack of professionalism, lack of regulatory framework, rampant corruption, poverty, poor citizen and stakeholder participation, inadequate political and fiscal decentralization, and unwillingness by decision makers to change existing transport systems 2. Apex framework is proposed to address these constraining factors with a single authority charged with responsibility for coordination and ensuring that all stakeholders adhere to accountability requirements

Research Designs

The main approach to designing and conducting research on public transport services has focused on a single theme in one city or country or part of these geographical units. While some studies take a temporal approach, tracing the development of a specific issue or several issues over time, others take a snapshot-cross sectional approach, examining how a specific theme or several topics vary from one urban area to another at a selected time period. Thus, a spatio-temporal approach is evident in several studies. Interviews, focus group discussions, and secondary sources are the dominant methods used for data collection.

Comparative analysis of two or more African cities has been limited in current and previous research. However, a key effort towards comparative analysis is in a book on paratransit operations that is based on primary research comparing regulation, operations, and reforms in Cape Town, Dar es Salaam, and Nairobi (Behrens et al., 2016). The book has chapters devoted to a specific city but there are also others that conduct a comparative analysis of the issues in three and more cities. For example, a chapter by Schalekamp et al. (2016) examines approaches to paratransit reform efforts in Cape Town, Nairobi, Dar es Salaam, Johannesburg, Lagos, Accra, Port Elizabeth, and Dakar.

Research methods or designs can replicate other studies or lead to improvement in existing ones. It is not enough for this chapter to basically describe designs in the studies reviewed. It is also important to determine the added value in research designs in the reviewed studies by addressing these two questions: (1) Is there anything being refined and created in the research designs in these studies? (2) Are these studies truly reflecting methodological approaches that depart from the conventional ones? Scholars from Africa and the Global South have been critical of transferring theories and methods developed in the Global North to the Global South, without meaningfully adapting them to the realities of the Global South or creating space for theories and methods generated from the Global South.

An innovation in research methods observed in the public transport research is in the establishment of a sampling framework. The exact date when this innovative approach was first used was not easy to establish from the studies reviewed but it seems to be widely used. African cities and countries do not have up to date directories of people, businesses, and organizations that can be readily used to generate a sampling framework. Transport scholars who use interviews or surveys have devised an approach to building a sampling framework. They begin with the incomplete directories or lists available with relevant organizations and individuals. They build on these lists to identify possible sampling frameworks. They then generate a complete list of individuals or ventures by physically visiting people and ventures in a selected geographical unit and thereafter compile a new list. They use this new list to select a sample. Research assistants are key in combing a selected site or a group of respondents to generate a new list. Virtually all the public transport studies synthesized in this chapter that utilized a survey had to start from scratch in creatively establishing a sampling framework using this generalized approach described in this paragraph. This innovation is not limited to transport research. It is also found in other disciplines like entrepreneurship, agriculture, industry, public health, and housing.

Theories

Conventional or existing theories are utilized in the studies reviewed. Most of the theories are applied to the African reality without a major modification to the original theory before or after its application. For example, institutional, demand and supply, business development and behavioural theories and models are used to generate concepts and variables for data collection and analysis. Collaborative, participatory, stakeholder engagement, and inclusion theories and concepts are drawn upon to develop research problems and shape methods of data collection and analysis for such studies as Kanyama and Cars (2009) and Klopp and Cavoli (2019).

What appears to have had limited attention is the use of empirical findings to revise and even formulate new theories and conceptual models or refine existing ones. There is in-depth description and analysis of the context in which public transport services have grown and developed in African cities. For example, the political and economic context that led to the emergence, operations, and organization of the paratransit or taxi industry in South African cities, *dala dala* in Dar es Salaam, *matatu* in Nairobi and mini-bus in Accra are fully described and analysed in Khosa (1992), Rizzo (2017), Kapila et al. (1981), Khayesi et al. (2015), and Behrens et al. (2016). The rise and decline of the bus system are well highlighted in these studies (Bruun et al., 2016) as is the rise and expansion of commercial bicycle and motorcycle services (Ehebrecht et al., 2018; Olvera et al., 2020). The introduction and spread of the bus rapid transit services in African cities is also receiving reasonable research attention (Wood, 2015). Inductively theorizing on these rich and in-depth contextual empirical findings to revise existing and even advance new research frameworks on, for instance, the moderating effect of African contextual variables on the interaction between dependent and independent variables in conventional frameworks is relatively inadequately developed in current research.

Does this situation imply that the need for African urban context informed transport research frameworks has not been raised? Yes, it has, and an example is in challenging an uncritical adoption of bus rapid transit systems in African cities. What is lacking is to systematize existing research into a framework that would help to explain how the African urban and national context affects the development of bus rapid transit systems.

The problem of not revisiting existing theories based on the rich contextual empirical findings is not limited to public transport research. It is also found in other subject areas like development studies and entrepreneurship. For example, there is substantial research on the informal economy in urban and rural Africa. However, a theory and model of African informality is yet to be derived from this rich empirical work. Mkandawire (1995, p. 80) discussed this challenging situation in which research by some African scholars is not anchored in major theoretical debates largely because of the poor state of access to literature in African universities. Mkandawire (1995, p. 80) noted that 'This produces the bizarre situation where "Africanists" publish materials with the latest bibliographical references but dated material while African scholars include the latest information on their countries but carry dated bibliographies'.

Empirical Results

Operations, Decline, and Revival of Bus and Commuter Train Services

Several studies point out the development, decline, and inadequacy of the bus and commuter services in African cities. Behrens et al. (2016) provide an overview of the development, operations, and decline of large-scale bus and tram services in African cities. They point out that these large-scale monopolistic bus companies dominated the transport services' provision in several African cities in the first half of the twentieth century. They consisted of fleets of large buses operating on networks of scheduled routes. Due to rapid urban growth, stagnant road capacity, and limited financial resources from the governments, Behrens et al. (2016) observe that this model of providing bus service faced a lot of pressure in the second half of the twentieth century, leading to their nationalization in the 1960s, with one significant outcome; the regulation of fares charged.

In the initial stages of nationalization, many of these state-owned bus companies were able to operate without government subsidies. With the passing of time, these companies faced financial challenges due to growing operating deficits and stagnation in subsidy budgets. Behrens et al. (2016, p. 10) vividly describe the result of these challenges as 'steady decline in both the quantity and quality of service'. Most of the public bus companies eventually failed, with many of the bankruptcies occurring in the 1990s, the period during which structural adjustment policies severely limited the availability of public funds for subsidy. This vacuum in public transport service was filled by paratransit transport services, which are discussed in the next sections.

With respect to individual studies that provide specific details, Khosa (1998) examines the development of urban passenger transport policy in South Africa in the period 1930–1986, placing the analysis within the context of changing economic and political climates in South Africa over the past seven decades. An important aspect of this study is the political context of urban passenger transport, showing how the delivery of essential services such as transport became an area of popular protests and political mobilization during key periods in

South Africa's development of the 1940s, 1950s, and 1980s. Even with transition from politics of protests to the politics of negotiation that ushered in a new era of inclusive and more transparent transport policy formulation in the 1990s, Khosa (1998) demonstrates that the national transport policy process has become another site of struggle, negotiation, and contestation.

Bruun et al. (2016) assessed the state of public transport systems in Cape Town, Dar es Salaam, and Nairobi. This study starts off by tracing the historical development of bus, commuter train, and paratransit services in the three cities, highlighting key turning points in planning and providing these services within a changing political economy. This evolution saw an initial public transport service that was dominated by either a bus and/or a commuter system give way to a mix of bus, commuter train, and paratransit systems as the three cities went through colonial, independence, and post-independence periods. The study then moves to compare several features of public transport services in the three cities such as daily trips per 1000 population, public transport space per 1000 population, accessibility of public transport services to all possible users and fares charged. Whereas the three cities share common characteristics such as predominance of paratransit in public transport modes, slow public transport systems with an average commute time of more than 50 min, and pursuit of efforts to reform the public transport systems in the three cities over the years, they also reveal significant differences in several features. For example, public transport fares in Cape Town are 10 times higher than in Dar es Salaam and Nairobi. On the other hand, 85 percent of the population in Cape Town is within 1 km of public transport facility compared to 73 percent in Nairobi. The average percent of household income spent on public transport is higher in Dar es Salaam (17 percent) compared with Cape Town (5–10 percent) and Nairobi (10–15 percent). The analysis reveals inefficiencies in the quality, reliability, and coverage of public transport systems in the three cities, thus pointing to the need for major reforms in these systems.

The analysis also reveals the existence of several organizations and agencies involved in the planning and delivery of public transport services and infrastructure in African cities. But a relevant question comes up as follow: how well are they delivering on their responsibilities? Having identified lack of effective coordination as a barrier, Kanyama and Cars (2009) have addressed this question by analysing factors that hinder institutional coordination in planning for public transportation in Dar es Salaam and Nairobi. The key factors, identified through interviews and secondary sources, include; lack of vision for cities, lack of effective city and public transport plans, lack of professionalism, lack of regulatory framework, rampant corruption, poverty, poor citizen and stakeholder participation, inadequate political and fiscal decentralization, and unwillingness by decision-makers to change existing transport systems. Based on the findings of their research, Kanyama and Cars (2009) proposed Apex framework to address these constraining factors, emphasizing the need for a single authority charged with responsibility for coordination and ensuring that all stakeholders adhere to accountability requirements.

In addition to intra-urban bus and commuter train services, there are inter-urban public transport services. There is substantial movement of people and goods between urban centres as well as rural and urban centres in Africa. However, insightful research is lacking on inter-urban large bus transport services though this sector is well developed in several African countries.

Paratransit Services
The origin, development, and operation of paratransit services in African cities are well documented in several of the studies reviewed. The focus in this section is on the mini-bus and mini-bus-taxi with varying seating capacities. Bicycle and motorcycle services, which are part of the paratransit system, are discussed in the next section. Building on an initial comprehensive definition of paratransit are passenger travel modes that fall between autonomous private transport, and scheduled, fixed-route public transport, Behrens et al. (2016) point out that in the developing world, paratransit services are provided at a larger scale for the general population. This is unlike in the developed world in which paratransit services are most commonly associated with demand-responsive transport systems in environments in which conventional public transport services are not viable. An intriguing feature of research on the paratransit services is the diversity of disciplines with an interest in this area of research. In addition to transport and urban planning, paratransit services are of interest to history, economics, religion, political science, literary studies, and business management.

I shall highlight results from three types of studies. The first are studies that focus on a specific topic or several topics on paratransit services in one city. The second are comparative studies of paratransit services in two or more African cities. The third are comparative studies of paratransit services in the world, including African cities.

With respect to a study focusing on one city or country, the book written by Khayesi et al. (2015) is illustrative of the insights and approaches that are found in several other studies. This study focuses on matatu entrepreneurship in Kenya, including cities like Nairobi and Eldoret as well as rural areas. It is based on secondary data sources such as Kapila et al. (1981) and Aduwo (1990) as well the authors' own primary investigation. The book presents details and discusses the origin, organization, conditions of work, contribution to the economy, business performance, and challenges facing the matatu industry in Kenya. Contrary to the widely held perception of a chaotic sector, the study found out that the matatu sector has grown over the years and become a self-organizing industry with a distinctive culture and strategy. The matatu industry is embedded into the political economy of specific cities in which it operates as well as that of Kenya as a whole. The study further indicates that the matatu industry is crucial in the movement of people and goods in both urban and rural areas of Kenya, accounting for 29 percent of daily trips in Nairobi in the 2000s. It offers both direct and indirect employment.

A study by McCormick et al. (2016) analysed matatu business strategies in Nairobi. The strategies identified are executed at two levels; overall strategy and business level strategy. Three overall strategies were identified as transport business, diversification, and daily income. Four business level strategies were also identified as brand and access, informed player, collective action, and resource-driven. The history of the matatu industry in Nairobi has been investigated and well documented by many scholars including researchers like Mutongi (2006, 2017).

The studies reviewed also examine the paratransit sector in individual African cities and countries, covering the same issues as those presented in Khayesi et al. (2015). Examples include Khosa (1992) for South African cities, Boateng (2020) in Ghana, and Rizzo (2002, 2017) in Dar es Salaam. An example of an effort to address challenges faced by women workers and travellers in the paratransit is provided by the recently established Flone Initiative in Kenya (https://floneinitiative.org/). There are other initiatives to address challenges faced not only by women but by the entire sector. Examples include trade unions, associations, negotiations, and strikes.

A line of investigation that goes beyond the origin, organization, business performance, and political economy of paratransit services has been pursued through collaborative mapping of paratransit routes and stops. Initial mapping was done in Nairobi (Klopp et al., 2015) and has been expanded to other African cities (Klopp & Cavoli, 2019). The mapping addresses a major gap in urban transport planning in Africa, for instance, lack of detailed data on the location and spread of paratransit routes and stops. Klopp and Cavoli (2019, p. 669) highlight the benefit of this investigation by stating the following:

"Establishing paratransit maps in Nairobi and Maputo facilitated more open discussion about minibus routes and stops as well as demand for services. Usually, such conversations happen behind closed doors between operators and the government around the issue of licensing rather than in an open planning process. Interestingly, in both cases, the minibus drivers and owners did not show resistance to mapping processes once the idea was explained to them. Indeed, the mapping served to highlight their substantial local and critical knowledge to contribute to transportation planning processes. The potential benefits of discussing formalisation in this context is that the maps create an opportunity to enhance and give visibility to the extent of paratransit service which is currently buried or unavailable in statistics, master plans and academic papers."

Another line of investigation that goes beyond origin, organization, business performance, political economy, and mapping of paratransit routes is by wa Mungai (2013), who has examined the matatu sub-culture in Kenya. Using literary analysis, he situates the observed behaviour of matatu workers such as reckless driving, loud music, and rough handling of passengers in the daily struggles of survival and competition. He shows that this competitive political economy context has led to matatu workers and industry constructing their identities and survival strategies.

With respect to comparative analysis of paratransit in African cities, the book edited by Behrens et al. (2016) stands out. The chapters are based on primary and secondary research conducted in Cape Town, Dar es Salaam, and Nairobi. Apart from being comparative, this book deviates from existing studies by focusing on regulations and reform of the paratransit in selected African cities. Findings from selected chapters from this book are presented and discussed in the following paragraphs.

A key policy effort in African cities has been on how to improve paratransit services to comply with the traffic law and ensure delivery of service for most of the people who rely on this mode of transport. Reforming paratransit services and operations is a recurring effort in an attempt to improve operations of this sector. Based on case studies and experiences of Cape Town, Johannesburg, Dar es Salaam, Port Elizabeth, Lagos, Accra and Dakar, Schalekamp et al. (2016) identify and discuss four main approaches to reforming paratransit services. The first consists of a comprehensive implementation of bus rapid transit in which paratransit is incorporated into operating companies. The second is a stepped process entailing paratransit operational improvements and paratransit corporatization, with the aim of their becoming the operators of future conventional large bus, or even bus rapid transit. The third is regulating competition in the paratransit market through franchising or concessioning agreements. The fourth is incrementally upgrading existing paratransit services without altering ownership or competition regulation mechanisms. Schalekamp et al. (2016) point out that these reform efforts have not been carried through and several have stalled or been delayed due to several reasons such as an overemphasis on infrastructure and technology transfer in the planning and design process, and an underemphasis on the existing system and incumbent operator capacities and constraints.

Regarding comparative studies of paratransit services in the world, including African cities, the research by Cervero (2000) is outstanding and reveals the following:

1. the existence of diverse informal transport services in African cities and rural areas like the two-wheeled bike taxis, motorcycle taxis, mini-buses, and tracks;
2. the essential role played by the informal mini-bus both in urban and rural public transport services;
3. informal public transport services exist in several unregulated operating environments;
4. the poor and non-existent public bus services; and
5. the multiple challenges faced in the informal public transport sector that includes crowded buses, long queues at bus and mini-bus terminals, poor vehicle maintenance, and road traffic crashes.

The pivotal contribution of Cervero (2000) is underscored in a statement by Behrens et al. (2016, p. 8) who observe the following:

> In perhaps the most comprehensive publication in the field, Cervero (2000) presented potential strategy options for rationalizing and upgrading paratransit services, ranging from operator organization, to regulation, financial support, infrastructure improvement, traffic management and operator training. From a spectrum of policy responses to 'informal transport' ranging from 'acceptance', to 'recognition', 'regulation' and 'prohibition', he argued that 'recognition' policies (in which rules and minimum standards focused largely on safety and insurance are enforced without public sector mediation of levels of supply) and 'regulation' policies (in which market entry and exit is publicly controlled) are most commonly appropriate.

A recent mapping of the paratransit and shared mobility at the global level by Institute of Transportation and Development Policy and Volvo Research and Educational Foundations (2021) reviewed over 100 publications and held consultations with 13 experts. The findings reconfirm the study by Cervero (2000) about the important role that paratransit and shared mobility services play in urban transport in different parts of the world. The study highlights issues related to the impacts of these services, management practices, and policy actions to improve them, which have been covered in several studies. This study also identifies gaps in knowledge, pointing out that while there is significant literature on these services broadly, there are under-studied areas in which additional examination is required to develop a more comprehensive research foundation, for example, employment and economic impacts of these transport services, government capacity requirements for effective management of public transport systems, effective business models for paratransit service, and use of government subsidies to spur service improvements.

A bibliometric analysis of 3295 publications on informal and shared mobility in the Global North and Global South by Behrens et al. (2021) provides details on trends in publications, themes or research fields, research activity, and authorship. The analysis focuses on publications produced in the period 2010–2020. The authors point out that during this period, the focus of research on informal public transport in sub-Saharan Africa was on analysing and mapping route networks, understanding business models, and improving and integrating informal services into 'hybrid' public transport networks (Behrens et al., 2021). The authors also point out the spread of shared mobility in African cities, beginning with the arrival of Uber in 2013 and development of local platforms. The two studies by Institute of Transportation and Development Policy and Volvo Research and Educational Foundations (2021), and Behrens et al. (2021) provide a review of studies in the world, an effort that shows developments in research since the well cited studies by Cervero (2000) and Cervero and Golub (2007).

Commercial Bicycle and Motorcycle Transport Services
In several cities in the world, the bus, commuter train, tram, and bus rapid transit are the main public transport services available. However, in African cities, the commercial bicycle and motorcycle services are a central component of public transport systems. A revealing question was asked and answered by Howe (1993). The question was whether the bicycle was a luxury or a necessity in Africa. The initial narrative on bicycle use was about its perception about being a mode of transport for the poor given its historical use during the colonial period. This initial view of the bicycle has somehow given some way to its evolving view as a necessity given a niche in transport that is not served by the formal transport system as well as the socio-economic reality and physical conditions that prevail in several African countries. Research and experience show that the bicycle plays a vital role in income-generation as well as movement of people and goods in African cities (Porter, 2014). Thus, the demand for a transport service for short-distance and low-volume goods identified in the preceding section has partly been filled by the commercial bicycle transport service.

The precise dates when commercial bicycle services were introduced in African countries are not known but Ehebrecht et al. (2018) observe that bicycle services had already been used in Senegal since the 1930s and had been established in East Africa in the 1960s, where they initially operated in the border region of Uganda and Kenya. Indeed, Uganda is among the African countries in which the bicycle mode was and continues to be extensively used for commercial transport of people and goods. A study conducted in Eastern Uganda in the 1990s found that the ownership and use of bicycles in this region met two household needs (Calvo, 1994). The first need was the personal transport requirements of male household members, and the second was that it was a means of generating income. Income generation was realized through the use of the bicycle as a transport service that people would pay for. The study found that the bicycle was mainly used for trips to markets and to local trading centres to purchase and sell food and households items. In addition, bicycles were also employed to take sick family members to the clinic. Beyond Uganda, the commercial use of the bicycle is now widespread in rural and urban Africa. The historical development and role of this mode of transport has been examined in some countries, showing its importance in filling up a gap in transport services as well as contributing to the extension of the activity space of individuals in pursuit of social and economic goals and further contributing to income-generation and employment of operators and owners (Njenga & Maganya, 1998; Olvera et al., 2012).

As pointed out by Porter (2014), the 1990s saw a dramatic change in rural transport services in rural Africa; namely, the expansion of motorcycle-taxi services, fuelled particularly by the availability of cheap imported Chinese motorcycles. The context and importance of this change is well captured by Porter (2014, p. 27):

"This development has special significance because it has occurred at roughly the same time as the expansion of mobile phone networks and the acquisition of handsets even in poor rural households. For the first time in African rural transport history, many—even very poor—rural dwellers may have the potential to summon transport when they need it."

There are several individual studies showing that the motorcycle taxis are a key feature of the transport and life space in both urban and rural areas in Africa and are known locally as *boda boda* in Uganda and Kenya, *aszemidjan* in Benin and Togo, *bendskin* in Cameroon, *kabu-kabu* in Niger, *okada* in Nigeria, and *alalok* and *oleyia* in Togo. It should also be noted that motorcycle taxis have grown in importance not only in Africa but also in other countries in the world (Kumar & Barrett, 2008; Vasconcellos, 2012). There are several reasons attributed to the growth of this mode of transport in Africa and beyond. The key reasons include having; inefficient transport services or systems in many developing countries; and also, a high level of unemployment that has forced the youths to turn to motorcycle transport as a source of income (Konings, 2006). The main features of the motorcycle that make them attractive for both transport and employment options are their affordability, availability, flexibility, and the ability to move on poor roads (Kumar, 2011). The commercial use of motorcycle transport has grown not only in rural areas as indicated by Porter (2014) but also in urban areas of Africa.

Though substantial research has been conducted on motorcycle taxis in Africa, a synthesis of these studies to provide an overview of this service has been lacking. Luckily, two recent literature reviews that summarize research and experience of motorcycle taxi services in African cities and rural areas have filled this gap in knowledge (Ehebrecht et al., 2018; Olvera et al., 2020). These two reviews provide insightful details of existing studies on the origin, geographical spread, demand, supply, governance, and challenges facing motorcycle taxi services in African cities.

Ehebrecht et al. (2018) reviewed 101 empirical studies and discussed findings from these studies with respect to: supply and demand aspects of motorcycle taxi service; actors, organization and politics; service regulation; and negative externalities. This study traces the emergence of motorcycle taxi services and factors that have influenced their expansion. Ehebrecht et al., (2018, p. 243) determined the approximate date or period when motorcycle-taxis appeared or emerged in selected African countries. They noted the following:

"Before moto-taxis gained momentum, in some places–primarily West and Central African countries–motorcycles had already to some degree been providing one of the public mobility alternatives: in Nigeria, the first appearance of moto-taxis dates back to the 1970s, while in countries such as Niger, Cameroon, Benin and Rwanda, the use of motorcycles for taxi services began in the 1980s; Chad, Kenya, Togo and Uganda followed in the 1990s. Other countries–for example, Angola, Ethiopia, Ghana–have seen rapid growth in these services since the 2000s."

Three examples of insights from the review by Ehebrecht et al. (2018, pp. 245, 250) are as follows:

- Working hours of drivers in samples taken in Douala, Lagos and Kampala amounted to 12 hours per day on average. In Accra, about 75 percent of drivers operated for 11–15 hours per day, while 94 percent of them worked for five to six days a week. In Aba, 94 percent of interviewed drivers were found to work at least six days per week;
- With regard to modal shares of moto-taxis, in Douala, 29 percent of respondents used moto-taxis either solely or in combination with other public transport modes. In Lomé, modal shares stood at almost 65 percent of trips for moto-taxis alone and aggregated to 83 percent when multimodal trips that included moto-taxi use were included. In various areas in Kampala, modal shares were in the range of ca. 20–40 percent, based on data from 2008; and
- Public regulation and formalisation of moto-taxi services in Calabar shifted from self-regulation to state regulation. The starting point for state regulation in this case was the creation of a regulatory authority that was tasked with the registration of all motorcycle drivers. This included a registration-renewal system that obliged all drivers to re-register every 12 months after payment of a registration fee, the distribution of standardised helmets and reflector vests, and the painting of vehicles in a standard colour.

I have reproduced the above three insights to show valuable detailed knowledge contained on the emergent research themes that have been synthesized by Ehebrecht et al. (2018). These insights are useful to researchers and policymakers as they help to determine gaps in knowledge and identify areas for intervention to enhance the quality of motorcycle taxi services, respectively.

Olvera et al. (2020) conducted an internet-based bibliometric analysis of motorcycle taxis and a field study in Lomé, Togo. Based on bibliometric analysis, these authors identify two main centres in the origin and spread of motorcycle taxis. The first is West Africa with Nigeria seeming to have been the first on the scene, supported by reports of motorcycle taxis in Calabar and Yola from the early 1970s, and in Port Harcourt and Kaduna in the first half of the 1980s at the latest. The authors trace the spread of this service to Benin, reaching Porto Novo in 1976 and Cotonou in 1991, Niger and Cameroon in the 1980s, and the rest of West Africa in subsequent years.

The second centre is East Africa on the Uganda–Kenya border. Bicycle taxis, which had been in use in this region from the early 1960s, were transformed into motorcycle taxis. From this border region, motorcycle taxis spread widely in both countries before further spreading to Rwanda and Tanzania. Olvera et al. (2020) identify the following factors as underlying the spread: proximity, landlockedness, type of economy inherited from the colonial period, cheap imports of motorcycles from China and India, and role of international bodies. These factors are similar to those summarized by Ehebrecht et al. (2018, pp. 243–245). The field work that was conducted by Olvera et al. (2020) in Lomé to understand how motorcycle taxis operate in practice identified main features governing the functioning of this service: the ambivalent approach or attitude of the state, the heterogeneous characteristics of the players, and the strong and multifaceted linkages of motorcycle taxis with formal activities.

In many rural and urban areas of Africa, bicycle and motorcycle transport services coexist, complementing each other, but at the same time competing with each other as well as with the informal and formal public transport buses. Alila et al. (2007, p. 301) succinctly summarize how *boda boda* transport service contributes to enhancing accessibility and the functioning of society in Africa:

> "In view of the fact that some of the remote rural areas may be inaccessible to motorised transport, *boda boda* plays an increasingly indispensable linkage role between rural localities and the outside world. Those travelling to and from urban centres are picked up and taken right to their gates/doorstep and/or furnished with vital information regarding their travel route and the transport available. In the rural towns, particularly on designated market days, one can observe a clearly marked division of labour between motorised and non-motorised transport operators and also a distinction between large and small traders and passengers. The merchandise, including maize, cabbages, beans, tomatoes and second-hand clothes, etc, arrive at the market in a pick-up or a lorry hired or owned by a large trader. The small traders then ferry small quantities to their kiosks/stalls using non-motorised transport. The options include handcarts, wheelbarrows, human porters, *boda boda* and boarding a matatu with the merchandise as personal luggage."

Bicycle and motorcycle transport services facilitate not only movement of people and goods in Africa but also contribute to socio-economic change through strengthening links and connections in rural and urban areas in Africa. By connecting places and people, these transport services broaden the action space for individuals who straddle between formal and informal sectors of the economy. Bicycle and motorcycle transport services are part of facilitators of the transactions in the informal–formal economy continuum in Africa (Khayesi et al., 2015).

While bicycle and motorcycle transport services continue to grow in importance not only in urban centres but also in rural areas in Africa, several studies have pointed out that despite an increase in bicycle and motorcycle taxis, formal transport planning has been slow in its response to this growing demand and supply of these services (Alila et al., 2007; Mutiso & Behrens, 2011). Though some efforts are being made to provide infrastructure or attend to the needs of *boda boda* transport service, research generally reveals that in both rural and the urban areas of Africa, there has been inadequate policy guidance to plan for bicycle and motorcycle routes and ensure safety standards are set and followed by motorcycle riders (Mitullah & Opiyo, 2016).

There are also other challenges with this form of transport, including security, safety, working environment for the operators, and cost of operating these transport businesses. There are recent efforts to develop non-motorized transport strategies for cities like Nairobi and Addis Ababa (Addis Ababa City Administration, 2018; Nairobi City County Government, 2015). If these strategies are fully implemented, the infrastructure and services for cycling and walking will be improved in these cities. Inadequacy in planning and governing is not limited to *boda boda* transport service in Africa. It is also observed in the informal economy specifically and the overall economy in general, despite the great potential Africa has with its natural and human resources (Moyo, 2009).

The Rise and Expansion of Bus Rapid Transit Systems
One of the options to address the need for mass public transport services is the promotion of bus rapid transit systems in African cities. The shift towards this mode of public transport is largely associated with external partners and donors. As Klopp et al. (2019, p. 3) observe, 'Often, the mass transit mode promoted is linked to which donor is contributing financing and related consulting'. The first bus rapid transport was opened in Lagos in 2008, with support from the World Bank. Since then, several bus rapid transit systems or projects have been initiated and are at different stages of development. Klopp et al. (2019) provide a review of the bus rapid transit system as a public transport reform in African cities. They observe that the growing urgency around improving and decarbonizing public transport is one of the driving forces leading to financial flows through climate funding towards bus rapid transit in African cities. Another issue that has been raised is whether bus rapid transit systems from South America can simply be transferred to the African context. Table 8.2 presents a summary of some key bus rapid transit projects in African cities.

From the work of Klopp et al. (2019), we draw the following insights:

1. There is very little independent analysis on the success and failures as well as the overall impacts of bus rapid transit in Africa. Thus, there is a knowledge gap with regard to rigorous evaluation and analysis of bus rapid transit projects, their political economy dynamics, and related institutional effects in Africa and elsewhere. Rizzo (2002, 2017) is described by these authors as one of the few political economy critiques of bus rapid transit, which he has characterized as a tool of neoliberalism, a vehicle for banks, construction companies, and private transport service operators to access Africa's private transport market.
2. There is poor integration between bus rapid transport and popular paratransit or mini-bus service because of the focus of the bus transit project to displace these popular transport services. As a result, bus rapid transit

Table 8.2 A summary of some key bus rapid transit projects in African cities

City/Metro area	Start date	BRT character/Stage	Governance	Financing
Lagos	2008 (first)	BRT-Lite 2nd phase started	Ministry at Transport Created LAMATA	World Bank Lagos Urban Transport Project (2003–2008) (2010–2017)
Johannesburg	2009	Full BRT (ITDP silver ranking) 2nd phase (1C)	City of Johannesburg responsible, Created Complex fragmented governance- no single metro transport authority	National Treasury City Support Programme Public Transport Network grants to cities, Global Environmental Facility, Brazilian Development Bank (BNDES) and some local sources
Accra	2016	BRT Stalled or faltering?	GAPTE (Greater Accra Passenger Transport Executive)	Ghana Urban Transport Project (2007–2015) World Bank, AFO (French Development Agent), GEF (Global Environmental Facility)
Dar es Salaam	2017	BRT first phase just launched but facing problems related to capture of operating company by political actors	DART (Dar Rapid Transit)	World Bank African Development Bank...
Addis		BRT project planning in progress	Addis Ababa Road and Transport Bureau (AARTB) consolidated fragmented agencies under one	World Bank Ethiopia: Transport Systems Improvement Project (TRANSIP) (2016–2023) Institutional support French Development Agent 2010, 2014, 2015 (BRT support)
Nairobi	Future	BRT -planned but moving slowly, new political pressures to move forward	NaMATA (just formed but contested)	World Bank African Development Bank...Government looking for other funders

(continued)

Table 8.2 (continued)

City/Metro area	Start date	BRT character/Stage	Governance	Financing
Dakar		Extensive capacity building/formalization process prior to BRT implementation	CETUD (longest existing transport authority in Africa) Capacity support (2000–2008)	World Bank Dakar Bus Rapid Transit Pilot Project (2017–2023) Urban Mobility Improvement Program project (2000–2008) (2010–2015)

Source Klopp et al. (2019, p. 5)

stations and terminals are not aligned with stops, stands, and stations of other modes as has been found in Dar es Salaam.
3. There is little discussion in existing studies about the politics of subsidies and financing of operations and maintenance of bus rapid transit systems. The focus of these studies is on planning, implementation, and the technical performance of bus rapid transit systems that are in operation. It is mainly in South Africa where there is growing discussion about fairness of subsidies and bus rapid transit systems.

An earlier study by Wood (2015) synthesized the experience of planning and developing bus rapid transit systems in South African cities. This study argued that bus rapid transit adoption was gradual, repetitive and at times delayed and not a rapid process. Starting with a published discussion of bus rapid transit in a conference report in 1973, the process witnessed a failed attempt to introduce a bus rapid transit in Cape Town in 2003, introduction of bus rapid transit in Johannesburg in 2009, Cape Town in 2011, and several South African cities in the 2010s. Another study by Agyemang (2015) examined the reasons for the failure of a bus rapid transit pilot in the Greater Accra that operated on a 20-km highway from 2005 to 2007. Reasons for the failure were given as follows; recurring traffic congestion, passengers' inadequate comfort and personal security, resistance from existing public transport operators, lack of legal status for a bus rapid transit system, and limited advertisement for the pilot.

Conclusion

This chapter has presented and discussed results of a synthesis of literature on public transport services with a focus on assessment of theories, research designs, planning approaches, and service provision. The chapter attempted to answer two questions: What are the dominant research designs and theories in research on public transport services in African cities? What does research reveal about the state of planning and provision of public transport services in African cities?

The dominant research designs used in the studies under review included: a temporal approach; tracing the development of a specific issue or several issues over time; and a snapshot-cross sectional approach, examining a specific theme or several topics at a given time. Interviews, focus group discussions, case studies and secondary sources were the dominant methods which were used for data collection. Institutional, demand and supply, business development, behavioural, collaborative, participatory, stakeholder engagement, inclusion theories and models were used to generate concepts and variables for data collection and analysis. What appeared to have had limited attention was the use of empirical investigation to interrogate existing concepts and theories and/or formulate new ones. Moreover, although in-depth description and analysis of the context in which public transport services have grown and developed in African cities were attempted, this effort did not yield much in terms of refining or generating new theories.

This review has demonstrated the existence of extensive research on public services that comprise bus, commuter train, mini-bus or paratransit, motorcycle, and bicycle. Also, several studies point out the development, decline, and inadequacy of the bus and commuter services in African cities, a gap that has been filled over the years by the emergence and spread of the use of minibuses, bicycles, and motorcycles. The bus rapid transit option, however, is a recent entry in the transport services matrix. Nevertheless, the mode is at different stages of adoption and development in African cities. While these modes provide key services to enhance accessibility by urban residents to activities and places, studies point to inadequate planning that would ensure optimal service delivery. Similarly, coordination of a wide range of actors involved in planning and providing public transport services, including state and non-state agencies, remains a challenge.

REFERENCES

Addis Ababa City Administration. (2018). *Addis Ababa non-motorized strategy 2019–2028*. Addis Ababa City Administration.

Aduwo, I. G. (1990). *The role, efficiency and quality of service of the matatu mode of public transport in Nairobi: A geographical analysis*. University of Nairobi.

Agyemang, E. (2015). The bus rapid transit system in the Greater Accra Metropolitan Area, Ghana: Looking back to look forward. *Norwegian Journal of Geography*, 69(1), 28–37.

Alila, P., Khayesi, M., Odhiambo, W., & Pedersen, P. O. (2007). Trade and transport: Business linkages and networks. In D. McCormick, P. Alila & M. Omosa (Eds.), *Business in Kenya: Institutions and interactions* (Chapter 12, pp. 281–309). University of Nairobi Press.

Behrens, R., McCormick, D., & Mfinanga, D. (2016). An introduction to paratransit in Sub-Saharan African cities. In R. Behrens, D. McCormick, & D. Mfinanga (Eds.), *Paratransit in African cities: Operations, regulation and reform* (pp. 1–25). Routledge.

Behrens, R., Newlands, A., Suliaman, T., et al. (2021). *Informal and shared mobility: A bibliometric analysis*. A report commissioned by the Volvo Research and Educational Foundations.

Boateng, F. G. (2020). 'Indiscipline' in context: A political-economic grounding for dangerous driving behaviours among Tro-Tro drivers in Ghana. *Humanities and Social Sciences Communications*, 7, 8. https://doi.org/10.1057/s41599-020-0502-8

Bruun, E., Mistro, R. D., Venter, Y., & Mfinanga, D. (2016). The state of public transport systems in three Sub-Saharan African cities. In R. Behrens, D. McCormick, & D. Mfinanga (Eds.), *Paratransit in African cities: Operations, regulation and reform* (pp. 26–58). Routledge.

Calvo, C. M. (1994) *Case study on intermediate means of transport bicycles and rural women in Uganda*. Sub-Saharan Africa Transport Policy Program (SSATP Working Paper No. 12).

Cervero, R. (2000). *Informal transport in the developing world*. United Nations Centre for Human Settlements.

Cervero, R., & Golub, A. (2007). Informal transport: A global perspective. *Transport Policy, 14*(6), 445–457.

Ehebrecht, D., Heinrichs, D., & Lenz, B. (2018). Motorcycle-taxis in sub-Saharan Africa: Current knowledge, implications for the debate on 'informal' transport and research needs. *Journal of Transport Geography, 69*, 242–256.

Howe, J. (1993, September 6–10) *The bicycle in Africa: Luxury or necessity?* Velocity conference 'The civilised city: responses to new transport priorities', Nottingham, UK.

Institute for Transportation and Development Policy and Volvo Research and Educational Foundations. (2021). *Future of paratransit and shared mobility* (Mapping Report). Institute for Transportation and Development Policy.

Kanyama, A. A., & Cars, G. (2009). *In search of a framework for institutional coordination in the planning for public transportation in sub-Saharan African cities: An analysis based on experiences from Dar es Salaam and Nairobi*. Royal Institute of Technology.

Kapila, S., Manu, M., & Lamba, D. (1981). *The matatu mode of public transportation in metropolitan Nairobi*. Mazingira Institute.

Klopp, J. M., & Cavoli, C. (2019). Mapping minibuses in Maputo and Nairobi: Engaging paratransit in transportation planning in African cities. *Transport Reviews, 39*(5), 657–676.

Klopp, J. M., Harber, J., & Quarshie, M. (2019). *A review of BRT as a public transport reform in African cities* (Governance of Metropolitan Transport Background Paper). VREF Research Synthesis Project.

Khosa, M. M. (1992). Routes, ranks and rebels: Feuding in the taxi revolution. *Journal of Southern African Studies, 18*(1), 232–251.

Khosa, M. M. (1998). "The travail of travelling": Urban transport in South Africa, 1930–1996. *Transport Reviews, 18*(1), 17–33.

Khayesi, M., Nafukho, F. M., & Kemuma, J. (2015). *Informal public transport in practice: Matatu entrepreneurship*. Ashgate Publishing Ltd.

Klopp, J. M., Williams, S., Waiganjo, P., Orwa, D., & White, A. (2015). Leveraging cellphones for wayfinding and journey planning in semi-formal bus systems: Lessons from digital matatus in nairobi. In *Planning support systems and smart cities* (Springer) in conjunction with the conference Computers in Urban Planning and Urban Management April 2015 MIT.

Konings, P. (2006). Solving transportation problems in African cities: Innovative responses by the youth in Doula, Cameroon. *Africa Today, 53*(1), 35–50. http://www.jstor.org/stable/4187755

Kumar, A. (2011). *Understanding the role of motorcycles in African cities: A political economy perspective* (SSATP Discussion Paper No. 13). Sub-Saharan Africa Transport Policy Program (urban transport series).

Kumar, A., & Barrett, F. (2008). *Stuck in traffic: Urban transport in Africa*. World Bank.

McCormick, D., Mitullah, W., Chitere, P., et al. (2016). Matatu business strategies in Nairobi. In R. Behrens, D. McCormick, & D. Mfinanga (Eds.), *Paratransit in African cities: Operations, regulation and reform* (pp. 125–154). Routledge.

Mitullah, W., & Opiyo, R. (2016). Effectiveness of institutional and policy framework for walking and cycling provision in Cape Town, Dar-es-Salaam and Nairobi.

In W. Mitullah, M. Khayesi, & M. Vanderschuren (Eds.), *Non-motorised transport integration into urban transport planning in Africa*. Routledge.

Mkandawire, T. (1995). The three generations of African academics: A note. *Transformation, 28*, 75–83.

Moyo, D. (2009). *Dead aid: Why aid is not working and how there is another way for Africa*. Penguin Books.

Mutiso, W., & Behrens, R. (2011). *Boda Boda bicycle taxis and their role in urban transport systems: Case studies of Kisumu and Nakuru, Kenya*. South Africa Transport Conference 2011.

Mutongi, K. (2006). Thugs or entrepreneurs? Perceptions of matatu operators in Nairobi, 1970 to present. *Africa, 76*(4), 549–568.

Mutongi, K. (2017). *Matatu: A history of popular transportation in Nairobi*. University of Chicago Press.

Nairobi City County Government. (2015). *Non-motorized transport policy*. Nairobi City County Government.

Njenga, P., & Maganya, J. (1998). Bicycles come to western Kenya. *Habitat Debate, 4*(2), 18–19.

Olvera, L. D., Plat, D., Pochet, P., & Maïdadi, S. (2012). Motorbike taxis in the 'transport crisis' of West and Central African cities. *EchoGéo*. Online since 13 July 2012, connection on 15 July 2013. http://echogeo.revues.org/13080; https://doi.org/10.4000/echogeo.13080

Olvera, L. D., Plat, D., & Pochet, P. (2020). Looking for the obvious: Motorcycle taxi services in Sub-Saharan African cities. *Journal of Transport Geography, 88*, 102476.

Pirie, G. (2018). *A sub-Saharan Africa transport research bibliography*. University of Cape Town.

Porter, G. (2014). Transport services and their impact on poverty and growth in rural sub-Saharan Africa: A review of recent research and future research needs. *Transport Reviews: A Transnational Transdisciplinary Journal, 34*(1), 25–45.

Rizzo, M. (2002). Being taken for a rise: Privatisation of the Dar es Salaam transport system 1983–1998. *Journal of Modern African Studies, 40*(1), 133–157.

Rizzo, M. (2017). *Taken for a ride: Grounding neoliberalism, precarious labour, and public transport in an African metropolis*. Oxford University Press.

Schalekamp, H., Golub, A., & Behrens, R. (2016). Approaches to paratransit reform. In R. Behrens, D. McCormick, & D. Mfinanga (Eds.), *Paratransit in African cities: Operations, regulation and reform* (pp. 100–124). Routledge.

Vasconcellos, A. E. (2012). Road safety impacts of the motorcycle in Brazil. *International Journal of Injury Control and Safety Promotion*. https://doi.org/10.1080/17457300.2012.696663

wa Mungai, M. (2013). *Nairobi's matatu men: Portrait of a subculture*. Goethe Institute.

Wood, A. (2015). Multiple temporalities of policy circulation: Gradual, repetitive and delayed processes of BRT adoption in South African cities. *International Journal of Urban and Regional Research*. https://doi.org/10.111/1468-2427.12216:568-580

Xie, Q., & Wagner, A. (2010). *Informal public transport: Recommended reading and links*. GTZ & Ministry of Economic Cooperation.

CHAPTER 9

Water Management

Gladys Moraa Marie Nyachieo and Martin M. Magu

INTRODUCTION

Water sustains life. Urban water management is key in ensuring the existence of sustainable towns, which are functional, efficient and productive. The continent of Africa is urbanizing rapidly and the demand for water in towns and cities is increasing. However, urban water management challenges have contributed to a crisis in demand and supply. The chapter assesses the study types, theories and empirical findings on water management in African cities. The chapter attempts to answer the following questions: What research designs are utilized in studies on urban water planning? What theories inform urban water management studies? What are the findings of empirical studies on water management?

METHOD

The first task was to come up with key words based on the study title 'Urban Water Planning in Africa'. The study made use of major electronic databases like ScienceDirect, JSTOR, ProQuest, ISI Web of Knowledge,

---

G. M. M. Nyachieo (✉) · M. M. Magu
Faculty of Social Science & Technology, Multimedia University of Kenya, Nairobi, Kenya
e-mail: gnyachieo@mmu.ac.ke

EBSCO, PubMed and Google Scholar among others to assemble all the relevant works in the area of urban water management and planning in Africa.

The study looked at studies and works from pre-colonial times in Africa to the present. As inclusion criteria, the study only focused on studies done in Africa on urban water. Therefore, relevant studies on water planning done outside Africa were not included. After assembling all the available evidence, using the key words generated from the chapter title, the authors did a preliminary reading of abstracts to confirm whether the selected evidence was relevant and whether it resonated with the inclusion criteria. The search identified 40 abstracts that were relevant to the theme of this chapter. These 40 abstracts were further examined and 21 found to be most appropriate to the aim of the chapter (Table 9.1).

Results and Discussion

Research Designs

The current study reveals that there are a number of designs that are used in urban water studies. The study highlighted the most commonly used designs.

A total of six studies are based on review of literature: Bahri and Vairavamoorthy (2016), Dos Santos et al. (2017), Kithiia and Majambo (2020), Monstadt and Schramm (2017), Adams et al. (2019), and McGarry et al. (2008). Case studies were the second most common designs with five studies based on them; Morinville and Harris (2014), Peloso and Morinville (2014), Nastar et al. (2019), Kobel and Del Mistro (2012), Sjömander-Magnusson and Van der Merwe (2005).

One study (Jacobsen et al., 2012) utilized comparative analysis; Household survey was conducted by Adams et al. (2019). Mixed methods as a research design were utilized in four studies: Mixed methods used by Bédécarrats et al. (2019); a descriptive, qualitative design utilized by Addo (2010), Itama et al. (2006) used experiment design; and a cross-sectional survey design was utilized by Dos Santos and Wayack-Pambe (2015).

Theories

There are a number of approaches, models or theories used in urban water planning and management. These models are utilized for different situations to help solve water management and planning problems as they explain the operations around water management and planning. The study will highlight some of the dominant approaches or models it identified as important. In addition, the current study will highlight a few theories that have been used in understanding urban water management in Africa.

Table 9.1 Summary of findings of studies reviewed

Author(s)	Focus	Geographical location	Study Design	Theories	Results
Jacobsen et al. (2012)	Water management	31 cities in sub-Saharan Africa with three case studies; Nairobi (Kenya), Mbale and Arua (Uganda)	Comparative analysis	Integrated Urban Water Management (IUWM)	Of the 31 cities in the study, in-depth investigations were conducted in three case studies; Nairobi (Kenya), Mbale and Arua (Uganda) Each urban of the identified urban area had different challenges; Nairobi was dealing with a gap between supply and demand and modelling the urban water cycle was a possible solution to reduce the cost; Mbale had limited institutional and financial capacities and rapid urbanization posed a problem; Arua's water supply had sustainability challenges due to unauthorized abstraction and pollution of water from the Enyua River
Bahri and Vairavamoorthy (2016)	Change management in implementing Integrated Urban Water Management	Three African cities of Mahé, Praslin, La Digue (Seychelles), Marondera (Zimbabwe), and Kinshasa (Democratic Republic of Congo)	Literature review	African Water Facility (AWF)	Effective involvement of a broad range of stakeholders enhances comprehensive IUWM plan. In addition, strong leadership and commitment from the national government, city policymakers and elected officials is vital in driving the IUWM process. Community leaders as well as sector professionals can play a key role in supporting IUWM efforts for scaling up consequently, there is need for a holistic and coordinated approach to city development. Technical assistance and capacity building is also crucial as it helps build capacity in IUWM
Dos Santos et al. (2017)	Urban water supply and access	Sub-Saharan Africa	Systematic Review	Not indicated	The estimated odds ratios from the multivariate analysis indicate that factors related to water access had a significant effect on the probability that the primary person responsible for fetching water was a woman over 16 years of age. This is particularly the case for the main source of drinking water. Other factors are type of container used for fetching water, time needed to access the water source, waiting time at the water source

(continued)

Table 9.1 (continued)

Author(s)	Focus	Geographical location	Study Design	Theories	Results
Kithiia and Majambo (2020)	Colonial and post-colonial status of water service provision	Mombasa, Kenya	Literature review and stakeholder analysis	Historical approach	Water and sanitation challenges trace back to pre-independence times in Mombasa. The colonial government designed and operated water infrastructure that secluded some neighbourhoods; these issues have not been addressed to date
Adams (2018)	Inequalities	Malawi	Household surveys	Community self-help and partnership models	Partnership-based models involving communities possess a huge possibility to fill water supply gaps in urban areas. This is more so for underserved areas and informal settlements where state-based public utilities, market-based solutions and public–private partnerships have not been able to improve access
Dagdeviren and Robertson (2011)	Changes in perspectives on public policy	Sub-Saharan Africa, e.g., Ghana, Kenya, Cameroon, Tanzania, Malawi, Nigeria, Sierra Leone	Meta synthesis	Not indicated	Piped water connected to cities' main network has the lowest tariffs per unit of water and the quality of water sourced by private providers from groundwater is highly dependent on the quality of sanitation services within the locale
In addition, the quality of access to water with small providers and community-managed schemes is most of the time inferior to the access from the public network
Moreover, where regulation is absent, which is often typical, prices may be subject to collusion between private providers, especially where either money has already been spent and cannot be recovered or a restricted number of licenses restrict market entry

Author(s)	Focus	Geographical location	Study Design	Theories	Results
Monstadt and Schramm (2017)	Technological and urban models in infrastructure planning	Dar es Salaam, Tanzania	Review of literature	Urban infrastructure planning models	The study found that since the colonial period, the circulating ideals of a networked city have considerably shaped the formal institutions, policies and aspirations of local administrator, international organizations utility companies and residents Mixed arrangements influenced by water planning and management shape urban environments of Dar es Salaam and also manifest unequal access to water
Morinville and Harris (2014)	Urban water governance and involvement	Accra (Ghana) and Cape Town (South Africa)	Case study, Empirical, Participatory strategies used	Participatory urban water governance	Grassroots participation may also be affected because of external influence Local Water Boards may amplify the affordability challenges. They may make it difficult to achieve higher connectivity levels because of complex bureaucracy and will increase the burden of meeting the cost to the poor and vulnerable by making them depend entirely on voluntary labour
Peloso and Morinville (2014)	Water access	Ashaiman in Accra, Ghana	A case study approach	Patchwork system of basic services	Informal water services supplement or 'patch up' gaps left by the sporadic water flow of the official service provider Basic water access is constructed through an assemblage of coping strategies and infrastructures
Nastar et al. (2019)	Politics of participation & water management Politics of access to water	Kampala, Uganda	Case study	Participatory approach	Barriers to water access in Kampala in Uganda will require that land title be changed from private ownership to communal ownership before water or sanitation facilities are installed to improve urban liveability

(continued)

Table 9.1 (continued)

Author(s)	Focus	Geographical location	Study Design	Theories	Results
Bédécarrats et al. (2019)	Decentralization of water services	Kinshasa	Mixed methods	Decentralized Water Systems (DWS)	The networks of public water utility are not spread in the whole land and city. In places where they exist, there is unreliable distribution of water supply leading to water problems. The demands for drinking water are met by a mosaic of operators
Addo (2010)	Institutional analysis of urban water supply	Accra, Ghana	A descriptive, qualitative design	Sector Wide Approach (SWAP)	The involved actors are generally disinterested in the urban water supply process. Others in the city are not involved in any process at all. In addition, there is no political will in making sure that initiated projects by previous governments continue uninterrupted as funds meant for the water sector are diverted to other activities and industries
Adams et al. (2019)	Water supply-policies and institutional arrangements	Sub-Saharan Africa Region, e.g., Zimbabwe, Côte d'Ivoire, Niger, Mozambique, Senegal and South Africa	Synthesizes the literature	Community self-help and partnership models	Improving urban water supply in sub-Saharan Africa requires innovative governance and institutional arrangements that blend the strengths of public, private and community-based water supply models There is no single institutional approach or policy to urban water supply

Author(s)	Focus	Geographical location	Study Design	Theories	Results
Banerjee et al. (2008)	Water supply	24 Sub-Saharan Africa countries; Benin, Cape Verde, Cameroon, Chad, Democratic Republic of Congo, Ethiopia, Kenya, Madagascar, Malawi, Mozambique, Burkina Faso, Namibia, Niger, Mali, Nigeria, Rwanda, Ghana, Senegal, Sudan, Tanzania, Côte d'Ivoire, Uganda, Zambia and South Africa	Conference paper	Not indicated	Sub-Saharan Africa lags behind other regions in terms of access to improved water sources with only 56 percent of the population enjoying access to safe water
Kobel and Del Mistro (2012)	Evaluation of water services	Kampala, Uganda	Case study	Multinomial choice model	As much as Kampala residents are sensitive to the cost of improving services in informal settlements, their decision will be influenced by four factors; 1. the proposed level of service to be implemented, 2. the expected reduction in diarrhoea infection, 3. the location of the informal settlement to be improved and 4. the means through which their contribution will be collected

(continued)

Table 9.1 (continued)

Author(s)	Focus	Geographical location	Study Design	Theories	Results
Itama et al. (2006)	Supplementary water supply	Ibadan, Nigeria	Experiment	Not indicated	The findings of this study reveal that 13 out of the 16 springs serve fundamentally as sources of drinking water in Ibadan, Nigeria. The amount of water from the springs was enough to meet the community needs. In addition, the physic-chemical quality met the recommended standards The PH values and temperature values ranged between 6.25–6.89 and 6.34–6.94, and 26.5–26.6 and 26.43–26.6 during the rainy and dry seasons, respectively. However, the average dissolved solids varied depending on the types of soil and the terrain
Sjömander-Magnusson and Van der Merwe (2005)	Policy design and urban water management	Windhoek, Namibia	Case study	Water Demand Management strategy (WDM)	A modified water management is required to incorporate the whole city along with the socio-economic changes in composition, income levels as well as the new water technology, and the extended water infrastructure There is also need to allocate funds continuously to allow the successful implementation of certain WDM measures There should also be a degree of flexibility among water users for successful strategic implementation

Author(s)	Focus	Geographical location	Study Design	Theories	Results
Dos Santos et al. (2015)	Water access and management	Three informal settlements of Ouagadougou (Polesgo, Nonghin and Nioko)	A Cross-Sectional Study	Not indicated	Even with a 91% access to improved water source, the prevalence of diarrhoea in children was high The main source of water was piped water from a standpipe located in a nearby formal neighbourhood (56%) or from their own private connection (4%) Heterogeneity in terms of sources of water lacks among the three neighbourhoods under study: Polesgo, Nonghin and Nioko
Bahri (2012)	Water partnerships	Sub-Saharan Africa Seychelles, Zimbabwe and Democratic Republic of Congo	Technical report	Integrated Urban Water Management (IUWM)	Integrated urban water management (IUWM) presents a better approach as compared to the current system In the current system, water and wastewater, and storm water as well as sanitation are managed by different entities All of the entities are also separated from economic development and land-use planning IUWM proposes that all the four entities align with urban development and basin management for successful attainment of sustainable economic, social and environmental goals
McGarry et al. (2008)	Water policy & governance	Africa cities, e.g., Algeria, Burundi, Djibouti, Egypt, Cape Verde, Kenya, Libya, Malawi, Rwanda, Tunisia, Morocco, South Africa and Somalia	Literature review in-country workshops	Not indicated	The sector's underlying policies, legislation and regulations provide the foundation for overall water governance. Key roles sector institutions and organizations need to fulfil in developing and carrying out the underlying legislation, policies and regulations that include; 1. strategic policy-making, 2. planning for water and related sectors, 3. conflict resolution and arbitration and 4. the regulation and monitoring of water users and service providers
Carden et al. (2009)	Water management	Cape Town, South Africa	Conference paper	Sustainability Index for Integrated Urban Water Management (SIUWM)	The research team did not reach a consensus on the merits of reporting a simple composite index versus the five components, or the twenty indicator scores in the study It was proposed that differences in indicator selection, composition and methods of aggregation be utilized to determine whether they have an effect on the overall index scores

Source Author compilation (2021)

Integrated Urban Water Management (IUWM)

Integrated urban planning is a modern planning approach closely connected with the complex nature of cities and the necessity of creating sustainable and resilient settlements. The Integrated Urban Water Management (IUWM) demands for the arrangement of urban development and basin management to achieve sustainable economic, social and environmental goals (Bahri, 2012). Integrated urban concepts are complex and must correspond with the local situation.

The IUWM approach has been analysed from various points of view with the focus being on its benefits and principles (Jacobsen et al., 2012). It has provided a platform for understanding how sources of water, sanitation, water supply, storm water and wastewater as well as solid water interact with one another.

The IUWM approach calls for the alignment of the basin management as well as urban development to achieve sustainable environmental, social and economic goals. It integrates water supply, wastewater, storm water and sanitation management with economic development and land-use planning (Bahri, 2012). It also assimilates water planning sector with other sectors in urban areas such as transport, energy, housing and land to avoid duplication and fragmentation in policy and decision-making (Jensen & Nair, 2019).

IUWM creates an environment where cross-sector relationships are strengthened, a common working culture is advanced, and collective benefits and goals are articulated. This means that differences in power and resources are easily negotiated. The model includes marginalized communities when dealing with urban informal sector challenges. Among other issues, IUWM principles include: protecting, conserving and exploiting water resources at their source; integrating water storage; treatment; recycling; distribution; and disposal. The principles also account for non-urban users among others (Wang et al., 2018). IUWM is housed within the broader framework of integrated water resources management (IWRM). In this study, a number of African cities have utilized this approach in water management and planning. They include Jacobsen et al. (2012), Bahri and Vairavamoorthy (2016) and Bahri (2012).

The African Water Facility Approach

The African Water Facility (AWF) strategic focus is on supporting Project Preparation, Water Governance and Water Knowledge projects designed to catalyse the development of the African water sector. Along with its grants, the AWF also provides technical expertise and knowledge to support project grantees all the way to project completion. The AWF approach aims at making sure that African countries are assisted in mobilizing and applying resources of water and sanitation sector to help in successfully implementing the Africa Water Vision 2025 (United Nations, 2007).

The approach focuses on strengthening water governance, meeting water needs, strengthening the financial base of African countries and improving water knowledge through increasing informed decision-making capacity in planning and managing water as well as in sanitation resources (Bahri, 2012). This approach addresses the growing challenges of urban water management. It also examines the entire water cycle and reconsiders how waste water and water can be reused and used, respectively.

The study by Bahri and Vairavamoorthy (2016) on water management utilized the AWF approach within the IUWM model as seen in the current study. The AWF approach is used to implement innovative solutions based on integrated urban water management (IUWM) in three African cities in Seychelles, the Democratic Republic of Congo and Zimbabwe. It describes the African Water Facility's experience in applying the approach to three cities. The study reports that although IUWM approaches have been extensively reported in the literature, their application has been limited.

Sustainability Index for Integrated Urban Water Management (SIUWM)

The Sustainability Index for Integrated Urban Water Management (SIUWM) is an approach that is used as an advocacy and management tool at both the national and local government level. This tool is employed in assessing and determining whether sustainability goals have been achieved. It is also used to measure the environmental state by focusing on variables and using a specific criterion to monitor relative changes (Carden et al., 2007). SIUWM focuses on institutional and social indicators of sustainability rather than doing so entirely on technology. It is designed using common Environmental Sustainability Index (ESI) aspects such as socio-cultural fairness and equitable distribution of resources; economically sound principles; environmental protection and preservation; international stewardship and political support; and technical capacity of the institution.

SIUWM can provide a more detailed analysis, which may be used to establish goals and inform strategic processes to influence support for improved water services. The different aspects of urban water management can be used to produce a greater awareness of the underlying issues by key decision makers thereby leading to appropriate action (Carden et al., 2009). In the current study, the model has been utilized by Carden et al. (2009) in a study in Cape Town, South Africa in which they hypothesized that the potential for long-term sustainability in urban water systems can be established through the application of a five component sustainability index.

Community Self-Help and Partnership Models

Community public partnerships are typically a partnership between a community or an elected body within a community and a public or state-owned water utility (Adams et al., 2019). Two studies in the current study utilize this approach. One is specific to a settlement in Lilongwe-Malawi (Adams, 2018) while the other represents the general areas of sub-Saharan Africa (Adams et al., 2019). These studies demonstrate that improving urban water supply requires innovative governance and institutional arrangements that combine the strengths of public, private and community-based water supply models.

The Community Self-Help and Partnership arrangements allow communities to form their own institutions for water delivery without formal connections or partnerships with utility operators as well as municipal governments. Community self-help initiatives tend to be smaller in scope than formal utility. In addition, they are likely to work in small towns (Bayliss & Adam, 2012).

Participatory Approaches

Participatory approaches in water management generally refer to processes that actively involve water managers and government officials as well as other interested parties. In the current study, studies that adopted participatory approaches are Morinville and Harris (2014) in Accra-Ghana and Cape Town, South Africa; and Nastar et al. (2019) in Kampala, Uganda. Participatory approaches show the importance of broadening participation among community members in order to make collective claims and pursue a common goal on water management in the urban area. The studies indicate the need to be proactive in long-term urban water governance.

Sector Wide Approach (SWAP)

The sector-wide approach (SWAP) supports a country-led programme to build the sector in a synchronized manner. In SWAP, funding for the sector, which comes from both government and donor is pooled to support a single sector policy and a sector expenditure programme. A sector-wide approach (SWAP) purposes for more efficient use of resources from national budgets, user contributions and development partners. This maximizes the overall investment in the water, for sustainable services for all. In SWAP, funding for the sector that is from both the government and donor, is pooled to support a single sector policy and a sector expenditure programme thereby supporting governments to lead their own development in a coordinated manner (Verhoeven, 2014).

In this study, SWAP is utilized by Addo (2010) in Accra, Ghana where the study results indicated that the involved actors were generally disinterested in urban water supply process. Some were not involved at all in any process. In addition, lack of political led to lack of support for the already initiated projects. There is therefore a need to adopt and implement a sector-wide approach (SWAP) to bring all stakeholders in the water sector on board to discuss water-related issues.

Empirical Findings

There are key themes or aspects that emerge from the studies examined. This section highlights these themes.

Water planning and management challenges in urban Africa can be attributed to some factors that include: colonial policies (Hungerford & Smiley, 2016); policy design (Dagdeviren & Robertson, 2011; Magnusson & van der Merwe, 2005; Sjömander-Magnusson & Van der Merwe, 2005); governance (Johannessen et al., 2019; Morinville & Harris, 2014); and planning and management (Brikké & Vairavamoorthy, 2016; Jacobsen et al., 2012) among others. All these issues influence urban water planning, and ultimately also influences water provision and access.

Water access in cities in sub-Saharan Africa is seen as relatively good when compared to water access in rural areas (Dos Santos et al., 2017). In many cities, most of the un-served are the urban poor population living in informal settlements. For example, countries like Senegal, Gabon, Uganda and South Africa are considerably increasing the number of new water connections as well as expanding delivery in urban areas (Dovi, 2007).

In most informal settlement in urban areas, people use alternative strategies for accessing water making these commonplace among the urban poor because of the absence of affordable and reliable state services. Many people meet their basic daily needs through a patchwork system of informal activities and networks (Peloso, 2014).

Urban Water Access

Africa's urban population is projected to double by 2030. This will exacerbate difficulties currently faced by African cities when it comes to the provision of sustainable water services (Jacobsen et al., 2012). Cities struggle to eradicate the backlog of water sanitation services. They are unable to meet increasing demand of water and are also unable to comply fully with wastewater standards. They depend entirely on power supply, and face challenges managing outdated water supply infrastructure in meeting developmental needs (Carden et al., 2009).

According to a study conducted by Peloso and Morinville (2014) in Ghana, there are no reliable and affordable state services to the urban poor. Those who are able to meet their basic daily needs do so through a patchwork system of informal networks and activities. The study respondents drew water from a variety of sources; for instance, sachet, buckets, rainwater and vendors as well as neighbours among others. They also face uncertainties in accessing water as the Ghana Water Company Limited (GWCL) who have been charged with the provision, distribution and management of urban water can only meet about 60 percent of the total water.

Statistics show that in sub-Saharan Africa, 42 percent of people are without basic water supply (WHO, 2017). In addition, Africa is urbanizing rapidly and its urban population is expected to increase from 345 million in 2014 to 1.3 billion people by 2050 (UN, 2014). Literature on public utilities in urban areas in developing countries demonstrate that only a proportion of urban population receive services while the rest are left to depend on alternative sources (Gulyani et al., 2005). The urban poor are inadequately served by the formal sector and are forced to make their own arrangements (which are inadequate) to meet basic survival needs (Carden et al., 2009).

A study conducted by Duflo et al., (2012) in Asia and Africa examined the coordination between governments and private sector in circumstances that governments opt for private sector management of urban services. It found that urban public utilities only serve a small fraction of the population. Therefore, majority of the people are underserved since many private companies and governments have failed to provide access services, especially to the poor.

Urban Sprawl and Access to Water

Governments as well as private companies have failed to provide access services in urban areas. They have also failed to address issues that undermine individual access to many services including water. Urban sprawl compounds the problem of urban water planning and management. Some studies observe that providers of water services cannot cope with rapid sprawl of the peri-urban interface, urban densification in poorest areas, and increasing population because of poor economic and planning capacities (Allen et al., 2006; Dos Santos et al., 2017; Furlong & Kooy, 2017; Jaglin, 2015). Other scholars have maintained that service fragmentation results in spatial, environmental and economic injustice in the poor neighbourhood thus increasing the cost gap of water supply and environmental degradation in highly inhabited places (Andreasen & Møller-Jensen, 2016; De & Nag, 2016; Domènech et al., 2013).

Water access is one of the key components of Sustainable Development Goals. However, Adams et al., (2019) note that population growth complicates access to water equation in sub-Saharan Africa. Dos Santos et al., (2017) project sub-Saharan population to triple by 2050. A study conducted by Wright et al., (2004) on the Global South found that most of the urban poor depend on water sources outside their premises that were often contaminated during transportation. The extent of contamination varied considerably between settings, but was proportionately greater where faecal and total coliform counts in source water were low. The study concluded that policies that aim at improving water quality through source improvements may be compromised by post-collection contamination. The study suggested that safer household water storage and treatment was necessary to prevent contamination, in addition to point-of-use water quality monitoring.

Kjellén and McGranahan (2006) and Adams et al., (2019) argue that the water available is sourced from small-scale vendors, tanker-truck services, sachet water, boreholes and public standpoints. It is not just costly and unsafe, but also used by many households and is insufficient (Dos Santos et al., 2015; Majuru et al., 2016; Price et al., 2019). Even in circumstances where there are improved water sources, some studies conducted in Africa, Latin America and Asia have established that they require long queuing times or run intermittently thus forcing consumers to supplement the water with unsafe alternatives (Dagdeviren & Robertson, 2011; Raina et al., 2019; Wutich et al., 2016). Brikké and Vairavamoorthy (2016) observe that climate change and urbanization will make it difficult for Africa to efficiently manage water sources. However, some studies have suggested that co-production and decentralization as well as flexibility may just be the solution to water accessibility (Domènech et al., 2013; Dos Santos et al., 2017; Furlong & Kooy, 2017).

Rapid Urbanization, Water Supply and Access

Urbanization process is associated with environmental, social and economic aspects. According to United Nations (2017, 2019), urbanization is linked to enhanced opportunities for political and cultural participation, greater access to economic and social services, better health conditions and higher levels of education and literacy. However, rapid and unplanned urbanization threatens suitable development thus resulting in environmental degradation, pollution and rapid sprawl. It also brings about unsustainable patterns of consumption (water, food and shelter) and production. According to Makinde (2012), rapid urbanization, high consumption rate and high population density in cities result in among other things, poor access to freshwater supply.

The global urban population is projected to reach 7.3 billion people by 2050 (UNDESA, 2015). The demand of water in the cities will grow from 15 percent to 20 percent to 30 percent in terms of global consumption. At the same time, the use of freshwater resources will remain unchanged. According to WWAP (United Nations World Water Assessment Programme) (2017), water infrastructure and resources are already experiencing pressure from the unprecedented concentration of demand. It has made it difficult to meet the ambitious goal of universal access to safe drinking water as well as decent sanitation for all people. Studies have demonstrated that cities are the leading source of contamination of freshwater resources (Nogueira et al., 2019).

Literature indicates that there are issues emanating from rapid urbanization such as pollution, environmental protection, housing for the poor, solid waste disposal, rising crime rates and urban poverty. Bahri (2012), while focusing on sub-Saharan Africa, found that decoupling water supplies development from the management of waste exerts unnecessary pressure on water resources thereby increasing challenges to the ecosystem and undermining reliability of water supplies. The study also found that integrated urban water management (IUWM) presents a better approach to water management. The study concluded that IUWM had iterative and adaptive process and adopting it would reduce the number of households without access to sanitation and water.

Water Demand

Household water demand entails aspects such as accessibility, availability, usage and quality. According to Osei et al., (2019), environmental factors resulting from hydrological changes affect availability of water. Timely availability, reliability and easy availability of fresh and safe water to meet basic human needs are essential to meeting not just water demand but also security (Koutiva & Makropoulos, 2016). The issue of being timely, easily available and reliable has to do with planning and management. Developing countries face serious challenges when it comes to managing high water demand because of increasing impacts of climate change on freshwater supply, urbanization and industrialization. Inman and Jeffrey (2006) note that urban water scarcity challenges may be addressed through demand-side or supply-side solutions; new sources of supply should be developed in conjunction with conventional approaches.

The United Nations Water Development Report projects that over 6 billion people will experience scarcity of water by 2050 because of increased demand for water that is driven by economic growth and dramatic population increase (Boretti & Rosa, 2019). But Zubaidi et al., (2020) note that these figures are underestimated since the scarcity of clean water may be worse by 2050 as the effects of its drivers are underrated. These drivers include needs, accessibility and unequal growth. The greater proportion of evidence on water demand management (WDM) is from the western world and entails fundamentally the measurement of income and price elasticity (Nauges & Whittington, 2010). However, most of these elasticity studies are not relevant to the developing countries since most developing countries deal with more basic problems such as reliability and affordability of water supply, clean water, reduced tax on water supply and metering of taps. These aspects facilitate the measuring of elasticity.

There is also little evidence on how developing countries manage urban water demand despite their fundamental challenges resulting from rapid economic growth and rapid urbanization (Butler & Memon, 2005). However, some studies have opined that performance of water utilities in developing countries is compared to coverage of water supply, availability of water, tariff average, public taps and metered connections as well as staff per 1000 connections and the money used on the management of water supply (Araral & Wang, 2013).

Conclusion

Urban water planning and management is complex. Many factors influence and are influenced by urban planning and management. These include policy designs and frameworks, governance, colonial policies and history and politics of stakeholder participation, among others. The current study has highlighted a number of approaches or theories/models that have been used by various scholars in urban water planning. Some of the approaches include; Integrated Urban Water Management (IUWM), The African Water Facility Approach, Sustainability Index for Integrated Urban Water Management (SIUWM), Community Self-Help and Partnership Models Participatory Approaches and Sector Wide Approach (SWAP). The findings emerging from these studies indicate that there is no single approach or model that can help in solving the problems of water planning in urban areas. However, integrated models would work best in solving urban water management and planning challenges in Africa.

Most literature indicate that the urban poor in informal settlements are more affected when it comes to water access and availability and have had to use other alternatives, mostly informal and patchwork system of basic services, to meet their demand for water. This has made water even more expensive especially given the on-going during the Covid-19 pandemic hygiene requirements that demand frequent hand washing and higher hygiene standards. In view of the rapid urban sprawl and increasing urbanization as well as the degradation of water towers in Kenya, water resources will be continuously scarce. This will present significant challenges in the planning, management and provisions of urban water services. There is need for more innovative ways of dealing with water planning and provision in African urban cities and towns.

References

Adams, E. A. (2018). Thirsty slums in African cities: Household water insecurity in urban informal settlements of Lilongwe, Malawi. *International Journal of Water Resources Development, 34*(6), 869-887. https://doi.org/10.1080/07900627.2017.1322941

Adams, E. A., Sambu, D., &, Smiley, S. L. (2019). Urban water supply in Sub-Saharan Africa: Historical and emerging policies and institutional arrangements. *International Journal of Water Resources Development, 35*(2), 240–263.

Addo, L. Y. (2010). *Institutional analysis of urban water supply in Ghana: The case of Accra Metropolitan assembly.* Aalborg.

Andreasen, M. H., & Møller-Jensen, L. (2016). Beyond the networks: Self-help services and post-settlement network extensions in the periphery of Dar es Salaam. *Habitat International, 53,* 39–47.

Allen, A., Dávila, J. D., & Hofmann, P. (2006). The peri-urban water poor: Citizens or consumers? *Environment and Urbanization, 18*(2), 333–351. https://doi.org/10.1177/0956247806069608

Araral, E., & Wang, Y. (2013). Water demand management: Review of literature and comparison in South-East Asia. *International Journal of Water Resources Development, 29*(3), 434–450.

Bahri, A. (2012). Integrated urban water management. *TEC Background Papers, 16*, 1–89.

Bahri, F. B., & Vairavamoorthy, K. (2016). Managing change to implement integrated urban water management in African cities. *ScienceDirect Aquatic Procedia 6*, 3–14, ISSN 2214-241X. https://doi.org/10.1016/j.aqpro.2016.06.002, https://www.sciencedirect.com/science/article/pii/S2214241X16300025

Banerjee, S., Skilling, H., Foster, V., Briceño-Garmendia, C., Morella, E., & Chfadi, T. (2008). *Africa-Ebbing water, surging deficits: Urban water supply in sub-Saharan Africa.* https://www.pseau.org/outils/ouvrages/aicd_ebbing_water_surging_defi cits_urban_water_supply_in_sub_saharan_africa_cross_country_annex_2008.pdf

Bayliss, K., & Adam, A. H. (2012). Where have all the alternatives gone? The shrinking of African water policy options. In D. McDonald & G. Ruiters (Eds.), *Alternatives to privation: Public options for essential services in the global south* (pp. 319–352). Routledge.

Bédécarrats, F., Lafuente-Sampietro, O., Leménager, M., & Sowa, D. L. (2019). Building commons to cope with chaotic urbanization? Performance and sustainability of decentralized water services in the outskirts of Kinshasa. *Journal of Hydrology, 573*, 1096–1108.

Boretti, A., & Rosa, L. (2019). Reassessing the projections of the world water development report. *NPJ Clean Water, 2*(1), 1–6.

Brikké, F., & Vairavamoorthy, K. (2016). Managing change to implement integrated urban water management in African cities. *Aquatic Procedia, 6*, 3–14.

Butler, D., & Memon, F. A. (Eds.) (2005). *Water demand management.* Iwa Publishing.

Carden, K., Armitage, N., Winter, K., Sichone, O., Rivett, U., & Kahonde, J. (2007). The use and disposal of greywater in the non-sewered areas of South Africa: Part 1–Quantifying the greywater generated and assessing its quality. *Water SA, 33*(4).

Carden, K., Winter, K., & Armitage, N. (2009). Sustainable urban water management in Cape Town, South Africa: Is it a pipe dream?. In Water, sanitation and hygiene-Sustainable development and multisectoral approaches: Proceedings of the 34th WEDC International Conference, Addis Ababa, Ethiopia, 2009. (pp. 18–22). cc WEDC, Loughborough University.

Dagdeviren, H., & Robertson, S. A. (2011). Access to water in the slums of sub-Saharan Africa. *Development Policy Review, 29*(4), 485–505.

De, I., & Nag, T. (2016). Dangers of decentralisation in urban slums: A comparative study of water supply and drainage service delivery in Kolkata, India. *Development Policy Review, 34*(2), 253–276.

Domènech, L., March, H., & Saurí, D. (2013). Degrowth initiatives in the urban water sector? A social multi-criteria evaluation of non-conventional water alternatives in Metropolitan Barcelona. *Journal of Cleaner Production, 38*, 44–55.

Dos Santos, S., Adams, E. A., Neville, G., Wada, Y., De Sherbinin, A., Bernhardt, E. M., & Adamo, S. B. (2017). Urban growth and water access in sub-Saharan Africa: Progress, challenges, and emerging research directions. *Science of the Total Environment, 607*, 497–508.

Dos Santos, S., Ouédraogo, F. D. C., & Soura, A. B. (2015). Water-related factors and childhood diarrhoea in African informal settlements. A cross-sectional study in Ouagadougou (Burkina Faso). *Journal of Water and Health, 13*(2), 562–574.

Dos Santos, S., & Wayack-Pambe, M. (2015). *The burden of fetching water for women: A cross-sectional study in informal settlements of the Ouagadougou-Health and Demographic Surveillance System (Burkina Faso).* https://paa2015.princeton.edu/papers/152275

Dovi, E. (2007). *Bringing water to Africa's poor.* Africa Renewal. https://www.un.org/africarenewal/magazine/october-2007/bringing-water-africa%E2%80%99s-poor

Duflo, E., Galiani, S., & Mobarak, M. (2012). *Improving access to urban services for the poor.* Abdul Latif Jameel Poverty Action Lab Report.

Furlong, K., & Kooy, M. (2017). Worlding water supply: Thinking beyond the network in Jakarta. *International Journal of Urban and Regional Research, 41*(6), 888–903.

Gulyani, S., Talukdar, D., & Mukami Kariuki, R. (2005). Universal (non) service? Water markets, household demand and the poor in urban Kenya. *Urban Studies, 42*(8), 1247–1274.

Hungerford, H., & Smiley, S. L. (2016). Comparing colonial water provision in British and French Africa. *Journal of Historical Geography, 52*, 74–83.

Inman, D., & Jeffrey, P. (2006). A review of residential water conservation tool performance and influences on implementation effectiveness. *Urban Water Journal, 3*(3), 127–143.

Itama, E., Olaseha, I. O., & Sridhar, M. K. C. (2006). Springs as supplementary potable water supplies for inner city populations: A study from Ibadan, Nigeria. *Urban Water Journal, 3*(4), 215–223.

JacJaglin, S. (2015). Is the network challenged by the pragmatic turn in African cities? Beyond the Networked City. *Infrastructure reconfigurations and urban change in the north and south.* Abingdon: Routledge, 182–203.

Jacobsen, M., Webster, M., & Vairavamoorthy, K. (Eds.) (2012). *The future of water in African cities: Why waste water?* The World Bank.

Jensen, O., & Nair, S. (2019). Integrated urban water management and water security: A comparison of Singapore and Hong Kong. *Water, 11*(4), 785.

Johannessen, Å, Gerger Swartling, A, Wamsler, C., Andersson, K., Arran, J., Hernández-Vivas, D., & Stenström, T. (2019). Transforming urban water governance through social (triple-loop) learning. *Environmental Policy and Governance.* https://doi.org/10.1002/eet.1843

Kithiia, J., & Majambo, G. (2020). Motion but no speed: Colonial to post-colonial status of water and sanitation service provision in Mombasa city. *Cities (london, England), 107*, 102867. https://doi.org/10.1016/j.cities.2020.102867

Kjellén, M., & McGranahan, G. (2006). *Informal water vendors and the urban poor* (pp. 978–981). International Institute for Environment and Development.

Kobel, D., & Del Mistro, R. (2012). Evaluation of non-user benefits towards improvement of water and sanitation services in informal settlements. *Urban Water Journal, 9*(5), 347–359.

Koutiva, I., & Makropoulos, C. (2016). Modelling domestic water demand: An agent based approach. *Environmental Modelling & Software, 79*, 35–54.

Majuru, B., Suhrcke, M., & Hunter, P. R. (2016). How do households respond to unreliable water supplies? A systematic review. *International Journal of Environmental Research and Public Health, 13*(12), 1222.

Makinde, O. O. (2012). Urbanization, housing and environment: Megacities of Africa. *International Journal of Development and Sustainability, 1*(3), 976–993.

McGarry, M., Mugisha, S., Hoang-Gia, L., Unheim P., & Myles, M. (2008). *Water sector governance in Africa. Volume 1 Theory and Practice.* https://www.afdb.org/fileadmin/uploads/afdb/Documents/Project-andOperations/Vol_1_WATER_SECTOR_GOVERNANCE.pdf

Monstadt, J., & Schramm, S. (2017). Toward the networked city? Translating technological ideals and planning models in water and sanitation systems in Dar es Salaam. *International Journal of Urban and Regional Research, 41*(1), 104–125.

Morinville, C., & Harris, L. M. (2014). Participation, politics, and panaceas: exploring the possibilities and limits of participatory urban water governance in Accra, Ghana. *Ecology and Society, 19*(3).

Nastar, M., Isoke, J., Kulabako, R., & Silvestri, G. (2019). A case for urban liveability from below: Exploring the politics of water and land access for greater liveability in Kampala, Uganda. *Local Environment, 24*(4), 358–373.

Nauges, C., & Whittington, D. (2010). Estimation of water demand in developing countries: An overview. *The World Bank Research Observer, 25*(2), 263–294.

Nogueira, G., Stigter, T. Y., Zhou, Y., Mussa, F., & Juizo, D. (2019). Understanding groundwater salinization mechanisms to secure freshwater resources in the water-scarce city of Maputo, Mozambique. *Science of the Total Environment, 661*, 723–736.

Osei, M. A., Amekudzi, L. K., Wemegah, D. D., Preko, K., Gyawu, E. S., & Obiri-Danso, K. (2019). The impact of climate and land-use changes on the hydrological processes of Owabi catchment from SWAT analysis. *Journal of Hydrology: Regional Studies, 25*, 100620.

Peloso, M. M. (2014). *Navigating water access and governance in peri-urban Ashaiman, Ghana: A case study.* Doctoral dissertation, University of British Columbia.

Peloso, M., & Morinville, C. (2014). "Chasing for water": Everyday practices of water access in peri-urban Ashaiman. *Ghana. Water Alternatives, 7*(1), 121–139.

Price, H., Adams, E., & Quilliam, R. S. (2019). The difference a day can make: The temporal dynamics of drinking water access and quality in urban slums. *Science of the total environment, 671*, 818–826. Progress on Drinking Water, Sanitation and Hygiene 2017 (Joint Monitoring Program, WHO).

Raina, A., Zhao, J., Wu, X., Kunwar, L., & Whittington, D. (2019). The structure of water vending markets in Kathmandu, Nepal. *Water Policy, 21*(S1), 50–75.

Sjömander-Magnusson, T., & Van der Merwe, B. (2005). Context driven policy design in urban water management: A case study of Windhoek, Namibia. *Urban Water Journal, 2*(3), 151–160.

UNDESA, U. N. (2015). *World population prospects: The 2015 revision, key findings and advance tables.* Working Paper No.

United Nations. (2007). The Africa Water Vision for 2025: Equitable and Sustainable Use of Water for Socioeconomic Development, Economic Commission for Africa, UN-Water/Africa. The National Water Services Strategy (NWSS) (2007 – 2015).

United Nation (2017). Waste Water: The Untapped Resources. Facts and Figure. *The United Nations World Water Development Report.*

United Nations. (2019). World Water Development Report. *Leaving no one behind*. https://en.unesco.org/themes/watersecurity/wwap/wwdr/2019#text=The%202019%20World%20Water%20Development,and%20for%20building%20prosperous%2C%20peaceful

United Nations, Department of Economic and Social Affairs, Population Division. (2014). World Urbanization Prospects: The 2014 Revision, Highlights (ST/ESA/SER.A/352).

Verhoeven, J. (2014). *IRC WASH*. https://www.ircwash.org/news/sector-wide-approach

WHO. (2017). *World health statistics: Monitoring health for the SDGs*. https://reliefweb.int/report/world/world-health-statistics-2017-monitoring-health-sdgs

Wang, H., Mei, C., Liu, J., & Shao, W. (2018). A new strategy for integrated urban water management in China: Sponge city. *Science China Technological Sciences, 61*(3), 317–329.

Wright, J., Gundry, S., & Conroy, R. (2004). Household drinking water in developing countries: A systematic review of microbiological contamination between source and point-of-use. *Tropical Medicine & International Health, 9*(1), 106–117.

Wutich, A., Beresford, M., & Carvajal, C. (2016). Can informal water vendors deliver on the promise of a human right to water? Results from Cochabamba, Bolivia. *World Development, 79*, 14–24.

Zubaidi, S. L., Ortega-Martorell, S., Al-Bugharbee, H., Olier, I., Hashim, K. S., Gharghan, S. K., & Al-Khaddar, R. (2020). Urban water demand prediction for a city that suffers from climate change and population growth: Gauteng province case study. *Water, 12*(7), 1885.

CHAPTER 10

Rural–Urban Linkages

Francis Nyongesa Wegulo

INTRODUCTION

The subject of rural–urban linkages has attracted persistent and growing interest among researchers, academicians as well as government decision-makers and planners (Akkoyunlu, 2015; Friedmann, 1966, 1988; Gebre & Gebremedhin, 2019; Somanje et al., 2020; Southall, 1978; Steinberg, 2014; Tacoli, 1998, 2003; UN, 2020; UN-Habitat, 2019). Several explanations have been given for this persistent interest, including development policies pursued by the state both in the colonial and post-colonial Africa which tended to favour urban areas with equal neglect for rural areas. According to Lipton (1977), these policies initiated a development dichotomy between the two spatial areas. Development policies in many African countries have thus tended to be pegged on the premise of a dual system; one for rural areas, and the other for urban areas. This duality has engendered spatial inequalities between rural and urban areas; a factor which has among other things precipitated massive population migration from rural to urban centres. A number of researchers have explained people's movement citing the discrepancies in social and economic conditions between the two (see for instance Wanyande, 2016).

Rural–urban linkages refer to the reciprocal and repetitive flow of people, goods, and financial as well as environmental services between specific rural,

F. N. Wegulo (✉)
Department of Geography, Egerton University, Nakuru, Kenya
e-mail: mununi1993@gmail.com

© The Author(s), under exclusive license to Springer Nature Switzerland AG 2022
M. Khayesi and F. N. Wegulo (eds.), *The Palgrave Handbook of Urban Development Planning in Africa*, https://doi.org/10.1007/978-3-031-06089-2_10

peri-urban, and urban locations (UN-Habitat, 2019). The dynamics of rural–urban linkages speak to the reality of socio-spatial arrangements in which a large number of households live, work in, and depend on both rural and urban ecosystems that sustain human life beyond political and administrative spheres creating places with distinct yet interwoven, socially constructed identities (UN-Habitat, 2019; Hatcher, 2017). While rural–urban linkages are usually defined as the spatial movement and exchange of goods, people, money, and information, they also have structural dimensions. The latter refers to exchanges and interactions between economic sectors, such as the manufacturing of inputs for agriculture and the processing, transport, and distribution of agricultural goods. Understanding and supporting positive rural–urban interactions require an examination that combines spatial and sectoral dimensions (Agergaard et al., 2019; Baffoe et al., 2021; Tacoli, 2003; UNCCD, 2017).

This chapter discusses findings of selected studies on research designs, theories, and role of the rural–urban relations in Africa's spatial development. It seeks to answer the following questions: What has been the overarching view regarding relations between rural–urban areas in Africa? How has such a view influenced spatial planning and regional development in Africa? Does this view find any precedent in other regions of the world? What factors have influenced this view in the past and current situation? What is the current perception among researchers, government decision-makers, and planners concerning rural–urban relations in Africa? How can this be explained? In what ways will and should relations between rural and urban areas inform future research, planning, and development policy of Africa's spatial economy?

Method

This study is based on a systematic review of literature focusing on the subject of rural–urban relations/linkages in Africa. The literature that forms the basis of the review was accessed from electronic databases such as Research Gate, Academia, Google scholar, JSTOR, Elsevier, Taylor and Francis Online, and IOSR. Also included in this study are policy documents and informed opinions and guidelines from organizations such as the United Nations and UN-Habitat. The search for the literature was guided by the use of the following key terms: 'rural–urban links'; 'rural–urban dynamics'; 'rural–urban development'; 'rural–urban connection', 'rural development'; 'decentralization' and 'rural development'; and 'integrated rural–urban development'.

Given the role of towns and market centres in facilitating the relations between rural and urban areas, selection of works was extended to the literature on this subject (see for example, the argument of Satterthwaite, 2016). It is important to state from the outset that rural–urban linkages or relations have attracted enormous research, academic and policy interest and hence there is a plethora of information in books, book chapters, dissertations, journals, grey literature, commissioned reports, conference proceedings, and indeed, in several other publications, both formal as well as informal. In view of this, selecting what to include and exclude was a daunting task. The following guidelines were therefore used: the works have a focus on developing countries in general, but more particularly to sub-Saharan Africa; works conducted in the last twenty years, although exceptions were made for inclusion of older but considered seminal and foundational to the subject under review. In selecting the sample works, care was also exercised to capture the predominant and emerging dimensions and perspectives that influence the dynamics of the rural–urban relations in the development matrix of rural and urban development in Africa. In particular, I was keen to include in the sample works that reflect sensitivity to issues of environment; how for instance, rapid growth of urban areas is impacting adjacent rural areas through what has come to be referred to as 'ecological footprint'.

Using the described exclusion and inclusion criteria, the large database of relevant works (well over 3000) was identified. This was further examined to fulfil the specific inclusion criteria, and subsequently, the works were scaled down to 100 or so, out of which only 28 have been selected to constitute the sample for review, analysis, and synthesis (see Table 10.1).

Results and Discussion

From the selected studies, relevant information was extracted and summarized in a data extraction matrix (Table 10.1). The items extracted included; name of author(s), geographical unit, study focus, data collection designs/method, conceptual and theoretical framework, and key study findings. It is worth noting that the studies are listed chronologically, from the earliest in 1979 to the latest in 2021. This is done deliberately with a view to facilitating the readers' appreciation of the changing focus, and scope in the study of rural–urban relations in Africa.

Research Designs

We highlight three aspects related to the nature of studies under review; namely, geographical distribution, designs used to collect the data/information by the scholars/researchers selected for this review, and the concepts and theories upon which the various studies are anchored.

Geographical Distribution of Sample Studies

Table 10.2 presents a summary of the geographical distribution of the selected studies. It is observed that studies conducted at the continental level (Africa) and those focusing on other developing countries constituted 28 and 25 percent, respectively, followed by those at national levels (Kenya, Zimbabwe, Ghana,) constituting 22 percent. An equal share of studies (22 percent were conducted at the local level (sub-national). Only one study was based on

Table 10.1 Results of reviewed studies

Authors	Area of focus	Geographical location of study	Data collection method (s)	Concept and theories	Results
Otite (1979)	Rural migrants as catalysts in rural development	Ondo State, Nigeria	Mixed research	Growth centres/Growth poles	The richer the diversity of economic resources in any given region, the greater the influx of immigrants with different talents to participate in their exploitation. A necessary condition for local population concentration to promote socio-economic development & the emergence of urban features is the degree to which immigrants & indigenous populations can access local resources. The rural hinterlands of Okitipupa division contribute to growth centres & emergent urban concentrations. Villages in turn derive various development incentives. Increased diversification of occupations leads to the transformation of rural life towards an urban system. Rural to urban migration is thus a desirable strategy to rural development and for the emergence of socio-economic growth centres; It should therefore be encouraged by government

Authors	Area of focus	Geographical location of study	Data collection method (s)	Concept and theories	Results
Kabwegyere (1979)	Small urban centres and growth of underdevelopment in rural Kenya	Kenya	Historical survey and expert views	Core–periphery	Development of central places & growth centres as part of national development aids the perpetuation and intensification of Third World exploitation and underdevelopment Small urban centres are a product of the large centres which developed as nodes in a transmission system of raw materials from Colonial Africa in exchange for manufactured goods (peripheral capitalism) Small urban centres in the rural areas serve as agents of penetration in an ever expanding periphery capitalist system whose aim is to deplete the meagre surplus generated under pre-capitalist relations. Rural areas are adjunct & the small urban centres mere nodes in the process of the further impoverishment of the country
Southall (1988)	Small urban centres in rural development: What else is development other than helping your own home town?	Developing countries: Africa, Asia, and Latin America	Expert views		Contrary to the fact that urban centres were the engine of growth, it is argued that small towns were the bases used by colonial powers, national elites, and multinational corporations, all of whom have sought to extract raw materials and exploit the rural poor Small towns are regarded as an extension of the exploitative arm of capitalism and an instrument of rural underdevelopment

(continued)

Table 10.1 (continued)

Authors	Area of focus	Geographical location of study	Data collection method (s)	Concept and theories	Results
Evans and Ngau (1991)	Rural–urban relations, & the contribution of household income diversification and agricultural productivity	Kutus, Kirinyaga-Kenya	Empirical survey	Rural–urban dynamics model	Kutus and its hinterland offer an excellent illustration of relations between the rural (agricultural sector) and small urban areas; Kutus town and other smaller towns in Kirinyaga County, Kenya. The said relations are largely dependent upon increase in agricultural output; which is itself influenced by existence of non-farm activities which are crucial for income diversification that contribute to making rural households more productive farmers. Besides the influence of non-farm income to increase in agricultural output and productivity, other factors considered important by farm households are diversified sources of income and readily liquidated capital assets. In Kutus area, these include engagement in salaried employment (in Kutus and other smaller towns), development of a non-farm business (in Kutus & other smaller towns), and acquiring livestock. Studies have shown the close connections between the agricultural sector and non-farm activities and by extension, the rural and urban sectors. Further, it is clear that rising farm incomes create opportunities for rural households to diversify their income; a significant proportion of it which is utilized in increasing productivity on their farms. Arising from these key findings, the authors put a premium on the role and contribution of the non-farm sector in improvement of agricultural production in the study area. Similarly, policies designed to develop local economies must recognize and seek to exploit and strengthen the synergies which exist between the rural and urban areas

Authors	Area of focus	Geographical location of study	Data collection method (s)	Concept and theories	Results
Tegegne (2001)	Rural–urban linkages under different farming systems	Ethiopia Robe Wereda & Limu Genet town	Empirical survey	Rural–urban dynamics, virtuous cycle model	Farm sector in the study areas shows consumption linkages expenditures on urban goods and selected social services. Hinterlands show limited marketing linkages in the sale of rural products to the small towns

The main rural products brought to the small towns are coffee in Limu Genet and grain in Robe Wereda. Most of the expected linkages such as input, financial and processing linkages between the hinterlands, and the small towns do not exist

The linkage of the urban households to the rural hinterland varies in each study site. In Robe town, urban households mainly derive their grain needs from the local market where local grains are sold. In Limu Genet town, however, though most of the urban households purchase grains from the local market in the town, these grains are not produced in the surrounding hinterland but are brought from far off places by urban traders

The urban traders in the study sites, though with limited capital, are mainly family-run. They, however, play an important role in connecting the city and the hinterland to the national markets for different products |

(continued)

Table 10.1 (continued)

Authors	Area of focus	Geographical location of study	Data collection method(s)	Concept and theories	Results
Tacoli (1998)	Review of recent literature on rural–urban interactions in the context of recent and current economic, social, & cultural transformations	South East Asia & Africa	Secondary data & expert review		Populations and activities described either as 'rural' or 'urban' are more closely linked both across space as well as across sectors Concepts of 'rural' and 'urban' do not have universal definitions; they vary from one country to another. This makes inter-country comparisons difficult For instance, households may be 'multi-spatial', with some members residing in rural areas and others in towns, as well as engaging in agriculture within urban areas or in non-farm activities in the countryside Flows of people, goods and wastes, and related flow of information and money, act as linkages across space between towns and the countryside Given the strong interrelations, the two sectors are equally impacted by economic reforms and structural adjustment programmes. Conventionally, the consequences arising from macro environment have been examined largely from the perspective of urban economies and labour markets; much to the neglect of rural areas SAPs, trade liberalization and the growth of export-oriented agriculture among African countries have adversely affected small farmers, prompting large numbers to migrate to towns in search of livelihoods On-going global social, economic, and political changes have instigated deepening economic and social differentiation, heightening poverty for both rural and urban populations. The manifestations of these are evident at the micro (household) as well as macro (regional and national) levels

Authors	Area of focus	Geographical location of study	Data collection method (s)	Concept and theories	Results
Chant (1998)	Household, gender, and rural–urban migration: reflections on linkages and considerations for policy	Africa, Latin America, Caribbean, and, Asia	Qualitative survey	Feminist theory	Households are not natural units with fixed meanings across space & time. But are socially constructed and inherently variable Household headship and composition in the study area is diverse, with a mixture of female and male headed. Among the female-headed households, some are *de jure* while others are de facto, thus having different rights to resources according to the social structures in place Neoclassical & Marxist researchers have not adequately addressed the gender aspect in their analysis of migration. They stress that gender differentiated access to resources is socially constructed & household organization affects decisions on migration & resource distribution Unlike in Caribbean & Latin America, women in Africa are restrained in matters concerning migration to urban areas De facto female-headed households, suffering poor access to labour & other constraints, may make their own migration decisions. But *de jure* female-headed households resulting from widowhood, divorce, or conjugal breakdown may be in a stronger position to make reference to a male partner

(continued)

Table 10.1 (continued)

Authors	Area of focus	Geographical location of study	Data collection method (s)	Concept and theories	Results
Kamete (1998)	Interlocking livelihoods: farm and small town	Zimbabwe	Empirical survey	Rural–urban interaction model	Small towns have the potential to positively impact their rural hinterland through provision of goods and services needed for agricultural production as well as serving as markets for the rural produced goods Small towns are an extension of the exploitative arm of capitalism and an instrument of rural underdevelopment Analysis is based on the livelihoods of low income people and is anchored on the economic interactions between the urban residents of Banket and its hinterland The interactions are divided into two channels. Channel one has the hinterland as a source of livelihoods, disaggregated into three activities; farm as a source of supplies, farm as a market, and farm as a place of employment. Channel two is focused on farm to town movement. This is disaggregated into the following activities: town as a source of provisions and services, and town as a market. Patterns of interactions are then presented showing the dynamics in the interaction between the rural and urban spheres (Kamete, 1998, pp. 28–33)

Authors	Area of focus	Geographical location of study	Data collection method (s)	Concept and theories	Results
Mulongo et al. (2010)	Articulation of key aspects with regard to: (a) rural–urban relations and (b) sustainability of urban areas	Western Kenya	Empirical survey	Urban–rural interlink model	The link demonstrated in the study area (Malaba town & its hinterland) is largely socio-economic. Rural people depend on Malaba & other small towns in rural regions for agricultural productivity, rural goods and services, and as centres of distribution for commodities. The prosperity of rural towns depends on widespread sharing of income generated by agricultural and rural production The hinterland areas are poorly connected to urban areas (especially to Malaba) and hence lack the capacity to compete in the regional, national, and international markets They also lack proper information and signals to produce, invest, raise productivity, diversify production, and engage in new activities Findings from the case study show significant rural–urban interlink between Malaba town and its hinterland. Further research is however needed to identify in more specific detail how the model could be used to elucidate the functioning of the elements in the model to promote production and marketing of goods
Kioko (2003)	Rural–urban linkages in the context of the spatial interaction of Machakos town and the hinterland	Machakos, Kenya	Empirical survey	Core–periphery, analysis of rank size & nearest-neighbour technique	Rural–urban linkages (in form of spatial interaction) enhance urban and regional planning Poor transport and communication networks hinder the effective functioning of the hierarchical organization of the urban network In addition, the hierarchical organization of urban network in Machakos District encourages the draining of income, population, and resources by the highest-level centre Focus on rural–urban linkages facilitates a clear understanding of the regional space economy; policies for strengthening small & intermediate urban centres will assist in this process

(continued)

Table 10.1 (continued)

Authors	Area of focus	Geographical location of study	Data collection method (s)	Concept and theories	Results
Bah et al. (2003)	Changing nature of rural–urban linkages	Sub-Saharan Africa; Mali, Nigeria, and Tanzania	Mixed methods Qualitative & participatory tools, intra-household matrices and mobility/migration matrices, commodity chain analysis; secondary data; & quantitative/empirical survey	Virtuous cycle (assumes that urban centres-through providing markets and services positively impact agricultural growth in their surrounding areas)	Farming is a primary activity in most of SSA & especially in the study countries: Mali, Nigeria, & Tanzania. Transformations in the agricultural sector therefore have potential to influence the scale & nature of rural–urban linkages & their relevance to the livelihoods of different groups in the community Increase in agricultural productivity is depended upon access to natural resources, financial capital, & information on market prices as well as their fluctuations. National policies, village level-characteristics, and socio-economic differences within & between households also matter, and these are dynamic and changing; for instance, occupational diversification & its effects on livelihoods of rural households is on the increase Evidence shows that despite the promise of the virtuous cycle in the rural–urban nexus, only two urban centres; Aba in south east Nigeria & Himo in northern Tanzania seem to play a role in the economic development of their respective regions. Both serve as markets for goods produced in the rural areas & as destinations for migrants & commuters engaged in non-agricultural employment Liberalization of international trade has adversely affected generation of local incomes. For instance, the importation of cheaper goods has undermined local vegetable oil production by women groups in Tanzania & traditional cloth weaving in Nigeria

Authors	Area of focus	Geographical location of study	Data collection method (s)	Concept and theories	Results
Tostensen (2004)	Rural linkages in sub-Saharan Africa: Contemporary debates and implications for Kenyan urban workers in the twenty-first century	Sub-Saharan Africa, Zambia, and Kenya	Historiography and developmental narratives	Circular migratory strategy	Analytical and binary designation of 'rural' and 'urban' cannot and should not be treated as a sharp dichotomy of discrete spheres, instead the links should be seen as interdependent Rural-urban relations are identified in forms such as movement of labour, natural resources, commodities, and finances Most rural households maintain close links with their urban counterparts and vice versa, taking the form of exchange of goods and services Many households pursue a circular migration strategy; straddling (they do not relinquish their roots on either side of the rural-urban divide) These findings corroborate the argument presented in the work of Ferguson (1999), in which he showed that workers in the copper mines towns had not progressed to being urban proletariats, thus severing their links with their rural homes. Instead, the urban migrants continued to depend on their rural areas for survival The study under review sees the possibility for the emergence of an urban proletariat in Africa, but only under conditions of high economic growth and concomitant creation of employment opportunities, a prospect that seems elusive for many countries in Africa today Given the low urban wage levels, declining agricultural production and increasingly smaller plots of land, households will seek to maintain straddling as a means of survival. This will serve to reinforce the rural-urban relations among the majority of African countries

(continued)

Table 10.1 (continued)

Authors	Area of focus	Geographical location of study	Data collection method (s)	Concept and theories	Results
Bryceson (2006)	Fragile cities: Fundamentals of urban life in East and Southern Africa	East and Southern Africa	Literature review	Review of literature	Evidence of 'urban carrying capacity' in many urban centres in Africa African urban populations have expanded without industrialization and national economic growth This has led to growing levels of unemployment and deprivation Author examines sub-Saharan Africa cities on the basis of past (colonial trajectories), post-colonial, early post-colonial. In each, details of the carrying capacity viewpoint are elaborated Fragility (shaky economic structures and associated welfare challenges) is shown to pervade Africa cities in all the eras especially in the post-independent
Foeken and Owuor (2008)		Nakuru, Kenya	Empirical Survey	Straddling/multi-spatial model	Farming is an important source of livelihood, especially for the poor. For this group, rural farming was more important as a livelihood source than urban farming The economic crisis of the 1980s and 1990s caused a major growth of urban farming; the urban poor engaged in the activity as a survival strategy. The crisis also prompted changes in urban–rural linkages; the urban poor increasingly became dependent on rural sources (especially food) for their livelihood; the urban poor has increasingly become multi-spatial or multi-local. In economic terms, households have their foothold in both the urban and rural areas This is contrary to many development theorists and practitioners who until recently viewed rural and urban areas as two mutually exclusive entities with unique populations, activities, problems, and concerns (p. 1988)

Authors	Area of focus	Geographical location of study	Data collection method (s)	Concept and theories	Results
Mylott (2009)	Urban–rural connections: A review of the literature	The United States, Canada, and Western Europe	Empirical Survey		Relationship between urban and rural areas is changing in countries over the world, both in developed and developing countries Land use types in all the countries are not mutually exclusive but rather lie on a continuum Rural–urban relations are recognized for their potential for poverty alleviation and sustainable rural development, improvement of living standards, and for creating employment opportunities for both rural and urban households Mutual benefits associated with the rural–urban relations have as yet not attracted adequate attention in planning and development practice Urbanization in sub-Saharan Africa is growing rapidly but without the associated growth and development benefits being spread around Regional development could be achieved through a settlement cluster which is anchored on the potential of small and medium towns that provide a link between the complex urban life and the rural sphere Small and medium towns, therefore, act as the instruments through which rural–urban linkages can be strengthened for sustainable urbanization
Alaci (2010)	Regulating urbanization in sub-Saharan Africa through cluster settlements approach	Ethiopia	Mixed Methods (Quantitative and Qualitative)	Settlement cluster	Urbanization in sub-Saharan Africa is growing rapidly but without the associated growth and development benefits being spread around. This is attributed to the lack of a spatial functional framework Better regional development tool-cluster formation is considered as the ideal. This is a settlement cluster with a focus on small and medium towns that provide a link between the complex and often sophisticated urban life, and the simple rural sphere. Small and medium towns therefore act as instruments for strengthening rural–urban linkages and fostering sustainable urbanization

(continued)

Table 10.1 (continued)

Authors	Area of focus	Geographical location of study	Data collection method (s)	Concept and theories	Results
Djurfeldt (2012)	Typologize and illustrate tendencies related to household-based rural–urban linkages in the south African region	Rusape town in Makoni district, eastern Zimbabwe	Mixed Methods	Variety of theories: multi-spatial livelihoods & sustainable livelihoods approaches; micro-level virtuous & vicious cycle linkages	Small towns are considered the focus of the exchange between rural & urban areas Linkages are both physical connections related to infrastructure & movement of goods, capital and people as well as more abstract interactions, e.g., the transfer of information, diffusion of innovations, & participation in social networks. Examples of the traditional connections take the form of urban remittances to rural livelihoods Strategies used by rural and urban households & individuals to straddle the rural–urban which depend on household access to economic and social resources are recognized Study is based on multi-spatial livelihoods model, which stresses trends & dynamics of survival & accumulation over both time and space The model focuses on flows mediated by the market as well as household-based linkages; a micro-level virtuous & vicious cycles of rural–urban linkages In the case of the virtuous cycle of rural–urban interaction, the household straddles both rural and urban spheres of production and consumption The vicious cycle of rural–urban interaction through the households' survival-centred activities both in the rural and urban spheres produces a situation in which the households' assets as well as productive resources such as land and labour are gradually depleted, eventually leading to deprivation & vulnerability

Authors	Area of focus	Geographical location of study	Data collection method (s)	Concept and theories	Results
					Rural linkages are maintained through rural land access and agricultural production. A quarter of the sample in urban areas met its entire maize needs through self-provisioned food or through food remittances from rural relatives
					Zimbabwean situation represents many African countries in which smallholder agriculture remains highly input dependent and with rapidly declining land sizes due to population growth. The urban areas have their own challenges; low & declining urban employment, which has led to reliance on the rural households for provision of food
Akkoyunlu (2015)	The importance of infrastructure, market and non-market institutions and trade in facilitating rural–urban linkages	Developing countries	Review of Literature	Rural–urban continuum & virtuous circle model	Rural–urban linkages are not only important in relation to the policies meant to address poverty reduction but also in relation to economic and sustainable development
					The nature of the linkages has changed from a separation and dichotomy towards close linkages between the two spheres; and also, towards more integrated systems and an urban system which are closely linked through the flow of people, production, commodities, capital & income, information, natural resources waste, & pollution
					Trade plays an important role in spreading and strengthening the rural–urban linkages & should therefore be emphasized
					A rise in the income levels of the rural population due to the diversification of their livelihoods increases demand for manufactured goods and services among these populations This in turn stimulates the growth of local towns and urban areas, & also triggers agricultural growth

(continued)

Table 10.1 (continued)

Authors	Area of focus	Geographical location of study	Data collection method (s)	Concept and theories	Results
					On the basis of the 'virtuous circle' model of regional development, urban centres through their provisioning of markets and services are considered to be the engines of agricultural growth for rural areas. This growth is then translated into an increase in non-farm employment and an increased demand for both agricultural and manufactured goods and services
					Mobility, the commuting between rural areas and urban centres, and migration are both important parts of livelihood strategies
					Migrants' remittances not only contribute to rural economies but are also important parts of household livelihoods; household income diversification and risk strategies
					Migrant remittances strengthen the financial linkages between urban and rural activities. Migrant remittances strengthen the financial linkages between urban and rural activities given the weak financial systems in many rural areas of Africa
					Policies that aim to stimulate rural–urban linkages should prioritize innovations in agriculture; transport and communications infrastructure; and the development of market institutions

Authors	Area of focus	Geographical location of study	Data collection method (s)	Concept and theories	Results
Steinberg (2014)	Paper addresses six key intellectual & policy issues relating to the relationship of urban centres with their rural hinterlands	Developing countries in Asia and Africa	Review of literature	Not stated	Urbanization recognized as a defining characteristic of the twenty-first century Majority of Africa's urban population live in intermediary and small cities The nature of linkages has changed from a separation and dichotomy towards close linkages between rural and urban areas, towards more integrated systems, a rural and urban system which are closely linked through the flow of people, production, commodities, capital and income, information, natural resources, waste, and pollution Urban complexities are on an increase. This presents a major challenge to achieve inclusions and resilience to climate change. Impacts may compel households to live multi-spatial lives—some residing in and working in rural areas, others in towns, engaging in non-farming activities in the countryside, or in urban agriculture

(continued)

Table 10.1 (continued)

Authors	Area of focus	Geographical location of study	Data collection method (s)	Concept and theories	Results
Mfune et al. (2016)	Changing Rural–Urban Linkages in Africa in a Globalizing Economy	Africa	Theoretical arguments, concepts, approaches and methodologies through an appraisal of published analyses on rural–urban interactions in Africa	Kizuna discourse & the rural–urban continuum framework	Africa is undergoing demographic and socio-economic shifts which are transforming the region and reconfiguring the nature of interactions between the rural and urban spaces. These shifts are attributed to poverty, increasing inequalities, environmental stresses, and shocks as well as food security Traditionally, these problems have been approached and treated as 'rural', 'urban', or even 'peri-urban'. However, the problems transcend these binary categories A case is made for 'Kizuna', a platform for understanding and promoting better strategies for sharing efforts and building strong bonds; it is seen as being able to drive rural–urban linkage for sustainable development The 'Kizuna' approach examines cities as part of a continuum embracing the rural–urban connections and hence transforming the rural, peri-urban, and urban areas Traditional treatment of the concepts of rural and urban as discrete categories and a basis for addressing Africa's development issues is questioned. The discrete and dichotomous approach to urban development as distinct from rural development no longer accords with the reality that is characterized in part by the changing demographic trends in Africa and its unique features A variety of literature is cited and articulated to trace elements of 'Kizuna' in rural–urban interactions in Africa. Arguments are made why building this rural–urban 'Kizuna' must be treated with a sense of urgency in order to accelerate poverty eradication and build sustainable African societies

Authors	Area of focus	Geographical location of study	Data collection method (s)	Concept and theories	Results
Mojoko and Fonjong (2018)	Examination of challenges to effective rural–urban interdependence	Meme Division of Cameroon	Empirical survey based on samples of farmers, non-farm and traders	Spatial interaction (complementarity, transferability & intervening opportunity)	Poor road infrastructure has inhibited effective rural–urban interactions. Farmers perceive the poor state of farm to market roads as a challenge to effective rural to urban food marketing in Meme; this raises the cost of transportation, as well as farmers' cost of production The poor state of the roads also impedes rural–urban trade and independence between the two sectors and spatial units Storage of food items such as cocoyams, vegetables, and fruits (all perishable commodities) present another challenge, especially during the heavy rains period. The study reports heavy losses by the farming community in view of this problem Other challenges that impede effective rural–urban linkages include inadequate supply of finances needed for farm improvement; absence of food processing machines that would add value to local produce and hence increase farm income; & inadequate market infrastructure for efficient trade

(continued)

Table 10.1 (continued)

Authors	Area of focus	Geographical location of study	Data collection method (s)	Concept and theories	Results
Agergaard et al. (2019)	Summarizes six studies which focus on the role of urbanization in economic, social and cultural change and the place of small towns in the process	Sub-Saharan Africa	Systematic review of literature	Rural–urban linkage	Six papers presented in this special issue revisit and provide an update on the dynamics of rural–urban linkages and emergence, and role of small towns (Agergaard et al., 2019). Steel et al. examine the changing role of rural–urban linkages and transformations in small town development in Africa from a livelihood viewpoint. This paper demonstrates how the different kinds of multi-locality and multi-activity develop and accelerate rural urbanization. Lazaro et al. explore how rural Tanzania is urbanizing by comparing settlement growth and local economic development in four emerging urban centres. It is shown in the paper how the four follow different trajectories based on their historical and geographical characteristics, and their respective crop value chain dynamics. In paper three, Baker shows how small towns in Ethiopia have been planned unlike the case in Tanzania. Baker highlights efforts by the government of Ethiopia in developing a new town, Bora, which has over time grown from a rural to an urban centre blending features of rurality and urbanism. The fourth paper by Ortenblad is focused on the Njombe region of Tanzania. The paper explores how the changing connections between the growing regional town and the rural hinterland are shaping patterns of rural transformation. Increased demand for Irish potatoes has impacted agricultural practices and rural livelihoods that involve livelihood diversification and social economic mobility. The paper underscores the strengthened rural–urban connections which manifest in intensification and commercialization of agricultural activities and the diversification of household activity portfolio. These are ushered into the Njombe region and its household economic growth and new livelihood opportunities

Authors	Area of focus	Geographical location of study	Data collection method (s)	Concept and theories	Results
					It is noted that barriers to entry into remunerative and accumulation of household activities, e.g., access to land, human capital, productive assets, gender, and age are causing a relatively large number of poor rural community not to benefit from the intensified rural–urban connections
					Focusing on periodic markets system in northern Ghana, it is acknowledged that close links between small town development and their rural hinterland exist
					The authors highlight the growing importance of small town development and rural–urban transformation process
					An analysis of small town development trajectories is shown to be linked to the history of the local markets and the characteristics of the commodity chains they host
Lynch (2018)	Discussion of past approaches to understanding development & rural–urban relations: the need to re-connect the two spaces	Developing countries	Collation of research work & theory relevant to interactions on urban–rural areas (review of secondary sources)	Various concepts & theories, e.g., modernization/core–periphery, mercantile model, & sustainable livelihoods	Earlier research on development focused on modernization diffusion which explored the relationship between the city and countryside using core–periphery (Friedman, 1966) or mercantile model (Vance, 1970)
					These theories focused on settlement hierarchies (urban bias) rather than the interaction between the urban and rural sectors
					Recent research has tended to shift away from a focus on the physical interface between urban and rural to the more important examinations of the connections between them

(continued)

Table 10.1 (continued)

Authors	Area of focus	Geographical location of study	Data collection method (s)	Concept and theories	Results
Gebre and Gebremedhin (2019)	The mutual benefits of promoting rural–urban interdependence through linked ecosystem services	Ethiopia	Systematic review of literature	The three magnets theory	Rural and urban areas are endowed with different amenities which bestow the two areas with advantages and disadvantages, ultimately influencing the different lifestyles in both rural and urban areas In spite of the unique differences, rural and urban areas are interlinked and not separated and discrete. The linkages take two forms: spatial linkages which connect people, goods, information; and sectoral linkages that connect agriculture, manufacturing industries and services Rural–urban linkage is important for both rural and urban areas. Rural and urban areas cannot stand alone without the mutual interdependence with one another. Ecosystems services provide a platform upon which to examine the interdependence. A set of issues against which to articulate the said relations are presented: the nature of the ecosystem services supplied by rural areas to urban areas; whether or not the ecosystem services contribute to the development of both rural and urban areas; the extent to which urban areas can survive in the absence of rural areas' ecosystem services; and how the rural–urban linkages can be enhanced through these ecosystem services Rural areas provide food, water, energy, raw materials, and other ecosystem services to urban areas. Water is critical for a range of different types of activities that include commercial and industrial as well as residential purposes. With the rapid growth of urban areas, the pressure on water resources will also increase. Water transfers and reallocations from rural to urban areas are therefore emerging areas of research

Authors	Area of focus	Geographical location of study	Data collection method (s)	Concept and theories	Results
					Rural areas also supply a diversity of raw materials which support industries and processing firms. Vegetable oils, rubber, and timber support urban-based industries. Farmers earn income from the sale of such products, which is used to improve agriculture and, in some cases, provide investment in non-farm activities as well as supporting employment and livelihoods
					Rural areas supply to urban areas, e.g., clean air, carbon sinks, sewerage disposal sites, temperature moderation as well as cultural services
					The cost benefit analysis of the supply and benefit to both rural and urban areas arising from the dynamics of ecosystems services is not provided
Graeme et al. (2019)	The nature of urban-rural linkages in the sub-Saharan region, and their efficacy in leveraging balanced development	Sub-Saharan Africa	Consensus study informed with expert views	Rural-urban continuum, virtuous & vicious cycles/models	Urbanization is on the rise in SSA. By 2050 most countries in the region will have surpassed the tipping point–more than 50 percent of their populations will live in towns & cities. This process has been and will continue to be driven by conflict, rural poverty (rural push), and better educational opportunities and higher urban wages (urban pull). Evidence shows that these dynamics have dramatically accelerated rural-to-urban transition over the past decades, as indeed they will in the coming future Viewing and examining these problems for policy-making is facilitated by distinguishing between rural and urban areas is useful although it can obscure the deep complexities and interconnections in the demographic, economic, and political shifts underway in many countries

(continued)

Table 10.1 (continued)

Authors	Area of focus	Geographical location of study	Data collection method(s)	Concept and theories	Results
					Urban and rural areas are interdependent to varying degrees, and rely on flows of individuals, capital, and information to sustain distinct ways of life
					Urban–rural linkages constitute the economic, social, cultural, and political relationships maintained between individuals and groups in urban and rural environments. These have potential distributional consequences, leading to either 'virtuous' and 'vicious' urban–rural linkages
					Attention to urban–rural linkages is also underscored in view of their canonization in the Sustainable Development Goals (SDGs) and the New Urban Agenda (NUA), courtesy of the Common African Position (CAP) on the SDGs, which emphasized the importance of moving beyond 'siloed' thinking on cities, and embracing their development within the frame of a wide, cohesive vision
					The views and broad objective are aligned to the African Union's (AU) Agenda 2063
					Three 'streams' of evidence related to urban–rural linkages; (1) productivity and livelihoods, (2) socio-cultural perceptions, and (3) power and accountability are identified and the related insights brought into policy and practice at all levels to help encourage the formation of virtuous urban–rural linkages

Authors	Area of focus	Geographical location of study	Data collection method (s)	Concept and theories	Results
UN-Habitat (2019)	Response by UN-Habitat to the growing spatial inequalities between urban and rural areas	Global, with reference to developing countries	Expert views & guidelines	Urban–rural continuum concept & functional territorial approach	The relationship between urban and rural communities is increasingly becoming important in view of the rapid process of urbanization. Disparities between rural and urban areas are key consequences Interrelations between rural and urban areas; e.g., repeated and reciprocal circular movements across the urban–rural continuum are real. The movements connect these areas and generate synergies between them thus contributing to functional, integrated territories and regions Territorial approaches are underscored for their efficacy in managing a comprehensive, interlinked, & participatory means to achieving sustainable development Urbanization and rural transformation are closely connected and should not be treated in isolation; rather, the processes that connect them should be seen to be mutually reinforcing The relationships can and should benefit from the UN Guiding Principles (GPs) which aim to inform pragmatic strategies and propose a framework for action to build an enabling environment for more inclusive and functional urban–rural linkages. GPs also seek to provide benchmarks for revising national and sub-national rural, urban, and territorial policy frameworks Adoption and application of GPs is expected to contribute towards creation of fair and sustainable livelihoods across the urban–rural continuum through strengthening the roles of local governments and other institutional partners. This will promote interdependence between rural and urban spaces and their respective activities

(continued)

Table 10.1 (continued)

Authors	Area of focus	Geographical location of study	Data collection method (s)	Concept and theories	Results
Klimzuk and Kochansk-Klimezuk (2019)	Review of selected theories & concepts of regional development	Various developing nations	Review of literature	Core–periphery model & world systems theory	Bring to attention to conflicting relations between centres and peripheries reduced to a dualism of dominant centres and weak peripheries (spatial determinants of development). Two theories are singled out; Core-periphery is attributed to Prebisch and world systems theory to Wallerstein Core–periphery is attributed to Prebisch in the 1950s. These notions (centre & periphery) are regarded as two broad and contrasting regional categories (the economically developed and the underdeveloped periphery) Friedman's version of core–periphery model offers an explanation of why some inner-city areas enjoy considerable prosperity while others show signs of urban deprivation and poverty; much the same pattern seen between advantaged urban areas over periphery rural areas The world systems theory attributed to Wallerstein shares the characteristics with Presbich's core–periphery but with additional features. The core in this case includes regions that are; innovative and play an active role in international trade; export capital; generate high incomes; and have high productivity and stability of political systems. They are also the site of the exchange of products

Authors	Area of focus	Geographical location of study	Data collection method (s)	Concept and theories	Results
Somanje et al. (2020)	Challenges and potential Solutions for Sustainable Urban–Rural Linkages in a Ghanaian Context	Ghana	Empirical Survey	Solution scanning framework	Increasing urbanization, challenges associated with population increase, climate change, food insecurity, unemployment and weak economic growth affect urban–rural linkages and sustainable development, and they must therefore be addressed holistically High inequality and gender gaps are found in the development of urban and rural areas The study noted poor basic and economic infrastructure resulting from, increased rural–urban migration, urban sprawl, industrial expansion, and increase in population growth. For instance, rural–urban increase has led to expansion of slum areas and their characteristic inadequate supply of amenities Urban-rural connectivity is also weak owing to poor and inadequate transport systems Although agriculture is the predominant source of livelihood for the majority of rural community, limited economic power combined with the effect of climate change have caused people to migrate for the purpose of searching for livelihoods Rural–urban linkages have also been weakened by lack of access to affordable finance, poor (or no) funding for business ventures, and low capacity building, especially among the youth and women Results show that gender inclusiveness was ranked first as a significant factor for enhancing sustainable urban–rural linkages. The other factors perceived to be significant are investment in economic infrastructure, modernization of agricultural systems, innovative financial inclusion, and the promotion of a decentralized system

(continued)

Table 10.1 (continued)

Authors	Area of focus	Geographical location of study	Data collection method (s)	Concept and theories	Results
Baffoe et al. (2021)	Urban–Rural linkages: effective solutions for achieving sustainable development in Ghana from an SDG interlinkage perspective	Ghana	Literature review/empirical survey, stakeholder consultations, SDG interlinkage analysis	Application of integrated approach through use of results from solution scanning exercise	Analysis re-affirms the findings that gender inclusiveness is a social element for addressing Ghana's urban–rural dichotomy Policies for improving gender inclusiveness generate synergistic spill over effect on several SDG areas (Goals 1, 2, 3, 4, 5 & 10, 6, 11) contributing to sound development in both rural and urban areas Significant urban–rural disparities are observed in basic services including access to food, water, energy, housing, and economic infrastructure On the basis of the SDG interlinkage analysis, improving agricultural productivity and increasing investment in rural infrastructure and agricultural extension services could generate synergies with some social and economic development indicators albeit with potential trade-offs, e.g., their negative impact on the environment Four SDG targets are identified to contribute to the promotion of innovative financial inclusion systems by increasing the access of small scale enterprises to financial services, and reducing transaction costs of migrant remittances on many social and economic sectors in Ghana in the study area—Ghana

Table 10.2 Geographical focus of reviewed studies

Geographical Unit	Frequency	Percentage
Local	7	22
National	7	22
Continental	9	28
Other Developing Countries (ODC)	8	25
Others (USA/CANADA & Europe	1	3

Note Frequency and per cent figures are not quoted because of overlaps

evidence from the United States, Canada, and Europe. From the information, it is clear that relations between rural and urban areas are a subject of interest among researchers and policy makers across the world. It is of particular note that rural–urban relations are considered important in the spatial economy and development in the African continent and other countries in the developing world as a whole.

Designs

How did the various authors derive the data and information on the basis of which they made their cases and arguments? Table 10.3 shows that as many as thirteen different techniques were utilized in the sample studies; this is a wide range for the small sample size in this study. By far the most commonly used design in the studies under review is the empirical survey method. This involved the selection of sample using rigorous scientific procedures (e.g., Evans & Ngau, 1991; Mulongo et al., 2010). Nearly a half of the studies employed this method in deriving their data. The following researchers used this method: Evans and Ngau (1991), Tacoli (1998), Kamete (1998), Bryceson (2006), Akkoyunlu (2015), Mulongo et al. (2010), Guneralp et al. (2017), Lynch (2018), Klimzuk-Kochanska and Klimezuk (2019), Somanje et al. (2020), Baffoe et al. (2021), Tacoli (2003), and Mojoko and Fonjong (2018).

Five studies by Otite (1979), Alaci (2010), Djurfeldt (2012), Gebre and Gebremedhin (2019), Bah et al. (2003) were based on review of documents (secondary data). In between, some researchers used 'mixed method'—a combination of quantitative and qualitative surveys. Studies that use this combination include those by Otite (1979), Alaci (2010), Djurfeldt (2012), Gebre and Gebremedhin (2019), Bah et al. (2003). Three studies, one by were based on historical survey; and the other by Tostensen (2004) using a combination of historiography and developmental narrative.

Consensus and expert views by Graeme et al. (2019); expert guidelines by UN-Habitat (2019); and qualitative and participatory research designs were

Table 10.3 Designs used for collection of data/information in the sample studies

	Designs used for data/information collection	Authors
1	Mixed research	Otite (1979), Alaci (2010), Djurfeldt (2012), Gebre and Gebremedhin (2019), Bah et al. (2003)
2	Historical	Kabwegyere (1979)
3	Narrative	Southall (1988)
4	Expert views	Southall (1988)
5	Quantitative survey	Evans and Ngau (1991), Tacoli (1998), Kamete (1998), Bryceson (2006), Akkoyunlu (2015), Mulongo et al. (2010), Cervero (2013), Guneralp et al. (2017), Lynch (2018), Klimezuk-Kochanska and Klimezuk (2019), Somanje et al. (2020), Baffoe et al. (2021), Tacoli (2003), Mojoko and Fonjong (2018)
6	Qualitative survey	Chant (1998)
7	Qualitative & participatory	
8	Historiography & developmental	Tostensen (2004)
9	Review of secondary data	Akkoyunlu (2015), Agergaard et al. (2019), Gebre and Gebremedhin (2019), Steinberg (2014), Southhall (1988)
10	Theoretical arguments, concepts	Mfune et al. (2016)
11	Consensus & expert views	Graeme et al. (2019)
12	Guidelines/Expert advice	UN Habitat (2019)

also used. These last three bring substantial innovativeness in the research design with the particular benefit of incorporating of wider stakeholders in the collection of the data, its analysis, and report preparation. These are important capacity building designs, especially for the groups which the research targets to benefit and empower.

Theories

This section presents the concepts and theories that have been used by various researchers and scholars to explain the different relationships between rural and urban areas in Africa (see useful details in Baker & Pedersen, 1992). As it may be observed in Table 10.4, a wide range of concepts and theories are used in the different studies under review. These are core–periphery by Kabwegyere (1979), and Kioko (2003), rural–urban dynamics model by Evans and Ngau (1991) and Akkayunlu (2015); Feminist theory by Chant (1998); urban–rural interlink model by Mulongo et al. (2010); virtuous cycle

Table 10.4 Concepts and theories used in the reviewed studies

	Anchor concepts and theories in selected readings	Authors
1	Core–Periphery	Kabwegyere (1979), Kioko (2003)
2	Rural–Urban Dynamics	Evans and Ngau (1991), Akkayunlu (2015)
3	Feminist Theory	Chant (1998)
4	Urban–Rural Interlink Model	Mulongo et al. (2010)
5	Virtuous Cycle	Bah et al. (2003), Akkayunlu (2015)
6	Circular Migratory	Chant (1998)
7	Multi-Spatial Model	Foeken and Owuor (2008), Djurfeldt (2012)
8	Settlement Cluster	Tostensen (2004)
9	Rural–Urban Linkage	Djurfeldt (2012
10	Kazina Discourse & Rural–Urban Continuum Framework	Mfune et al. (2016)
11	Spatial Interaction	Mojoko and Fonjong (2018)
12	Rural–Urban Continuum	Graeme et al. (2019), UN Habitat (2019)
13	Modernization	Lynch (2018)
14	Three Magnets Theory	Gebre and Gebremedhin (2019)
15	Virtuous & Vicious Cycle	Graeme et al. (2019)
16	Functional Territorial Approach	UN Habitat (2019)
17	Solution Scanning Framework	Somanje et al. (2020), Baffoe et al. (2021)
18	Integration Approach	Baffoe et al. (2021)

model by Bah et al. (2003), Akkayunlu (2015); 'virtuous' and 'vicious' cycle by Graeme et al. (2019); and 'circular migratory' strategy by Chant (1998), Potts and Mutambirwa (1990). Others used are multi-spatial model by Foeken and Owuor (2008), Djurfeldt (2012), settlement cluster model by Tostensen (2004); rural–urban linkage by Djurfeldt (2012); the 'Kazina' discourse and rural–urban continuum framework by Mfune et al. and Graeme et al. (2019); and the spatial interaction model by Mojoko and Fonjong (2018).

The following models and theories have also been used in various studies: Modernization theory by Lynch (2018); the three magnets theory by Gebre and Gebremedhin (2019); rural–urban continuum by Graeme et al. (2019) and UN Habitat (2019); the functional territorial approach by UN Habitat (2019), the solution scanning framework by Somanje et al. (2020) and Baffoe et al. (2021); and the integration approach by Baffoe et al. (2021). It is worth noting that a number of researchers have relied on more than one model or theory in their studies. The purpose is to widen the scope of reach to the data required as well as to ensure triangulation thereby increasing the accuracy of the information to be derived.

A number of questions are pertinent with respect to the models and theories used in the studies under review. First, what factors explain the wide range/diversity? Two, how relevant are the models and theories in offering explanations of the relationships between rural and urban areas in an African context? Three, is there any evidence of innovative ideas-cutting edge conceptualization, modelling, and theorizing that reflect the reality of rural–urban relations in an African context? We return to these questions in a subsequent section, but suffice it to state the following: the studies under review focus on changing and broadening scope of aspects that currently speak to the reality of the rural–urban relations; namely, social, economic, political, and increasingly environment. Not surprisingly, the relations between rural and urban areas embrace many more issues than was the case a few decades ago. But, to what extent are the models and theories relevant to the realities found in African cities and towns? This last question could have been better answered by the researchers themselves through evaluations (and or disclaimers) of the efficacy(ies) of the methods used. In my reading and evaluation of the studies reviewed, I did not encounter any such critique.

Generally, researchers in Africa and other developing countries have, however, tended to rely upon models and theories developed in the north for conceptual and theoretical guidance in pursuit of their research. But this could soon change given sentiments as those of Wiardaa (1983: Abstract) who opines that:

> There is widespread rejection of the Western model of development, suggesting that there are many new and existing efforts on the part of intellectuals and political elites throughout these areas to assert new and indigenous models of development. These efforts represent serious and fundamental challenges to many cherished social science assumptions and understandings and to the presumption of a universal social science of development.

Conceptualizing Rural–Urban Relations

Rural–urban linkages refer to the flows of people, goods, and wastes, and the related flows of information and money across space between towns and countryside (Steinberg, 2014). A distinction has been made between sectoral and spatial linkages. Rural–urban interactions include (1) linkages across space (such as flows of people, goods, money, information, and wastes), and (2) linkages between sectors (for example, between agriculture and services and manufacturing). Rural–urban interactions can also include 'rural' activities taking place in urban centres (such as urban agriculture) and activities often classified as 'urban' (such as manufacturing and services) taking place in rural settlements (Mfune et al., 2016; Tacoli, 1998).

Graeme et al. (2019) elaborate on this conceptualization of rural–urban relations pointing out that:

urban-rural linkages constitute the economic, social, cultural, and political relationships maintained between individuals and groups in urban and rural environments , and these have potential distributional consequences, leading to either 'virtuous' and 'vicious' urban-rural linkages.

Assumptions undergirding the virtuous cycle suggest that urban centres, through providing markets and services, positively impact agricultural growth in their surrounding areas. The failure of this to happen; that is, urban centres not being able to provide the incentives for economic growth, leads to the 'vicious cycle' (Bah et al., 2003).

The main argument in the rural–urban linkage model is that there are close and practical relations between urban and rural areas. Rural areas depend on urban areas for secondary schools, post and telephone, credit, agricultural expansion services, farm equipment, hospitals, and government services. Rural areas on the other hand supply towns with food needed to satisfy the growing consumption, raw materials for manufacturing and processing industries, and human labour among other flows. These relations have over the time been greatly expanded in view of greater access to information technology, better roads, improved education and changing economic realities. All these have served to increase the movement of people, goods, and services.

Scholars are, however, divided as to whether towns play parasitic or generative roles in their relations with their rural hinterlands. Some scholars vouch for mutual and synergetic flows; the markets centres and towns being seen to support the development of their rural hinterlands (Rondinelli, 1988). Several others led by Southall (1988) argue to the contrary, suggesting that towns exploit their rural hinterlands.

Conceptualization of rural–urban relations has also been approached differently in the literature, with a focus on either rural or urban of the two. Traditional treatment of the concepts of rural and urban as discrete categories and a basis for addressing Africa's development issues is questionable on grounds of ground reality. It has been aptly argued that an approach that treats urban development as distinct from rural development is not aligned to Africa's reality, given the continent's changing demographic trends and its unique features (Mfune et al., 2016). This is what Tacoli says on conceptualization of rural–urban areas:

The distinction between 'rural' and 'urban' is probably inescapable for descriptive purposes; however, it often implies a dichotomy which encompasses both spatial and sectoral dimensions. (Tacoli, 2003)

And the World Cities Report had this say:

Urbanization should not be at the expense of rural development. In fact, both should be symbiotic and mutually enhancing. (UN-World Cities Report, 2020)

It is for this reason that many researchers do not recognize the distinction between 'rural' and 'urban' in terms of their populations and activities, choosing to them rather as more closely linked both across space as well as across sectors (Steinberg, 2014; Tacoli, 1998). This position is reinforced by those who argue that rural–urban relations are reciprocal; they flow across—to and from each area and each supports the other (Graeme et al., 2019; Steinberg, 2014, p. 12). These researchers have argued that rural and urban areas are interdependent to varying degrees, and rely on flows of individuals, capital, and information to sustain distinct ways of life.

Nevertheless, distinctions between the rural and urban areas may be considered to hold from the viewpoints of livelihoods and economy approach, which is prevalent in geographical literature (Rigg, 2007 cited in Mfune et al., 2016, p. 111). This approach suggests that the rural is dominated by primary production and agricultural livelihoods, while on the other hand, the urban is dominated by manufacturing and non-farm activities. Application of these binaries however denies the co-existence of the rural and urban areas. The work of Owuor (2006) shows the widespread nature of non-farm activities in rural areas, while urban agriculture is a dominant feature of African cities (Bah et al., 2003). Steinberg (2014) goes further to argue that the concepts 'rural' and 'urban' do not have universal definitions; their meanings vary from one country to another. This has important implications; one, inter-country comparisons are rendered difficult, and two, interpreting and applying the concepts in various geographical situations and in time can run into serious challenges. Moreover, there are far reaching policy implications depending on how the rural and urban relate and interact.

Changing Rural–Urban Relations in Africa

Like many other developing regions of the world, Africa is also undergoing demographic and socio-economic shifts. Population growth is on the upward trend in the rural but more significantly, urban areas. Urbanization is on the rise in the sub-Saharan region (Alaci, 2010). By 2050, most countries in the region will have surpassed the tipping point-more than 50 percent of their populations will live in towns and cities (Graeme et al., 2019). These dynamics are transforming the region and reconfiguring the nature of interactions between the rural and urban spaces. The changes are attributed to a variety of factors including poverty, increasing inequalities, environmental stresses and shocks as well as food security (Mfune et al., 2016). Traditionally, these problems have been approached and treated using the categories; 'rural', 'urban', or even 'peri-urban' (e.g., modernization theorists). However, the problems experienced in Africa transcend these discrete and binary categories. Examining and treating rural and urban areas as distinct units may at times be useful; for instance, for deriving descriptions, and more importantly policy intervention, but the separation can serve to obscure the deep complexities and interconnections in the demographic, economic, and political shifts underway in many countries (Graeme et al., 2019). It is noted, however, that although urbanization in sub-Saharan Africa is growing rapidly, the associated growth and development benefits are not being spread around (Mylott, 2009).

Besides increase in population, other factors include the changing political governance dynamics in the region. An example is the wave of decentralization and devolution across many African countries. This has served to encourage more development resources to be shifted to smaller territorial regions and the small towns in their midst. Although this phenomenon has yet to attract much research evidence, this shift in governance policy will significantly impact the dynamics of rural–urban relations in the nations pursuing this policy.

Increase in the incidence of poverty is yet another factor contributing to the changing scenarios in many African countries and in their towns. The manifestation of poverty in both spheres; rural and urban, has direct and indirect implications to the nature and relations in both rural and urban areas.

The concepts and to some extent the theories, vary in scope and diversity. Moreover, the conceptualisation of the relations between rural and urban areas is informed by the economic, social, and political histories of various African countries. The commonly used labels for the relations between rural–urban areas include rural–urban interactions, rural–urban relations, rural–urban development, rural–urban dynamics, and rural–urban balance. For this, we can refer to: Tacoli (1998), Satterthwaite and Tacoli (2003), Gebre-Egziabher and Tegegne (2010), Mushi (2003), Ngau (1989), Mulongo et al. (2010), Hinderink and Titus (2008), Zeleke et al. (2008), Trutmann et al. (2007), Evans (1992), Oucho (2004), Wegulo and Obulinji (2001), and Gaile (1992).

A question that may arise is as follows: 'To what extent do these theories illustrate the efficacy of the linkages between urban centres and development of their rural hinterlands?' This question is best answered by looking at selected studies with empirical verifications (Karaska, 1999; Mason, 1989; Mushi, 2003; Ngau, 1989; Wegulo & Obulinji, 2001). These studies demonstrate the existence of fairly dynamic relations between rural areas and the small towns. The study however, underscores the weak linkages existing between the rural agricultural hinterland and Dar es Salaam. The weaknesses are attributed to several factors; including, limited local institutional development, and its interplay; inadequate provision of social, physical, and economic infrastructure; and ineffective regional planning machinery in the impact region (Mushi, 2003).

Role of Rural–Urban Relations

Rural–urban relations in Africa need to be examined in relation to urban settlements at various levels. These settlements at various scales play important roles and functions in facilitating the backward and forward linkage functions in terms of resource movements and use between the rural and urban areas. Urban centres, especially those at the lower end of the hierarchy such as market centres and small towns, mediate various linkages between rural and urban settlements. Without this mediation, the regional spatial economy in various African countries, and indeed elsewhere would not function (Agergaat et al., 2019; Hinderink & Titus, 2002).

Studies reviewed in this chapter, and others elsewhere demonstrate the importance of mutual and symbiotic relations between rural and in urban centres (UN-Habitat, 2017; Friedmann, 1979; Friedmann, 1996; Hinderink & Titus, 2008; Potts & Mutambirwa, 1990; Okpala, 2003). The study of the impact region of Dar es Salaam by Mushi (2003), for example, unveils the latent potentials of rural–urban linkages (in terms of livelihood enhancement) between the rural and urban sectors. Behind the movement and transfer of goods and services between the two spheres are systems of organizations and production that involve coordinating labour, finance, and management resources. Through interrogating these relations, valuable insights are gained as to how economies; regional and national function. These insights, therefore, provide the basis and framework for planning and development of the resources in rural and urban areas sustainably.

Results from studies conducted in Kutus in Kirinyaga in Kenya and reported variously by Ngau (1989), Mason (1989), and Karaska (1999) equally demonstrate the potential benefits of linkage between towns and their rural hinterlands. It is observed that the Kutus exchange system has several key ingredients briefly described as income multiplication, production and marketing generated revenue, and consumption expenditure. These flows benefit both the agricultural sector (rural) and town. However, like in the case of the Dar es Salaam impact study area, the agricultural sector and by extension the farm households remain the most critical factor in driving the Kutus regional economy.

The study by Wegulo and Obulinji (2001) provides further elaboration of the links between the rural-based agricultural sector (sugarcane production), and market centre and small town based activities (trading, artisanal and provision of a wide range of services). It is evident from the study results that the rural economy and its development are largely dependent upon the agricultural sector.

Challenges Facing the Rural–Urban Dynamics

The role or importance of rural–urban relations notwithstanding, various authors have pointed out challenges that limit the effective functioning of the movement and transfer of resources between and within the two interdependent sectors. Of these, poor infrastructure (roads), lack of storage facilities for fragile produce, lack of value addition and therefore limited income earnings for the producers deserve to be addressed. Others are economic recession and structural adjustment in the decades of the 1980s and 1990s. These caused inter-related changes in the nature of rural–urban relations in many African countries (Foeken & Owuor, 2008).

Evidence from the studies reviewed in this chapter point to some of the challenges. A study conducted by Mojoko and Fonjong (2018) in Meme division of Cameroon draws attention to several bottlenecks that frustrate the communities engaged in agricultural production in that area. The leading challenges are poor infrastructure, especially road connections between the producing areas and the market centres. This is compounded by poor storage facilities and lack of value addition mechanisms that would be instrumental to lessening damage and wastage of fragile commodities such as vegetables and fruits. Value addition could also increase farmer earnings and offer to rural communities other trading and business related employment opportunities. These sentiments are replicated in the study by Somanje in Ghana (Somanje et al., 2020). In this study, the authors observed poor basic and economic infrastructure which was attributed primarily to increased rural–urban migration, urban sprawl, industrial expansion and population increase in the country. In addition, they observe that urban–rural connectivity is weak as a result of poor and inadequate transport (Somanje et al., 2020, p. 7).

Conclusion

This chapter set out to review a select number of published materials on the subject of rural–urban relations in Africa. In total, 32 papers which met the inclusion criteria were selected, read, and interrogated with respect to the nature of study; author, year of publication, focus of the study (what the study is about), geographical unit in which the study was conducted or which area it represents (in the case of secondary data). Also interrogated were the research design used for collecting the data; the concepts and theories which formed the anchor of each study, and key findings from each of the papers reviewed.

The synthesis shows that each of the sample papers has contributed in enriching the sum of the views presented in this chapter on rural–urban relations in Africa. The entirety of the information generated from the individual papers provides an invaluable pool of information on the concept and nature of the relations between rural and urban areas in the continent of Africa. The review has shown that the relations are complex and dynamic, and cannot be restricted to the binary and dichotomous 'rural' and 'urban'. It is equally clear from the results that the relations that connect rural and urban areas are not static in place and time; they are in constant flux depending on the socio-economic, and political environments in the various parts of Africa. The relations also play an important role in shaping social and economic affairs of the regions in which they exist. As such, the nexus between the two sectors and spheres that constitute the rural and the urban allows researchers and policy makers an excellent opportunity to examine and understand the workings of the regional economics under review. Policy makers have a better opportunity to make appropriate interventions to counter development challenges such as poverty, unemployment, and the incidence of climate change in both rural and urban areas. Equally important is the behaviour and practices that communities engage in, in order to mitigate the impact of these problems; for instance, migration, straddling between the rural and urban spheres and in different ways; and the survival strategies used, especially by the poor and economically disadvantaged persons to leverage their ways out of these problems.

This review has in many ways shown the importance of examining the activities people engage in to produce and exchange goods and services across the rural and urban interfaces. The interrogation of such must be a continuing engagement by researchers given the ever changing economic, social, and political environments in Africa. The challenges prompted by the dynamics mentioned will only get more and not less daunting. Of these, poor infrastructure (roads), lack of storage facilities for fragile produce, lack of value addition and therefore limited income earnings for the producers deserve to be addressed. Governments, development partners, and the local communities ought to forge multi-purpose and multisectoral partnerships and approaches to identify and address the emerging and future challenges affecting Africa as revealed through the micro-cosmic sample studies interrogated in this chapter. Increasingly, policy interventions should recognize the virtue of holistic and integrated planning of rural and urban areas in Africa.

The findings presented in this chapter contribute to on-going theoretical and practical understanding of the spatial and sectoral dimensions of rural and urban relations in Africa. The chapter makes reference to the continuing complexities inherent in the relations between the two sectors. Indeed a 'paradigm shift' is eminent, following research findings from the late 1980s onwards about interactions and linkages between rural and urban areas. During this period, analysis of rural and urban 'development' was seen not as separate issues, but expressing a growing awareness of the importance of rural–urban relationships, and dissatisfaction with urban-based centralized models of development.

This chapter also draws attention to sustainable development of the rural–urban system in view of the urban footprint concept. Given the emerging trends in urban expansion of the future in Africa, relations between rural and urban areas will continue to manifest and accordingly shape future spatial development in Africa. Undergirding these ramifications are three factors: First, the ever growing urban population evident in many African countries which places new challenges upon both rural and urban areas. Second, is the globalized economy whose dynamics and ramifications affect the organization and functioning of the rural and urban economies in different ways. Third, African countries are signatories to various global conventions, declarations, and treaties that stipulate how our social and economic affairs should be organized and developed (e.g., MDGs/SDGs, climate change). All these require consolidated and synthesized information that allows African governments at various scales and levels to make relevant and appropriate policy decisions required for the planning and implementation of sustainable development of our countries.

REFERENCES

Agergaard, J., Tacoli, C., & Steel, G. et al. (2019, January). Revisiting rural–urban transformations and small town development in sub-saharan Africa. *European Journal of Development Research, 31*, 2–11. https://doi.org/10.1057/s41287-018-0182-z. Published 21 November 2018.

Akkoyunlu, S. (2015). The potential of rural-urban linkages for sustainable development and trade. *International Journal of Sustainable Development & World Policy, 4*(2), 20–40.

Alaci, D. S. A. (2010). *Regulating urbanization in Sub Saharan Africa through cluster settlement: Lessons for urban managers in Ethiopia*. Retrieved from http://www.um.ase.ro/No14/2/2pdf

Baffoe, G., Zhou, X., Moinuddin, M., Somanje, A. N., Kuriyama, A., Mohan, G., Saito, O., & Takeuchi, K. (2021). Urban–rural linkages: Effective solutions for achieving sustainable development in Ghana from an SDG interlinkage perspective. *Sustainability Science*. https://doi.org/10.1007/s11625-021-00929-8

Bah, M., Cisse, S., Diyamett, B., Diallo, D., Lerise, F., Okali, D., Okpara, D., Olasoye, J., & Tacoli, C. (2003, April). Changing rural-urban linkages in Mali, Nigeria and Tanzania. *Environment and Urbanization, 15*(1), 13–24.

Baker, J. & Pedersen, P.O. (Eds.). (1992). The rural-urban interface in Africa: Expansion and adaptation. *Seminar Proceedings No. 27*, Copenhagen: The Scandinavian Institute of Africa Studies in Cooperation with the Centre for Development Research.

Bryceson, D. (2006). Fundamentals of urban life in east and southern Africa. In D. F. Bryceson & D Potts (Eds.), *African urban economics: Viability, vitality or vitiation* (pp. 3–38). Palgrave Macmillan.

Cervero, R. (2013). Linking urban transport and land use in developing countries. *Journal of Transport and Land Use, 6*(1), 7–24.

Chant, S. (1998). Households, gender and rural-urban migration: Reflections on linkages and considerations for policy. *Environment and Urbanization, 10*(1), 5–22.

Djurfeldt, A. A. (2012). Virtuous and vicious cycles in rural-urban linkages: Cases from Zimbabwe. *Africa Review 4*(2), 136–156.

Evans, H. E. (1992). A virtuous circle model of rural-urban development: Evidence from a Kenyan small town and its hinterland. *Journal of Development Studies, 28*(4), 640–667.

Evans, H. E., & Ngau, P. (1991). Rural-urban relations, household income diversification and agricultural productivity. *Development and Change, 23*(1991), 519–545.

Ferguson, J. (1999). *Expectations of modernity: Myths and meanings of urban life on the Zambian Copperbelt*. University of California Press.

Foeken. D. W. J. & .Owuor, S. (2008) Farming as a livelihood source for the urban poor of Nakuru, Kenya. *Geoforum 39*(6): 1978–1990. https://doi.org/10.1016/j.geoforum.2008.07.011

Friedman, J. (1966). *Regional development policy: A case study of Venezuela*. MIT Press.

Friedmann, J. (1979). Basic needs, agropolitan development, and planning from below. *World Development, 7*(6), 607–613.

Friedmann, J. (1996). Modular cities: Beyond the rural-urban divide. *Environment and Urbanization, 8*(1), 129–131. https://doi.org/10.1630/095624796322752975

Gaile, G. L. (1992). Improving rural-urban linkages through small town market-based development. *Third World Planning Review, 14*(2), 131–148.

Gebre, T., & Gebremedhin, B. (2019). The mutual benefits of promoting rural-urban interdependence through linked ecosystem services. *Global Ecology and Conservation, 20,* e00707.

Gebre-Egziabher, T., & Ayenew, M. (2010). *Micro-and small enterprises as vehicles for poverty reduction, employment creation and business development: The ethiopian experience.* Forum for Social Studies (FSS), Addis Ababa FSS Research Report No. 6.

Graeme, S. W., Sewankambo, N., Mwendwa, S., Kayom, W. (2019). *Owning our urban future: Urban-rural linkages for balanced regional development in Africa.* Uganda National Academy of Sciences.

Guneralp, B., Lwasa, S., Mwasundire, H., Parnel, S.,& Seto, K. C. (2017). Urbanization in Africa: Challenges and opportunities for conservation. *Environment Research Letters.* (2018). https://doi.org/10.1088/1748.9326/aa94fe

Hatcher, C. (2017). *Rural-urban linkages in the context of sustainable development and environmental protection.* United Nations Centre to Combat Desertification. Global land Outlook Working Paper.

Hinderink, J., & Titus, M. (2008). Paradigms of regional development and the role of small centres. *Development and Change, 19*(3), 401–423. https://doi.org/10.1111/J.1467-7660

Hinderink, J., & Titus, M. (2002). Small towns and regional development: Major findings and policy implications from comparative research. *Urban Studies, 39*(3), 379–391.

Kabwegyere, T. B. (1979). Small urban centres and the growth of underdevelopment in rural Kenya. *Africa Journal of the International African Institute, 49*(3), 308–315.

Kamete, A. Y. (1998, April). Interlocking livelihoods: farm and small town in Zimbabwe. *Environment and Urbanization, 10*(1).

Karaska, G. J. (1999). The regional structures of third world economies: Rural-urban dynamics in Kenya and Madagascar. *Environment and Planning, 31*(5), 767–781.

Kioko, K. M. (2003). *The role of rural-urban linkages in urban and regional planning: A case study of the spatial interaction of the municipality of Machakos and its umland.* PhD dissertation at university of Nairobi. erepository.uonbi.ac.ke

Klimzuk, A., & Klimezuk-Kochanska, M. (2019). Core-periphery model. In R. S. Thapa & P. M. Marton (Eds.), *The Palgrave encyclopaedia of global security,* 1–8. Cham: Springer. https://doi.org/10.1007/978-3-319-74336-3_320-1

Lipton, M. (1977). *Why poor people stay poor: Urban bias in world development.* Temple Smith.

Lynch, K. (2018). Rural-urban interaction and development in Africa. In *The Routledge handbook of African development.* London: Routledge International Development/ Routledge/Taylor & Francis.

Mason, J. P. (1989). *The role of urbanization in national development: Bridging the rural-urban divide.* AID Program Evaluation Discussion Paper No. 27. Washington, DC: US Agency for International Development.

Mfune, O., Mutisya, E., Popoola, I., Mungai, D., Fuh, D. & Olayide, O. E. (2016). Changing rural urban linkages in Africa in a globalizing economy. *AJSD, 6*(2).

Mojoko, F. M., & Fonjong, L. (2018). Challenges to effective rural-urban linkages in meme division of Cameroon. *Journal of Asian Scientific Research*. https://doi.org/10.18488/journal.2.2018.82.42.51

Mulongo, L. S., Erute, B. E., & Kerre, P. M. (2010). Rural-urban interlink and sustainability of urban centres in Kenya; Malaba Town. *46th ISOCARP Congress*, Nairobi, Kenya.

Mushi, N. S. (2003). *Regional development through rural-urban linkages: The Dar es Salaam impact region*. A PhD Thesis submitted to the Faculty of Spatial Planning, University of Dortmund in fulfilment of the requirement of the award of a Dr. rer. pol. Degree.

Mylott, E. (2009). *Urban-rural connections: A review of the literature*. Available from: https://ir.library.oregonstate.edu/apa/rb68xb945. Accessed in October 2021.

Ngau, P. M. (1989). *Rural-urban relations-Kutus, Kenya*. Unpublished PhD Dissertation. University of California, Los Angeles.

Okpala, D. C. L. (2003). *Promoting the positive rural-urban linkages approach to sustainable development and employment creation: The Role of UN-HABITAT*. https://www.fig.net/resources/proceedings/fig_proceedings/morocco/proceedings/PS1/PS1_1_okpala.pdf. Accessed 2 Apr 2017.

Otite, O. (1979). Rural migrants as catalysts in rural development: The Urhobo in Indo State, Nigeria. *Africa 49*(3), 226–234.

Oucho, J. (2004). *Rural-Urban Linkages: Biharamulo town (Mtwara Region of Tanzania and its Immediate Hinterland)*. https://www.google.com/search?q=Oucho%2C+J.+%282004%29.+Rural-Urban+Linkages%3A+Biharamulo+town+%28Mtwara+region+of+Tanzania%29+and+its+immediate+hinterland&ie=utf-8&oe=utf-8&client=firefox-b. Accessed 2 Apr 2018.

Owuor, S. O. (2006). *Bridging the urban-rural divide: Multi-spatial livelihoods in Nakuru town, Kenya*. Unpublished PhD Thesis, University of Amsterdam, The Netherlands.

Potts, D., & Mutambirwa, C. C. (1990). Rural-urban linkages in contemporary Harare: Why migrants need their land. *Journal of Southern African Studies, 16*(4), 676–698.

Rondinelli, D. (1988). Market towns and agriculture in Africa. The role of small urban centres in economic development. *African Urban Quarterly, 3*, 1–2.

Satterthwaite, D. (2016). *Small and Intermediate urban centres in sub-Saharan Africa*. Working Paper No. 6. International Institute for Environment and Development, UK.

Satterthwaite, D., & Tacoli, C. (2003). *The urban part of rural development: The role of small and intermediate urban centres in rural and regional development and poverty reduction*. International Institute for Environment and Development.

Somanje, A. N., Mohan, G., Lopes, L., Mensah, A., Gordon, C., Zhou, X., Moinuddum, M., Saitu, O. K., & Takeuchi, T. (2020). Challenges and potential solutions for sustainable urban-rural linkages in a Ghanaian context. *Sustainability, 12*, 507. https://doi.org/10.3390/su12020507

Southall, A. (Ed.). (1978). *Small urban centres in rural development in Africa*. African Studies Program, University of Wisconsin.

Southall, A. (1988, December). Small Urban centres in rural development: What else is development other than helping your own hometown? *African Studies Review, 31*(3).

Steinberg, F. (2014). *Rural-urban linkages: An urban perspective*. Document No. 128. Working Group: Development with Territorial Cohesion for Development Program. Rimisp, Santiago, Chile.

Tacoli, C. (1998, April). Rural-urban interactions: A guide to the literature. *Environment and Urbanization, 10*(1), 147–166

Tacoli, C. (2003). The links between urban and rural development. *Environment and Urbanization, 15*, 3. https://doi.org/10.1177/095624780301500111

Tegegne, G. E. (2001). *Rural-urban linkages under different farming system*. Social Science Research Report Series, No. 2.

Tostensen, A. (2004). *Rural-urban linkages in sub Saharan Africa: Contemporary debates and implications for Kenyan urban workers in the 21st century*. WP 2004: 4. Chr. Michelsen Institute Development Studies and Human Rights.

Trutmann, P., Zeleke, G., & Denekew, A. (2007). Fostering new development pathways: Harnessing rural-urban linkages (RUL) to reduce poverty and improve environment in the Highlands of Ethiopia. http://hdl.handle.net/123456789/2107

Vance, J. E. (1970). *The merchant's world: The geography of wholesaling*. Prentice Hall.

Wanyande, P. (2016). *Devolution and territorial development inequalities: The Kenyan experience*. Working Paper Series No. 187. Rimisp, Santiago, Chile.

Wiardaa, H. J. (1983). Toward a nonethnocentric theory of development: Alternative conception from the third World. *Journal of Development Areas., 4*, 433–452.

Wegulo, F. N., & Obulinji, H. W. (2001). Link between sugarcane farming and small enterprise development. In P. O. Alila & P. O. Pedersen (Eds.), *Negotiating social space: East African micro enterprises* (pp. 223–252). African World Press Inc.

UNCCD. (2017). *United Nations convention to combat desertification in Africa: Economic report on Africa 2017—Urbanization and industrialization for Africa's transformation*. Bonn: UNCCD

UN-Habitat. (2017). *Implementing the new urban agenda by strengthening urban-rural linkages: Leave no one and no space behind*. Nairobi: United Nations Human Settlements Programme.

UN Habitat. (2019). *Urban-rural linkages: guiding principles: Framework for action to advance integrated territorial development*. Nairobi: UN Habitat

UN-World Cities Report. (2020). *The value of sustainable urbanization*. Nairobi: UN Habitat.

Zeleke, G., Alemu, D., Bewuket, W., Alemu, B., Assefa, Y., & Trutmann, P. (2008). *Poverty gradient along the rural-urban transect in Ethiopia: The case of Addis Ababa-Bahir Dar Gradient*.

Websites: Videos and You Tube Materials

Videos and YouTube Web Materials on Rural-Urban Relations
Thinking rural and urban areas together contribute to achieve several SDGs. Available at https://www.youtube.com/watch?v=-uGVi6FlV00

Training Guides on Rural-Urban Relations
Training Manual for Applying the Urban-Rural Linkages-Guiding Principles. Available at: https://urbanrurallinkages.files.wordpress.com/2020/03/url-training-manual.pdf

CHAPTER 11

Recreation Planning and Management

Wycliffe W. Simiyu Njororai

INTRODUCTION

Recreation provision has become an important service designed to meet significant physical, social and emotional needs of all community residents and their families (Kraus & Curtis, 1990). According to Mogajane et al. (2014), recreation provision may be affected by the nature and structure of leadership in government, be it local or national. Planning for recreation services is also driven by changes in technology, socioeconomics, politics, new opportunities and changes in family structures (Edginton et al., 2004). Urban parks and open spaces are locations that provide opportunities for a wide range of leisure, sports and recreational activities. While parks alone cannot solve our current urban problems such as air pollution, noise, health risks and amenity loss, they are crucial for the economic health of our cities and to the citizens' quality of life for several reasons (del Saz Salazar & Menéndez, 2007).

Park and recreation programmes in urban areas can contribute to the promotion of public health and safety by encouraging physical and mental fitness and by providing an effective antidote to the stress of urban living (del Saz Salazar & Menéndez, 2007; Wolf, 2017). According to Wolf (2017), scientific evidence should be the basis of future efforts to make cities more sustainable and sustaining. Wolf adds that green space directly contributes to quality human habitat and is profoundly important for the health of the

---

W. W. S. Njororai (✉)
Department of Kinesiology, University of Texas at Tyler, Tyler, TX, USA
e-mail: wnjororai@uttyler.edu

mind and body. Integrating parks and infrastructure goals can provide more opportunities for the nearby nature experiences that promote good health and sustain wellness in African cities. This chapter presents and discusses evidence on trends and status of recreational and physical activities and their management in African cities, critically assessing the specific theories, research designs, planning approaches and outcomes that have been studied. The chapter highlights some of the studies and reports done on the planning and availability of recreation resources and services in some African urban areas.

One of the most important components of recreational activities is physical activity (PA). PA is a health-enhancing behaviour with many benefits to an individual. Regular PA has been shown to reduce the risk for a range of chronic diseases (Amusa et al., 2012; Dhurup & Grobler, 2012; Dvorak et al., 2012; Ferreira et al., 2006; Strydom, 2013). Among young people, PA offers prospects for building strong bones, healthy joints, a strong heart, a good mental health and prevents today's major public health concerns; obesity (Amusa et al., 2012; Kohn & Booth, 2003). Despite these health benefits, many people, especially the young ones, are not engaging in recommended levels of PA to maximize these benefits. One of the reasons for low participation is the absence of recreational facilities for people to fully engage safely in their movement endeavours. This is noticeably so in urban areas where space is at a premium and opportunities for physical movement are scarce.

Nevertheless, physical inactivity has been associated with the Western, affluent and industrialized societies (Aarts et al., 2011; Dvorak et al., 2012; Ziraba et al., 2009), with serious problems and several unfavourable health consequences. However, similar negative consequences are reported to be on the increase in Africa. There is increasing evidence showing that high levels of physical inactivity are becoming a major lifestyle among adults and children throughout Africa (April et al., n.d.; Dumith et al., 2011; Dvorak et al., 2012; Guthold et al., 2008, 2011; Kamau et al., 2011; Njororai & Njororai, 2018; Onywera et al., 2012, 2013, 2016; Strydom, 2013; Ziraba et al., 2009). This chapter summarizes the evidence on recreation and related physical activity planning in urban areas of Africa.

Methods

Published peer-reviewed articles, commissioned reports and academic theses on recreation and physical activity planning pertaining to urban areas in Africa were the focus of the study. Published articles/reports/theses on recreation planning were searched in electronic databases. These included Medline, CINAHL, Sport Discus, Health Source, Health Reference Centre and Academic Consumer Health. Additionally, google search was done. The key words used in the literature search included recreation planning, physical activity, African countries, health promotion, leisure, African cities, urbanization, green spaces and urban playgrounds. The search strategy was restricted to English language papers published between 1995 and 2020.

Initially, titles and abstracts of studies uncovered by the electronic searches via data bases were examined on the screen. Papers which could not be excluded based on the title and abstract were obtained in full and reviewed for possible inclusion. Over 1569 titles showed up, out of which the titles and abstracts of 120 articles were initially reviewed, yielding 50 that were printed and examined further. Twenty-one publications (see Table 11.1) were found appropriate and selected, based on sample characteristics or nature of study, study type, data collection method, study focus, findings and conclusions and recommendations, for deeper conceptual, methodological and contextual analysis.

Results and Discussion

Table 11.1 shows the summary of the reviewed publications including the author(s), year of publication, sample characteristics, geographical unit, nature of the study, study type, data collection method, study focus, findings and conclusions and recommendations.

Nature of Studies

Table 11.1 has presented a summary of the reviewed publications including the author(s), year of publication, sample characteristics, geographical unit, type of study or design, data collection method, study focus, findings and conclusions and recommendations. Out of the 21 studies reviewed, 20 of them were published between 2011 and 2020 (Cirolia & Berrisford, 2017; Daniel, 2016; Daniel & Strickland, 2017; Dhurup & Grobler, 2012; Goslin et al., 2015; Kimengsi & Fogwe, 2017; Kumelachew, 2020; Makworo & Mireri, 2011; Mboumba, 2017; Mogajane et al., 2014; Munien et al., 2015; Oosthuizen & Burnett, 2019; Owen, 2016; Shackleton et al., 2018; Tibesigwa et al., 2020; Turpie et al., 2016; Urmilla & Maharaj, 2015; van Der Merwe, 2012; Vansintjan, 2020; UN-Habitat, 2016). Only one was published in 1995 (Kaarsholm, 1995). There seem to be an upsurge in literature on African cities and provision of green spaces and recreation services in the last ten years.

In terms of geographical units. South Africa led the way with 8 studies (Dhurup & Grobler, 2012; Goslin et al., 2015; Mogajane et al., 2014; Munien et al., 2015; Oosthuizen & Burnett, 2019; Shackleton et al., 2018; Urmilla & Maharaj, 2015; van Der Merwe, 2012); followed by 3 Global ones (Daniel & Strickland, 2017; UN-Habitat, 2016; Vansintjan, 2020); 2 from Kenya (Makworo & Mireri, 2011; Owen, 2016); two multi-nations (Cirolia & Berrisford, 2017; Daniel, 2016); and one each from Gabon (Mboumba, 2017); Cameroon (Kimengsi & Fogwe, 2017), Zimbabwe (Kaarsholm, 1995), Ethiopia (Kumelachew, 2020), Tanzania (Tibesigwa et al., 2020) and Uganda (Turpie et al., 2016). It is apparent that South Africa had more studies than any other country. This may be due to more established disciplines that focus

Table 11.1 Summary of results on recreation in African cities

Author (year)	Study focus	Geographical unit	Sample characteristics	Theories	Study type/design	Data collection method	Results
Mogajane et al. (2014)	Availability of recreation policies and strategies for the provision of recreation service delivery	North Western province, SA	20 local recreational managers	Strategic planning and quality life	Mixed Methods approach	Focus group and questionnaire	Majority (75 percent) of the local governments are in the rural settings while 25 percent are located in urban areas with limited resources. All local governments (100 percent) do not have recreation strategic plans. Policy statements concerning finance (80 percent), provision of human resources (90 percent), provision of recreation facilities (65 percent), provision of recreation programme (80 percent), coordination, planning or implementation of recreation programmes (85 percent), the lease of recreation facilities (75 percent), the appointment of administrative or supportive service (95 percent) or the use of volunteers (80 percent) were not available

Author (year)	Study focus	Geographical unit	Sample characteristics	Theories	Study type/design	Data collection method	Results
van Der Merwe (2012)	Locating opportunities for Outdoor action and Adventure Recreation and Tourism in the Western Cape, SA	Western Cape Province of South Africa	Twenty-seven relevant criteria were selected from 80 available mapped variables	Modern spatial computing technology in developing spatial policy for, and planning of outdoor action and adventure recreation and tourism (OAART)	Quantitative	Geographical information system (GIS) applications	This research gives strategic direction to developers and marketers of OAART in the Western Cape. The deliverable is an indicator of potential spatial recreationist product opportunities, spatially represented in map format at a resolution of 1 km^2 and offered as a valuable planning and development tool and aid. It identifies, exposes and explains key elements of the natural, cultural and social and policy environments in which OAART operations and endeavours exist in the Western Cape
Goslin et al. (2015)	Eight dimensions of management and project design of a facility	City of Tshwane, SA	8 recreation and sport facility managers	Management capacity and quality of life	Quantitative case study	Capacity Analysis Tool self-administered questionnaire consisting of 88 sub-elements	Results indicated that the internal systemic management capacity of the particular department in this investigation measured unsatisfactory ($x = 2.50$) in five of the eight management dimensions. While three dimensions scored satisfactory ($x = 2.50$) the overall collective management capacity score for all eight dimensions was unsatisfactory at $x = 2.33$
Urmilla and Maharaj (2015)	Tourism infrastructure and services available	Durban central beachfront, South Africa	Tourists visiting parks and recreational facilities	Recreation infrastructure and service provision	Mixed methods approach	Observation and survey	Study identifies several infrastructure needs linked to transport, ablution facilities, safety and security and maintenance issues

(continued)

Table 11.1 (continued)

Author (year)	Study focus	Geographical unit	Sample characteristics	Theories	Study type/design	Data collection method	Results
Oosthuizen and Burnett (2019)	Community mapping and creating safe spaces for physical activity	Mamelodi East, Ekurhuleni municipal district, SA	School kids, coaches, stakeholder and community representative	Safe environments or spaces	A multi-method research design	Interviews	Spaces simultaneously exist on a continuum of safe and unsafe in articulation with supportive and unsupportive environments
Munien et al. (2015)	Conceptualization and use of green spaces in peri-urban communities	Inanda, KwaZulu-Natal, SA	Former African reserve settlement	Safe public spaces	Mixed methods approach	Structured surveys and a focus group	Local community members use green spaces for a range of recreational and livelihood purposes such as relaxation, hiking, biking, playing sports and the collection of resources. Also, even though limited levels of scientific knowledge were noted, respondents displayed significant levels of environmental awareness

11 RECREATION PLANNING AND MANAGEMENT 297

Author (year)	Study focus	Geographical unit	Sample characteristics	Theories	Study type/design	Data collection method	Results
Kaarsholm (1995)	Discusses urban development, culture and politics in Bulawayo, Zimbabwe	Bulawayo, Zimbabwe's second biggest city	The last hundred years' social history of urban development	Authentic vs eclecticism culture	Qualitative/essay	Archival research	Policies before independence fluctuated between attempts at keeping African urban residents 'temporary' and underlining their basically rural identities and modernizing efforts at integrating them in town and establishing forms of social control that would discourage them from developing political demands for rights and citizenship equal to those of white urbanites. The culture and politics of Bulawayo's African townships were influenced significantly by initiatives to adapt to, or resist such policies, and the article seeks to trace lines of continuity between the way in which people reacted to urban conditions and policies of urbanization in colonial times and what stand out as important issues of articulation and self-understanding in what is today called 'high-density suburbs' and provide political culture in Bulawayo with its special liveliness

(continued)

Table 11.1 (continued)

Author (year)	Study focus	Geographical unit	Sample characteristics	Theories	Study type/design	Data collection method	Results
Shackleton et al. (December 2018)	How important is green infrastructure in small and medium-sized towns?	South African Towns	Location of green infrastructure across nine towns	Urban green infrastructure or social-ecological	Quantitative	GIS mapping	The results show significant use of green infrastructure for a range of provisioning and cultural services as well as its contribution to spiritual and mental well-being. Provisioning contributions are both in regular support of livelihood needs as well as increased use after a covariate shock (a flood), both of which help reduce household vulnerability. Lastly, our results show the expressed level of support and willingness to pay or work among urban residents for green infrastructure and the services it provides

Author (year)	Study focus	Geographical unit	Sample characteristics	Theories	Study type/design	Data collection method	Results
Kumelachew (2020)	Attitude and perception of residents towards the benefits, challenges and quality of neighbourhood parks	Addis Ababa, Ethiopia	Household survey of residents and three focus group discussions	Urban green space/ecosystem/socio-cultural	Mixed Methods Approach	Survey and focus group discussions	Respondents recognize the environmental, socio-cultural and economic benefits provided by neighbourhood parks. However, the socio-cultural and environmental benefits are perceived as more important than the economic benefits. The socio-demographic characteristics of age, gender and education level were found to have no significant effect on perceptions or attitudes. The cost of managing neighbourhood parks and the attraction of nuisance insects were the two most important challenges. The majority of respondents rated the quality of the existing neighbourhood parks as excellent or good, with the existing safety condition and the presence of high plant diversity receiving the highest number of high scores. The availability of park facilities was the aspect of park quality considered poor by the most respondents

(continued)

Table 11.1 (continued)

Author (year)	Study focus	Geographical unit	Sample characteristics	Theories	Study type/design	Data collection method	Results
Makworo and Mireri (2011)	Threat to public open spaces by congestion and deterioration	Nairobi City, Kenya		Spatial planning and public green space	Qualitative	Archival/document analysis	According to the 1948 Master Plan for the city, city planning was premised on the neighbourhood concept with ample provision of public open spaces. However, after Kenya's independence in 1963, the implementation of the Master Plan was largely abandoned. Rapid and uncontrolled urbanization meant that public open spaces that were intended to serve a population of 250,000 now serve over 3 million people. Public open spaces in the city suffer from degradation, overcrowding and insecurity, thus denying city residents access to the much-needed recreation and leisure facilities
Kimengsi and Fogwe (2017)	Opportunities and challenges of urban greening	Bamenda City, Cameroon	Residents	Urban green growth/ecological/green space	Mixed methods approach	Interviews, content analysis and focus groups	Initiative will provide opportunities for employment, generate revenue for the City Council and prevent uncontrolled city sprawl against the backdrop of the relatively unstable nature of the foothills (due to mass wasting processes) and land-use competition, largely driven by population growth and the daunting task of relocating prior users. We therefore argue in favour of the effective application of urban development policies to restrict encroachment around the area and to engage in slope stabilization where necessary

Author (year)	Study focus	Geographical unit	Sample characteristics	Theories	Study type/design	Data collection method	Results
Tibesigwa et al (2020)	Valuing recreational ecosystem services in developing cities	Dar es Salaam, Tanzania	A random survey of households residing	Urban ecosystem services	Survey/quantitative	Questionnaire	Marginal willingness to pay is highest for nature parks, followed by multi-use parks and neighbourhood parks. Willingness to pay for neighbourhood parks decreases as distance increases. Specifically, and depending on the assumptions, the marginal willingness to pay for nature parks ranges between US$0.40 and US$0.79 per month. Households are willing to pay between US$0.27 and US$0.69 per month for multi-use parks. Under neighbourhood parks, this value is $0.10 to US$0.47

(continued)

Table 11.1 (continued)

Author (year)	Study focus	Geographical unit	Sample characteristics	Theories	Study type/design	Data collection method	Results
Owen (2016)	Highlights the role of recreation as a governing and community interest that shaped the development of urban policy and land use in Nairobi and Mombasa; Kenya's two largest cities	Mombasa and Nairobi, Kenya	Residents	Negotiation, struggle and production of built environments	Mixed methods approach	Interview and document analysis	Through the allocation of land for clubs, the state affirmed its authority as an arbitrator of multiple interests and constituencies. During the 1940s and 1950s, the state, viewing African boredom as a cause of social delinquency, promoted the development of new spaces of leisure such as social halls, playing fields and public gardens. Rather than reaffirming the state's position as the paternalistic guardian of African interests, these spaces were sites of social and cultural negotiation between urban Kenyans and colonial welfare officers. By independence, Kenyans recognized playgrounds, parks and other recreational amenities as fundamental requisites of city life, connecting them with ideas of propriety, legitimacy and dignity. My dissertation chronicles the struggles of urban Kenyans for recreational spaces in the midst of competing demands for urban space, extension of state authority and the social effects of privatization and neoliberalism

Author (year)	Study focus	Geographical unit	Sample characteristics	Theories	Study type/design	Data collection method	Results
Mboumba (2017)	Determine the tourism impacts of the 2012 Africa Cup of Nations (AFCON) in Gabon	Libreville and Franceville, Gabon		Sports tourism	Quantitative research approach (descriptive design)	Questionnaires	The results show that there is a huge deficiency of awareness in terms of responsible tourism, with the local residents not seeming to have an appreciation of its meaning, importance and advantages. The question also arises as to whether the Gabon local government officials are aware of their responsibility towards the future generation in this respect. However, the Gabonese government has certainly made the development of the tourism sector a priority through the adoption of different policies, regulations, programmes and strategies that have been created, most notably in the case of the Gabonese greening strategies. Nevertheless, there seems to be an extensive gap between the policies and strategies adopted, and their actual implementation. This should be seen in the light of the Cape Town Declaration recognizing that responsible tourism is about 'making better places for people to live in and better places for people to visit'. Such tourism entails that travel agencies, governments, tours operators, tourists, hoteliers and local communities take responsibility for actions that go towards making tourism more sustainable than it has been in the past

(continued)

Table 11.1 (continued)

Author (year)	Study focus	Geographical unit	Sample characteristics	Theories	Study type/design	Data collection method	Results
Turpie et al. (2016)	Green Urban Development	Kampala, Uganda	Report	Green urban spaces	Case study	Project rehabilitation	Current functioning and capacity of the Nakivubo wetland requires interventions to restore the wetland to a level where economic benefits could be realized. The primary objectives were defined as (1) effecting a measurable improvement of water quality passing out of the Nakivubo wetland into Inner Murchison Bay, (2) ensuring sustainable management of the Nakivubo wetland, (3) reducing water quality impacts on human health and (4) opening up opportunities for safe recreational use of the lower wetland. A sequential set of interventions (treatment train) was recommended to achieve these objectives, and included both infrastructure upgrades and wetland rehabilitation and conservation measures as well as investment in recreational facilities

Author (year)	Study focus	Geographical unit	Sample characteristics	Theories	Study type/design	Data collection method	Results
Girolia and Berrisford (2017)	Unpacks how plans are implemented in three African cities	Nairobi, Addis Ababa and Harare	Three planning implementation instruments	Comparative spatial planning/negotiated planning	Case study	Document analysis	It is clear that planning implementation is different in each of the cities discussed. However, in each case, planning is not simply an ad hoc process, with no sense or logic. Instead, planning implementation reflects the unique and particular context, context and ongoing negotiation among the stakeholders implicated in realizing urban plans
Dhurup and Grobler (2012)	Effects of community environments on health conditions such as physical inactivity	Southern Gauteng, SA	148 respondents in a semi-urban township	Community environments/ecological	Cross-sectional/quantitative	Questionnaire	Results indicate that respondents' physical activity participation ranged from mild to moderate with majority of the respondents not meeting the minimum physical activity guidelines (30 minutes or more a day, most days of the week of at least moderate physical activity). In addition, the results indicate that the built environment or the lack thereof play an influential role in physical activity participation. Perceived access to various destinations, street planning in the neighbourhood, places for walking and cycling, neighbourhood surroundings, safety from traffic and safety from crime seem to prohibit residents from participating in physical activity

(continued)

Table 11.1 (continued)

Author (year)	Study focus	Geographical unit	Sample characteristics	Theories	Study type/design	Data collection method	Results
Daniel and Strickland (2017)	Policies that preserve, protect and enhance important community assets	Global	Open public spaces in Cities	Open public space/liveable city	Case studies	Document analysis	Open public spaces have numerous environmental benefits. The increase in hard surfacing and the reduction of green spaces is resulting in higher temperatures in cities than in the surrounding countryside. Parks that include plants and trees help to balance this effect by cooling the air, providing shade and absorbing air pollutants. This is especially beneficial in cities with hot climates and can assist in lowering the need for air conditioning, resulting in improved air quality. Additionally, parks improve the quality of water, and can decrease the effects of flooding by allowing water to infiltrate the ground

Author (year)	Study focus	Geographical unit	Sample characteristics	Theories	Study type/design	Data collection method	Results
Vansintjan (2020)	High quality, accessible and genuinely public green and open spaces in cities	Global	Public and private spaces	Open public space/liveable city	Case study report	Document analysis	According to the Charter of Public Space agreed upon by all parties present at the 2013 Biennial of Public Space convened by UN-Habitat, public spaces are important because they: Support the movement of and interaction between people; Host accessible commercial and public activities; Offer space for recreation, leisure, exercise and regeneration; Promote education and culture; Promote conviviality, encounter and freedom of expression; Are important for individual and collective memory and community identity; Are vital in the integration of ecosystems and architecture and determine the image of the city; Are one of the main tools available to governments to build social and economic wealth and upgrade urban space

(continued)

Table 11.1 (continued)

Author (year)	Study focus	Geographical unit	Sample characteristics	Theories	Study type/design	Data collection method	Results
Daniel (2016)	Research and Implementation Agenda for Public Spaces in African Cities	Kenya, SA, Ghana, Niger, Uganda, Tanzania	18 researchers, governments and civil society	Change theory and public spaces	Archival	Document analysis	In Africa, like in many other places in the world, public spaces are used for public life, commerce and interaction. However, lack of funds, planning and maintenance, as well as priority for motorized vehicles, has turned many public spaces into unsafe, unforgiving and unconnected places. In addition, many public spaces are difficult to access, especially for those living in vulnerable situations. Public spaces are a key element of individual and community well-being and are critical for the historic, environmental, social and economic functioning of cities and ultimately for people's quality of life. This document outlines a suggested agenda for key public spaces, research and implementation priorities for researchers, civil society, government and funders in Africa. It can be used as a starting point to develop research strategies and funding programmes for the creation and support of public spaces in African cities

Author (year)	Study focus	Geographical unit	Sample characteristics	Theories	Study type/design	Data collection method	Results
United Nations Human Settlements Programme (UN-Habitat) (2016)	Toolkit is to guide policies and strategies at city level and to provide examples linking policies to practices	Global	Cities/experts	Public spaces	Case studies	Expert groups	Since 2012, UN Habitat's Urban Planning and Design Branch (UPDB) and Office of External Relations have jointly embarked on the development and implementation of a Global Programme on Public Space, which is organized around three main areas: (1) Partnerships for public space; (2) City-wide strategies and pilot/demonstration projects; and, (3) Knowledge management, tools and advocacy. UN-Habitat is also mobilizing partners to work with cities around the globe in improving the quality, supply and reach of public spaces. A special focus is on cities in developing countries, and cities with high percentages of their population living in slums and in underprivileged circumstances. Public space is often referred to as 'the poor man's living room' which hints at its particular importance for the recreation, social and economic development of vulnerable groups

on recreation and the emerging concept of smart cities with a focus on green spaces, tourism and recreation.

In terms of study type or designs, 7 used mixed methods approaches (Kimengsi & Fogwe, 2017; Kumelachew, 2020; Mogajane et al., 2014; Munien et al., 2015; Oosthuizen & Burnett, 2019; Owen, 2016; Urmilla & Maharaj, 2015). Six were quantitative in nature (Dhurup & Grobler, 2012; Goslin et al., 2015; Mboumba, 2017; Shackleton et al., 2018; Tibesigwa et al., 2020; van Der Merwe, 2012), three qualitative/archival/historical (Daniel, 2016; Kaarsholm, 1995; Makworo & Mireri, 2011) and five case studies (Cirolia & Berrisford, 2016; Daniel & Strickland, 2017; Turpie et al., 2016; UN-Habitat, 2016; Vansintjan, 2020). There were therefore diverse study designs, geographical scope and data collection approaches that shed light on the state of recreation with implications for urban planning in Africa in the period spanning 1995–2020.

Theories and Conceptual Models

Globally, there is increasing interest as well as extensive research which reveals that recreational ecosystem services, such as urban parks, playgrounds and other green spaces, provide benefits both directly and indirectly to the user (Bernath & Roschewitz, 2008; Chaudhry, 2013; Daniel, 2016; Daniel & Strickland, 2017; del Saz Salazar & Menéndez, 2007; Dhurup & Grobler, 2012; Goslin et al., 2015; Henderson-Wilson et al., 2017; Kimengsi & Fogwe, 2017; Kumelachew, 2020; Makwaro & Mireri, 2011; Munien et al., 2015; Oosthuizen & Burnett, 2019; Owen, 2016; Shackleton et al., 2018; Tibesigwa et al., 2020; Turpie et al., 2016; UN-Habitat, 2016; van Der Merwe, 2012; Vansintjan, 2020). This is made urgent by the rapid urbanization that Sub-Saharan Africa is experiencing.

It is projected that urban areas will host 50 percent of the African population within the next two decades (Shackleton et al., 2018). This rapid change calls for proactive preparation in terms of planning for services that include recreation. Many of the studies conceptualize recreation planning in different ways including the following: Strategic planning and quality life (Mogajane et al., 2014); Modern spatial computing technology in developing spatial policy for, and planning of outdoor action and adventure recreation and tourism (OAART) (van Der Merwe, 2012); Management capacity and quality of life (Goslin et al., 2015); Recreation Infrastructure and service provision (Urmilla & Maharaj, 2015); Safe environments or spaces (Munien et al., 2015; Oosthuizen & Burnett, 2019); Authentic vs eclecticism culture (Kaarsholm, 1995); Urban Green Infrastructure or Social-ecological (Kumelachew, 2020; Makworo & Mireri, 2011; Shackleton et al., 2018); Urban Green Growth/Ecological/Green space/ecosystem (Kimengsi & Fogwe, 2017; Tibesigwa et al., 2020; Turpie et al., 2016); Negotiation, struggle and production of built environments (Owen, 2016); Sports tourism (Mboumba, 2017); Comparative spatial planning/Negotiated planning (Cirolia & Berrisford, 2017); Community environments/ecological (Dhurup & Grobler, 2012); Open public space/liveable city (Daniel & Strickland, 2017; UN-Habitat, 2016; Vansintjan, 2020); Change theory and public spaces (Daniel, 2016).

Daniel (2016) in the 'Bellagio Accord for public spaces in African cities', outlines the agenda for implementation by researchers, civil society, government and funders in Africa in order to create and support recreational spaces using the theory of change approach. The Theory of Change is essentially a comprehensive description and illustration of how and why a desired change is expected to happen in a context. It is focused on mapping out what a programme or change initiative does (its activities or interventions) and how these lead to desired goals being achieved. It does this by first identifying the desired long-term goals and then works back from these to identify all the conditions (outcomes) that must be in place (and how these related to one another causally) for the goals to occur. These are all mapped out in an Outcomes Framework (Theory of Change, n.d.). This theory of change uses 'The Outcomes Framework' to provide the basis for identifying what type of activity or intervention will lead to the outcomes identified as preconditions for achieving the long-term goal (Theory of Change, n.d.).

Through this approach, the precise link between activities and the achievement of long-term goals are more fully understood. This leads to better planning, in that activities are linked to a detailed understanding of how change happens (Theory of Change, n.d.). It also leads to better evaluation, as it is possible to measure progress towards the achievement of longer-term goals that go beyond the identification of program outputs (Theory of Change, n.d.). The 'Bellagio Accord for public spaces in African cities' report (Daniel, 2016) can therefore be used as a starting point to develop research strategies and funding programmes for the creation and support of public spaces in African cities.

One key component in the change process is the articulation of an overall goal for recreational spaces in African cities followed by a description of the conditions and actions that must be in place for the goal to be realized. The major goal is that set by the Sustainable Development Goals (SDG) number 11 is to make cities and human settlements inclusive, safe, resilient and sustainable (Daniel, 2016; Daniel & Strickland, 2017; del Saz Salazar & Menéndez, 2007; Dhurup & Grobler, 2012; Goslin et al., 2015; Henderson-Wilson et al., 2017; Kimengsi & Fogwe, 2017; Kumelachew, 2020; Makwaro & Mireri, 2011; Munien et al., 2015; Oosthuizen & Burnett, 2019; Shackleton et al., 2018; Tibesigwa et al., 2020; Turpie et al., 2016; UN-Habitat, 2016; van Der Merwe, 2012; Vansintjan, 2020).

According to Daniel (2016), provision of safe, accessible and inclusive green and public spaces for all people is a key precondition for the achievement of SDG 11. This would require significant investments in urban planning for public open spaces, as well as the creation of mobility and urban planning policies that focus on encouraging walking and cycling, playgrounds, green spaces, entertainment sites and on urban policies that support local markets. To accomplish this goal, intermediate goals must be emphasized including services that are people-centred, accessible, inclusive, safe and have multiple uses. To achieve the goal and outcomes, specific actions need to be implemented by researchers, civil society and governments in African cities (Daniel, 2016). These actions fall under three formative pathways that represent the greatest opportunity for impact and change. The three pathways and associated actions are:

1. Increase Understanding (Conduct collaborative research, Initiate community-led studies, translate/share knowledge);
2. Align Policy (Re-allocate resources, formalize the processes for citizen engagement, identify decision-maker champions); and
3. Strengthen Collaboration and Impact (Create inter-departmental collaboration, develop partnerships, raise awareness, support and build capacity).

It is evident that the growing urbanization of Africa calls for new approaches to planning for recreational services. The old Master plans drawn up during the colonial era are now outgrown and new perspectives that are informed by green spaces, open and public services, safe playgrounds, mapping technology, negotiated strategic planning in consultation with the service consumers, researchers, civil society, private sector and the government, are the way forward.

Policy and Recreation Planning

According to Mogajane et al. (2014), Makworo and Mireri (2011) and Owen (2016), the promotion of recreation and leisure through coherent strategies and policy development is a significant move towards changing the quality lives of communities living in cities. However, the unavailability of recreation strategies and policies are associated with negative effect on the delivery of recreation services in Africa. Using South Africa as an example, Scholtz and Meyer (1990) and Scholtz et al. (1996) argue that changes in technology, urbanization, cultural diversity and related aspects have instigated the demand for specialized recreation service. Recreation service delivery is an important part of community life, and the role of local government is critical. Many African countries tend to have local governments that preside over the planning, implementation, management and development of urban areas. The authority of these local governments is vested in elected council members as they are tasked with delivering services to satisfy certain needs and demands of residents (Scholtz et al., 1996). One of the major concerns in Africa is the rapid urbanization that is taking place.

Many youths tend to migrate to cities in search of job and career opportunities thereby putting pressure on the existing infrastructure. Indeed, many urban residents are concerned about the areas where they live, access to services and economic opportunities, mobility, safety, pollution and congestion and lack of proximity to social and recreational facilities (Ikawa, 2015; Mogajane et al., 2014). Local government can have an impact on all these facets of people's lives including recreation services (Goslin et al., 2015; Naidoo, 2005). The local government will need to continue to be an important player if recreation is to be developed and services improved. The multiple benefits of recreation at the following levels: personal (relaxation, self-esteem and image); economic (small investment in recreation that can yield big economic returns); environmental (environmental health) and social (building strong communities, promoting ethnic and cultural harmony) are sufficient proof that it forms an important part of our everyday life (Collins & Kay, 2003).

Recreation policies and strategies are critical in the provision and delivery of service in local government (Mogajane et al., 2014; Naidoo, 2005; Scholtz et al. 1996). Problems pertaining to recreation service delivery such as lack of adequate strategies, policies, the provision of recreation facilities, programming, financing and human resources still exist at the local government level. Mogajane et al. (2014) studied the availability of recreation policies and strategies in South Africa. They discovered among other things that all local governments (100 percent) did not have recreation strategic plans. They also found that policy statements concerning finance (80 percent), provision of human resources (90 percent), provision of recreation facilities (65 percent), provision of recreation programme (80 percent), coordination, planning or implementation of recreation programmes (85 percent), the lease of recreation facilities (75 percent), the appointment of administrative or supportive service (95 percent) or the use of volunteers (80 percent) were not available.

According to Goslin (2003), decision-makers' understanding of the role and value of recreation is still lacking. Singh and Burnett (2003) indicated that there is confusion regarding the roles and functions of local government in the implementation of policies. Naidoo (2005) indicates a lack of recreation policies as a major problem for local governments. Even in South Africa, which had the highest number of reviewed studies, the state of recreation planning and service provision in urban areas needs improvement. For example, after 1994, the White Paper on Sport and Recreation (2002) identified the shortcomings in the South African recreation system such as the need for a national recreation body, provincial recreation structures and lack of insight into the problem of participation by the majority of the people in physical activity. It also found that there was a lack of resources needed for ensuring involvement in physical activity.

The Constitution of the Republic of South Africa, 1996 (South Africa, 1996) states that everyone has the right to a safe and healthy environment. Local government must therefore develop a policy framework for the governance of recreation at the local level; that is, in concert with the national and provincial sport and recreation policy and must make recreation accessible to all people in the local area (White Paper on Sport and Recreation, 2002). Therefore, the development of recreation strategies and policy formulation by local governments is an obligation as mandated by the White Paper on Local Government (1998), White Paper on Sport and Recreation (2002) and the Constitution of the Republic of South Africa, 1996 (South Africa, 1996).

Conversely, whereas the Constitution in Kenya is silent on recreation as a human right, the Sports Act, 2013 (Kenya, Republic of, 2013) captures the strategic significance of sports and recreation. Kenya's Sports Act (2013) clearly spells out that the Government; would be on the forefront of managing and maintaining selected sports facilities; establish, manage, develop and maintain its sports facilities, including convention centres, indoor sporting and recreational facilities; adopt, develop, plan, set stadia standards and licence and regularly inspect stadia for sporting and recreational use; establish and maintain a sports museum; participate in the promotion of sports tourism; provide the necessary amenities or facilities for persons using the services or facilities provided by Sports Kenya; operate sports facilities on public grounds in such a manner that it deems necessary; collaborate with county governments, learning institutions and other stakeholders concerned with sports and recreation; inculcate the sense of patriotism and national pride through sports and recreation; create awareness on matters of national interest through sporting events; create awareness on the benefits regular participation in sports for healthy living; and provide advisory and counselling services to athletes.

However, Kenya's Achilles heel is the lack of implementation of policy, which is evident in the City of Nairobi. Makworo and Mireri (2011) declared that public open spaces in the City of Nairobi were under threat which runs counter to its slogan of being the Green City in the sun. Their investigation revealed that public open spaces in Nairobi City have been increasingly threatened by congestion and deterioration as a result of the rapid rate of urbanization (5–7.5 percent), poor planning, weak management and illegal alienation. Citing the 1948 Master Plan for the city, Makworo and Mireri argue that 'city planning was premised on the neighbourhood concept with ample provision of public open spaces' (p. 1107). However, it appears that after Kenya's independence in 1963, the implementation of the Master Plan was largely abandoned. The non-compliance with the Masterplan instigated rapid and uncontrolled urbanization which meant that public open spaces that were intended to serve a population of 250,000 now serve over 4 million people. The uncontrolled growth of the city due to an influx of migrants from the rural areas in search of job opportunities has driven the public open spaces in the city to suffer from degradation, over-crowdedness and insecurity, thus denying city residents access to the much-needed recreation and leisure facilities.

A study of Nairobi, Addis Ababa and Harare by Cirolia and Berrisford (2017) shows that planning implementation is different in each of the cities. However, in each case, planning is not simply an ad hoc process, with no sense or logic. Instead, planning implementation reflects the unique and context, contest and ongoing negotiation among the stakeholders implicated in realizing urban plans. This dependency on discretion leaves room for corruption and manipulation.

Access to Recreation Facilities

Public open spaces are an integral part of city life (Cirolia & Berrisford, 2017; Fataar, 2017; Makworo & Mireri, 2011). Such spaces meet the social, political, economic and aesthetic needs of the city residents and visitors including both local and foreign tourists. The type and scale of public open spaces provided in a city typically affect a country's level of development. Urban public open spaces serve multiple functions, including recreation; providing amenities that attract and retain jobs, a vibrant culture and talented people; and protecting the visual character, heritage and beauty of a city (Makworo & Mireri, 2011). Public urban open spaces are also created to satisfy a human being's desire to commune with nature, and they play a significant role in preserving community identity (Smith & Riggs, 1974). Owen (2016) further asserts that playgrounds, parks and other recreational amenities are fundamental requisites of city life, connecting them with ideas of propriety, legitimacy and dignity.

In the African urban setting, the built environment can be perceived both as a facilitator and a barrier to physical activity participation as well as other recreational pursuits. In a study by Dhurup and Grobler (2012) on the built environment and PA participation in a city in South Africa, it was noted that respondents were inactive. They established that the built environment or the lack thereof, plays an influential role in physical activity participation. Some of the prohibitive aspects of urban planning related to perceived accessibility of various destinations, street planning in the neighbourhood, places for walking and cycling, neighbourhood surroundings, safety from traffic and safety from crime. It is therefore absolutely necessary that various levels of Government, policymakers and environmental planners need to take cognizance of future planning in the development of user-friendly environments so that residents can meaningfully participate in physical activity and other recreational pursuits (Oosthuizen & Burnett, 2019).

According to Oosthuizen and Burnett (2019, p. 85), 'creation of safe spaces may aid in improving the use of space through the provision and safeguarding of spaces, understanding the integrated dimensions and multifunctionality'. They argue that the greatest tangible challenge encountered by children that inhibited them from walking through public spaces included cars parked on designated walkways. Once again, this confirms that when the designated use of a space does not match the functionality, the space may become unsafe. When the designated use of a space does not align with the functionality of space through a lack of policy enforcement, the physical space is perceived to be one that is unsafe.

April et al. (n.d.) list some of the key barriers to recreational sites as road safety and neighbourhood crime. However, there are also opportunities for physical activity including walking to recreational facilities that are nearby such as school playgrounds; common life activities such as cycling and walking paths; and walking to bus stops and shopping centres. Goslin et al. (2015) investigated how well sports and recreation services were managed in a city in South Africa on eight dimensions of management. They enumerated these dimensions as: leadership, governance and strategy; administration and human resources; finances and budget of the facility; project design, management and evaluation; technical capacity; advocacy and networking; community ownership and accountability; and fundraising. Results indicated that the internal systemic management capacity of the department of recreation and sports in this investigation measured unsatisfactory.

Kumelachew (2020) on the other hand highlights the importance of place-based studies for assessing the perceived benefits that attract people to use urban parks as well as the challenges that deter use. According to Kumelachew, Addis Ababa's use of public participation in urban parks development and management provides a good model that cities in Sub-Saharan Africa could draw from in the development and management of neighbourhood parks. As Owen (2016) points out, recreational spaces in the form of clubs, parks, playgrounds, social halls and other similar venues are important features that give urban dwellers a stake in the city and shape their engagement with the state.

The way cities are designed with respect to proximity and connectivity to local destinations, including schools, parks and shopping centres and the presence of footpaths becomes a determinant of whether people are able to access recreational services locally (Njororai et al., 2015). A growing body of evidence shows that the built environment can positively influence physical activity and other recreation services. According to the social-ecological framework of behaviour change, people's behaviours are influenced by many factors including family, friends, local surroundings, built environment and community (Sinnett et al., 2011). To enhance recreation infrastructural use, the supporting environments and policies must be changed to make it easier for people in those environments to make healthy choices (Onywera et al., 2016).

In 2015, Kenya through the National Council for Children's Services published a National Plan of Action for Children (Kenya, 2016). The plan is anchored on the United Nations Convention on the Rights of the Child (UNCRC) which Kenya signed in 1990. The plan recognizes the right of all Kenyan children to leisure, play and recreation that are appropriate to the age of the child. According to Ikawa (2015) whose study aimed at establishing the impact of policies on the Development and Management of Recreational Spaces in Nairobi (Kenya), a resident has 22 m^2 of recreational space on average from a high of 159 m^2 at independence. This translates to 2.162 acres per thousand residents compared with the best practice in the United States and Europe of 6–10 acres per thousand. Only 5 percent of Nairobi County is currently available for recreational spaces.

Ikawa (2015) further found that due to large geopolitical neglect, the management and development of recreational spaces has been left wanting, and in the process, various private sector arrangements are leading the way in design and management. Ikawa also observed that education affects the type of space visited, indicating social and political differences in access. Access to spaces is largely skewed to the higher social classes who have access to 'members only' parks and golf courses. On average, the Nairobi County residents take between 22 and 90 minutes to access recreational spaces (Ikawa, 2015). However, more studies are needed to explore the reality of recreation and access to playgrounds in most African cities as it is apparent that only countries such as South Africa, Mauritius, Kenya, Ghana, Tanzania, Ethiopia, Uganda, Zimbabwe, Mozambique and Nigeria have attracted scholarly attention and the corresponding emergence of cardiovascular diseases as a major public health concern (April et al., n.d.; Onywera et al., 2012, 2013; WHO, 2008).

Examples of Best Practices for Recreation Provision

All around the world, the way cities are built, managed and planned is changing rapidly (Kiggundu, 2014). Several major transformations are underway globally including new kinds of urbanization, changing environment for investment and the desire for green space and public areas for recreational use (Vansintjan, 2020). Since 2012, UN-Habitat's Urban Planning and Design Branch (UPDB) and the Office of External Relations have jointly embarked on the development and implementation of a Global Programme on Public Space, which is organized around three main areas: Partnerships for public space; City-wide strategies and pilot/demonstration projects and Knowledge management, tools and advocacy. UN-Habitat is also mobilizing partners to work with cities around the globe in improving the quality, supply and reach of public spaces.

A special focus is on cities in developing countries, and cities with high percentages of their population living in slums and in underprivileged circumstances. Public Space is often referred to as 'the poor man's living room' which hints at its importance for the recreation, social and economic development of vulnerable groups. Open public spaces have numerous environmental benefits. The increase in hard surfacing and the reduction of green spaces is resulting in higher temperatures in cities than in the surrounding countryside. Parks that include plants and trees help to balance this effect by cooling the air, providing shade and absorbing air pollutants. This is especially beneficial in cities with hot climates and can assist in lowering the need for air conditioning, thereby resulting in improved air quality. Additionally, parks improve the quality of water, and can decrease the effects of flooding by allowing water to infiltrate the ground (Daniel & Strickland, 2017). A good city should be an inclusive city; one that provides spaces for social engagement and fosters social cohesion, tackling poverty and inequality through the provision of inclusive, safe and accessible public spaces, especially for marginalized groups (UN-Habitat, 2015).

According to the Charter of Public Space that was agreed upon by all parties present at the 2013 Biennial of Public Space convened by UN-Habitat, public spaces are important because they:

1. Support the movement of and interaction between people;
2. Host accessible commercial and public activities;
3. Offer space for recreation, leisure, exercise and regeneration;
4. Promote education and culture;
5. Promote conviviality, encounter and freedom of expression;
6. Are important for individual and collective memory and community identity;
7. Are vital in the integration of ecosystems and architecture and determine the image of the city; and
8. Are one of the main tools available to governments to build social and economic wealth and upgrade urban space (Vansintjan, 2020).

In Africa, like in many other places in the world, public spaces are used for public life, commerce and interaction. However, lack of funds, planning and maintenance, as well as priority for motorized vehicles, has turned many public spaces into unsafe, unforgiving and unconnected places. In addition, many public spaces are difficult to access, especially for those living in vulnerable situations. Public spaces are a key element of individual and community well-being and are critical for the historic, environmental, social and economic functioning of cities and ultimately for people's quality of life. Government, policymakers and environmental planners need to take cognizance of future planning in the development of user-friendly environments so that residents can meaningfully participate in recreation and physical activity (Daniel, 2016; Dhurup & Grobler, 2012; Njororai et al., 2015, 2016).

Politics and Corruption

One of the challenges that African cities face, especially the civil servants in charge of planning, is the political and corrupt nature of both local and national governments and the manipulation as well as evasion of established policies and procedures. Makworo and Mireri (2011) clearly decry the fact that provision of public open spaces in Nairobi City is threatened by a rapid rate of urbanization against the weak capacity of city authorities to cope with the growth. It is evident that while the population of Nairobi City has rapidly increased, particularly since independence in 1963, little effort has been made to conserve the existing public open spaces, never mind the creation of new ones. The city, which was originally premised on a neighbourhood concept with approximately 30 percent of the city devoted to public open spaces, has cascaded into one characterized by tall buildings and the attendant slums for the poor.

The Master Plan was meant to serve the city up to 1975 with an optimal population of 250,000 (Makworo & Mireri, 2011). Despite the rapid urban growth, the 1948 Master Plan has not been revised to date and attempts to revise it have failed because of competing political interests. Public open spaces, which were meant to serve 250,000 people, are now serving 4.397 million, exemplifying the serious shortage of public open spaces in the city. The disheartening part is that key players in destroying the public spaces and illegal alienation of public open spaces are both the state and members of the public. According to Makworo and Mireri, 'the political leadership with the active engagement of technocrats have presided over the illegal alienation of public open spaces for private use' (p. 1122). On the other hand, the history of African cities cannot be divorced from the discriminatory nature of recreation and sports access that African workers experienced during colonial days. Some practices that separated the indigenous from the settler categories (Badenhorst & Mather, 1997; Owen, 2016) provides a colonial legacy that shaped the eventual recreation and sports industry witnessed in current cities in Africa.

Conclusion

Studies reviewed on recreation planning in Africa reveal growing scholarly interest particularly in South Africa, Kenya and other cities in Sub–Saharan Africa. Most of the published research occurred in the twenty-first century. Studies reviewed approached recreation in urban Africa using diverse study designs, geographical scope and data collection methods that shed light on the state of recreation with implications for urban planning in Africa. Despite the diverse approaches, there is increasing interest as well as extensive research which reveals that recreational ecosystem services, such as urban parks, playgrounds and other green spaces provide benefits both directly and indirectly to the user. This realization is informed by the Sustainable Development Goals (SDG) number 11 which is to make cities and human settlements inclusive, safe, resilient and sustainable. Obviously, the provision of safe, accessible and inclusive green and public spaces for all people is a key precondition for the achievement of SDG 11. Accomplishing this goal would require significant investments in urban planning for public open spaces as well as the creation of mobility and urban planning policies that focus on encouraging walking and cycling, playgrounds, green spaces, entertainment sites and urban policies that support local markets. Unfortunately, many studies reveal either the absence of policies or the poor implementation of existing recreation policies. These failures hamper the service delivery of recreation facilities and services in urban Africa.

Recreation policies and strategies are critical in the provision and delivery of service in cities. Problems pertaining to recreation service delivery such as lack of adequate strategies, policies, the provision of recreation facilities, programming, financing and human resources still exist in African countries including South Africa, Kenya, Tanzania, Ethiopia, Zimbabwe and Uganda. Coupled with the absence of policy or coordinated service delivery structures, is poor access to the recreation facilities due to limited investments in the recreational spaces required to enhance the well-being of urban residents. The lack of public investments has given rise to the call for public and private partnerships to meet the recreational needs of the people. It is for this reason that Habitat's Urban Planning and Design Branch (UPDB) and the Office of External Relations have jointly embarked on the development and implementation of a Global Programme on Public Space, which is organized around three main areas: Partnerships for public space; City-wide strategies and pilot/demonstration projects and Knowledge management, tools and advocacy. UN-Habitat is also involved in mobilizing partners to work with cities around the globe in improving the quality, supply and reach of public spaces with a special focus on cities in developing countries. Provision and access to recreational space are important, especially to the under-resourced. Such space is often referred to as 'the poor man's living room' which hints at its importance for the recreation, social and economic development of vulnerable groups.

Recreation spaces, both public and private, are an integral part of city life and African cities need to aggressively provide for them. Such spaces meet the social, political, economic and aesthetic needs of the city residents and visitors including both local and foreign tourists. The type and scale of recreational spaces provided in a city typically affect a resident's health and well-being. Urban public open spaces serve multiple functions that include recreation; providing amenities that attract and retain jobs, a vibrant culture and talented people; and protecting the visual character, heritage and beauty of a city. Therefore, as the urbanization of Africa intensifies, there is need for new approaches to planning for recreational services. The old Master plans drawn up during the colonial era are now outgrown and new perspectives informed by green spaces, open and public services, safe playgrounds, mapping technology, negotiated strategic planning in consultation with the service consumers, researchers, civil society, private sector and the government are the way forward. Africa's urban population is growing at an exponential rate. This rapid growth is putting cities' infrastructure under tremendous pressure.

Additionally, demands for establishing new industrial complexes and other commercial spatial needs have made it difficult for land to be set aside for community use for recreation and natural aesthetics. The recent emphasis on urban planning that prioritizes open safe spaces, green spaces, parks, museums, playgrounds, mega sports infrastructure for hosting international and national events and so on, adds value to the health and well-being of urban residents. It is important that urban planners in local and central government prioritize this overarching need for recreation spaces to enhance the health and well-being of their urban residents, visitors and tourists. Government, policymakers and environmental planners need to bear in mind that future planning in the development of user-friendly environments is vital for residents to meaningfully participate in physical activity and other recreational endeavours.

Efforts geared towards improving the provision of recreation, both public open and private spaces in African cities, should therefore consider the following measures.

1. Preparation of either new Master plans or strategic plans for urban areas as a plausible means of creating new public open spaces to not only improve access to open spaces but also decongest the existing ones.
2. Lobby the city authorities to improve resource allocation (personnel and facilities) for parks, playgrounds and other entertainment management areas. This is important in empowering the city authorities to appreciate the importance of public open spaces, and making them be aware of the need for effective management and the resource requirement.
3. Consider innovative approaches to recreation and leisure management that may include both the public and private sector recreation providers and users. Recreation and leisure management could be improved through public and private partnership, which could be done by creating a commission/trust for engaging the stakeholders in decision making. This would facilitate active engagement of key stakeholders in recreation management, especially government, park and playground users, the private sector and civil society organizations.
4. All community-based stakeholders may collaborate and play a vital role in implementing safety measures and strategies in providing surveillance for safe corridors within the public space to enhance active living. In turn, schools and NGOs offering sports and physical activity programmes would benefit from community mapping so as to identify safe (green) spaces for the mobility of their participants that will influence the numbers of active participants (Oosthuizen & Burnett, 2019).
5. Given the important role that parks play in improving health, quality of life, supporting local economies and improving the environment, it is important to develop policies that preserve, protect and enhance these important community assets.
6. Deliberate effort should be directed at addressing the data deficit on recreation planning, management and usage by the residents to inform proper planning and implementation of desirable programmes. Additionally, the unavailability of policies affecting recreation service delivery should challenge local governments to generate recreation strategies and policies that address recreation service delivery while elaborating on the collaboration among the different stakeholders to ensure effective recreation service delivery.

References

Aarts, M. J., Schuit, A. J., Van de Goor, L. A. M., & van Oers, H. A. M. (2011). *Feasibility of multi-sector policy measures that create activity-friendly environments for children: Results of a Delphi study*. http://www.implementationscience.com/content/6/1/128

Amusa, L. O., Toriola, A. L., & Goon, D. T. (2012). Youth, physical activity and leisure education: Need for a Paradigm shift. *African Journal for Physical, Health Education, Recreation and Dance (AJPHERD), 18*(42), 992–1006.

April, M., Kolbe-Alexander, T., Draper, C., & Lambert, E. V. (n.d.). *Physical activity and public health in Africa: A review of the problem and strategies for primordial prevention of non-communicable diseases*. Report from UCT Research Unit for Exercise Science and Sports Medicine, Dept of Human Biology, Faculty of Health Sciences, University of Cape Town.

Badenhorst, C., & Mather, C. (1997). Tribal recreation and recreating tribalism: Culture, leisure and social control on South Africa's gold mines, 1940–1950. *Journal of Southern African Studies, 23*(3), 473–489.

Bernath, K., & Roschewitz, A. (2008). Recreational benefits of urban forests: Explaining visitors' willingness to pay in the context of the theory of planned behaviour. *Journal of Environmental Management, 89*, 155–166.

Chaudhry, P. (2013). Valuing recreational benefits of urban forestry: A case study of Chandigarh city of India. *International Journal of Environmental Sciences, 3*(5), 1785–1789.

Cirolia, L. R., & Berrisford, S. (2017). 'Negotiated planning': Diverse trajectories of implementation in Nairobi, Addis Ababa, and Harare. *Habitat International, 59*, 71–79.

Collins, M. F., & Kay, T. (2003). *Sport and social exclusion* (p. 304). Routledge.

Daniel, K. (2016). *Bellagio accord for public spaces in African cities*. Liveable Cities: HealthBridge Foundation of Canada. www.healthbridge.ca

Daniel, K., & Strickland, E. (2017). *Policies that support parks and open public spaces global examples*. Livable cities: HealthBridge Foundation of Canada. www.healthbridge.ca

del Saz Salazar, S., & Menéndez, L. G. (2007). Estimating the non-market benefits of an urban park: Does proximity matter? *Land Use Policy, 24*(1), 296–305. https://doi.org/10.1016/j.landusepol.2005.05.011

Dhurup, M., & Grobler, W. C. J. (2012, December). The built environment and physical activity participation in a semi-urban area in Southern Gauteng. *African Journal for Physical, Health Education, Recreation and Dance (AJPHERD), 18*(Supplement 1:2), 414–430.

Dumith, S. C., Hallal, P. C., Reis, R. S., & Kohl, H. W. (2011). Worldwide prevalence of physical inactivity and its association with human development index in 76 countries. *Preventive Medicine, 53*(2011), 24–28.

Dvorak, J., Fuller, C. W., & Junge, A. (2012). Planning and implementing a nationwide football-based health-education Programme. *British Journal of Sports Medicine, 46*, 6–10. https://doi.org/10.1136/6bjsports-2011-090635

Edginton, C. R., Hudson, S. D., Dieser, R. B., & Edginton, S. R. (2004). *Leisure programming: A service centred and benefits approach* (4th ed., p. 534). McGraw-Hill.

Fataar, R. (2017). *Public spaces in African cities.* Retrieved at https://www.citiestobe.com/public-spaces-in-african-cities/. Accessed 30 Jan 2021.

Ferreira, I., van der Horst, K., Wendel-Vos, W., Kremers, S., van Lenthe, F. J., & Burg, J. (2006). Environmental correlates of physical activity in youth: A review and update. *Obesity Reviews, 8,* 129–154.

Goslin, A. (2003). Assessment of leisure and recreation research in Africa. *African Journal for Physical, Health, Education Recreation and Dance, 25*(1), 35–46.

Goslin, A. E., Sere, M. G. O., & Kluka, A. (2015). Management capacity at sport and recreation facilities on local government level. *African Journal for Physical, Health Education, Recreation and Dance, 21*(4:1), 1290–1303.

Guthold, R., Ono, T., Strong, K. L., Chatterji, S., & Morabia, A. (2008). Worldwide variability in physical inactivity: A 51-country survey. *American Journal of Preventive Medicine, 34*(6), 486–494.

Guthold, R., Louazani, S., Riley, L. M., Cowan, M., Bovet, P., Damasceno, A., Sambo, B. H., Tesfaye, F., & Armstrong, T. (2011). Physical activity in 22 African countries: Results from the World Health Organization STEPwise approach to chronic disease risk factor surveillance. *American Journal of Preventive Medicine, 41*(1), 52–60.

Henderson-Wilson, C., Sia, K. L., Veitch, J., Staiger, P. K., Davidson, P., & Nicholls, P. (2017). Perceived health benefits and willingness to pay for parks by park users: Quantitative and qualitative research. *International Journal of Environmental Research and Public Health, 14*(5), 1–18, 529.

Ikawa, J. V. (2015). *The impact of policies on the development and management of recreational spaces in Nairobi, Kenya.* Retrieved at https://www.semanticscholar.org/paper/The-Impact-of-Policies-on-the-Development-and-of-in-Ikawa/90f2f3e53c4bc770536a344cd31963a721711fb4. Accessed 2 Feb 2021.

Kamau, J. W., Mwangi, P. W., Njororai, W. W. S., & Wamukoya, E. K. (2011). Prevalence of overweight and obesity among primary school children in Nairobi province, Kenya. *African Journal for Physical, Health Education, Recreation and Dance (AJPHERD), 17*(2), 312–327.

Kaarsholm, P. (1995). Si Ye Pambili-Which way forward?: Urban development, culture and politics in Bulawayo. *Journal of Southern African Studies, 21*(2), 225–245.

Kenya, Republic of. (2013). The Sport Act. *Kenya Gazette Supplement No. 39,* Acts No. 25, pp. 673–719.

Kenya, Republic of. (2016). *National plan of action for children in Kenya.* https://www.google.com/search?q=Republic+of+Kenya.+National+Plan+of+Action+for+Children+in+Kenya&ie=utf-8&oe=utf-8&client=firefox-b. Accessed 2 Feb 2021.

Kiggundu, A. T. (2014). Constraints to urban planning and management of secondary towns in Uganda. *Indonesian Journal of Geography, 46*(1), 12–21.

Kimengsi, J. N., & Fogwe, Z. N. (2017). Urban green development planning opportunities and challenges in Sub-Saharan Africa: Lessons from Bamenda City Cameroon. *International Journal of Global Sustainability, 1*(1), 1–17.

Kohn, M. R., & Booth, M. (2003). The worldwide epidemic of obesity in adolescents. *Adolescent Medicine, 14,* 1–9.

Kraus, R. G., & Curtis, J. E. (1990). *Creative management in recreation, parks and leisure services* (5th ed., p. 494). WCB/McGraw-Hill.

Kumelachew, Y. (2020). Attitude and perception of residents towards the benefits, challenges and quality of neighbourhood parks in a sub-Saharan City. *Land, 9,* 450. https://doi.org/10.3390/land9110450

Makworo, M., & Mireri, C. (2011, October). Public open spaces in Nairobi City, Kenya, under threat. *Journal of Environmental Planning and Management, 54*(8), 1107–1123.

Mboumba, G. N. (2017). The tourism impacts of the 2012 confederation of African football (CAF) nations cup in Gabon. Dissertation submitted in fulfilment of the requirements for the degree Master of Technology in Tourism and Hospitality Management in the Faculty of Business and Management Sciences at the Cape Peninsula University of Technology. Retrieved at https://core.ac.uk/download/pdf/156958081.pdf

Mogajane, V. S., Meyer, C., Toriola, A. L., Amusa, L. O., & Monyeki, M. A. (2014). The availability of recreation policies and strategies for the provision of recreation service delivery in the North West Province, South Africa. *African Journal for Physical, Health Education, Recreation and Dance (AJPHERD), 20*(1), 24–39.

Munien, S., Nkambule, S. S., & Buthelezi, H. Z. (2015, December). Conceptualisation and use of green spaces in peri-urban communities: Experiences from Inanda, KwaZulu-Natal, South Africa. *African Journal for Physical, Health Education, Recreation and Dance, 21*(Supplement 1), 155–167.

Naidoo, M. (2005). *The role of the provincial department of sport and recreation in collaboration with the local government to promote recreation as an essential service*. Paper presented at the Institute of the Environment and Recreation Management Conference held on 9–10 June, p. 4 (Unpublished).

Njororai, F. J., & Njororai, W. W. S. (2018). Physical activity. In M. Khayesi (Ed.), *Rural development planning in Africa* (pp. 199–248). Palgrave Macmillan.

Njororai, W. W. S., Njororai, F. J., & Jivetti, B. A (2016). Walkability in upper East Texas cities and implications for physical activity and health. *International Journal of Human Sciences, 13*(1), 487–499. https://doi.org/10.14687/ijhs.v13i1.3438

Njororai, W. W. S., Njororai, F., & Jivetti, B. A. (2015). Walkable scores for selected three east Texas counties: Physical activity and policy implications. *International Journal of Human Sciences, 12*(2), 674–687.

Onywera, V. O., Adamo, K. B., Sheel, A. W., Waudo, J. N., Boit, M. K., & Tremblay, M. S. (2012). Emerging evidence of the physical activity transition in Kenya. *Journal of Physical Activity and Health, 9*, 554–562.

Onywera, V. O., Héroux, M., Jáuregui Ulloa, E., Adamo, K. B., Taylor, J. L., Janssen, I., & Tremblay, M. S. (2013). Adiposity and physical activity among children in countries at different stages of the physical activity transition: Canada, Mexico, and Kenya. *African Journal for Physical, Health Education, Recreation and Dance (AJPHERD), 19*(1), 132–142.

Onywera, V. O., Muthuri, S. K., Hayker, S., Wachira, L. M., Kyallo, F., Mang'eni, R. O., Bukhala, P., & Mireri, C. (2016). Kenya's 2016 report card on physical activity for children and youth. *Journal of Physical Activity and Health, 13*(Suppl 2), S195–S200. https://doi.org/10.1123/jpah.2016-0359

Oosthuizen, Y., & Burnett, C. (2019). Community mapping and creating safe spaces for physical activity in a South African context of relative poverty. *South African Journal for Research in Sport, Physical Education and Recreation, 41*(1), 77–91.

Owen, C. E. (2016). Lands of leisure: Recreation, space, and the struggle for urban Kenya, 1900–2000. Unpublished Dissertation submitted to Michigan State University in partial fulfilment of the requirements for the degree of History-Doctor of Philosophy. Retrieved at https://d.lib.msu.edu/etd/4530

Scholtz, G. J. L., & Meyer, C. D. (1990). Provision of leisure resources and services by local authority in the RSA and Namibia-1984/85. Potchefstroom: PU vir CHO.

Scholtz, G. J. L., Saayman, M., & Meyer, C. D. (1996). *Policy document for the provision of recreation in the North West Province*. PU for CHE, Institute for Tourism and Leisure Studies.

Shackleton, C. M., Blair, A., De Lacy, P., Kaoma, H., Mugwagwa, N., Dalu, M. T., & Walton, W. (December 2018). How important is green infrastructure in small and medium-sized towns? Lessons from South Africa. *Landscape and Urban Planning, 180*, 273–281.

Singh, C., & Burnett, C. (2003). The Tshwane metropolitan municipality and strategic partnership in sport and recreation. *African Journal for Physical, Health, Education, Recreation and Dance, 9*(3), 78–88.

Sinnett, D., Williams, K., Chatterjee, K., & Cavill, N. (2011). Making the case for investment in the walking environment: A review of the evidence. *Technical Report*. Living Streets.

Smith, E. E., & Riggs, D. S. (Eds.). (1974). *Land use, open space, and the government process: The San Francisco Bay area experience*. Praeger.

South Africa. (1996). *Constitution of the Republic of South Africa*. http://www.info.gov.za/documents/constitution/index.htm. Accessed 30 Jan 2021.

Strydom, G. L. (2013). Physical activity, health and well-being: A strategic objective of the National Sport and Recreation Plan (NSRP) of South Africa. *African Journal for Physical, Health Education, Recreation and Dance (AJPHERD), 19*(4:2), 980–992.

Theory of Change. (n.d.). https://www.theoryofchange.org/what-is-theory-of-change/

Tibesigwa, B., Ntuli, H., & Lokina, R. (2020, November). Valuing recreational ecosystem services in developing cities: The case of urban parks in Dar es Salaam, Tanzania. *Cities, 106*, 102853, 18 pages.

Turpie, J., Liz, D., Dambala, G. K., Gwyneth, L., Chris Roed, C., & Forsythe, K. (2016). A preliminary investigation of the potential costs and benefits of rehabilitation of the Nakivubo Wetland, Kampala. *World Bank Other Operational Studies 26425*, The World Bank. Retrieved at https://ideas.repec.org/p/wbk/wboper/26425.html. Accessed 30 Jan 2021.

UN-Habitat. (2015). *Habitat III Issue Paper No. 22-Informal Settlements*. http://unhabitat.org/wp-content/uploads/2015/04/Habitat-III-Issue-Paper-22_InformalSettlements-2.0.pdf

UN-Habitat. (2016). *Global public spaces toolkit: From global principles to local policies and practice*. http://unhabitat.org/wpcontent/uploads/2015/10/Global%20Public%20Space%20Toolkit.pdf

Urmilla, B., & Maharaj, A. (2015). An examination of tourism infrastructure and services available at the Durban central beachfront locality, South Africa. *African Journal for Physical Health Education, Recreation, and Dance, 21*(sup-2), 13–23.

van Der Merwe, J. H. (2012). Locating opportunities for outdoor action and adventure recreation and tourism in the Western Cape: A GIS Application. *South African Journal for Research in Sport, Physical Education and Recreation, 34*(2), 197–214.

Vansintjan, A. (2020). Open public space and the private sector: A toolkit for overcoming barriers and best practices final report. HealthBridge Canada, 33 pages.

White Paper on Local Government. (1998). Department of Constitutional Development, South Africa. http://www.hst.org.za/pphc/Phila/summary/vol4_no1.htm. Accessed 30 Jan 2021.

White Paper on Sport and Recreation. (2002). National Department of Sport and Recreation. South Africa. http://www.info.gov.za/whitepapers/1998/sports.htm. Accessed 30 Jan 2021.

Wolf, K. L. (2017). The health benefits of small parks and green spaces. *Parks & Recreation Magazine*. Retrieved at https://www.nrpa.org/parks-recreation-magazine/2017/april/the-health-benefits-of-small-parks-and-green-spaces/. Accessed 2 Feb 2021.

World Health Organization. (2008). Review of best practice in interventions to promote physical activity in developing countries. Background Document prepared for the WHO Workshop on Physical Activity and Public Health 24–27 October 2005: Beijing, People's Republic of China.

Ziraba, A. K., Fotso, J. C., & Ochako, R. (2009). Overweight and obesity in urban Africa: A problem of the rich or the poor? *BioMedCentral* at http://www.biomedcentral.com/1471-2458/9/465. Accessed 30 Jan 2021.

CHAPTER 12

Air Quality

William S. W. Busolo and Victor Isanda Njabira

INTRODUCTION

The world has undergone tremendous changes since the beginning of the urban revolution in the ancient towns, and cities have been termed as engines of social modernization and economic advancement. Rural–urban migrations have promoted growth of the urban populations which in turn lead to growth of megacities. Today, 55 percent of the world's population live in urban areas, with Africa contributing approximately 13 percent of the current total world's urban population. By 2050, it is estimated that the world's urban population would have increased to 68 percent (United Nations, 2018 Revision of world urbanization prospects).

However, as much as cities are perceived to be breathing new life to its residents, the reality is otherwise. Urbanization has impacted negatively the quality of our environment pushing the ambient environment quality standards (EQSs) way past the stipulated thresholds. The world is also currently experiencing the effects among which global warming and climate change and its effects are the most popular. This chapter therefore focuses on air quality and provides evidence of a constrained environment characterized by

---

W. S. W. Busolo · V. I. Njabira (✉)
Intershelter Sullivan Architects, Nairobi, Kenya
e-mail: victorisanda@gmail.com

W. S. W. Busolo
e-mail: busolo@intershelterarchitects.com

extremely high concentrations of particulate matter (PM) in African cities, adverse effects on public health, and high economic costs in efforts to curb the impacts.

Method

An extensive search for literature from databases and personal enquiry yielded 152 publications. Studies were sourced using the PubMed, Google Scholar and Electronic Theses and Dissertation (ETD) databases. Search terms included the following: ambient air pollution in Africa; household air pollution in Africa; source of Air pollutants; epidemiological studies on effects of air pollution; mitigation measures/solutions to air pollution; the economic impact of air pollution in Africa; and vulnerability to air pollution. These publications were further screened and trimmed to 50 studies that satisfied the inclusion criteria. The publications selected were only those that:

1. Did not exceed 10 years;
2. Were published in a recognized paper or journal in accordance with research paper documents layout;
3. Focused on urban centres in developing countries and must have included at least a few centres in Africa with at least a population of 2 million people;
4. Focused on urban environmental pollution, effects and mitigation measures; and
5. Focused on urban environmental planning.

A detailed examination was conducted on all selected studies and findings on air quality were extracted with respect to:

a. Air pollution and Fine Particulate matter monitoring;
b. Air pollutants and their Sources;
c. Effects of air pollution, relation to public health and economic impact;
d. Mitigation measures;
e. Extreme air pollution cases; and
f. Urban planning approaches and conceptual models.

The information looked for included trends observed in the researches reviewed and variables such as objectives of study, research methodology, findings, recommendations, author, and publication dates. Declarations, frameworks, and policies by various bodies were also reviewed. Only those that focused on long-term urban planning and design solutions to air pollution were selected. These bodies had to be world-recognized bodies accredited to formulate policies or take state governments into declarations and oversee implementation of these policies with the aim of building smart cities.

Table 12.1 provides a summary of the findings of the studies synthesized. The table shows a list of reviewed researches, their authors, years of publications, and their findings.

Results and Discussion
Air Pollution

Air pollution, the release of toxic substances into the atmosphere, is a major environmental risk to the health of the urban population. Ambient air pollution in Africa has been attributed to rapid urbanization and industrialization resulting in increased concentration levels of pollutants that are broadly referred to as particulate matter (PM). These are tiny particles in the air that reduce visibility and cause the air to appear hazy when levels are elevated. With its growing cities and limited regulatory frameworks, a study or report by WHO (2016a) shows that Africa is home to some of the world's most polluted cities. Onitsha in Nigeria, the worst-ranked city globally; it recorded 30 times more than the WHO recommended levels of particulate matter (PM) concentration. Other cities that were highly polluted as per the reviews, included Cairo in Egypt; Capetown, Pretoria; Johannesburg and Durban in South Africa; Nairobi in Kenya; Algiers in Nigeria; Tunis in Tunisia; Harare in zimbabwe and Accra in Ghana.

The data that exists is not always publicly available or strategically communicated. The unavailability of this data which includes government publications means that there is a lack of access to information to the public which also reduces effective policy making. Thus, the challenge is multifaceted. Even in the presence of air quality standards in many African countries, the lack of air monitoring data blocks enforcement. Routine PM monitoring does not exist in most African cities and only a few studies have reported annual mean levels of $PM_{2.5}$ and PM_{10}. Lack of consistency in PM monitoring in the few countries with PM monitoring stations is also a big challenge in determining the actual quality of air in the region. This is evident from the contradicting report by WHO, listing Algeria, Botswana, Ghana, Madagascar, Mauritius, Nigeria, Senegal, South Africa, Tanzania, Egypt and Tunisia as the only countries that conducted particulate monitoring. This listing omitted Ethiopia and Zimbabwe that had been listed along with Ghana, Madagascar and Tanzania as the only five Sub-Sahara African (SSA) countries, in a 27 countries initial survey by World bank (Petkova et al., 2013; WHO, 2013). Additionally, Dieter (2012) reported on phased air quality programmes in sub-Saharan Africa. For example, both the Regional Air Pollution in Developing Countries and Air Pollution Information Network for Africa which were funded by the Swedish International Development Cooperation Agency were discontinued in 2009.

In Northern Africa, studies conducted reported that mean PM levels exceeded annual and 24H WHO guidelines. The high levels of PM were

Table 12.1 Summary of review of empirical research studies on urban air quality

Author(s)	Geographical setting	Theory	Method	Focus	Results
Dieter (2012)			Review	Causes and effects of air pollution on health and economy	Rapid urbanization translates into population growth, increase in motorization and industrialization which in turn leads to increased air pollution because of increased pollutant emissions. There is also a link between air pollution and poverty hence an obstacle to economic development of a nation
Amegah and Agyei-Mensah (2017)			Policy research	Sustainable international mitigation policy framework for urban air pollution and associated health impacts in SSA	Exposure to ambient air pollution is a major threat to public health in SSA, therefore, there is need of formulating and implementing policies to reclaim our cities, make them liveable, and have new developments to be sustainable
Kgabi (2014)	Angola, Zambia, Zimbabwe, South Africa		Quantitative research	Legislation frameworks to monitor and control air pollution	There is inadequate PM monitoring in southern Africa. There is need for science-led research in proper planning and implementation of air quality legislation since the concentration of pollutants vary from one place to another depending on various variables

Author(s)	Geographical setting	Theory	Method	Focus	Results
Heiberg and Mashishi (2019)	South Africa		Quantitative research	Urban PM monitoring	Much of the African continent lacks sufficient measured air quality data, thereby leaving nearly a billion people without information about their pollution exposure
Dionisio et al. (2010)	Accra, Ghana		Quantitative research	Spatial, socio-economic status (SES), and temporal patterns of ambient air pollution in Accra	Low-income and densely populated neighbourhoods and traffic sites recorded highest PM concentration than high-income and middle-income residential neighbourhoods
Odhiambo et al. (2010)	Nairobi, Kenya		Quantitative research	PM monitoring	Transport nodes are hot spots of urban polluted air
Hersey et al. (2015)	South Africa		Quantitative research	PM monitoring	Ground monitoring indicates that low-income township sites experience by far the worst particulate air quality in South Africa, with seasonally averaged PM_{10} concentrations as much as 136 percent higher in townships that in industrial areas
Peter et al. (2012)			Quantitative research	PM monitoring	Increased motorization because of urbanization results in increased toxic emissions hence polluting the air in urban areas

(continued)

Table 12.1 (continued)

Author(s)	Geographical setting	Theory	Method	Focus	Results
Linden et al. (2012)	Ouagadougou, Burkina Faso		Quantitative research	PM monitoring	Spatial aspects, weather and climatic conditions of regions dictate the variability of PM concentrations from place to place
Safar and Labib (2010)	Cairo, Egypt		Quantitative research	PM monitoring	Cairo recorded high PM levels with soil dust contributing between 30 and 45 percent of the particulate matter. This is due to the arid climate and very low rainfall due to the area being surrounded by the Sahara Desert
Adeleke et al. (2011)	Lagos, Nigeria		Quantitative research	PM monitoring and health impact assessment	A huge percentage of Lagos' (Nigeria) population is exposed to a fatal health risk due to extremely high pm levels recorded that exceed WHO guidelines
Meko (2019)			Quantitative research	PM monitoring	Africa's diverse climate exerts a strong influence on PM levels
Gaita et al. (2014)	Nairobi, Kenya		Quantitative research	Source apportionment and seasonal PM variation, SSA, Nairobi	There is poor understanding of long-term variations of airborne particulate matter (PM) in SSA and little is known about its sources, elemental constituents, and seasonal variation. This is due to lack of long-term measurement data
Kinney et al. (2011)	Nairobi, Kenya		Quantitative research	Traffic impacts on PM levels	Lack of effective transport and land-use planning has resulted in increased motorization in Nairobi, making roads an air pollution hotspot due to harmful emissions hence increased PM concentrations

Author(s)	Geographical setting	Theory	Method	Focus	Results
Egondi et al. (2013)			Cross-sectional study	Household air pollution in slums	People residing in slums are exposed to high PM levels within their homes mainly from cooking and lighting fuels. Housing and social related problems also contribute to degree of exposure to residents
Singh et al. (2020)	Kampala, Addis Ababa, Nairobi, in East Africa		Quantitative and qualitative research	Visual impact	Conversion of visibility to extinction coefficient suggests that the PM levels of Kampala, Nairobi and Addis Ababa have increased by 162, 182 and 62 percent, respectively, since the 1970s
Landrigan et al. (2018)			Quantitative research	Health analysis	Pollution is the largest environmental cause of disease and premature death in the world today. Diseases caused by pollution were responsible for an estimated 9 million premature deaths in 2015–16 percent of all deaths worldwide
HEI (2018)			Quantitative research	Air pollution and health analysis	Air pollution is the leading environmental risk factor, contributing to more deaths than malaria or HIV/AIDS
NASA (2019)			Quantitative and qualitative research	Air pollution and health analysis	Majority of deaths due to poor air quality are caused by particulate matter carried by the Sahara Desert dust storms

(continued)

Table 12.1 (continued)

Author(s)	Geographical setting	Theory	Method	Focus	Results
Petkova et al. (2013)			Literature review	PM pollution	Rapid urban population growth, air pollution emissions, and changing patterns of disease in African cities may increase the burden of air pollution-related morbidity and mortality in coming decades. Yet, air monitoring is limited across the continent and many countries lack air quality standards
Pope et al. (2018)	Nairobi, Kenya		Quantitative research	PM monitoring	Calibrated low-cost sensors can be successfully used to measure air pollution in cities like Nairobi. It demonstrates that low-cost sensors could be used to create an affordable and reliable network to monitor air quality in cities
Cohen et al. (2017)			Quantitative research	Health analysis	Ambient $PM_{2.5}$ was the fifth-ranking mortality risk factor in 2015. Exposure to $PM_{2.5}$ caused 4.2 million deaths which has increased over the past 25 years
Shaddick et al. (2018)			Quantitative and qualitative research	PM concentrations	The global population-weighted annual average $PM_{2.5}$ concentrations were threefold higher than the 10 μg/m³ WHO guideline, driven by exposures in Asian and African regions. Estimates in regions with high contributions from mineral dust were associated with higher uncertainty, resulting from both sparse ground-based monitoring, and challenging conditions for retrieval and simulation
Simwela et al. (2018)	Nairobi, Kampala, Addis Ababa, East Africa		Review	Visual impact	PM hygroscopicity has decreased over time in three cities in Africa, Nairobi, Kampala & Addis Ababa, which is consistent with increasing emissions of PM with hygroscopicity lower than the ambient background. A large urban increment in PM is observed, with poor visibility typically occurring when the wind brings air from densely populated urban areas
Schwander et al. (2014)	Kampala, Uganda		Quantitative research	Air quality	Air quality in Kampala, the capital of Uganda, has deteriorated significantly in the past two decades. Exposure to ambient air in Kampala may increase the burden of environmentally induced cardiovascular, metabolic, and respiratory diseases including infections

Author(s)	Geographical setting	Theory	Method	Focus	Results
Rajé et al. (2018)	Nairobi, Kenya		Review	Traffic pollution	There is a detrimental effect of traffic congestion on cities. There should be awareness that this affects productivity, competitiveness, and sustainability. Resolution of congestion is key to amelioration of traffic related air pollution
Kalisa et al. (2019)			Quantitative research	Urban aerosols	PM exposure in Africa exceeds World Health Organization (WHO) safety limits. Carcinogenic PAHs/NPAHs and pathogenic microorganisms are the major components of PM aerosols. However, information on the role of aerosols in disease association in Africa remains scarce
Ekeh et al. (2014)	Kampala, Uganda		Quantitative research	Greenhouse gases	Charcoal burning has greatly influenced the increase in GHG emissions hence contributing to the deterioration of air quality in Kampala, Uganda
Egondi et al. (2013)	Nairobi, Kenya		Cross-sectional study	Community perception on air pollution	The perceived air pollution level and related health risks in the study community in Nairobi were low among the residents indicating the need for promoting awareness on air pollution sources and related health risks
deSouza (2020)			Quantitative research	PM monitoring	Low-cost air quality sensors have the potential to bridge the need for more air quality monitoring systems in Africa to monitor the deteriorating air quality

(continued)

Table 12.1 (continued)

Author(s)	Geographical setting	Theory	Method	Focus	Results
Simwela et al. (2018)			Review	Air quality	Pollution caused by fine particles is of a great concern in Africa because of its high magnitude and its physicochemical characteristics. There is a great need to improve monitoring networks in Africa
Williams et al. (2012)			Quantitative research	African biomass burning	biomass burning is categorized as the leading contributor of $PM_{2.5}$ in the Southern Hemisphere, resulting in reduced visibility with concurrent enhancement in aerosol concentrations and associated reduction in photochemical activity
Bauer et al. (2019)			Review	Outdoor air pollution and health	Air pollution in Africa leads to the premature death of about 800,000 people per year, with particulate matter ($PM_{2.5}$). Natural aerosols and anthropogenic pollution are major contributors to air pollution
Roy (2016)			Quantitative research	Cost analysis	The estimated economic cost of premature deaths from ambient particulate matter pollution in Africa in 2013 was ≈ USD 215 billion. The estimated economic cost of premature deaths from household air pollution was ≈ USD 232 billion
Habtamu et al. (2014)	Addis Ababa, Ethiopia		Quantitative research	Indoor air pollution	Average $PM_{2.5}$ concentration measured in homes using fuels exceeds WHO guidelines

Author(s)	Geographical setting	Theory	Method	Focus	Results
Croitoru and Sarraf (2017)	Casablanca, Rabat; Tangier and Marrakesh in Morocco		Quantitative research	Cost analysis	The health impacts of $PM_{2.5}$ exposure is a pressing environmental challenge in Morocco, costing society US$1.14 billion, or 1.05 percent of the country's GDP in 2014
Garland et al. (2017)			Quantitative research	Air quality management	Use of air quality indicators can be used as a simplified mode of communication with detailed information to all stakeholders including the public. This information is inclusive of the potential impact on human health and the ecosystem
UNEP and CCAC (2020)			Quantitative research	Climate change	Air pollution from toxic gases including oxides of nitrogen, carbon, sulphur, and methane are key contributors to greenhouse effect which is the main cause of air pollution
UNICEF (2019)			Quantitative and qualitative research	Children exposure	Only 6 percent of the total children population in Africa live within a proximity of 50 km radius from monitoring stations that provide real-time data on the quality of air they are breathing. Increasing the base of reliable, local, ground-level measurements would greatly aid effective responses to this poorly understood killer of children across the continent
WHO (2016a, b)			Quantitative research	PM levels and exposure	More than 80 percent of people living in urban areas that monitor air pollution are exposed to air quality levels that exceed the World Health Organization. Degradation of urban quality leaves its residents exposed to health risks with populations in low-income cities being most impacted

influenced by the desert climate characterized by sandstorms and hot and dry summers, high traffic roads as well as a substantial concentration of industries. Egypt's capital, Cairo (one of the two megacities on the continent) and the delta cities take the lead in high PM levels, with annual mean $PM_{2.5}$ concentration levels above 75 μg/m³ thereby exceeding the recommended WHO guideline values of 10 μg/m³. Other cities that recorded high PM levels included Algiers, the capital of Algeria; Sfax and Tunis in Tunisia and Kenitra in Morrocco. Two PM monitoring networks have been established by the Egyptian environmental affairs agency in Cairo as a part of the Cairo Air Improvement Project with the support of the United States Agency for International Development (Safar & Labib, 2010). Despite a downward trend, Safar and Labib reported that annual PM_{10} levels remain very high, in excess of 150 μg/m³ at industrial, traffic, and some residential sites (Safar & Labib, 2010). The pollutant concentrations are presumed high in this region over the industrialized regions (Morocco, North Algeria, Tunisia and Eastern Algeria) thus accounting for about 60–70 percent of the total sulphate in the Saharan air layer (SAL).

In Western Africa, studies reported that mean PM levels were also found to exceed the annual and 24-h WHO guidelines. PM levels were particularly high in Nigeria, although very high levels were also recorded in Burkina Faso as well as among populations of lower socio-economic status in Ghana. As a part of a health impact assessment study (City of Lagos, Nigeria with a population of over 20 million), Adeleke et al. (2011) performed 5 months of integrated sampling and reported extremely high levels of up to 272.8, 617.4, and 1171.7 μg/m³ for $PM_{2.5}$, PM_{10} and TSP, respectively (Adeleke et al.). In yet a different study, researchers carried out field studies to analyse the spatial and temporal variability of air pollution and climate in Ouagadougou, Burkina Faso, where they focused on the relationship between atmospheric stability and pollutant levels. PM_{10} and $PM_{2.5}$ levels were substantially higher during highly stable atmospheric conditions compared to moderately stable atmospheric conditions across selected locations with various land cover, land use and traffic density. For instance, the average urban PM_{10} was 162 μg/m³ during extremely stable conditions compared to 69 μg/m³ during moderately stable conditions (Linden et al., 2012).

In the most recent scientific study to date examining urban air quality in Africa, researchers carried a PM monitoring in Accra, Ghana, to examine the within-neighbourhood spatial variability of PM concentrations in communities of varying socio-economic status. Mean annual particulate matter values across all traffic and residential sides, excluding days with the strongest Harmattan winds, ranged between 30 and 70 μg/m³ for $PM_{2.5}$ and between 57 and 108 μg/m³ for PM_{10}. PM variability was greater across neighbourhoods than across traffic sites and the highest PM level was observed in a densely populated low-income neighbourhood (Dionisio et al., 2010).

In Eastern Africa, studies reported the highest PM levels in Kenya and lowest in Tanzania with mean PM levels that were below or only slightly exceeding the 24-h $PM_{2.5}$ and PM_{10} guidelines, respectively. Nairobi, the capital of Kenya and the fourth most congested city in the world, is in many ways typical of the fast-growing cities of sub-Saharan Africa. Nairobi depicted an alarming increase of PM levels. Previous studies recorded TSP measurements ranging between 30 and 80 $\mu g/m^3$ between December 1993 and October 1994. Subsequently, Odhiambo et al., (2010) recorded a PM_{10} mean of 239 $\mu g/m^3$, measured once a week for 8 h during a 3-month period in 2003. However in the most recent studies, by use of portable filter-based air samplers to take measurements, Kinney et al., (2011) reported mean 11-h average (0730–1830 hours) $PM_{2.5}$ concentrations between 58.1 and 98.1 $\mu g/m^3$ at four traffic sites. With only two monitoring stations, Addis Ababa in Ethiopia also recorded unhealthy PM levels.

Major pollutants like PM_{10}, NO_2, SO_2, Troposphere ozone, and CO recorded a maximum level of 285 $\mu g/m^3$, 97 ppm, 20 $\mu g/m^3$, 45 ppb and 2.8 ppm/15 mins, respectively. These values exceed the WHO stipulated standards of tolerable concentrations and even further aggravate during the dry seasons (Mekonnen & Tigist, 2018). Measurements taken in Khartoum, Sudan, by the US embassy, recorded AQI above 150 on most of the days, which the US Environmental Protection Agency (EPA) considers unhealthy particulate concentrations. In Kampala, Uganda, PM collected in teflon-membrane filters, depicted concentrations above 100 $\mu g/m^3$ for both $PM_{2.5}$ and PM_{10}, thus indicative of unhealthy air attributed to heavy urbanization and other anthropogenic activities. $PM_{2.5}$ Mass concentrations recorded in Kampala were at least three times the US 24-hr National Ambient Air Quality Standards, NAAQS 35 $\mu g/m^3$ and the WHO Air Quality standards 25 $\mu g/m^3$ (Schwander et al., 2014).

In Southern Africa, according to reviewed studies, it is South Africa which is the only African country that appears to have established well-defined standards and a comprehensive monitoring network (Hersey et al., 2015; Kgabi, 2014). Despite having an advanced monitoring network including satellite-based air quality management systems, only 20.9 percent of South African cities met WHO targets for annual $PM_{2.5}$ exposure in 2019 hence denying a healthy environment to a bigger percentage of the urban population This is because of heavy industrialization, coal mining and use as well as urbanization in South Africa (Heiberg & Mashishi, 2019; WHO, 2019a). Zimbabwe and Zambia contributed significantly to this region's air pollution. This is mainly due to the rapid growth of the two cities that is characterized by heavy industrialization (such as cement production industries) and high traffic hence increased emissions. Regional hot spots for atmospheric brown clouds include southern Africa, extending southwards from sub-Saharan Africa into Angola, Zambia and Zimbabwe (Kgabi, 2014). It had been established that air pollution concentrations in southern Africa exceed thresholds of 40 ppb (parts per billion) at which plant damage can occur. The Environmental Sustainability Index estimated countrywide pollutant concentrations in $\mu g/m^3$ for South

Africa as 44.03, 22.37, 111.9; Zambia as 26.35, 19.52, 147.0; and Zimbabwe as 38.55, 5.35, 144.6; for NO2, SO2, and TSP respectively.

Although many researches rely on technical methods to quantify PM concentrations and monitor air quality in the cities across the globe, one of the PM study conducted in East Africa used visibility as a proxy for air quality (Singh et al., 2020). This was linked to a lack of sufficient monitoring programmes and techniques to evaluate the air quality in the cities under study. The study points out that a large urban increment in PM can be observed, with poor visibility more pronounced when the wind brings air from densely populated urban areas. Singh et al. (2020). argue that there has been a significant loss in East African visibility since the 1970s to date, with Nairobi having the greatest loss at 60 percent compared to Kampala at 56 percent and Addis Ababa at 34 percent. This has been associated with increased anthropogenic PM emissions, whose levels have tremendously increased by 182 percent in Nairobi, 162 percent in Kampala and 62 percent in Addis Ababa. Singh et al. further investigated PM hygroscopicity by comparing visibilities under different RH conditions, with results showing a decrease in this property, which is consistent with increasing emissions of PM with lower hygroscopicity lower than ambient backgrounds. Due to changing PM sources and sinks in rainy and dry seasons over time, distinct variations in seasonal visibility are also observed (Singh et al., 2020). Sadly, Gaita et al., (2014), in their study on source apportionment and seasonal PM variation in Nairobi, Kenya, mention that there is little knowledge on such PM variations mentioned above, and elemental constituents of PM, all attributed to poor monitoring (Gaita et al., 2014).

Air Pollutants and Their Sources

Ambient air pollution in urban areas has mainly been attributed to energy production and use. This mostly includes the burning of fossil fuels in industries and vehicles contributing to outdoor air pollution. In addition to energy production and use, other sources include poor waste management and particulate matter (any mixture of solid particles or liquid droplets that remain suspended in the atmosphere for appreciable time periods). However, depending on spatial and infrastructural aspects such as densities, weather and climatic condition of regions, the main sources of air pollutants and their concentrations in air vary from place to place. For instance, in Northern and Western Africa, studies showed that dust was the major air pollutant contributing to 45 percent of particulate matter concentrations. This is mainly because of the dust storms rising from the matrix, the Sahara Desert (Linden et al., 2012; Meko, 2019; NASA, 2019; Safar & Labib, 2010).

According to Haslett et al., (2019) and Owili et al. (2017), biomass burning is the key source of air toxic pollutants in Central Africa. In Eastern Africa, increased motorization and industrialization is the main source of air pollution while in southern Africa, coal mines, industries and vehicle emissions were major sources of air pollutants (Heiberg & Mashishi, 2019; Hersey et al., 2015; Kgabi, 2014; WHO, 2019a). It is important to note that Africa's diverse climate and landscape characteristics exert a strong influence on PM levels. This is evident from pronounced seasonal fluctuation in particulate matter levels, with higher levels recorded during the dry season. In addition, long-range transportation of pollutants is often associated with high PM concentrations in particular regions away from their sources.

Indoor or household air pollution, referring to the concentration of the chemical, biological and physical contaminants in the air inside a building, is primarily caused by heavy consumption of biofuels such as wood and charcoal, fossil fuels mainly paraffin/kerosene and coal. When burnt indoors in open fires or rudimentary appliances, the incomplete combustion of these fuels releases high amounts of toxic pollutants. Indoor pollutants also originate from building materials and carpets, tobacco smoke, asbestos products, pesticides, and household cleaning products. They may also penetrate from outdoor environments by forced ventilation, diffusion, or infiltration and vice versa (meaning HAP, can also contribute to outdoor air pollution). These factors result in high concentrations of respirable particulates within the indoor environment that are significantly higher than PM_{10} and $PM_{2.5}$ experienced in the ambient environment.

Traffic Related Pollution

Rapid urbanization in developing countries of Africa has caused a large-scale proliferation in motorization. For instance, Nairobi, the 4th most traffic congested city in the world recorded an increase of up to 77 percent in the number of newly registered vehicles in 2018. The National Transport and Safety Authority registers up to 90,000 vehicles yearly. It is projected that by 2030, the number of vehicles in Nairobi (excluding motorcycles, farm and earth moving machineries) is likely to hit 1.35 million (Kenya National Bureau of Statistics, 2018).

In Addis Ababa, Ethiopia, with an estimated population of 3.6 million, the rate of vehicular increase is estimated at 9.88 percent annually which is beyond even the holding capacity of the road networks under construction with an estimated annual growth rate of 8.22 percent. This city houses almost 70 percent of the total number of vehicles registered in Ethiopia (Mekonnen & Tigist, 2018). In Cairo, Egypt, the number of cars in 2014 rose by 12 percent, hitting 2.2 million cars, with private cars representing 91 percent of the total. National wide, the country registered 7.9 million cars in that year (Central Agency for Public Mobilization and Statistics [CAPMAS], 2014).

In South Africa, the country with the highest number of cars per capita and the largest vehicle market in the African continent, there was a total of more than 12 million registered vehicles by end of 2017 according to the electronic National Administration Traffic Information System (eNatis) while in Nigeria, according to National Bureau of Statistics (NBS), the total number of cars hit 11.8 million in 2018. Liberia, a rubber-powered economy, has one of the highest car-to-population ratios in the continent, despite being one of the poorest countries with poor infrastructure in the region. Other countries in the African continent with high number of cars per capita include Morocco, Tunisia, Ghana, Tanzania, Cameroon and Mauritania. Togo, Sao Tome and Principe are the countries with the least number of cars per capita in the region.

According to the UNEP (2017), there were more than 45 million vehicles (LDVs and HDVs) in Africa by 2015, and the numbers of LDVs are projected to rise by more than 137 million in 2040. The significance of road transport on social-economic development of a country cannot be undermined, particularly nowadays when both time and cost of delivery of goods is critical. However, given the contemporary desire of people to relocate and to carry goods which has brought about significant changes in road transport, the rapid increase in spatial distribution densities of vehicles in the cities of Africa is resulting in swarming conditions exerting externalities on the quality of the urban environment, urban mobility, and life on broader scales. This could spell disaster if not addressed.

Despite improving accessibility and reducing transportation costs, increased motorization has made African cities increasingly congested and largely polluted. Between 2000 and 2016, transport emissions are reported to have increased by 95 percent in North Africa and by 75 percent in sub-Saharan Africa (UNEP, 2017). This is evident from extremely high levels of PM concentrations above WHO guidelines recorded in various highways and carriageways under study in African cities. For instance, PM studies conducted in Nairobi, Kenya, found that roadway concentrations of $PM_{2.5}$ were estimated to be about 20-fold higher than those from the urban background sites while black carbon concentrations differed by tenfold. In Douala, Cameroon, roadside PM concentrations exceeded stipulated WHO guidelines by approximately 300 percent. While in Accra, Ghana, roadside $PM_{2.5}$ and PM_{10} concentrations were estimated to be as high as 200 $\mu g/m^3$ and 400 $\mu g/m^3$, respectively (Dionisio et al., 2010; Kinney et al., 2011; Odhiambo et al., 2010; Petkova et al., 2013; UNEP, 2017).

Industrial Pollution

Mineral exploration and production have constituted significant parts of Africa's economies since the emergence of industrialization in early 1920s. Africa is richly endowed with bauxite, cobalt, industrial diamond, phosphate rock, platinum-group metals (PGM), vermiculite, zirconium, aluminium, chromite, copper, gold, iron ore, steel, lead, manganese, zinc, cement, graphite, natural diamonds, mineral fuels, and uranium. This makes Africa the richest continent as it constitutes over 30 percent of the world's global mineral reserves, besides being the matrix on which the Congo Basin, the world's second-largest surviving rainforest lies. Based on the current trends, the continent is on the verge of an unprecedented mining boom, and is now attracting billions of dollars in foreign investment to boost a less than 5 percent of the total global mineral exploration and extraction budget invested in the continent.

Despite the fact that this will play a critical role in regional socio-economic growth, there is a great concern about environmental degradation associated with the current industrial and mining-related activities in Africa. This has been attributed to heavy consumption of fossil fuels and coal, use of highly toxic chemicals, deforestation and loss of vegetation cover (resulting in loss of biodiversity due to habitat destruction, soil erosion, dust emissions and implications on the hydrological cycle, carbon cycle and nitrogen cycle), formation of sinkholes, and industrial discharges of untreated effluents that contribute significant amounts of environmental pollutants resulting in air, soil, and water quality degradation. These industrial emissions may include but are not limited to oxides of carbon, nitrogen, hydroxides, heavy metal fumes, particulate matter, benzene, organic and inorganic waste. As much as most of these natural resource exploitation activities take place in the rural contexts, the high PM concentration levels recorded in various urban centres of Africa are also attributed to long-range transportation of the pollutants from their sources in rural areas.

A study on air quality in southern Africa Region comprising South Africa, Zambia, Angola, Botswana, Zimbabwe, and Mozambique (Kgabi, 2014; Morakinyo et al., 2020) showed that most industries produce very toxic emissions into the atmosphere owing to their over-reliance on coal as a main source of energy. Coal combustions contribute substantial amounts of CO_2, mercury, lead, sulphur dioxide and nitrogen oxides. Dust emissions associated with mining activities and cement production in these countries, also contribute significantly to this region's air pollution. South Africa is the most industrialized country in southern Africa and gets 90 percent of its electricity from coal-fired power plants contributing to 66 percent of the total industrial sulphur emitted in the region. Greenpeace (2019) examined satellite data on air quality and the results showed that South African air has the highest concentration of NO_2 in the world which is attributed to coal plants and coal-powered industries. Greenpeace also revealed that most of these coal plants in South Africa often failed to meet even the emission standards set forth by the government. Zimbabwe, the second most industrialized country in the Southern African Development Community(SADC), has most of its industries concentrated around Harare, with ore smelters located close to the ore sources (principally along the Great Dyke) and their emissions are a posing threat to the ambient air quality of the city.

Results from an examination of the chemical composition of particulate matter of samples collected at North Atlantic free troposphere at Izana Global Atmospheric suggest a vital industrial contribution to regional and global ambient air pollution. Emissions mainly consist of carbon oxides, nitric oxides, sulphur oxides, heavy metals and ammonium from crude oil refineries, fertilizer manufacturing industries, phosphate mines and power plants. These are found on the Atlantic coast of Morocco, Northern Algeria, Eastern Algeria and Tunisia. These emissions contributed a significantly large portion of the mix desert dust (in form of nitrates, sulphates, ammonium compounds, etc.) which is the lead pollutant in the Northern and Western Regions of Africa (Rodríguez et al., 2011). Studies have singled out industrial emissions in these regions to be contributing 60–70 percent of the total sulphate concentrations.

The production of polyamide, nylon, and polyester which is a synthetic petroleum-based fibre in large scale textile industries of Egypt, Botswana and Ethiopia involves the use of harmful toxic chemicals whose emissions are carcinogenic. Petroleum refineries are a major source of hazardous and toxic air pollutants. Nigeria, an oil-powered economy and the largest oil and gas producer in Africa, along with Angola, Algeria, Libya, Egypt, DRC, Ghana, Gabon, Libya, Equatorial Guinea, Chad, Cameroon, Sudan Ivory coast, Tunisia, Congo, Niger and Morocco suffer significant ambient air pollution attributed to emissions from their crude oil refineries. Noteworthy, the Petroleum Refineries Sector is the second-highest ranked sector in terms of greenhouse gas (GHG) emissions per facility, with an average of 1.22 million metric tons of carbon dioxide equivalent (MMT CO_2e), behind only the power plant sector. These refineries produce substantial amounts of particulate matter, sulphur oxides, hydrofluorocarbons, chlorofluorocarbons, carbon monoxide, nitrogen oxides, BTEX compounds (benzene, toluene, ethylbenzene, and xylene), methane and volatile organic compounds (VOCs) for each ton of crude processed. Even as oil exploration still goes on in Africa with hopes to find more and more oil reserves, there is a need for formulation and implementation of mitigation measures and policies to curb air pollution attributed to oil refining.

Urbanization is generally associated with the increased consumption of industrially manufactured goods. This has resulted in increased consumption of household chemicals across many upcoming urban areas in Africa. There is a rapid increase in chemical industries in Africa. This is occasioned by the demand for agricultural production (for food, biofuel, fibre and pharmaceutical), and the need to control insect-borne diseases and petroleum products. The current global chemical production capacity is estimated at 2.3 billion tonnes and is projected to double by 2030. These industries have continually emitted hazardous chemicals to the environment in large quantities thus degrading its quality and posing a health risk to residents in the neighbourhoods (UN, 2018). Most of these industries are set up either in urban areas or near them because of the good infrastructure and readily available markets.

In most developing countries of Africa, unplanned industrial growth is a major challenge to environmental degradation. In these countries, air pollution control policy and regulatory frameworks are weak, and emission reduction technologies as well as cleaner fuels are too expensive or not available. Most industries still rely on old technologies that are not environmentally friendly as they produce a lot of untreated emissions and waste. Despite the formulation of international frameworks to mitigate air quality degradation, implementation progress has been uneven hence creating more gaps in efforts to mitigate industrial pollution. Cheap labour, availability of resources and weak environmental management capacities provide an economic opportunity for relocation of some industries from industrialized countries to Africa, for example, lead-acid battery recycling tanneries. Studies showed that most industries get a way through without conducting a comprehensive environmental impact assessment and audit (EIA & EA). This resulted in most industries not having a detailed environmental management plan (EMP) to monitor, assess and mitigate degradation of the environment. This has also been linked to corruption among policymakers, policy implementation bodies, and developers.

Waste Related Air Quality

Waste generation has been rapidly increasing owing to rapid population growth (hence increased consumption), urbanization and industrialization. In 2016, the world's cities generated 2.01 billion tonnes of solid waste, amounting to a footprint of 0.74 kilograms per person per day. It is projected that annual waste generation is expected to increase by 70 percent from 2016 levels to 3.40 billion tonnes in 2050. According to Bello and colleagues, the developmental rates of any country/region are directly proportional to the amounts of MSW generated (Bello et al., 2016). Africa, the least developed region in the world, produces 125 million tonnes of municipal waste annually, and this value is expected to triple by 2050 due to rapid socio-economic growth in both SSA and North Africa (WHO, 2019a). Before the emergence of industrial revolution and urbanization, the world's population was still low and most of the wastes produced was biodegradable and was effectively managed within households. Therefore, waste contribution to environmental degradation and deterioration of public health was extremely low almost negligible.

History has depicted attempts by the developing countries of Africa in the 1900s, to manage their wastes that were aimed at maintaining public health. These attempts included efficient waste collection methods and proper disposal at designated sites was in operation. During the colonial period, waste management was very efficient and centralized with the introduction of refuse trucks that would collect wastes from points of generation and deposit them at designated sites. However, after gaining independence, most of the African countries neglected these measures resulting in a decline of waste management system.

Most recent studies reported most urban governments in many African countries facing serious problems with the management of solid waste. They reported relatively poor management practices characterized by indiscriminate dumping of raw waste in water bodies and isolated places often associated with open burning. In some cases, advanced technology characterized by the use of incinerators has been deployed but the ashes, which are full of contaminants, are still buried in landfills. These malpractices of waste management have adverse effects on the environment and social-economic status of Africa's urban population. The problem of widespread indiscriminate waste disposal in the cities of Africa has been associated with several factors including ineffective and inefficient policy frameworks, lack of adequate financial resources, lack of awareness, infrastructure and land-use planning which are not matched with the urban growth rates as well as a long-term lapse in the enforcement of urban planning and environmental laws.

Emenike et al., (2013) examined waste generation and management in four popular, densely populated, and economically significant cities, with each city representing the four regions of the continent. These cities included Cairo in Egypt (pop. 9.12 million, Northern Africa), Lagos in Nigeria (pop. 11 million, West Africa), Nairobi in Kenya (pop. 3.1 million, Eastern Africa) and Johannesburg in South Africa (pop. 4.4 million, Southern Africa). The results of these studies showed that the average per capita waste generation across the cities is 0.7 kg/day, and is characterized by low recycling rates at 10 percent of total waste, and incessant disposal of waste on streets and use of uncontrolled landfills.

Another study by Bello et al., (2016) reveals that apart from Municipal solid wastes (MSWs), African cities struggle with the collection, disposal and management construction and demolition waste, end-of-life Vehicles (EoLV), biomass wastes, healthcare wastes, and electronic wastes (e-waste). However, residential neighbourhoods are the highest waste generators. For instance, in Uganda, residential wastes contribute up to between 52 and 80 percent of total wastes produced. In Kenya, a case study of four cities (Nairobi, Mombasa, Kisumu and Nakuru) reveals that residential waste contributed up to 60 percent of total waste produced. This is characterized by huge amounts of biodegradable organic materials; mainly kitchen remains, and minor portions comprised of paper, plastics, and ceramics. Industries also contribute a substantial percentage of total wastes produced in cities of Africa. However, the constituents of the wastes vary from country to country or region to region, depending on the rate of economic growth, distribution of raw materials, and type of industries in the regions. For example, Egypt, Ethiopia and Botswana focus on textile industry, Tunisia in clothing industry, while Nigeria, Senegal and South Africa are well known for their food industries.

Increased motorization in cities of Africa and advancements in technologies has also resulted in rapid increase in production of End-of-Life Vehicles (EoLV), more so their tyres, and e-waste. These are poorly managed so they contribute in polluting the environment. For instance, South Africa produces over one million waste tyres annually. When burnt, these wastes such as dioxins emit huge amounts of toxic matter into the atmosphere thereby degrading the air quality and contributing to climate change (Emenike et al., 2013; Nkosi et al., 2013).

Waste can contain volatile organic compounds (VOCs), polychlorinated biphenyls (PCBs), heavy metals, radioactive materials, and pharmaceuticals that are very harmful and toxic. Burning of waste, particularly organic waste which in most cases contributes up to 50 percent of total waste generated in Africa; with a significant amount of GHG gases and other amounts to particulates thus contributing to the greenhouse effect and ambient air pollution. Dumping of waste into water further aggravates the already low sanitation levels in these countries. These also contribute to the degradation of aquatic ecosystems. Waste constituents such as plastics and scrap metal that take too long to decompose also contribute to soil pollution. These may also include the release of heavy metals, metalloids, and other chemicals into soils either directly through leachate and chemical reactions or indirectly through acidic rains contaminating soils and water bodies. Landfills majorly use a plastic liner system, which deteriorates over time allowing leachate contaminated by the buried waste with all the potential toxins, to get into soils and underground water. The alternatively used clay or compacted soil liners also become increasingly porous over time releasing contaminants into the environment. All of these aspects contribute significantly to the deterioration of public health and has an economic cost implication (African Development Bank [ADB], 2017; Bello et al., 2016; Emenike et al., 2013; UNEP, 2018a, b).

In relation to urban air quality, open burning of waste or use of incinerators resulting in emissions of GHGs into the atmosphere results in increased PM levels degrading the urban air. A study conducted by Tadesse (2020) in Addis Ababa, Ethiopia, reveals that the maximum concentration of $PM_{2.5}$ in the case of Hidar Sitaten was 215 µg/m^3, 8.6 times higher than the WHO air quality guideline standard of daily allowance, with a maximum AQI value recorded at 184. Tadesse also report the recorded highest values of air quality index and $PM_{2.5}$ concentrations at 171 and 106 µg/m^3, and mean values at 112 and 44.2 µg/m^3, respectively, in 2017 on the same cultural days. In 2018, a total of 177 was recorded as the maximum AQI value, with concentrations of $PM_{2.5}$ reaching as high as 176 µg/m^3.

As much as the use of incinerators might be termed as advanced technologies in waste management not only in Africa but in the entire world, they also produce ultra-fine particulate matter that enters the air after escaping pollution control technology. Both methods emit toxins such as VOCs, heavy metals, dioxins, sulphur dioxide, carbon monoxide, mercury, carbon dioxide, and furans into the air. Most of these toxins are persistent chemical pollutants and are also highly poisonous. For instance, dioxins can remain in the environment for very many years before its radioactivity falls to half its original level. Decomposing waste in landfills produces a bad smell due to the presence of hydrogen sulphide and mercaptans, and depending on the constituents, it may generate methane gas which is explosive and contributes to the greenhouse effect. Other gases generated in landfills include toxins such as phenols and chlorobenzenes as well as carcinogens such as benzene and methylene chloride.

Environmentally, sound waste management strategies are very critical in the development of sustainable, resilient, and liveable cities. However, lack of enough solid waste management funding, inadequate technological and infrastructural advancements remain to be major challenges in solid waste management in Africa. This explains why only 10 percent of waste produced can be effectively managed through recycling. There also exists an information gap on solid waste generation and management in most developing cities of Africa. These hinder the formulation and implementation of effective waste management policies to mitigate environmental pollution and socio-economic implications.

Desert Storms

Africa is the matrix on which the world's largest hot desert, the Sahara Desert, sits. Other deserts within the continent include Kalahari and Namib deserts. Deserts across the world have been characterized by extremely heavy and frequent sandstorms and desert emissions. Studies point out desert regions in the Northern Africa to be the largest source of soil dust suspended in the earth's atmosphere, with emissions ranging from 300 to 1600 Tg y^{-1}. These amounts are 2–3 times larger than those generated in the Asian deserts, which are the second most important dust sources and account for more than 60 percent of global desert dust emissions. Rodríguez et al., (2011) mention that regional dust production and exportation in the Northern Africa experience a marked seasonal evolution activated in the summer monsoon. The Bodélé depression in the Sahara Desert is one of the most prolific sources of dust in the world. Other studies have highlighted areas located at the south of the southern slope of the Atlas Mountains to be significant sources of dust advected towards the Atlantic in the summer on the northern edge of the Saharan air layer.

The heavy sandstorms and dust emissions occurring in the deserts of Africa and other drought-prone regions contribute significant amounts of PM not only within their regions of location but to other parts of the world. However, PM concentrations experience a large variability throughout the year, with the most predominant season being the non-dusty period, termed as 'clean free troposphere', depicting concentrations within a range of 1–5 $\mu g/m^3$, whereas during intense dust emissions, PM_{10} concentrations could reach as high as 150 $\mu g/m^3$, and 120 $\mu g/m^3$ and 700 $\mu g/m^3$ for $PM_{2.5}$ and TSP, respectively as 8-h or 24-h average (Rodríguez et al., 2011). In some intense cases, TSP concentrations can exceed 800 $\mu g/m^3$ (Bhattachan et al., 2012; Middleton & Kang, 2017).

According to PM studies conducted in Northern and Western Africa, dust from the Sahara Desert was the major component in the samples collected in various cities, including Cairo in Egypt, Algiers in Algeria, Sfax and Tunis in Tunisia, Lagos in Nigeria, Ouagadougou in Burkina Faso and Kenitra in Morocco. Mineral dust contributed up 45 percent of particulate matter

(Meko, 2019; Safar & Labib, 2010; van Donkelaar et al., 2016). The results from an examination of the chemical composition of PM, depict that desert mineral dust contribute to the highest percentage of phosphorous content in the Saharan air layer. Soil emissions of evaporite minerals such as Al, Ca, Fe, Mg, Mn, Ti, Rb, P, Sr, La, V, Ni, Co, Cr, As, and K combine with other emissions from anthropogenic activities (mainly industrial) to form mix desert dust with high concentrations of toxic particulate pollutants such as nitrates, sulphate, and ammonium compounds (Rodríguez et al., 2011). Compounds such as sulphates depicted highest concentration in regions with abundance of crust of salts on topographic lows and salt dry lakes, as well as in regions characterized by intensive anthropogenic emissions of $SO_2/SO_X/H_2SO_4$.

In Southern Africa, Namib and Kalahari Deserts contribute substantial amounts of dust from interdune areas thus increasing PM levels in the region. A high concentration of dust in the air is characterized by dark brown to reddish hazy skies that reduce visibity as observed in Southern Africa cities including Johannesburg, Pretoria, Capetown and Alexander Bay in South Africa; Gaborone, Tshane and Ghanz

i in Botswana; Windhoek, Walvis Bay and Swakopmund in Namibia; Lusaka in Zambia; Namibe in Angola (Bhattachan et al., 2012; Heiberg & Mashishi, 2019; Kgabi, 2014; WHO, 2019a) More comprehensive studies are required to evaluate the chemical profile of dust emissions from these two deserts as well as other drought-prone regions to determine their effect on air quality, climate change and biogeochemistry processes. These occurrences of intense dust emissions, and pollutants mixing with those from other anthropogenic sources, form the toxic mix of desert mineral dust and contribute to high PM levels in cities under study. This explains why Sahara dust is the leading cause of premature deaths in Northern, Western, and some parts of Central Africa (Adeleke et al., 2011; Bauer et al., 2019; Linden et al., 2012/2017; NASA, 2019).

Hot and dry climatic conditions characterized by low amounts of rainfall received in these regions are responsible for the formation of dust. Additionally, studies have highlighted climate change, land-use change, industrial activities such as mining, poor water management systems, heavy motorization, and other unsustainable anthropogenic activities such as overgrazing, poor soil tenure systems to be influencing the frequency and intensity of sandstorms as well as dust emission rates. These paradigms have a complex interconnection and greatly influence changes in surface wind and vegetation growth which in turn modify sandstorms and dust emissions. Strong winds that blow across are responsible for transporting the dust particles and suspending them in air. The hot temperatures are responsible for depriving desert soils of any moisture content thus making their particles too light and are therefore suspended in the air for a long period of time.

In addition to affecting air quality, studies have shown an association between dust emissions and processes affecting climate change as well as biogeochemistry. Given the scattering and absorbing radiative properties of dust, its presence greatly influences energy distribution in the atmosphere. Dust particles could significantly influence cloud and rain radiative properties, as they may act as cloud condensation nuclei. In regard to biogeochemistry, dust deposition in the oceans and other water bodies, has greatly influenced the production rate of ammonium and nitrates by cyanobacteria that utilize iron in their metabolism. Noteworthy, iron, Fe, is one of the many soils evaporite minerals contained in the soil dust. Additionally, Fe and P, contained in dust deposited in high nutrient and low chlorophyll oceanic regions may be limiting nitrogen fixation by phytoplanktons, consequently modulating the carbon cycle.

Biomass Burning and Other Agricultural Emissions

Global and regional air pollution resulting in accumulations of GHGs in the atmosphere has always been associated with emissions because of anthropogenic activities in industrialized and urbanized regions. However, studies have revealed that biomass burning is also a key contributor to ambient air pollution through trace gas emissions and generation of tropospheric nitric oxides, NO_x. Biomass burning is mainly associated with fuel production and various land-use activities including the burning of vegetation (mainly savannah and forest burning), forest clearing for settlement and cultivation, and agricultural waste combustion. Although most of the fires are human-induced, natural wildfires also do occur. Studies have pointed out lightning, falling rocks as well as extremely hot and dry weather conditions, as key natural causes of wildfires.

In Southern Africa, the hot and dry Berg winds blowing from mountains to the coast and vast dry grasslands have been greatly associated with wildfires in the region. It is important to note that both natural and human-induced fires are frequent during the hot and dry seasons whose onsets and offsets vary from region to region within the continent. For example, in western Africa, biomass burning seasons are between November and January while in Angola, Congo, and Zambia, it is pronounced between June and September. Noteworthy, according to NASA (2019), out of approximately 10,000 fires burning across the world, 70 percent are experienced in Africa.

Despite assumptions that these activities/fires do not contribute significantly to net emissions, biomass burning is one of the largest sources of oxides of carbon in Africa. Past studies revealed that biomass contributed approximately 337 Tg C of CO_2 representing 18 percent of global biomass burning CO_2 total of 1906 Tg C/yr and 90 percent of total CO produced in the continent. The 96 TgC/yr of CO emitted annually on the continent constituted 20 percent of the global all source total. Between 2000 and 2005, wildfires are reported to have accounted for almost 45 percent of total CO_2 emitted by land-use sector in Africa. Globally, biomass burning also contributed 45, 37, 32 and 5 percent of total sources of ethylene, ethane, propylene, and other non-methane hydrocarbons (NMHCs), respectively. Geoffrey et al., (2018) estimates a combined total of 194, 113, 270 tCO_2-e of emissions in early and late dry seasons of savannah and forest fires in 29 African countries.

Moreover, biomass burning emissions play a critical role in global photochemical ozone formation, contributing up to 35 percent. Ambient air pollution studies conducted in West Africa show seasonal persistence of ozone on the equatorial West African coast owing to both the intensity and duration of biomass burning in tropical Africa whereas in central Africa, studies revealed that surface ozone rises by 50 ppbv during the biomass burning seasons. In a recent publication by Vijay Shankar under SciDev.Net's Global edition (2016), scientists have claimed that the burning down of forests in Africa and South East Asia causes ozone pollution in the air as far as the western Pacific Ocean, thereby contradicting the thought that ozone-rich air over the ocean was a natural phenomenon leading to development of wrong global climate models. In another study by Williams et al., (2012), biomass burning is categorized as the leading contributor of $PM_{2.5}$ in the Southern Hemisphere, resulting in reduced visibility with concurrent enhancement in aerosol concentrations and associated reduction in photochemical activity. It is worth noting that although the ozone protects us from dangerous ultraviolet radiations from the sun, long-term exposure to ground-level ozone can result in irreversible damage to lungs, heart, and eye tissues.

Most recent satellite measurements of the tropospheric ozone have revealed that large amounts of air pollution associated with biomass burning comes from tropical Africa, thus taking the lead by 50 percent of global biomass burning which contributes to about 4 percent to the global overall CO_2 budget. Despite much of these activities majorly happening in rural areas in which Africa's largest percentage population reside, the fires are so profuse in some regions, especially Central, Southern and Western Africa. Smoke and soot emissions from these fires radiate across the whole continent and streams south and southeast covering the urban air space too, and contributing to particulate pollution. Prevailing winds across the continent are responsible for long-range transportation of the emissions. The smoke and soot not only constitute CO_2 but also CO, CH_4, VOC, H_2, NO, N_2O, NH_3, SO_2, COS, CH_3Cl, and CH_3Br. Similar emissions have been associated with veld fires in Eastern South Africa, contributing significantly to air pollution as well as translating to socio-economic and environmental losses such as destruction of infrastructure, loss of homes, stock and grazing field losses, loss of biodiversity as well as loss of vegetation.

Schwander et al., (2014) examined the air quality in Kampala. The results depicted high PM concentrations in the city attributed to both heavy motorization and biomass burning. In this study, elevated water-soluble potassium to total potassium ratio in all $PM_{2.5}$ samples collected was evidence of abundance biomass burning during the study period. For this reason, this study highlighted the need for analysis of organic and elemental carbon as well as carbon speciation to further understand source attributions and implications on public health. Additionally, Rodríguez et al., (2011) also mentions that dust particles exported in the winter tropical SAL are often externally mixed with carbonaceous and inorganic trace species such as K^+, linked to biomass burning in Sahel during the dry season.

Haslett et al., (2019) and Maranan et al., (2017) provide evidence of biomass burning aerosols dominating Southern-West African air pollution. In this study, the Dynamics-Aerosol-Chemistry-Cloud Interactions in West Africa (DACCIWA) aircraft campaign aimed to analysing gas and aerosol properties in the region to assess anthropogenic and other influences on the atmosphere. The study was conducted over the upwind Atlantic Ocean air layer bordering the south-west coastline, along the coastline on which most of the cities are located including Accra in Ghana, Lomé in Togo, Abidjan in Côte D'Ivoire and Cotonou and Porto Novo in Benin as well as in a portion of air layer into the continent. Samples were collected and submicron aerosol chemical composition was measured using Aerodyne compact Time-of-Flight Aerosol Mass Spectrometers (AMS) mounted on board all the aircrafts used. The results depicted the presence of a significant mass of aged accumulation mode aerosol in the southern West African boundary layer, over both the ocean and the continent. Having displayed similar chemical composition, lack of variability in the accumulation mode concentration and chemical composition was evidence that much of the aerosols observed were of similar origin source.

Even in the urban air layer along the coastline, mass spectral features associated with near-field urban sources such as internal combustion engines were less prominent than would be expected from pure urban aerosol. The observations on the aerosol composition during this campaign depicted high concentrations of biomass burning aerosols. This large-scale mass of homogeneous aerosol in this Southern West Africa region was attributed to biomass burning plumes in Central and Southern Africa, which are advected northwards after being entrained into the monsoon layer over the eastern tropical Atlantic Ocean. After a detailed evaluation of organic aerosol mass spectra, biomass plumes were regarded as a primary source of accumulation mode aerosols in the region contributing up to 80 percent of the region's total during the monsoon season.

From the study by Haslett et al., (2019) just discussed, it is important to note that urban heavy ambient air pollution is not only confined to the region's dry seasons characterized by high PM concentrations because of the Sahara Desert dust storms and local biomass burning but also long-range transportation of particulate pollutants throughout much of the year. The vital contribution of long-range emissions towards the regional influx of aerosols polluting the growing Southern West African coastal cities poses a great challenge to air quality policy formulation and implementation.

Beside biomass burning, agricultural activities such as land tilling, harvesting, land preparation, and fertilizer and chemical treatment could be potential sources of significant amounts of particulates and gaseous emissions. Crop farmlands are key sources of pollens and spores that form significant parts of PM-associated bioaerosols in agricultural intensive regions (Kalisa et al., 2019). It is worth noting that as Africa industrializes and urbanizes, modernization in agriculture is expected. This would be characterized by heavy machinery use as well as heavy consumption of chemicals to boost production to meet the demands of the rapidly growing populations in the African continent. In return, there is an anticipated increase in industrial activities to also meet demand for these implements. In the case of no intervention characterized by heavy consumption of heavily polluting fuels and lack of clean production technologies in both sectors, the amounts of toxic emissions generated are likely to skyrocket, further degrading the air. Studies have linked the increase in the generation of waste amounts to modernization in agriculture, besides urbanization, industrialization, and population growth. Given the burning of crop residues as a waste management strategy, long-range transportation of pollutants from this unsustainable activity is set to result in increased PM concentrations in the cities of Africa.

Aircraft Related Pollution

There is limited documented research on the impact of aircraft emissions on air quality. However, according to the International Civil Aviation Organization (ICAO), aircrafts often travel for longer distances at varying altitudes and generate emissions that can potentially affect local, regional, and international air quality. These emissions include PM, CO_2, NO_2, CO, SO_2 and VOCs. The amounts of these emissions vary depending on fuel specifications, the number of aircraft operations such as landing and take-off cycles, aircraft fleet mix and the length of time that aircrafts spend in each of the modes of operations; take-offs, climb out, approach and idle.

There is growing use of air transport in small and large scale (domestic and international levels), across the world. Aircrafts are not only being used to transport people and goods but have also been deployed in some agricultural activities such as the spraying of chemical essentials on crops. Given the emissions associated with aircraft operations, there is need for comprehensive research on the contribution of this sector to the degradation of air quality as well as solutions to mitigate air pollution. This will greatly help to reduce health effects associated with exposure to these toxic pollutants as well as climate change.

Indoor Air Pollution

Global degradation of air quality is not only attributed to outdoor air pollution, but also indoor air pollution which is mainly characterized by heavy household consumption of biofuels (charcoal, firewood, dung & agricultural wastes) and fossil fuels, particularly kerosene (Amegah & Agyei-Mensah, 2017; Ekeh et al., 2014). Nearly half the world's population burns solid fuels as their principal household fuel for cooking, heating and lighting. In homes where these activities are pronounced, 24-hour mean indoor airborne concentrations of $PM_{2.5}$ and PM_{10} routinely reach several hundred micrograms per cubic meter and may peak as high as 10,000 µg per cubic meter during cooking (WHO, 2010). Indoor air pollution in Africa is higher than anywhere else in the world. It is estimated that approximately 80 percent of African households depend on biomass fuels (wood fuel and charcoal accounting largest shares), kerosene and coal as a major source of energy, meeting over 70 percent of their energy needs through combustion in rudimentary appliances, due to limited access of less polluting types of fuels (UNEP, 2017; UNEP CSD-14; Simwela et al., 2018). Only a small proportion of the population in the continent use clean fuel as a primary source of energy. 'The problem of widespread, inefficient use of solid biomass in households is linked to several factors, among which poverty and the geographical remoteness of rural population are only the most evident' (Hafner et al., 2018).

The energy ladder model points out electricity as the cleanest and safest fuel in terms of indoor air quality. This is followed by LPG and natural gas, while biomass fuels mainly wood, crop residues and dung are the most unsafe occupying the bottom of the ladder, which are finally followed by transition fuels that are mainly charcoal, coal and paraffin. In SSA, Kerosene is often advocated as a cleaner alternative to solid fuels, biomass, and coal for cooking. At the same time, kerosene lamps are frequently used when electricity is unavailable. Globally, an estimated 500 million households still use fuels, particularly kerosene, for lighting (Lam et al., 2012).

In most of the developing countries of Africa, electricity, natural gas and LPG are expensive owing to the low socio-economic standards of the largest portion of the population. These sources of energy are also unreliable due to inadequate infrastructural facilities and household appliances required for their supply and use. Other studies have highlighted a remarkable growth in access and use to clean cooking fuels, with LPG currently being consumed by more than half of those gaining access to clean cooking in SSA cities. However, population growth in entire Africa, outpaces the increase in access to non-solid fuels, resulting in over 900 million people lacking access to clean fuels for cooking (IEA, 2019).

As much as heavy consumption of biofuels and kerosene is attributed to the largest percentage of populations residing in rural areas with minimal alternative energy sources, there is greater concern over the rapidly growing urban poor populations (low and middle-low income residents), with over 200 million people living in slums representing approximately 50 percent of Africa's urban populations (Rabat, 2010). This segment of the population are heavy consumers of these fuel sources, whose emissions contribute significantly to both local and regional air pollution. Of the 900 million lacking access to clean cooking, over 30 percent are projected to be residing in the African cities. Rapid growth of the urban poor populations has resulted in increased charcoal and firewood production and consumption to meet the ever-growing fuel demand; this has also contributed to the reduction of global forest cover. Besides primary uses of fuel wood for cooking and heating in the residential sector, sizable amounts are also used by small and medium-size industries for metal processing, food processing and brick making.

The predominance of inefficient rudimentary appliances for cooking with wood and charcoal use of these inefficient cooking fuels and technologies (such as leaky stoves) produce high levels of household air pollution with a range of health-damaging pollutants that includes small soot particles that penetrate deep into the lungs. In addition to the above-stated biomass burning emissions, production and consumption of biofuels account for the largest amounts of CO_2 emissions at 50 percent of the total biomass burning CO_2 emissions. Biofuels also release very toxic compounds, mainly Polycyclic Aromatic Hydrocarbons (PAHs) and Nitric-Polycyclic Aromatic Hydrocarbons (NPAHs) that were recorded as present in both $PM_{2.5}$ and PM_{10} during chemical analysis of PM. Burning kerosene emits high amounts of fine particulate matter, carbon monoxide, nitric oxides, sulphur dioxide, benzene, radon, trichloroethylene, tetrachloroethylene, naphthalene, Formaldehyde and PAHs (Lam et al., 2012; WHO, 2010).

Kalisa et al., (2019) conducted a review on the chemical and biological components of urban aerosols in Africa. In this review, most studies recorded a mean concentration of atmospheric $PM_{2.5}$ and PM_{10} in Africa. These recordings greatly exceeded the WHO guideline value of the annual and 24-h mean. The mentioned organic pollutants were major components of PM. Both PAHs and NPAHs concentrations exceeded WHO recommended standards of 1 $\mu g/m^3$. Senegal, Kenya, and South Africa recorded the highest amounts of PAH concentrations, while Rwanda, Algeria and Egypt recorded the highest amounts of NPAHs concentrations. Mali, Uganda and Sierra Leone also recorded significant concentration amounts of these pollutants. A chemical analysis conducted on these organic pollutants revealed that benz (g, h, i) perylene (BPe), phenanthrene (Phe), fluoranthene (Flu), BaP, indeno (1,2,3-cd) pyrene (IDP) and benzo(b)fluoranthene (BbF) were the main constituents of PAH, while 9-nitroanthracene (9-NA) and 1-NP were most abundant in NPAHs in the African cities' air layer. The high concentrations of these pollutants have been attributed to domestic fuel burning, biomass burning, coal combustion, and diesel engine emissions in both rural and urban areas of Africa.

In a study undertaken by Habtamu et al., (2014) to assess the magnitude of indoor pollution from household fuel use in Addis Ababa (total pop. 3,709,000), Ethiopia, the mean geometric $PM_{2.5}$ concentration was found to be approximately 818 $\mu g/m^3$ with a standard deviation of 3.61 from WHO guideline standards. The researchers recorded 1134 $\mu g/m^3$, 637 $\mu g/m^3$, and 335 $\mu g/m^3$ as the highest values (24-h geometric mean) in households that used predominantly solid fuel, kerosene and clean fuel. The findings of this study point out indoor air pollution attributed to household biofuel and kerosene use as a major environmental and health hazard in Addis Ababa.

In South Africa, despite high household electrification rate and relatively low household coal reliance at national levels, studies still reveal heavy coal consumption in high-density urban settlements. For instance, 55 percent of households in informal settlements in the 'Vaal Triangle' areas of Sasolburg, Vereeniging and Vanderbijlpark are reliant on coal. The availability of low-cost coal within the areas makes it the fuel of choice for heating and cooking purposes within low-income settlements. Kerosene consumption also remains a major concern in the poor urban environments of South Africa. Studies revealed that approximately 62 percent of total households in Cato Manor (Durban), Alexandra (Johannesburg), Lady Grey (North Eastern Cape), Benoni (Gauteng), Gugulethu (Western Cape) and Galashewe (Northern Cape) were reliant on kerosene for cooking. Energy use varies seasonally with higher consumption of solid fuels during the winter leading to increased particulate loading (Barnes et al., 2009; Hersey et al., 2015).

In Nigerian cities, most household pollution is attributed to emissions from small capacity fossil-fuelled electric power, operated averagely for 6 h daily and heavy consumption of firewood as fuel among the urban and rural residents. Household activities contribute significantly to outdoor pollution which is attributed to high levels of emissions released into the air owing to the huge population densities in cities of Nigeria. For instance, Abuja had a population of 2,442,000 with a growth rate of 6.13 percent, while Onitsha had a population of 1,109,000 with a growth rate of 4.92 percent (Godson et al., 2015). In Morocco, per capita energy consumption was estimated at 0.54 tons of oil equivalent (toe) in 2012, which is very low compared to the global average 1.9toe/capita and that of Africa 0.67 toe/capita. Wood and coal accounted for 25 percent of the total energy consumption in the same year (Croitoru & Sarraf, 2017).

In addition to the major sources of indoor pollutants already discussed, studies conducted in Egypt highlight other critical components in residential buildings that should be taken into consideration in urban residential planning and developments to address Indoor Environmental Quality (IEQ) which of concern in the fast-growing cities of Africa. Indoor air pollution may also be ascribed to increased use of manufactured building materials, finishes, furniture, heating, ventilation and air conditioning (HVAC) systems, and various building chemicals. Indoor elements such as paints, solvents, adhesives, matters, fabrics, fibres and building materials are key sources of VOCs emissions. Soils and rocks on which buildings are constructed, some building materials, water, and natural gas are major sources of indoor radon. Radon gas usually finds its way into the houses through cracks in the concrete, floor, weeping tiles, mortar and wall joints, foundations, pores and cracks in blocks and penetrations of loose-fitting pipe among others.

It is important to note that basements allow more infiltration of soil gas entry than slab-on-grade foundations. Fine mineral-fibre emissions from synthetic vitreous fibres (consisting of mainly glass wool, rock wool, slag wool, glass filaments and ceramic fibres) are also toxic when inhaled in long exposure and are of great environmental health concern due to their carcinogenicity attributed to their chemical composition. In addition, moisture drift from cooling towers, containing minerals (including salts such as chlorine, sulphates, and carbonates), dissolved gases including oxygen, hydrogen and carbon dioxide, metal ions (such as iron and manganese ions) or any dissolved or suspended solids, can get into the makeup air, building vents and other outdoor air intakes, contaminating the air before it gets into the buildings' circulation systems (Konbr, 2017).

As much as other studies only point at the urban poor and rural populations as the vulnerable group to indoor pollution, these indoor pollutants sources are majorly pronounced in middle-high and high-income urban residents, therefore, making them vulnerable too. In the case of indoor fire occurrences or building fires, the toxic fumes produced contribute to outdoor pollution by raising PM concentrations. Incineration of industrial foams used as construction materials such as insulators, results in the emission of formaldehyde, carbon dioxide and other toxic gases in huge amounts. These can cause death within few seconds of exposure.

Poor housing conditions in high density urban settlements such as congested slums and poor house typology designs in rural areas that are often characterized by minimal or no ventilation and chimneys may result in increased concentration of emissions with time within a household. Ventilations, defined as the intentional introduction of outdoor air into an indoor space to control indoor air quality by diluting and displacing indoor pollutants hence treating the Sick Building Syndrome (SBS), depends on the occupation and pollution ratio (ventilation rate/capita) through the fresh air quality. Noteworthy, inadequate ventilation causes around 52 percent of SBS. With no space to escape out, and fresh outdoor air to flow in, indoor PM concentration levels can get up to 100 times the acceptable levels hence increasing health risk to the occupants owing to long exposure to the toxic emissions (WHO, 2016a, b). Even when the emissions get out eventually, the highly congested structures in slums and high-rise buildings in the urban context become barriers to wind flow hence hindering dispersion of the emissions resulting in prolonged exposure. Exposure is particularly high among women and young children, who spend the most time near the domestic hearth. However, since the emissions are characterized as hot air, which is less dense than the ambient air, they still rise slowly above the structures, and get dispersed into the atmosphere contributing significantly to outdoor air pollution thus affecting all populations. It is important to note that as much as ventilations can be an effective solution to indoor pollution, they can also be a channel through which other pollutants get into households. This can be attributed to anthropogenic activities and natural occurrences in the immediate residential neighbourhoods, resulting in toxic emissions polluting the outdoor air.

Besides the chemical composition of particulate matter highlighted from the sources of air pollution, Kalisa et al., (2019) mention that bioaerosols such as bacteria, fungi and viruses contribute a significant portion of the mass coarse of PM_{10} and fine $PM_{2.5}$ particles. These biological components of airborne particulate matter can exist as individual particles or agglomerates of particles as they can attach to PM from other sources such as industries, soils, and biomass. Fungi, like pollen and spores, account for large proportions of airborne PM, but some other components such as fungal spores belong to fine fractions of PM. Fungal spores and pollen contribute 4–11 percent of the total mass concentration of $PM_{2.5}$. However, the concentration of fungal spore loadings on PM are higher in PM_{10} than in $PM_{2.5}$ air samples since the aerodynamic diameters of a fungal spore agglomerate are between 2.5 μm and 10 μm.

Airborne bacteria can be found in the air as isolated microorganisms but are more likely to be attached to other particles such as soil or leaf fragments or found as conglomerates of a large number of bacterial cells. Airborne bacteria can also be associated with small size particles. Up to 80 percent of the total viable concentration of bacteria (5036 CFU/m^3) in the atmosphere is found in particles with diameters less than 4.7 μm. Studies point out that the relative abundance of microbial allergens and pathogens associated with PM, increase with an upsurge in the concentration of PM. Detection of viruses in airborne biological contaminants is a heavy task due to their size and difficulty in collecting and analysing procedures. Citing Cao et al. (2014) who used metagenomic methods to analyse the microbial composition of Beijing's PM pollutants, Kalisa et al., (2019) showed that airborne dsDNA viruses can however be identified at the species level. Human adenovirus C (6.5 percent) was the most dominant pathogenic airborne virus identified in the $PM_{2.5}$ and PM_{10} samples.

Effects of Air Pollution on Health and Economy

PM remains a major public health concern (Amegah & Agyei-Mensah, 2017) globally, but its impact on population health in developing countries remains unclear. With minimal systematic ambient air pollution (AAP) monitoring in SSA, and a lack of reliable primary AAP data for the vast majority of the populations, there is limited evidence of adverse health effects associated with AAP. Moreover, the limited exposure data that are available have been obtained by independent research teams covering only small geographical areas or multilateral institutions like the United Nations Environmental Programme (UNEP). Nevertheless, the existing information indicates that the levels of exposure and pollutant concentrations, exceed WHO guidelines, hence supporting the findings of the few epidemiological studies in Africa, in relation to AAP.

In Morocco, recent epidemiological studies associated $PM_{2.5}$ with mortality related to five diseases; namely, ischemic heart disease, stroke, chronic obstructive pulmonary disease, lung cancer, and Acute Respiratory Infections(ARIs). Over 70 percent of the cases recorded originated from the major cities of Morocco (Casablanca, Rabat, Tangier and Marrakesh). In 2014, over 6000 deaths were attributed to AAP, with an economic cost implication of US$1.14 billion, or 1.05 percent of the country's GDP (Croitoru & Sarraf, 2017).

In South Africa, increased number of cases of bronchitis, bronchial hyperreactivity BHR, asthma, pneumonia, emphysema, wheeze, cough, shortness of breath, phlegm, rhinitis, rhino-conjunctivitis and Cardiorespiratory comorbidities has been associated with exposure to high levels of PM. In a case-crossover study in Capetown, the risk of dying from respiratory diseases (RD), cardiovascular diseases (CVD) and cerebrovascular diseases (CBD) was associated with the 24-h average levels of AAP, with even higher estimates than those reported in developed countries. Interquartile range, IQR, an annual increase of PM_{10} [12 µg/m^3] and NO_2 [12 µg/m^3] increased CBD mortality by 4 and 8 percent, respectively, while IQR annual increase of NO_2 [12 µg/m^3] and SO_2 [8 µg/m^3] resulted in 3 percent increase of CVD mortality (Nkosi et al., 2016; Wichmann & Voyi, 2012). In addition, South Africa has the deepest mines in the world and the industry employs half a million people and continual exposure to mineral dust in mine shafts has resulted in high rates of silicosis.

Researchers in South Africa argue that some of these health effects are aggravated by gene composition in the bodies. In support of this, a study was conducted among children by Reddy et al., (2012) and modification of pollutant effects by genes in relation to RD was revealed. TNF-α-308 G/A polymorphism alone was not significantly associated with intraday variation of FEV1. However, carriers of this gene had increased deterioration of lung function upon exposure to NO and SO_2. Similarly, glutathione-S-Transferase M1 gene (GSTM1), and glutathione-S-transferase P1 gene (GSTP1), both known to increase susceptibility to asthma, alone were not associated with FEV1 variation. However, interacting with pollutants, GSTP1(AG/GG) genotype modified the effect of three days prior 24 hr average PM_{10} and SO_2 and increased FEV1 variability. In addition, CD14 CT/TT genotype showed a reverse effect of respiratory phenotype following exposure to NO_2 and NO (Makamure et al., 2016, 2017; Patrick et al., 2019; Reddy et al., 2012). The World Health Organisation estimates that air pollution kills at least 20,000 people a year in South Africa, with more than 50 percent of these deaths attributed to heavy consumption of biofuels, mainly wood and coal. The economic cost implication of these deaths was $20 billion, or 6 percent of South Africa's 2012 GDP.

In Namibia, with minimal literature on the burden of environmental-related respiratory diseases, 10 percent of all deaths per year as in 2004 was attributed to outdoor air pollution with PM_{10} in urban areas reported at 50 µg/m^3. With rapid industrialization and motorization, the value has been estimated to have doubled, hence increasing the burden of diseases and deaths. In 2009, WHO reported the Namibian prevalence rate for chronic obstructive pulmonary diseases (COPD) and asthma was at 0.5 and 1.7 per 1000 people for the general population respectively.

In the most recent study to estimate the prevalence of respiratory symptoms and assess respiratory health risks associated with PM exposure among Windhoek resident (Hamatui & Beynon, 2017), cough (43 percent), shortness of breath (25 percent), and asthma (11.2 percent) were more prevalent in high density residential regions characterized with high PM levels and high exposure led to an increased odds ratio (OR) for episodes of phlegm and cough as it causes irritation of the airway. However, despite recording high PM levels (outdoor) across all suburbs under study, no statistically significant association to health problems was observed. This is a contradiction to past studies that suggested that PM concentrations were generally associated with acute and long-term poor pulmonary related health outcomes.

Among all assessed respiratory diseases, only an episode of cough and phlegm was found to be associated with PM concentration. This supported findings of past studies that associated episodic respiratory symptoms with PM concentrations, while cough symptons were mainly associated with the type of energy consumed with households such as paraffin, gas, charcoal and coal that degrade indoor air quality. Analysed findings of this study point out individual characteristics such as gender, age, socio-economic factors (including environmental and history of occupational exposure to dust or chemical and habits such as smoking), and health status increase vulnerability to respiratory diseases (RD) and exposure to high PM levels outdoor aggravate the situation. Therefore, poor respiratory health outcomes among Windhoek residents are not entirely based on PM concentrations alone, but also on poor indoor air quality both at home and workplaces, and other factors already highlighted.

Nigeria, the most polluted country in Africa, suffers a significantly high burden of fatalities from air pollution (ranked highest in West Africa). With an annual mean concentration of PM, extremely exceeding the WHO recommended levels, the cities of Nigeria have experienced increased hospitalization of their residents. A study conducted in the Niger Delta and analysis of 5 years hospital records revealed a high prevalence of respiratory diseases such as emphysema, bronchitis, lung damage, and asthma and other chronic diseases attributable to exposure to toxic air pollutants (Ana et al., 2014). Nigeria has also recently recorded the highest maternal mortality in the world, aggravated by air pollution in the country (WHO, 2019b; 2018a). According to a World Bank study in 2018, exposure to ambient air pollution resulted in more than 11,500 deaths in Lagos, causing losses estimated at $2.1 billion. This represented about 2.1 percent of Lagos State's GDP (World bank, 2013).

In Egypt, over 67,000 deaths have been attributed to air pollution, translating to economic losses of more than $31.5 billion, representing 3 percent of the GDP. In 2012, air pollution attributed diseases (acute lower respiratory, chronic obstructive pulmonary disease, stroke, ischemic heart disease (IHD) and lung cancer) claimed over 43,000 Egyptian lives. In 2016, Kenya also recorded a high number of these cases, including miscarriages, diabetes, tuberculosis (TB) and mental disorders, (with $PM_{2.5}$ recorded at 25.8 $\mu g/m^3$, 2.5 times the WHO recommended guidelines of 10 $\mu g/m^3$) killing over 18,000 with an economic implication of US$ 1.9 billion, translating to 2.2 percent of the GDP. In Uganda (whose Capital, Kampala, has the worst PM_{10} pollution in Africa, and 15th in the global $PM_{2.5}$), the mortality rate for air pollution increased from 70.5 deaths/100,000 people to 155.7 deaths/100,000 people in 2016, with over 24,000 children mortality cases per year (under age of 5 years) attributed to pneumonia (with a large percentage of cases associated with AAP) as in 2016 (Muntaka, 2019).

Polycyclic aromatic hydrocarbons (PAHs) and Nitro-polycyclic aromatic hydrocarbons (NPAHs) are of greatest environmental health concern due to their carcinogenicity and mutagenicity. Therefore, with these organic pollutants and other heavy metals (such as cadmium, lead, and mercury) forming a major part of urban aerosols in Africa (Kalisa et al., 2019), the populations face a lifetime cancer risk exceeding WHO guideline values and with increased levels of DNA adducts, they are likely to succumb to more chronic diseases such as kidney and bone diseases. Types of cancer attributable to these pollutants include lung cancer, breast cancer, gastric cancer, bladder cancer and skin cancer (WHO, 2018). This compounds also exhibit high direct-acting mutagenic potency on viruses, fungi, and bacteria such as Salmonella and can exacerbate health problems associated with such microorganisms.

WHO also reports of increased rates of low birth weights (LBW) at less than 2500 g, pregnancy complications, maternal mortality, premature/preterm births and perinatal mortality/still births in Africa. This is attributed to pregnant women and infants being exposed to household air pollution majorly from solid fuels and environmental tobacco smoke (WHO, 2018b, c). However, during early stages of pregnancy, women also get exposed to outdoor pollution, increasing their vulnerability to these adverse effects. Noteworthy, LBW remains a very important risk factor for pneumonia and other serious adverse health outcomes for infants in the continent. In 2017, pneumonia killed approximately 1 million children worldwide, accounting for 15 percent of all deaths of children below the age of 5 years. Upon exposure, children can also potentially have chronic low lung function, which is associated with an increased risk of cardiovascular disease and mortality in adulthood, neurodegenerative diseases (caused by oxidative stress, a result of magnetic charge on pollutant particles such as ultra-fine magnetite that enter the body through the olfactory nerve and the gut) and neuro-inflammation (a result of damaged blood–brain barrier). Pollutants such as PAHs can also damage areas in the brain that are critical in helping neurons communicate since it is the foundation for children's learning and development.

Maternal exposure to environmental oxidants such as VOC, CO, NO_2, heavy metals, and PAHs increase the risk of pregnancy complications through stimulation of the formation of methemoglobin and carboxyhemoglobin. As a result, this may lead to hypoxia and hypoxemia in pregnant women. This has an important influence on maternal health as well as placental and foetal development, hence increased risk of foetal underdevelopment and neonatal mortality. In addition, formaldehyde (HCHO), NPAHs and PAHs, has been associated with adverse reproduction effects including, reduced fertility (depending on levels of exposure, pollutants may result in reduced fecundability in women and lower sperm count, lower percentage of motile sperm and lower percentage of sperm with normal morphology in men), spontaneous abortion, foetal growth (such as reduced biparietal diameter), and birth malformations. With the ability to cross the placenta and enter foetal tissues, these pollutants are likely to cause genotoxicity, oxidative stress, disruption of the protein, enzyme and hormonal activity and DNA methylation on the developing foetus. NPAHs and PAHs metabolites can also exhibit estrogenic and antiestrogenic activity, thus affecting fertility in women.

In a study to determine the associations between types of ambient $PM_{2.5}$ and Under-Five and Maternal Mortality in Africa (Owili et al., 2017), the results demonstrated that $PM_{2.5}$ was significantly associated with under-five and maternal mortality in Africa where the exposure level usually exceeds the WHO standards. Biomass $PM_{2.5}$ increased the rate of under-five mortality in Western and Central Africa, each by 2 percent, and maternal mortality in Central Africa by 19 percent. Anthropogenic $PM_{2.5}$ increased under-five and maternal deaths in Northern Africa by 5 percent and 10 percent, respectively, and maternal deaths by 4 percent in Eastern Africa. Dust $PM_{2.5}$ increased under-five deaths in Northern, Western, and Central Africa by 3, 1, and 10 percent, respectively. Mixture $PM_{2.5}$ only increased under-five deaths and maternal deaths in Western (incidence rate ratio = 1.01, $p < 0.10$) and Eastern Africa (incidence rate ratio = 1.06, $p < 0.01$), respectively.

Exposure to PM-associated bioaerosols has been linked with a wide range of human health problems including infectious diseases, acute toxic effects, allergies, and cancer. Exposure to fungal spores loading in PM has been associated with respiratory diseases, allergies, and asthma. Studies have pointed out *Cladosporium s., Aspergillus sp., and Alternaria sp.*, to be the most predominant genera of fungi identified in airborne PM samples, and they are commonly associated with respiratory tract allergies. Pollens and spores from trees and grasses have been termed to exacerbate respiratory diseases such as asthma and rhinitis. Microbial allergens and pathogens depict similar effects as fungal spores on human health. $PM_{2.5}$ concentrations have been reported to have a significant association with human influenza virus. Exposure to airborne viruses plays a critical role in microbial ecology and some infectious diseases.

Additionally, studies have revealed an association between viruses and bacteria that cause respiratory infections, particularly in children, thus aggravating the conditions. An example of such interactions is that of Pneumococcus bacteria and influenza bacteria. It is important to note that most of these studies were based in other regions outside Africa, and in order to ascertain the actual synergistic health impacts of bioaerosols associated with PM in the continent, there is a need for comprehensive research.

In Africa, air pollution causes more than 900,000 premature deaths annually (Bauer et al., 2019; NASA, 2019, WHO, 2018), with an estimated economic cost implication of USD 215 billion (deaths caused by ambient particulate matter pollution) and USD 232 billion (deaths caused by household air pollution) (Roy, 2016). According to another study, the cost of air pollution in African cities can be as high as 2.7 percent of the continent's GDP (UNEP, 2017). Studies have revealed that mix desert dust with toxic chemical composition (Rodríguez et al., 2011) from the Sahara Desert is the lead contributor to these air pollution attributed deaths in Africa. Exposure to natural emissions, primarily fine particulate matter in dust, caused 556,475 premature deaths on the continent in 2016 with about 43,489 of this number occurring in West Africa. Industrial emissions caused 182,398 deaths while biomass burning caused 43,374 deaths (Bauer et al., 2019).

With 90 percent of African households depending on biomass fuels as the major source of energy, it is worth noting that exposure to household air pollution resulting from the use of these fuels, such as wood, charcoal and agricultural residues, and coal, could be the primary cause of disease which is aggravated upon exposure to the other sources of pollutants. However, over time, and as the region continues to urbanize and industrialize, the relative contributions from natural versus anthropogenic emissions are likely to change. In addition, with the minimal infrastructure needed to map in detail, the pollutant concentration levels to which people are exposed and their effect on public health in Africa, this number of deaths could be an underestimate.

In conclusion, although there is sufficient evidence globally to confirm the association between PM and poor health outcomes, such evidence is limited to studies conducted in Africa whose pollution levels and sources vary from one country to another. In addition, a review study (Patrick et al., 2019) points out various contradictions and weaknesses of epidemiological findings in relation to PM in various studies (some highlighted above) in Africa, based on poor assessment methodologies. For instance, in Benin, motorcyclists were not at significantly higher risk of cough, or phlegm and no difference in forced expiratory volumes (FEV1) was observed compared to neighbourhood controls (Lawin et al., 2016), which contradicts the findings of a community study in Ibadan, Nigeria (Ana et al., 2014) to establish lung function impairment and PM_{10} relationship where PM_{10} was five-fold, six-fold, seven-fold and eight-fold higher than WHO standards (20), in an academic area, high traffic area, industrial area and commercial area, respectively, and FEV1 and PM_{10} were negatively co-related across study locations ($r = -0.37$, $p < 0.05$).

In the reviewed studies (Patrick et al., 2019), exposure and health outcomes were often assessed via questionnaires or estimated via aggregated data and rarely by representative individual measurements or GIS-based models. Minimal studies were based on reliable mortality or morbidity statistics at regional and national levels. The majority of studies conducted in Africa are cross-sectional surveys, thus precluding an assessment of temporality, let alone casuality. These factors contribute to shallow outcomes that cannot be considered sufficient to estimate the true impact of AAP on the health of African populations.

Apart from studies by WHO, most of the other studies only report on RD which are also not very comprehensive, yet other diseases have been extensively documented in other continents. With a lack of sufficient monitoring data, knowledge on health effects associated with exposure to AAP are unavailable to the public. Considering the fact that some chronic disease take long to manifest, use of inapproapriate methodologies to assess PM concentration levels, exposure levels, and associated health outcomes (such as questionnaires among study community) might result in vague information. Taking into consideration the rapid economic growth in Africa, establishing current pollution levels as well as health-related effects is necessary to provide evidence to inform public health policy and planning aimed at ambient air pollution control and monitoring. This also plays a critical role in the achievement of sustainable development goals (SDGs) and millennium development goals (MDGs) including universal health care and wellbeing as well as improving maternal health, reducing child mortality and eradication of poverty.

Conclusion

Degradation of air quality is becoming a great concern in the world owing to its adversities among which climate change and adverse human health impacts are most evident. Africa emits a paltry amount of GHG gases, estimated at 3 percent which is the lowest across the globe. However, the continent's industrialization, urbanization, and population growth rates exceed that of any other region in the world. The growth rate of cities in Africa is estimated at 4 percent per annum, with a projection of half a billion population increase by 2040. These growth rates are expected to play a significant role in increased amounts of emissions in a no intervention scenario. Noteworthy, indoor air pollution in Africa is higher than anywhere else in the world, owing to over-reliance on traditional biomass as well as other dirty fuels such as kerosene and coal.

Studies have pointed out Africa to be the most vulnerable to the effects of climate change, and yet ironically, it is the same continent that lags in the fight against climate change. Africa's current state depicts lack of consistent monitoring of PM, consequently leaving a vast majority of the population with no data on the quality of air they breathe and also a lack of adequate regulatory and legislative frameworks to counter the currently rising air pollution trends in African cities. The few studies conducted in Africa have pointed out increased motorization, industrial emissions, poor waste management, and large-scale burning of biomass as key sources of air pollution in the urban areas. Long-range transportation of pollutants across the continent has also played a significant role in increased PM concentration in the cities of Africa.

Given the severe adversities of air pollution that is spiralling out of control, there is a call for action to mitigate air pollution. The upcoming trend of 'smart cities', a concept of green developments, proposes a shift from fossil-fuelled cities to renewables, climate-friendly transport, incorporation of Integrated Solid Waste Management into mainstreams of waste as well as clean and efficient industrial processes, as solutions to Ambient Air Pollution. Given these solutions, Africa has a good chance to pursue fewer carbon developments and attain the UN's SDGs and MDGs ahead of the rest. This has been associated with facts such as the availability in the abundance of renewable energy resources in Africa whose generation potential could meet the current and future world energy demands; over-reliance on NMT as a key mode of transport in the cities; upcoming recycling culture; and the current status of economic developments that are likely to adapt to new changes. However, these measures would need to be complemented with the right mix of legislation frameworks, good governance as well as good stewardship on allocated development resources if they are to succeed.

The concerns over the leading killer in the continent, 'mix desert mineral dust' and the transboundary hazard has resulted in intensive research to provide solutions to sand and dust storms whose intensity and frequency have increased owing to climate change. The proposed mitigation strategies provide a great chance to harness massive resources from Africa's extensive deserts and dry lands, with extremely huge socio-economic and environmental co-benefits.

From this study, it is evident that mitigating air pollution in the cities of Africa cannot be considered a sole solution to the deteriorating air quality across the world, rather, regional and continental-scale sources of particulate must be considered. The quest for clean air in Africa demands, not only having partnerships and collaborations of all stakeholders such as the energy departments, transport, land-use planners, urban planners, private sectors, Non-Governmental Organizations (NGOs) and Community-Based Organizations (CBOs), general public, governments at national, and regional levels but also doing so on global scales. Domestication of international and regional conventions and treaties that aim at addressing air pollution and other environmental concerns is vital. The effectiveness of these concerted efforts in addressing air pollution demands a focus on problem-specific solutions and commitment to feasible timelines for implementation. Besides the huge resource potential, most of Africa's challenges are great opportunities that could be utilized to spur the continent's transformations from 'The poorest and most vulnerable continent in the world' to 'the most sustainable continent in the World'.

After review of the various studies regarding air pollution, this study identified the following gaps that require more research:

1. What are the contributions of other natural sources of emissions such as volcanic mountains, soils, seas and oceans as well as PM-associated bioaerosols such as biogenic volatile organic compounds to degradation of air quality and relation to human health?
2. What are the contributions of Kalahari and Namib deserts to degradation of air quality, climate change as well as impacts on global biogeochemistry processes?

3. What is the contribution of water, air, and railway transport to air pollution?
4. What is the contribution of other chemical aerosols such as insecticides, herbicides, termiticides and fungicides to air pollution? Given that they are used in large scale in agricultural farmlands in rural setups, does long-range transportation of pollutants play a role in increasing PM concentrations? What are their chemical properties and impacts on environment as well as human health?
5. Do stakeholders conduct any assessment on the effectiveness of existing legislation frameworks and mitigation measures against air pollution in Africa? If so, what are the results?
6. What are the governments of net exporters of hazardous wastes, and second-hand cars that do not meet the recommendable European emission standards and safety standards doing to protect Africa from such harmful trends?
7. Are there any health-associated problems of air pollution particular to Africa, given the variations in issues such as climate, geographical characteristics and races across the globe?
8. Are there any cases of eye complications reported in Africa that are linked to exposure to PM?
9. How far are the African countries in domestication of signed international and regional convention treaties aimed at eradicating air pollution?
10. The study identified commitments to particular developments such as renewable energy and Mass-Rapid-Transport (MRT) using electric buses by African states that could potentially help in solving air pollution. How far are the states in achieving them? If not yet started, or implementation depicts an extremely slow pace, what are the faced challenges and solutions?
11. What have been the impacts/contributions of air pollution to, or on the breakout and spread of the most recent pandemics experienced, particularly COVID-19 across the world?
12. How can we best monitor indoor air pollution?

References

Adeleke, M. A., Bamgbose, J. T., Oguntoke, O., Itua, E. O., & Bamgbose, O. (2011). Assessment of health impacts of vehicular pollution on occupationally exposed people in Lagos metropolis, Nigeria. *Trace Elements and Electrolytes, 28*(2), 128–133.

African Development Bank. (2017). The new deal on energy Africa. A Transformative partnership to light up and power Africa by 2025. *Environmental Research Letters, 15*(202), 084002. https://doi.org/10.1088/1748-9326/ab8b12

Amegah, K., & Agyei-Mensah, S. (2017). Urban air pollution in sub-Saharan Africa: Time for action. *Environmental Pollution* 220 (PtA) Air Pollution in Africa. https://doi.org/10.1016/j.envpol.2016.09.042

Ana, G. R. E. E., Odeshi, T. A., Sridhar, M. K. C., & Ige, M. O. (2014). Outdoor respirable particulate matter and the lung function status of residents of selected communities in Ibadan, Nigeria. *Perspectives in Public Health, 134*(3), 169–175. https://doi.org/10.1177/1757913913494152

Barnes, B., et al. (2009). Household energy, indoor air pollution and child respiratory health in South Africa. *Journal of Energy in Southern Africa, 20*(1), 4–13. https://doi.org/10.17159/2413-3051/2009/v20i1a3296

Bauer, S. E., et al. (2019). Desert dust, industrialization, and agricultural fires: Health impacts of outdoor air pollution in Africa. *Journal of Geophysical Research: Atmospheres, 124*(7), 4104–4120. https://doi.org/10.1029/2018JD029336

Bello, I. A., Ismail, M. N. B., & Kabbashi, N. A. (2016). Solid Waste Management in Africa: A Review. *International Journal of Waste Resources, 6*, 216. https://doi.org/10.4172/2252-5211.1000216

Bhattachan, A., D'Odorico, P., Baddock, M. C., Zobeck, T. M., Okin, G. S., & Cassar, N. (2012). The Southern Kalahari: A potential new dust source in the Southern Hemisphere? *Environmental Research Letters, 7*(2), 024001. https://doi.org/10.1088/1748-9326/7/2/024001

Boman, J., Lindén, J., Thorsson, S., Holmer, B., & Eliasson, I. (2009). A tentative study of urban and suburban fine particles (PM2.5) collected in Ouagadougou, Burkina Faso. *X-Ray Spectrometry, 38*(4), 354–362.

CAPMAS. (2014). *Central agency for public mobilization and statistics.* https://www.egyptindependent.com/capmas-egypt-s-licensed-vehicles-rose-12-2014-reaching-79-million/

Climate and Clean Air Coalition (CCAC). (2020). Climate and clean air coalition annual report 2019–2020.

Cohen, A. J., Brauer, M., Burnett, R., Anderson, H. R., Frostad, J., Estep, K., ... & Forouzanfar, M. H. (2017). Estimates and 25-year trends of the global burden of disease attributable to ambient air pollution: An analysis of data from the Global Burden of Diseases Study 2015. *The Lancet, 389*(10082), 1907–1918. https://doi.org/10.1016/S0140673617305056

Croitoru, L., & Sarraf, M. (2017). Estimating the health cost of air pollution: The case of Morocco. *Journal of Environmental Protection, 08*(10), 1087–1099. https://doi.org/10.4236/jep.2017.810069

deSouza, P. (2020). Air pollution in Kenya: A review. *Air Quality, Atmosphere & Health, 13*(12), 1487–1495. https://doi.org/10.1007/s11869-020-00902-x

Dieter, S. (2012). Review of urban air quality in sub-Saharan Africa Region—Air Quality profile of SSA countries (Rep.). http://documents.worldbank.org/curated/en/936031468000276054/pdf/677940WP0P07690020120Box367897B0ACS.pdf

Dionisio, K. L., Rooney, M. S., Arku, R. E., Friedman, A. B., Hughes, A. F., Vallarino, J., & Ezzati, M. (2010). Within-neighborhood patterns and sources of particle pollution: Mobile monitoring and geographic information system analysis in four communities in Accra, Ghana. *Environmental Health Perspectives, 118*(5), 607–613.

Egondi, T., Kyobutungi, C., Ng, N., Muindi, K., Oti, S., Van de Vijver, S., Ettarh, R., & Rocklöv, J. (2013). Community perceptions of air pollution and related health risks in Nairobi slums. *International Journal of Environmental Research and Public Health, 10*(10), 4851–4868.

Ekeh, O., Fangmeier, A., & Müller, J. (2014). Quantifying greenhouse gases from the production, transportation and utilization of charcoal in developing countries: A case study of Kampala, Uganda. *The International Journal of Life Cycle Assessment, 19*(9), 1643–1652. https://doi.org/10.1007/s11367-014-0765-7

Emenike, C. U., Iriruaga, E., Agamuthu, T. I., & Fauziah, S. H. (2013). *Waste generation in Africa: An invitation to wealth generation*. A conference paper 2013. https://www.researchgate.net/publication/265511623 environment; Impact of local environment and vehicles on particle number concentrations. Science of the Total Environment volume 688. https://doi.org/10.1016/j.scitotenv.2019.06.309

Environmental impacts of Geothermal Energy. www.ucsusa.org/resources/environmental-impacts-geothermal-energy

Gaita, S. M., Boman, J., Gatari, M. J., Pettersson, J. B., & Janhäll, S. (2014). Source apportionment and seasonal variation of PM 2.5 in a sub-Saharan African city: Nairobi, Kenya. *Atmospheric Chemistry and Physics, 14*(18), 9977–9991.

Garland, R. M., Naidoo, M., Sibiya, B., & Oosrhuizen, R. (2017). *Air quality indicators from environmental performance index: Potential use and limitations in South Africa*. https://doi.org/10.17159/2410-972X/2017/v27n1a8

Geoffrey, J., Nicholas, H., & Edward, T. (2018). Emissions mitigation opportunities for savanna countries from early dry season fire management. *Nature Communication*. https://doi.org/10.1038/s41467-018-04687-7.www.nature.com/communications

Godson, R., Oyewale, M., & Gregory, A. (2015). *Indoor air quality and risk factors associated with Respiratory complications in Nigeria*. https://doi.org/10.5772/59864. https://www.intechopen.com/books/current-air-quality-and-risk-factors-associated-with-respiratory-conditions-in-nigeria

Greenpeace. (2019, August 19). Mpumalanga SO2 pollution as bad as NO2, new study finds [Press release]. https://www.greenpeace.org/africa/en/press/7678/mpumalanga-so2-pollution-asbad-as-no2-new-study-finds/

Habtamu, S., Araya, A., & Abera, K. (2014). Indoor air pollution in slum neighbourhoods of Addis Ababa, Ethiopia. *Atmospheric Environment, 89*. https://doi.org/10.1016/j.atmosenv.2014.01.003

Hafner, M., Tagliapietra, S., & de Strasser, L. (2018). Prospects for renewable energy in Africa. In *Energy in Africa*. SpringerBriefs in Energy. Springer. https://doi.org/10.1007/978-3-319-92219-5_3

Hamatui, N., & Beynon, C. (2017). Particulate matter and respiratory symptoms among adults living in Windhoek, Namibia: A cross sectional descriptive study. *International Journal of Environmental Research and Public Health, 14*(2), 110. https://doi.org/10.3390/ijerph14020110

Haslett, S. L., Taylor, J. W., Evans, M., Morris, E., Vogel, B., Dajuma, A., Brito6, J., Batenburg, A. M., Borrmann, S., Schneider, J., Schulz, C., Denjean, C., Bourrianne, T., Knippertz, P., Dupuy, R., Schwarzenböck, A., Sauer, D., Flamant, C., Dorsey, D., ... Coel, H. (2019). *Remote biomass burning dominates southern West African air pollution during the monsoon*. https://doi.org/10.5194/acp-2019-38

HEI. (2018). State of global air 2018. *Special Report*. Health Effects Institute.

Heiberg, T., & Mashishi, N. (2019, June 10). *South African government sued over coal and industrial air pollution*. Retrieved February 17, 2020, from https://www.reuters.com/article/ussafrica-coal-idUSKCN1TB1Q7

Hersey, S. P., Garland, R. M., Crosbie, E., Shingler, T., Sorooshian, A., Piketh, S., & Burger, R. (2015). An overview of regional and local characteristics of aerosols in South Africa using satellite, ground, and modeling data. *Atmospheric Chemistry and Physics, 15*, 4259–4278. https://doi.org/10.5194/acp-15-4259-2015

IEA. (2019). https://www.iea.org/reports/africa-energy-outlook-2019

Kalisa, E., Archer, S., Nagato, E., Bizuru, E., Lee, L., Tang, N., Pointing, S., Hayakawa, K., & Lacap-Bugler, D. (2019). Chemical and biological components of urban aerosols in Africa: Current status and knowledge gaps. *International Journal of Environmental Research and Public Health, 16*(6), 941.

Kenya National Bureau of Statistics. (2018). http://www.knbs.or.ke

Kgabi, N. K. (2014). *Air quality policy and scientific research in Southern Africa.* https://doi.org/10.2495/AIR120141.www.witpress.com

Kinney, P. L., Gichuru, M. G., Volavka-Close, N., Ngo, N., Ndiba, P. K., Law, A., Gachanja, A., Gaita, S. M., Chillrud, S. N., & Sclar, E. (2011). Traffic impacts on PM2.5 air quality in Nairobi, Kenya. *Environmental Science & Policy, 14*(4), 369–378.

Konbr, U. (2017). Studying the indoor air pollution within the residential buildings in egypt as a factor of sustainability. *Journal of Engineering Sciences, 45*(5), 722–741. https://doi.org/10.21608/jesaun.2017.116874

Lam, N. L., Smith, K. R., Gauthier, A., & Bates, M. N. (2012). Kerosene: A review of household uses and their hazards in low-and middle-income countries. *Journal of Toxicology and Environmental Health, Part B, 15*(6), 396–432. https://doi.org/10.1080/10937404.2012.710134

Landrigan, P. J., Fuller, R., Acosta, N. J., Adeyi, O., Arnold, R., Baldé, A. B., Bertollini, R., Bose-O'Reilly, S., Boufford, J. I., & Breysse, P. N. J. T. L. (2018). The Lancet commission on pollution and health. *Lancet, 391*, 462–512.

Lawin, H., Agodokpessi, G., Ayelo, P., Kagima, J., Sonoukon, R., Ngahane, B. H. M., ... & Fayomi, B. (2016). A cross-sectional study with an improved methodology to assess occupational air pollution exposure and respiratory health in motorcycle taxi driving. *Science of the Total Environment, 550*, 1–5.

Linden, J., Boman, J., Holmer, B., Thorsson, S., & Eliasson, I. (2012). Intra-urban air pollution in a rapidly growing Sahelian city. *Environment International, 40*, 51–62.

Makamure, M. T., Reddy, P., Chuturgoon, A. A., Naidoo, R. N., Mentz, G., Batterman, S., & Robins, T. G. (2016). Tumour necrosis factor α polymorphism (TNF-308α G/A) in association with asthma related phenotypes and air pollutants among children in KwaZulu-Natal. *Asian Pacific Journal of Allergy and Immunology*. https://doi.org/10.12932/AP0677

Makamure, M. T., Reddy, P., Chuturgoon, A., Naidoo, R. N., Mentz, G., Batterman, S., & Robins, T. G. (2017). Interaction between ambient pollutant exposure, CD14 (-159) polymorphism and respiratory outcomes among children in Kwazulu-Natal, Durban. *Human & Experimental Toxicology, 36*(3), 238–246. https://doi.org/10.1177/0960327116646620

Maranan, I., Rosenberg, M., & Schlueter, A. (2017). A meteorological and chemical overview of the DACCIWA field campaign in West Africa in June–July 2016. *Atmospheric Chemistry and Physics*. https://doi.org/10.5194/act-2017-345

Meko, K. (2019). *We're at the peak of the global fire season.* Retrieved February 17, 2020, from https://www.washingtonpost.com/climateenvironment/2019/08/30/were-peak-global-fire-season/?arc404=true

Mekonnen, M. T., & Tigist, Y. G. (2018). Trends of ambient air pollution and the corresponding respiratory diseases in Addis Ababa. *Res Rep Toxi, 2*(1), 5.

Middleton, N., & Kang, U. (2017, June). Sand and dust storms: Impact mitigation. *Sustainability, 9*(6), 1–22. MDPI.

Morakinyo, O. M., et al. (2020). Ambient gaseous pollutants in an urban area in South Africa: Levels and potential human health risk. *Atmosphere, 11*(7), 751. https://doi.org/10.3390/atmos11070751.www.mdpi.com/journal/atmosphere

Muntaka, C. (2019). Air pollution in Uganda: Causes, effects and solutions, *ATC MASK*.

NASA. (2019). https://www.giss.nasa.gov/research/features/201905_dust/

Nkosi, V., Wichmann, J., & Voyi, K. (2013). Chronic respiratory disease among the elderly in South Africa: Any association with proximity to mine dumps? *Environmental Health: A Global Access Science Source, 14*(2015). https://doi.org/10.1186/s12940-015-0018-7

Nkosi, V., Wichmann, J., & Voyi, K. (2016). Comorbidity of respiratory and cardiovascular diseases among the elderly residing close to mine dumps in South Africa: A cross-sectional study. *South African Medical Journal, 106*(3), 290–297.

Odhiambo, G. O., Kinyua, A. M., Gatebe, C. K., & Awange, J. (2010). Motor vehicles air pollution in Nairobi, Kenya. *Research Journal of Environmental and Earth Sciences, 2*(4), 178–187.

Owili, P. O., Lien, W. H., Muga, M. A., & Lin, T. H. (2017, March 30). The associations between types of ambient $PM_{2.5}$ and under-five and maternal mortality in Africa. *International Journal of Environmental Research and Public Health, 14*(4), 359. https://doi.org/10.3390/ijerph14040359. PMID: 28358348; PMCID: PMC5409560.

Patrick, D. M. C., Katoto, L. B., Brand, A. S., Mokaya, J., Strijdom, H., Goswami, N., De Boever, P., Nawrot, T. S., & Nemery, B. (2019). Ambient air pollution and health in Sub-Saharan Africa: Current evidence, perspectives and a call for action. *Environmental Research, 173*, 174–188. https://doi.org/10.1016/j.envres

Petkova, E. P., Jack, D. W., Volavka-Close, N. H., & Kinney, P. L. (2013). Particulate matter pollution in African cities. *Air Quality, Atmosphere & Health, 6*(3), 603–614.

Pope, F. D., Gatari, M., Ng'ang'a, D., Poynter, A., & Blake, R. (2018). Airborne particulate matter monitoring in Kenya using calibrated low-cost sensors. *Atmospheric Chemistry and Physics, 18*(20), 15403–15418. https://doi.org/10.5194/acp-2018-327

Rabat, K. R. (2010). Towards African cities without slums, *Africa Renewal*.

Rajé, F., Tight, M., & Pope, F. D. (2018). Traffic pollution: A search for solutions for a city like Nairobi. *Cities, 82*, 100–107.

Reddy, P., Naidoo, R. N., Robins, T. G., Mentz, G., Li, H., London, S. J., & Batterman, S. (2012, December). GSTM1 and GSTP1 gene variants and the effect of air pollutants on lung function measures in South African Children. *American Journal of Industrial Medicine, 55*(12), 1078–1086. https://doi.org/10.1002/ajim.22012. Epub 6 Janary 2012. PMID: 22228263; PMCID: PMC3414676.

Rodríguez, S., Alastuey, A., Alonso-Pérez, S., Querol, X., Cuevas, E., Abreu-Afonso, J., Viana, M., Pérez, N., Pandolfi, M., & de la Rosa, J. (2011). Transport of desert dust mixed with North African industrial pollutants in the subtropical Saharan Air Layer. *Atmospheric Chemistry and Physics, 11*(13), 6663–6685. https://doi.org/10.5194/acp-11-6663-2011

Roy, R. (2016). *The cost of air pollution in Africa*.

Safar, Z. S., & Labib, M. W. (2010). Assessment of particulate matter and lead levels in the Greater Cairo area for the period 1998–2007. *Journal of Advanced Research, 1*(1), 53–63.

Schwander, S., Okello, C.D., Freers, J., Chow, J.C., Watson, J.G., Corry, M. and Meng, Q. (2014). Ambient particulate matter air pollution in Mpererwe District, Kampala, Uganda: A pilot study. *Journal of Environmental and Public Health, 2014*, 1–7. https://doi.org/10.1155/2014/763934

Shaddick, G., Thomas, M. L., Amini, H., Broday, D., Cohen, A., Frostad, J., Green, A., Gumy, S., Liu, Y., Martin, R. V., & Pruss-Ustun, A. (2018). Data integration for the assessment of population exposure to ambient air pollution for global burden of disease assessment. *Environmental Science & Technology, 52*(16), 9069–9078.

Simwela, A., Xu, B., Mekondjo, S. S., & Morie, S. (2018). Air quality concerns in Africa: A literature review. *International Journal of Scientific and Research Publication, 8*, 588–594.

Singh, A., William, R., & Pope, F. D. (2020). Visibility as a proxy for air quality in East Africa. *Environmental Research Letters, 15*(8), 084002. https://doi.org/10.1088/1748-9326/ab8b12

Tadesse, W. (2020). Impact of open burning refuse on air quality: In the case of 'Hidar Sitaten' at Addis Ababa, Ethiopia. *Environmental Health Insights, 14*, 1178630220943204.

UNEP. (2017). 'Atlas of Africa Energy Resources'. United Nations Environment Programme.

UNEP. (2018a). *Africa waste management outlook*. https://wedocs.unep.org/bitstream/handle/20.500.11822/25515/Africa_WMO_Summary.pdf?sequence=1&isAllowed=y

UNEP. (2018b). *Air pollution and development in Africa: Impacts on health, the economy, and human capital*. https://wedocs.unep.org/bitstream/handle/20.500.11822/36717/APDA.pdf

UNICEF. (2019). Silent suffocation in Africa, *UNICEF*.

United Nations. (2018). Revision of world urbanization prospects. *United Nations, Department of Economic and Social Affairs*.

van Donkelaar, A., Martin, R. V., Brauer, M., Hsu, N. C., Kahn, R. A., Levy, R. C., ... & Winker, D. M. (2016). Global estimates of fine particulate matter using a combined geophysical-statistical method with information from satellites, models, and monitors. *Environmental Science & Technology, 50*(7), 3762–3772.

WHO. (2010). *Indoor Air Pollution (IAP)*. https://energypedia.info/wiki/Indoor_Air_Pollution_(IAP)#cite_note-WHO:_Air_quality_and_health.2C_Fact_sheet_N.C2.B0313_http:.2F.2Fwww.who.int.2Fmediacentre.2Ffactsheets.2Ffs

WHO. (2016a). *WHO's Urban Ambient Air Pollution Database-Update 2016*. World Health Organization.

WHO. (2016b, September 27). *Who releases country estimates on air pollution exposure and health impact*. Retrieved February 17, 2020, from https://www.who.int/news-room/detail/27-09-2016-who-releases-country-estimates-on-air-pollution-exposure-and-health-impact

WHO. (2018, October 29). *More than 90% of the world's children breathe toxic air every day*. Retrieved February 17, 2020, from https://www.who.int/news-room/detail/29-10-2018-more-than-90-of-theworld%E2%80%99s-children-breathe-toxic-air-every-day

WHO. (2019a). *Africa, air pollution.* https://www.afro.who.int/health-topics/air-pollution

WHO. (2019b) *Maternal mortality.* https://www.who.int/news-room/fact-sheets/detail/maternal-mortality

Wichmann, J., & Voyi, K. (2012). Ambient air pollution exposure and respiratory, cardiovascular and cerebrovascular mortality in Cape Town, South Africa: 2001–2006. *International Journal of Environmental Research and Public Health, 9*(11), 3978–4016.

Williams, J. E., Van Weele, M., Van Velthoven, P. F., Scheele, M. P., Liousse, C., & Van Der Werf, G. R. (2012). The impact of uncertainties in African biomass burning emission estimates on modeling global air quality, long range transport and tropospheric chemical lifetimes. *Atmosphere, 3*(1), 132–163. www.mdpi.com/journal/atmosphere

World Bank. (2013). https://www.worldbank.org/en/topic/environment/publication/the-cost-of-air-pollution-in-lagos

World Health Organization (WHO). (2013). *Review of evidence on health aspects of air pollution—REVIHAAP project.* WHO. http://www.euro.who.int/data/assests/pdf file/0020/182432/e96762-final.pdf

World Health Organization. (2016). *Ambient air pollution: A global assessment of exposure and burden of disease.* World Health Organization.

World Health Organization. (2018a). *Ambient (outdoor) air quality and health.* World Health Organization. https://www.who.int/news-room/fact-sheets/detail/ambient-(outdoor)-air-quality-and-health

World Health Organization. (2018b). Burden of disease of household air pollution for 2016. https://www.who.int/airpollution/data/HAP_BoD_results_May2018_final.pdf

World Health Organization. (2018c). *Household air pollution and health.* WHO. https://www.who.int/news-room/fact-sheets/detail/household-air-pollution-andhealth

Index

A

Accessibility, 188, 197, 209, 217, 222, 239, 240, 315, 342

Africa, 2–4, 11, 12, 14, 17, 18, 25, 26, 29, 31, 33, 34, 43, 44, 49, 50, 53, 54, 56, 58–60, 63–68, 70–73, 76, 77, 88, 93, 95, 96, 98–100, 105, 107, 112, 114, 119, 120, 122–124, 130–134, 141–145, 150, 157, 159, 161, 162, 165–167, 173, 176, 177, 180, 186–188, 191, 192, 198, 200–202, 206, 208, 209, 213–218, 221, 225–227, 230, 231, 233–235, 237–239, 247, 248, 251, 255, 259–261, 265, 266, 268, 280–283, 286, 292, 293, 303, 310–312, 316, 319, 320, 327–329, 332, 335–337, 339–349, 351–356, 359, 361–366

Africa development, 3

African cities, 10–12, 14, 17, 18, 50–53, 55, 58, 61–63, 66, 75–78, 94, 96–98, 100, 101, 106–109, 119, 121, 128, 130, 142, 144–147, 154, 155, 159–162, 165, 166, 171, 176–178, 186, 190, 191, 197, 198, 200, 202, 204–215, 218, 219, 221, 222, 225, 227, 234, 235, 237, 280, 282, 292–294, 305, 308, 311, 312, 317–321, 328, 329, 334, 339, 342, 346, 354, 355, 363, 364

Air pollution, 14, 88, 157, 161, 291, 328–341, 343, 344, 350–357, 359–366

Authorities, 10, 11, 27, 31, 37–40, 50–52, 54, 56, 58, 60, 66, 67, 69, 71, 72, 78, 82, 91, 96–98, 101, 105, 107, 108, 110, 112–123, 126–128, 130, 135, 136, 142, 160, 162, 173, 189, 318, 321, 341

B

Bicycle, 12, 197, 207, 210, 214, 216–218, 222

Bus, 12, 69, 124, 197, 198, 201–205, 207–210, 212, 214, 217, 218, 222, 316

Bus rapid transit (BRT), 12, 124, 198, 201, 202, 204, 207, 212, 214, 218, 219, 221, 222

C

City(ies), 4, 9–12, 14, 15, 19, 20, 24, 25, 27, 31–33, 36, 38–40, 42, 43, 49–57, 59–72, 75, 78, 80, 81, 83, 88, 91, 93, 94, 96–100, 106–109, 111, 114, 115, 118–121, 124, 125, 127, 128, 130, 135, 136, 141–144, 146, 150–152, 154–157, 159–161, 166, 169, 171, 173, 177, 179–181, 186–189, 192, 197–200, 203–206,

374 INDEX

209, 210, 218, 225, 227–230, 232–235, 237, 239, 241, 253, 260, 265, 266, 269, 271, 272, 282, 291, 297, 300–302, 305–321, 327–330, 334, 335, 337–343, 345, 346, 348, 349, 351–354, 356, 358, 360, 364, 365
Complexity, 41–43, 59, 60, 62, 64, 94

D
Development, 1–6, 11, 12, 17–20, 24, 26–34, 37–43, 52, 57, 58, 65–68, 72, 78, 90, 95, 96, 105–109, 111, 113, 115, 116, 118–123, 130–136, 142, 143, 148, 151, 153, 154, 157, 159–161, 166, 170, 171, 173, 177, 179, 183, 184, 187–190, 192, 198–200, 202, 203, 205–210, 213–215, 218, 221, 222, 227, 233, 234, 236, 239, 240, 247–252, 258, 260, 261, 263, 264, 266, 268–277, 280, 281, 283–286, 295, 297, 300, 302–304, 309, 312, 314–318, 320, 321, 330, 342, 348, 351, 356, 361, 364–366

E
Ecosystem, 6, 14, 239, 248, 270, 271, 299, 301, 307, 310, 318, 319, 337, 347
Environment, 5, 6, 12, 19, 40, 60, 61, 64, 66, 69, 79, 83, 84, 88, 96, 109, 120, 122, 123, 133, 142, 162, 173, 175, 182, 185, 187, 190, 192, 205, 210, 212, 218, 229, 234, 249, 254, 272, 273, 276, 280, 281, 295, 296, 302, 305, 310, 311, 313, 315–318, 321, 327, 339, 341, 342, 344–347, 356, 366

F
Financing African cities, 11, 101, 108, 119, 121, 130
Financing sustainable urban development, 108, 110
Financing urban infrastructure, 110, 122, 131

Fiscal decentralization, 209
Food security, 78–80, 82, 84, 89, 90, 92, 94–96, 98, 100, 178, 185, 187, 266, 282

G
Governance, 6, 10, 26, 28, 32, 49–51, 53, 55–58, 60–63, 65, 67–72, 105, 106, 108, 119, 122, 126, 130, 133, 134, 155, 184, 189, 191, 192, 200, 201, 205, 215, 229, 230, 233–237, 241, 283, 313, 316, 365
Green City, 314

H
Households, 11, 12, 34–37, 39, 43, 52, 58, 78–86, 88–100, 125, 130, 135, 145, 150–157, 166–170, 172–175, 178–192, 203, 209, 214, 215, 226, 228, 238–240, 248, 252–255, 258–265, 268, 269, 284, 298, 301, 328, 336, 341, 344, 345, 353–357, 360, 361, 363

I
Ideology, 17, 21, 22, 24, 25, 29, 32, 33
Industrialization, 151, 240, 260, 329, 330, 339, 340, 342, 345, 353, 359, 364
Institutions, 4–6, 19, 25, 27, 28, 30, 32, 43, 50, 54, 62, 97, 106, 113, 122, 131, 166, 168, 175, 184, 185, 190, 191, 229, 233, 235, 236, 263, 264, 314, 358

K
Knowledge, 1–8, 18, 19, 81, 86, 90, 149, 169, 191, 199, 201, 211, 213, 215, 216, 218, 225, 234, 235, 296, 309, 312, 317, 320, 340, 364

L
Land rights, 76, 95
Leisure, 11, 55, 99, 291, 292, 300, 302, 307, 312, 314, 316, 318, 321

Literature review, 2, 7, 8, 18, 56, 78, 80, 87, 91, 92, 147–149, 154–158, 198, 199, 215, 227, 228, 233, 260, 276, 334

M
Management, 10–14, 27, 32, 35, 38, 41, 42, 49–51, 53, 57, 62, 67–70, 72, 79, 82, 86, 97, 115, 120–122, 125, 128, 131, 133, 135, 141–146, 155, 159, 161, 162, 165, 166, 171, 177, 180, 181, 184, 186, 187, 190, 192, 199, 210, 213, 225–227, 229, 232–241, 284, 292, 295, 304, 309, 310, 312, 314, 316, 317, 320, 321, 337, 339, 340, 345–349, 353, 364
Managing poverty, 12
Method, 1, 4, 5, 7, 14, 18, 24, 41, 50, 55, 106, 108, 117, 124, 128, 145, 146, 149, 152–156, 161, 166, 169–183, 185, 191, 198–207, 221, 226, 230, 233, 249–277, 280, 293–296, 299, 300, 302, 310, 319, 330–337, 340, 345, 347, 358
Migration, 12, 95, 117, 143–146, 150, 151, 154, 155, 157–159, 161, 171, 176, 187, 190, 192, 247, 250, 255, 258, 259, 264, 275, 285, 286, 327
Motorcycle, 12, 130, 197, 198, 200, 202, 205, 207, 210, 212, 214–218, 222, 341

N
Nature of poverty, 166

O
Outdoor space, 357

P
Paratransit, 198, 199, 201, 203, 204, 206–213, 218, 222
Particulate matter (PM), 14, 328, 329, 332, 333, 336, 338, 340, 341, 343, 344, 347, 355, 357, 358, 363
Physical activity (PA), 292, 296, 305, 313, 315, 316, 318, 321

Planning, 1–6, 9, 11, 13, 14, 17–20, 23–34, 36, 38–44, 52, 54, 56, 66, 67, 78, 93, 98, 100, 107, 123, 136, 141–150, 152, 157, 161, 162, 165, 166, 169, 172, 173, 175, 176, 184, 187, 189–192, 197, 201, 202, 205, 209–212, 218, 221, 222, 225, 226, 229, 233, 234, 237, 238, 240, 241, 248, 257, 261, 283, 284, 286, 291, 292, 294, 295, 300, 305, 308–315, 318–321, 328, 330, 332, 346, 356, 364
Planning culture, 9, 17, 18, 20, 23–28, 31–34, 38, 39, 41–43
Planning theory, 18, 23, 54
Policy, 1–4, 11, 12, 14, 27, 28, 30, 32, 51, 52, 57, 58, 62–67, 70, 75, 76, 79, 82, 83, 85, 87, 91, 92, 94, 96–101, 107, 108, 111, 114, 116, 123, 127, 129, 132, 136, 142, 146, 148, 149, 154, 155, 157–161, 166, 168, 169, 171–173, 176, 177, 182–184, 186, 188–193, 197–199, 204, 208, 209, 212, 213, 218, 228–230, 233, 234, 236–238, 241, 247, 248, 252, 255, 257, 258, 263, 265, 272, 273, 276, 282, 283, 286, 294, 295, 297, 300, 302, 303, 306, 309–316, 318–321, 328–330, 344–346, 348, 352, 364
Policy-maker, 82, 181, 277, 285, 318, 321, 345
Population, 7, 11, 14, 24, 27, 35, 36, 39, 49, 51, 54, 58, 66–69, 76, 98, 99, 107, 116, 117, 134, 141–143, 145–150, 152, 155–157, 159–162, 165, 169, 171, 173, 186, 190, 203, 209, 210, 231, 237–240, 247, 250, 254, 257, 263, 275, 282, 283, 285, 300, 309, 310, 314, 317–319, 327, 328, 330, 332, 337, 338, 341, 342, 345, 353, 354, 356–359, 363, 364
Practice, 5, 6, 9, 17, 18, 20, 22–25, 27–30, 32–34, 41, 43, 44, 61, 66, 71, 83, 90, 93, 95, 99, 108, 111, 112, 114, 117, 123, 126, 129, 133, 142, 156, 181, 199, 200, 205, 217, 261, 268, 272, 286, 309, 316, 319, 345

R

Recreation, 6, 14, 91, 291–295, 300, 302, 307, 309, 310, 312–321
Research, 1–7, 9, 10, 14, 18, 21–24, 39, 50–60, 63, 69, 72, 73, 75–92, 95, 106, 107, 141, 145, 147, 158, 169, 170, 173, 175, 177, 180, 190–192, 197–199, 202, 206–210, 212–217, 221, 222, 225, 226, 233, 248, 250, 257, 269, 270, 277, 278, 280, 283, 285, 286, 292, 295–297, 303, 308, 310–312, 319, 328, 330–337, 353, 358, 362, 365
Resource movement, 13, 283
Rural, 1, 13, 27, 69, 75, 109, 129, 141, 143, 146, 150, 151, 154, 157, 159, 165, 176, 181, 189, 191, 205, 208, 210, 212, 214, 215, 217, 237, 247–254, 256–273, 275–286, 294, 297, 314, 343, 351, 354–357, 366
Rural-urban relations, 13, 248, 249, 252, 257, 259, 261, 269, 277, 280–285

S

Slums, 30, 32, 34–36, 49, 66, 69, 70, 145, 152, 156, 159, 161, 165, 172, 174, 181, 186, 189, 275, 309, 317, 319, 333, 354, 357
Social-economic and political environments, 13, 285, 286
Society, 2, 6, 20, 35, 40, 49, 50, 53, 61, 62, 64, 65, 67, 69, 70, 144, 185, 217, 266, 292, 308, 311, 312, 320, 321, 337
Study design, 14, 76, 77, 106, 144–158, 180, 227–233, 310, 319
Synthesis, 1, 4, 5, 7, 8, 17, 18, 25, 169, 186, 197, 198, 204, 205, 215, 221, 228, 249, 285

U

Urban, 1–6, 10–14, 17, 19, 20, 24, 27–38, 42, 49–73, 75, 76, 78–88, 90, 92–98, 100, 105–113, 115–120, 122, 123, 125, 126, 128–130, 132–136, 141–146, 150, 151, 154–162, 165–173, 175–193, 197–199, 205–208, 210, 212–215, 217, 222, 225–227, 229, 230, 232–241, 247–276, 278, 280–286, 291, 292, 294, 297, 298, 300, 302, 304, 305, 307, 310–313, 315, 316, 318–321, 327, 328, 330, 331, 334, 335, 337, 338, 340, 342–347, 351, 352, 354–357, 361, 364, 365
Urban agriculture (UA), 11, 75–100, 177, 188, 190, 193, 265, 280, 282
Urban farmers (UF), 11, 76, 78, 80, 82–87, 89–92, 94–96, 98–101
Urban finance, 11, 106, 116, 136
Urban housing, 11, 34, 52, 56, 71, 98, 173, 189, 192, 234, 357
Urbanization, 50, 54–56, 63–65, 67, 68, 70, 72, 75, 87, 98, 99, 107, 150, 157, 158, 165, 171, 176, 183, 184, 186, 190, 192, 227, 239–241, 261, 265, 268, 271, 273, 275, 282, 283, 292, 310, 312, 317, 320, 327, 329–331, 339, 341, 344, 345, 353, 364
Urban parks, 14, 291, 310, 316, 319
Urban plots, 11, 76
Urban population, 11, 12, 69, 72, 95, 96, 98, 141, 142, 144, 145, 150, 157, 158, 160, 162, 165, 180, 186, 192, 197, 237–239, 254, 260, 265, 286, 320, 327, 329, 334, 339, 346, 354
Urban Poverty Analysis (UPA), 181

W

Water, 6, 13, 35, 39, 40, 49, 51, 61, 71, 78, 79, 81, 96, 97, 99, 100, 105, 109, 113, 119, 124–126, 134–136, 151, 154, 155, 157, 159, 160, 174, 176, 178, 181, 182, 186, 187, 192, 225–241, 270, 276, 304, 306, 317, 343, 345, 347, 349–351, 356, 366